Engendering Romance

Engendering Romance

Women Writers and the Hawthorne Tradition
1850–1990

Emily Miller Budick

Yale University Press

New Haven and London

Designed by Sonia L. Scanlon
Set in Berkeley type by Marathon
Typography Service, Inc., Durham, North Carolina
Printed in the United States of America by
BookCrafters, Inc., Chelsea, Michigan

Library of Congress Cataloging-in-
Publication Data

Budick, E. Miller.
Engendering romance : women writers and
the Hawthorne tradition, 1850–1990 /
Emily Miller Budick.
p.   cm.
Includes bibliographical references (p.) and
index.
ISBN 0-300-05557-9 (alk. paper)
1. American fiction—Women authors—
History and criticism.   2. American
fiction—20th century—History and
criticism.   3. American fiction—19th
century—History and criticism.
4. Feminism and literature—United
States—History.   5. Women and
literature—United States—History.
· 6. Hawthorne, Nathaniel, 1804–1864—
Influence.   7. Influence (Literary, artistic,
etc.)   8. Romanticism—United States.
9. Sex role in literature.   I. Title.
PS374.F45B83   1994   93-37419
813'.085099287—dc20   CIP

The catalogue record for this book is available
from the British Library.

The paper in this book meets the guidelines for
permanence and durability of the Committee on
Production Guidelines for Book Longevity of
the Council on Library Resources.

10 9 8 7 6 5 4 3 2 1

For Yochanan, 1977–1992

Contents

Acknowledgments

A major concern in this book is acknowledgment—how we accept and affirm a world of
doubts and differences. It is appropriate, therefore, that I should begin with acknowledgments
of a simpler but no less important variety.

As in all books of literary criticism, debts are
specified here in the form of citations. But some
academic debts go beyond this. Sacvan Bercovitch and Stanley Cavell have encouraged me in
this project from the beginning. At every point
in my reading of the Hawthorne tradition their
thinking informs my own. I hope that, even as I
have rendered them objects of inquiry, my admiration and affection for them are evident.

Portions of this project were first presented
as working papers to the Hebrew University
Workshop on the Institutions of Interpretation,
directed by Wolfgang Iser and Sanford Budick.
The three meetings of this workshop put me in
contact with a series of extraordinary scholars
from Israel, Germany, France, England, and the
United States who have helped me refine and
deepen my thinking. I am indebted to all of
them, as I am to my colleagues at the Hebrew
University of Jerusalem and especially to Sharon
Baris of Bar Ilan University, who have listened to
me in both formal and informal contexts. In June
1991 the Kennedy Institute for North American
Studies of the Free University of Berlin supported
me in a month's research. Winfried Fluck was an
exceptional host and colleague, and I wish to
thank him and his wife, Brigitte Fluck, and the

institute itself. The staffs at the Princeton and Harvard libraries were gracious and helpful. Grants from the Hebrew University and from the Israel Academy of Arts and Sciences also helped further my work. Mary Pasti of Yale University Press made reviewing the edited manuscript a truly illuminating experience.

Portions of my introduction first appeared in PMLA 107 (1992): 78–91; a portion of Chapter 1 in New Literary History 22 (1991): 199–211; and a portion of Chapter 10 in Arizona Quarterly 48 (1992): 117–38, which is reprinted by permission of the Regents of the University of Arizona. I thank the journals for permission to reprint.

My greatest debt is to my husband, Sanford Budick, and to my children, Rachel, Ayelet, and Yochanan. My children have engendered me as surely as I have engendered them; this book is intended in part as a tribute to them, and to their father, my partner and co-parent in life and literature both.

Yochanan did not live to see the completion of this work, in which he was, as in all things, a concerned citizen and lively trooper. He continues to abide in our every thought and prayer — a strength beyond our own which was delivered for a short time into our merely mortal keeping. He has not for a moment left us, and we miss him terribly.

Engendering Romance

Introduction

Until recently the romance tradition dominated American literary studies. Despite important revisions in our understanding of the canon, it continues to play a crucial role in criticism and theory. As conventionally defined, the tradition consists primarily of the writings of Edgar Allan Poe, Nathaniel Hawthorne, and Herman Melville, with Charles Brockden Brown and James Fenimore Cooper, Henry James and William Faulkner variously associated with them, fore and aft. The tangential connection of Ralph Waldo Emerson and Henry David Thoreau in philosophy and Walt Whitman and Emily Dickinson in poetry is also implied. I suggest that at least four important twentieth-century women authors inherit this tradition: Carson McCullers, Flannery O'Connor, Toni Morrison, and Grace Paley.[1]

My claim is that these four writers—and some other women writers to whom I will briefly refer —write into an originally male, not female, tradition. I do not intend this claim to be hostile to recent feminist interventions into the canon.[2] My thinking has been profoundly influenced by the reconceptualization of literary study that feminist criticism has effected. Nonetheless, I insist on two things. The first is that male authors may be just as sensitive to issues of gender as female authors. The second is that female authors might recognize the gender-consciousness of texts by male authors and—for this or other reasons— choose to cast their lot with a male rather than a female tradition. My interest here is in a particular literary tradition in America—the romance tradition. The existence of this tradition does not preclude the existence of other competing traditions—realist, naturalist, African American, women's, and so on.

For a good number of critics today, whether they write according to principles of deconstruction or New Historicism or feminism or psychoanalysis or New Criticism, literature seems on some level to constitute a testimony to our entrapment by all of the conditions that pertain to the human situation: economics, politics, gender, race, generation, psyche, language, even aesthetic theory. Less and less, it seems to me, are critics willing to trust the notion that authors and readers might control or intend meanings or that, whatever struggles the writings evince, authors are capable of making decisions and (to invoke the thinking of the Americanist philosopher Stanley Cavell) assuming responsibility for what and how their words mean. The American romance tradition self-consciously resists such capitulation to what Ralph Waldo Emerson variously calls *conformity* and *fate.* As embodied in both its male and its female writers, the tradition has intimately to do with questions of choice and responsibility—in particular, with choosing a place within history and tradition and with assuming responsibility both for oneself and for one's progeny.

To be sure, the relation between history and tradition on the one hand and the idea of choice and consent on the other is fraught with complexities, paradoxes, and contradictions. For this reason the romance tradition of American fiction has recently come under intensive scrutiny by a group of critics who are convinced that conservative ideological power pertains as much to romance texts as it does to all other works of literature and literary criticism. In 1957, building on earlier work in canon formation and literary theory, Richard Chase argued that nineteenth-century American fiction constituted a genre distinct from the novel. This genre, which he called romance, was distinguished by an antimimetic, allegorical, and symbolic structure. In Chase's view and in the views of a long line of scholars who followed him, this structure permitted texts to avoid directly representing sociopolitical institutions. It allowed them to escape direct engagement with politics and ideology.[3] Although some recent critics have called into question Chase's fundamental distinction between the novel and the romance, most have been far more concerned to dispute the second implication of Chase's theory, that the American romancers intended to create a "world elsewhere" (to use Richard Poirier's phrase)—a world "out of space—out of time" (Poe) or between the "Actual and the Imaginary" (Hawthorne).[4] According to contemporary New Americanist critics (as Frederick Crews has dubbed them), critics in the Chase tradition neglected the sociopolitical implications of American literature.[5] Because they were responding to the pressures of World War II and the Cold War, the argument goes, they sought to disengage Americans from what they perceived as the deadly consequences of ideology and thus to find in the American tradition the unassailable bases of democracy, individualism, and pluralism. Because their own ideological agenda remained invisible to them, they failed to recognize the ideology concealed in the works that they analyzed.

For some critics the job of American literary criticism is to expose the racial, class, and gender biases of nineteenth-century writers in order to demonstrate how the romancers and then their critics unwittingly reinscribed those biases.[6] And yet surely there is significance in the attempt of the nineteenth-century romancers and their twentieth-century critics to move outside the cultural frame that contains and limits them. How might we specify, preserving the distinctness of differing traditions, the relation between ideology, culture, and tradition on the one hand and, on the other, an act of literary composition that self-consciously places itself in an oppositional, or what I call (following Stanley Cavell) aversive, relation with society? *Ideology* can, and usually does, refer to a particular political, social, religious agenda. The term can also, however, mean what Sacvan Bercovitch calls the "ground and texture of consensus . . . the system of interlinked ideas, symbols, and beliefs by which a culture—any culture—seeks to justify and perpetuate itself; the web of rhetoric, ritual, and assumption through which society coerces, persuades, and coheres."[7] In Bercovitch's view, as in the view of a good number of New Americanists, writers and readers cannot break out of ideology. Ideological circumscription is simply the condition of our lives in culture. Insidership, however, need not imply social enslavement (although in some societies it can mean this). It can facilitate our involvement in society as consenting participants. In Bercovitch's view the ideology of America produces the circumstance through which the American citizen-writer-reader resists passive acceptance of a status quo and instead interprets and consents to social consensus. For Bercovitch, this is what Hester's return at the end of *The Scarlet Letter* dramatizes.

Traditionally Hawthorne's text has been understood as celebrating individualism and human aspiration. Like other New Americanists, Bercovitch enables us to see that the story takes place within an environment of political constraints which are implicit in the text and which it does not explicitly acknowledge; the author aims at goals that he does not fully confess. Like the protagonist, Hester Prynne, *The Scarlet Letter* may not embody resistance or rebellion, as generations of readers have assumed. Rather, Bercovitch suggests, the book may serve instead as an "agent of socialization." It compels our participation in the social compact: "The silence surrounding Hester's conversion to the scarlet letter is clearly deliberate on Hawthorne's part. It serves to mystify Hester's choice by forcing us to represent it for ourselves, by ourselves." To force representation, however, is not, Bercovitch insists, to impose meaning. "Having given us ample directives about how to understand the ways in which the letter had not done its office, Hawthorne now depends on us to recognize, freely and voluntarily—for he would not *impose* meaning upon us—the need for Hester's return. In effect, he invites us to participate in a liberal democracy of symbol-making. He elicits our interpretation in order to make our very search for meaning the vehicle of our accommodation to society."[8]

My argument concerning the Hawthorne tradition of romance fiction is that although it largely consists of a resistance to particular ideologies (such as racism, classism, and patriarchy—the ideology that will most concern me here), it in no way suggests the possibility of escaping from society, history, and tradition. Romance fiction does not deny culture or what Stanley Fish calls interpretive community.[9] Rather, it discovers ways of recommitting oneself to the world and to other people without yielding to mindless consensus and conformity. How one *chooses* tradition is, I suggest, the subject of Hawthorne's romance. The key to such choosing—indeed, the key to the socialization, interpretation, and consent that Bercovitch describes—is an idea of philosophical skepticism.

As I argued in *Fiction and Historical Consciousness: The American Romance Tradition,* American romance fiction is fundamentally skepticist. Its evasion of explicit sociopolitical reference and its antimimetic mode of representation produce a text that insists, with an intensity unlike that of other forms of literary writing, on challenging the reader to enter into an interpretive relationship with it. The meaning of the major romance texts seems to have less to do with what they say—about the world, about history, about philosophy and psychology—than with the way they say it. Romance fiction proceeds by questioning whether and what we can know.[10]

Under the pressure of deconstructionist thought, this skepticist tendency of the romance tradition has seemed to some critics to render the romance text open-ended or indeterminate.[11] In raising the question Can we know the world and other people in it? romance fiction responds with a resounding no.

But as the philosopher Stanley Cavell stresses, skepticism refrains from offering answers to the existential and epistemological questions that it raises. The power of skepticism lies in its reenactment of a question to which it does not offer an answer. In this way, skepticism facilitates the reexperiencing of doubt. It opens up the possibility of living with and through what cannot be known. The consequence of skepticism thus understood is not, or at least not necessarily, to produce either despair or a sense of the indeterminacy or unknowability of the world. Rather, skepticism can promote the turn from knowledge toward acknowledgment, toward accepting responsibility for words and for the world they create. It can also make human beings turn to one another in an attempt, in the face of doubt, to create and sustain together a world of human manufacture.[12]

Sacvan Bercovitch suggests why reading must take place within a common-sense understanding of how ideology affects interpretation and, therefore, why even American romance fiction must be understood in a sociopolitical context. Cavell indicates why reading—which is also, especially in the romance tradition, as much a philosophical and psychological activity as it is a political one—must also take place within a commonsense understanding of language. For Bercovitch ideology in America is rooted in language. Cavell's ordinary language philosophy may help reveal how Bercovitch's ideology of interpretation allows individuals to move beyond consensus to active consent.

For Cavell language has to do with accepting that "there is such a thing as language" and "(1) that every mark of a language means something in the language, one thing rather than another; that a language is totally, systematically meaningful; (2) that words and their orderings are meant by human beings, that they contain (or conceal) their beliefs, express (or deny) their convictions; and (3) that the saying of something when and as it is said is as significant as the meaning and ordering of the words said." He explicates: "Words come to us from a distance; they were there before we were; we are born into them. Meaning them is accepting that fact of their condition. To discover what is being said to us, as to discover what we are saying, is to discover the precise location from which it is said; to understand why it is said from just there, and at that time."[13] Therefore, a key concept in Cavell's philosophy of language is assuming "responsibility" for words. Such responsibility does not represent one's placement within a status quo to which one cannot help consenting. Responsibility is instead the consequence of a choice and a decision made available by the indeterminacies and imprecisions of language. Responsibility is the powerful response that human beings can make to the "ineluctable fact" that they cannot know. This responsibility extends to words as well as to deeds; and it results in a relationship to the world defined, not by knowing, but rather by what Cavell calls acknowledgment.[14]

This relationship to society, in Cavell's view, stands at the center of Ralph Waldo Emerson's achievement:

> The relation of Emerson's writing (the expression of his self-reliance) to his society (the realm of what he calls conformity) is one, as "Self-Reliance" puts it, of mutual aversion: "Self-reliance is the aversion of conformity." Naturally Emerson's critics take this to mean roughly that he is disgusted with society and wants no more to do with it. But "Self-reliance is the aversion of conformity" figures each side in terms of the other, declares the issue between them as always joined, never settled. But then this is to say that Emerson's writing and his society are in an unending argument with one another—that is to say, he writes in such a way as to *place* his writing in his unending argument (such is his loyal opposition)—an unending turning away from one another . . . hence endlessly a turning *toward* one another. So that Emerson's aversion is like, and unlike, religious conversion.[15]

The question that Cavell moves us to ask, the question, he insists, that Emerson pushes us to ask is, *why* this word in this place and at this time. For Cavell the freedom to turn away, which becomes the basis for a decision not to turn away, can be preserved only if it is unconditional, if its threat to the unity and continuity of culture remains undissipated. Dissent can lead to consent only if dissent can be taken all the way to disorder and disaffiliation. But by locating this freedom within language, Cavell also indicates why such freedom tends to reaffirm rather than destroy social relatedness. *Aversion* attests to Emerson's dissent in two distinct ways. The term testifies to his resistance to American conformity. It also, however, dramatizes how words, because they are unstable, open up further, continuing pathways to interpretive freedom. The reader may also turn away from Emerson as Emerson turns away from America. But by figuring each side in terms of the other, by declaring the issues between himself and America and between himself and his reader as always joined, and thus by placing his writing in an unending argument with America, Emerson also asserts the conditions of language that make our agreeing to "meet" upon the word, which is to say our consent, not only possible but probable.[16]

Consent as meeting on the word is what Hawthorne dramatizes at the end of *The Scarlet Letter*. When Hester returns and takes up the letter "of her own free will, for not the sternest magistrate of that iron period would have imposed it" on her, she enacts what Cavell describes as Emersonian aversion.[17] She assumes responsibility for her words and consents to place them within community and tradition. Hester's return is specifically to speech: she speaks literally. By way of acknowledging this, Hawthorne attributes the final words of the story to Hester: "So said Hester Prynne, and glanced her sad eyes downward at the scarlet letter" (264). Having learned to speak for herself, Hester becomes the voice of the text. To emphasize that this speaking is uncoerced, Hawthorne positions Hester's return in relation to her daughter's decision not to return to New England. Hester's earlier decision to remain in New England also represents a choice (itself affirming the possibility of consent). Hawthorne is explicit that Hester is "kept by no restrictive clause of her condemnation within the limits of the Puritan settlement." She is "free to return to her birthplace, or to any other European land" (79). Choosing to remain in New England, however, and choosing to return there at the end are not merely two different choices. Staying is distinguished from leaving and returning by the force of return itself, which produces a special kind of speaking.

When Hester returns to New England and chooses to speak, the text emphasizes that her speaking is not only vocal, directed to her audience, but also oblique and cryptic, made through the letter. As important as Hester's decision to return to her community and to language is where she places her words in relation to her audience. From the beginning of the story, the eyes of the community are on Hester. At the end, her placement of the *A* on her breast redirects the public gaze there and acknowledges the public perception of her shame. In glancing downward at her breast, she confesses that she sees herself as the community does. But by placing the *A* on her breast, Hester also accuses and resists the community. She exposes its shamelessness when it refused to avert its gaze from her body. Hester, then, involves the community members in a form of aversive seeing. By averting her own glance from them, she both sees herself as they see her and confesses to them that she so sees herself. But because her seeing is upside down, her viewers also see that she redirects toward them their own accusatory glances. She reverses what they see and reflects or turns it back to them. Furthermore, in averting her eyes from her audience (creating a line of obliqueness that replicates the letter's own diagonals), Hester does not focus attention exclusively on the meanings that her words directly or indirectly convey or conceal. Rather, she defines lines of relationship with her audience. Hester's *A* establishes that the issue between her and the Puritans is, as Cavell says about Emerson, always joined, never settled, in an unending argument between them. The ideological power packed in Hester's letter serves the purposes of consent (and not of conformity) when individuals, recognizing that they will never settle the issues between them, nonetheless choose to meet upon the word, to turn simultaneously away from and toward each other, allowing themselves to catch and deflect, brave and be embarrassed by, each other's gazes. Aversive seeing eschews the articulation of any sociopolitical ideology. But its indirection is turned as much toward as away from community, and it results in a kind of speaking that does not simply define or inform but establishes relationships of commitment and acknowledgment.

For the largest part of the story, Hester's letter does not speak in this way, even though Hester, from the beginning, attempts to make the *A* speak for her. The letter, as text, fails for two reasons. Insofar as it represents a quotation of the public consensus, it serves only to reiterate the status quo. But even as a radical assault on the Puritans' *A*, Hester's letter fails to speak. As a celebration of open-ended ambiguity, the letter produces a cacophony of opposing meanings that drowns out all possibility of personal voice. During the larger part of the book Hester's scarlet letter is a text inadequate to the task of communication because, by alternately closing and expanding the space between meaning and interpretation, it baffles conversation.

For Hawthorne consent is no simple statement of affirmation, like a pledge of allegiance or a declaration of independence or the recitation of a catechism. Nor is it, however, an unwritten or unspoken law, which (as Hester puts it) has "a consecration all its own" (195). It is not a secret, not even part of the secret workings of something like an ideology or teleology. Instead, it is a decidedly public event, much in the way that children (like Pearl, the scarlet letter incarnate) are public events. Like children, consent conveys private feelings, even doubts and uncertainties, into the social arena. There, even though such expressions of consent inevitably deviate from their intrinsic meanings (such as they are), they are nevertheless owned. A consenting adult, like a parent, assumes personal responsibility despite doubt. Consent voices a relation between radical doubt and the necessities of public commitment.[18]

In the following pages I bring together a set of remarkable American texts that, in speaking to us and to each other, constitute a literary tradition rich in philosophical thought and humane intention. This tradition of skepticist, romance fiction is as powerful as the individuals—male and female, African American and white, Christian and Jewish—who create it. My analyses proceed through readings of individual texts. Like the human community that it figures forth, the skepticist romance tradition derives its power from its willingness, not simply to permit difference (gender, racial, ethnic, and religious) but to celebrate the experience to which such difference commits us and to affirm responsibility for the future that such difference produces. The American romance tradition conducts a conversation predicated on the possibility of conversation itself.

I

The Antipatriarchal Romance

1

The Romance of the Family

Nathaniel Hawthorne

Throughout *The Scarlet Letter* one particular question generates the action. It is on everyone's lips, spoken and unspoken, from beginning to end; it is asked the moment that Hester Prynne steps onto the scaffold in the public square. It is reformulated in various ways, not only by the different characters in the novel but also by the reader. Whose child is Pearl? The question does not express some trivial curiosity about Pearl's paternity. Insofar as it also means "what kind of being is Pearl, mortal or divine?" it represents one of the primary questions that the Puritans must decide in order to preserve their sense of themselves as a chosen people, a new Israel reincarnated in a new England. Pearl's paternity, in other words, is as much a historical-theological as a social-moral concern. It expresses the Puritans' desire to discover within themselves evidence of their inner grace and to locate a single line of descent, moving directly from God the Father through the patriarchs of ancient Israel to the (male) leaders of the American polity.

The illegitimate child (female to boot) threatens that historical continuity. By interrupting the lines of spiritual genealogy Pearl calls into question the principle of visible sanctity on which the Puritan community founded itself. Nowhere is this emblematized more clearly than in the early, ironic portrait of Hester as "the image of Divine Maternity . . . that sacred image of sinless motherhood, whose infant was to redeem the world."[1] In imitation of the Christian paradigm, the Puritans would prefer to constitute their world as an unadulterated continuity of the divine in which the body of the mother is only the incidental vehicle of, and not itself a sexual partner in, the divine birth of a male progeny. The question Whose child is Pearl? exposes a problem of historical and religious consciousness inextricably linked to an issue in skepticism. The community wishes to resolve any and all doubts about its essential nature. By tracing in its history an unambiguous line of divine inheritance, it would confirm a straightforward relation between physical evidence and spiritual reality.

To a degree that may at first startle us, The Scarlet Letter is organized as a response to the question of Pearl's paternity. This question leads into one major area of concern in Hawthorne's romance: the woman-mother in patriarchal society. That Hester returns at the end of the novel and that she takes her place within Puritan society (not to mention within the tradition of American letters) has largely to do with what Hester and Hawthorne both learn about patriarchy and the woman, for the politics of history and community within the book are inseparable from the recovery of the woman-mother and of the family (not to mention the nation) that she helps to create.

Hawthorne's Critique of Patriarchy

In the view of nineteenth-century romance writers, patriarchal society (which is to say society as we know it) is defined by the desire of men to eliminate doubt from their lives. To some extent this critique of patriarchy has nothing to do with issues of gender. It is part and parcel of the romantic commentary on the conservative, authoritarian structure of society. But philosophical skepticism, the romancers realize, has implications for thinking about gender. Indeed, it may well be that the relation of men to women is a response to a doubt that women engender in men. Although many critics have been severe in their evaluation of the apparent feminism of Hawthorne's novel, The Scarlet Letter constitutes one of the most powerful literary critiques of the misogyny of patriarchal society.[2] Hawthorne mounts this critique by discovering the link between skepticism and the woman or, more precisely, between the desire of traditional societies to close down the space of skeptical reflection and the kinds of doubts women inevitably, biologically, introduce into the world. Long in advance of feminist thinking on this matter, Hawthorne notes the way certain principal social institutions, such as marriage, may have evolved as strategies to secure formally or legally what men can never secure biologically—knowledge of their genetic relationship to their children.

Like all political, psychoanalytic, and linguistic theories, Mary O'Brien's description of the "politics of reproduction" must be subjected to serious scrutiny.[3] But O'Brien's idea, now shared by many feminist critics, is that the terms of human reproduction produce a troubling asymmetry between mothers and fathers vis-à-vis their ability to prove or know as biological fact their genetic relationship to their children. Therefore, male society may want to control female reproduction in order to secure for themselves a knowledge that women naturally possess. Another idea popular in psycholinguistic feminist criticism, which also must remain tentative, is the Law of the Father, or the law of symbolic consciousness: "the 'myth of language'" as "theorized by Freud and Lacan," which holds that "'language and culture depend on the death or absence of the mother and on the quest for substitutes for her. . . . Women are identified with the literal, the absent referent' . . . which makes possible the (male) child's entry into the symbolic or Law of the Father."[4]

Although a final verdict on these attempts to understand the relation between patriarchal tradition and women must await some future moment, a significant number of informed and thoughtful critics concur that—either because of the biological features of human reproduction or because of the role that mothers play in the child's early psycholinguistic development—women generate some kind of epistemological problem for men. To men and women both, it has seemed that women have access to knowledge about their children's biological connection to them that the fathers of those children cannot have. Furthermore, the mother, as the first object of love and desire, may well pose a problem for psychosexual development. Western patriarchy can therefore be understood as a strategy on the part of men to control female reproduction and to limit the effects of mothering on culture. It may constitute an attempt by men to attain as closely as possible—through the intervention of law and tradition—a knowledge that women seem inherently to possess, and to make the word or the name (the patrinomial, which belongs to the father, not the mother) the determinant of social continuity.

The politics of reproduction and the myth of language make the relationship between men and women more deeply disturbing and fraught with anxiety (for men) than women's vague and indescribable difference from men. Current discussions of the woman as other, whether these discussions recur specif- ically to the term *skepticism* or not, represent a variety of skepticist discourse. Femaleness, we are reminded by the word *other,* is something male conscious- ness cannot know. It demands a willingness on the part of men to loosen their grasp on the knowability of reality.[5] But the romancers, I suggest, resist think- ing of the woman simply as other. They realize that to do so is not to correct the abuses of patriarchal society but to reinscribe them. As David Leverenz points out, what is other about the woman from the man's point of view is not other from the woman's point of view[6]—not that women do not have, or do not have to develop, their own sense of the otherness of others (the otherness of men, for example, or the otherness of their children). Nonetheless, if part of the contest between men and women has to do with reproductive specificity and a kind of knowledge to which women and not men seem able to attain, then to reincorporate women into society on the basis of their otherness is to repeat, not repeal, the law of male discourse. Some prominent feminist critics have suggested that because of their reproductive role, women may be less inclined than men to feel at home in a symbolic universe. If so, then to force women into the position of otherness is to co-opt them, once again, to play a male-defined role in a male world.

Both male and female authors in the romance tradition recognize that a much more important issue between women and men than the otherness of the woman (or, for that matter, the otherness of men) is the unknowability and utter physical realness of what they together create: the child. Whatever the otherness of the woman, whatever the otherness of other people, the direct consequence of the relationship between men and women is the offspring they create and, beyond that, the family, community, and history they produce. The issue between men and women is much more practical, even political, than poetical. It has fundamentally to do with tangible others, who, for fathers at least, are the source of considerable doubt and uncertainty.

In *The Scarlet Letter,* given the preoccupation with the question of Pearl's paternity, it is not surprising that the major focus of the prefatory sketch is the world of New England fathers. In the Salem Custom-House, Hawthorne begins his exploration of the implications of patriarchy in connection with philosoph- ical skepticism, women, and art. The Custom-House, so aptly named for Hawthorne's purposes, is "a sanctuary into which womankind, with her tools of magic . . . has very infrequent access" (7). Some feminist critics have taken the absence of female presences in the Custom-House sketch as signifying

Hawthorne's unrelenting male bias.[7] Hawthorne, it has seemed to them, would reconstitute the phenomena of being "native" (8, 12) and "natal" (11) as representing purely male affairs. At the most, the sketch would seem to testify to Hawthorne's working through of the death of his mother, who died shortly before he began work on the novel, and even of certain facts about her history: her first child was conceived before her marriage to Hawthorne's father; Hawthorne's father died early, leaving his mother a single parent (more on this later).[8] Yet for Hawthorne the world of the Custom-House is no ideal repository of the ancestral past. For some reason, which cries out for discovery, it fails to institute the customs that Hawthorne craves.

The striking fact about the Custom-House of Hawthorne's "great-grandsires" (10) is its sterility. Hawthorne goes out of his way to emphasize this dead-endedness, even inverting father-son relationships, making himself the father of this "patriarchal body" (12) of Custom-House officials and, by implication, of the fathers from whom they inherit their offices. Hawthorne accounts himself "paternal and protective" to these "children" (15) in his keeping, even to the "patriarch," the "father of the Custom-House," who is the "legitimate son of the revenue system" (16), a "patriarchal personage" (18) who has been "the husband of three wives [and] the father of twenty children, most of whom" have died (17). Painful circularity and deathliness, not power, emerge from Hawthorne's Custom-House sketch. Fathers dominate sons; sons dominate fathers and make them into sons. These are regressive relationships that lead nowhere.[9]

The sterility of the patriarchal Custom-House is closely related to another issue in the sketch: Hawthorne's painfully confessed inability to write. To write, Hawthorne makes clear, is not to inscribe the words that establish one's place and rank in the Custom-House. Since he has taken up his position in the Custom-House, Hawthorne has traveled the road of social, political conformity. As a consequence, his words have become the static record of male customs and duties. Like Hester's A early in the novel, Hawthorne's words and letters, however much he has tried to embroider them, are no more than quotations of the status quo; they are the alphabet of social (paternalistic) conformity.

Hawthorne must relocate himself in some more "domestic scenery" than the public space of the Custom-House can afford (35). He must abandon the "narrow circle" of the Custom-House, with its minimum of "lettered intercourse" (27) and get on to what he calls the "second story of the Custom-House" (28; literally, the second floor). This second story is the story of the repressed history, which, as Walter Benjamin has taught us, it is our responsibility to recover.[10] In this novel the second story is the story of the woman and of her marginalization by male culture. On the second floor of the Custom-House, Hawthorne discovers the manuscript of Surveyor Jonathan Pue with its very different kind of intercourse and its very different kind of letter(s). Hester does not introduce into the Custom-House some merely abstract quality of the feminine, some general otherness. She introduces a specific feature of male-female relationships—what Hawthorne calls in relation to the question of Pearl's paternity a "labyrinth of doubt" (99). She engenders uncertainty.

In the second story of the Custom-House, in other words, Hawthorne discovers the relation between the origins of speech and the laws of grammar that attempt to control its meaning, the relation between sexuality and the historical paradigms that try to regulate it, and, finally, the relation between letters and sexuality (writing and history or creativity and procreation). This second story, then, is not the story of custom and tradition that society ordinarily tells itself. Rather, it is the story of culture's origins in the uncertainties and even illegitimacies of sexual intimacy, which custom and tradition would deliberately repress.

In spite of its sterility and deathliness, the patriarchal Custom-House still contains this second story, where the "forgotten" letter, kept from the "knowledge of [its] heirs" (30), purloined by history, is concealed.[11] Hawthorne would reform society, specifically in relation to women; he would not overturn it. Nonetheless, in the first instance, Hawthorne recognizes that male society must recover the woman, whom it has repressed and denied. It must recover the second story in order that the dominant story itself make sense. For this reason, the "letter" that Hawthorne discovers—which suggests both language and documentary history—contains the secret of the same loins punningly alluded to in the title of the Poe story, which Hawthorne's title may well be echoing. Poe's "Purloined Letter" also has to do with sexual secrets and with the relation between those secrets and the mysteries of writing.[12] Poe and Hawthorne produce different kinds of fictions. Both, however, are concerned with retrieving their female ancestors whose identities have been kept a secret (whose letters have been purloined) because of their potential to disrupt official, familial, masculinist history. More than one Poe narrator conjures the female not as physical woman but as spiritual principle, that is, as an extension of himself. The narrator buries her within himself, to the mutual extinction of both of them. Poe's house of Usher, like Hawthorne's Custom-House, cannot abide the living woman and annihilates itself. The Custom-House threatens the same collapse, the same end to creativity and procreation both—until Hawthorne finds Hester's letter.

Hawthorne realizes that to begin writing he must do more than discover a spiritual or literary ancestor. He must do more even than discover an appropriate father—although, following the paradigm of the Freudian family romance, "The Custom-House" sketch surely represents such a search for paternity as well. Rather, Hawthorne must locate his biological origins in a female predecessor. He must come to understand that the act of writing both names a relationship to a past encoded in words and names and also raises doubts about it. In other words, he must recover the mother who has always existed in the Custom-House but whose presence has been denied there; he must recover the fact of the sexual union that gives birth both to life and to the uncertainties that life embodies. Many critics have understood "The Custom-House" as expressing Hawthorne's gender-related anxieties about writing, his fear, specifically, that writing is a feminine activity.[13] Such tensions undoubtedly produce much of the vitality of the prefatory sketch. Given Hawthorne's anxieties, it is remarkable that his quest in "The Custom-House" is for a female ancestor.

In recovering the A and what it signifies, Hawthorne recovers as well the origins of self and culture in uncertainty. He confronts men's skepticism concerning their biological offspring. Reversing direction, he also faces the inascertainability of the knowledge of the biological father (and hence the knowledge of history): fathers may be official ancestors rather than genetic ones, and, therefore, the son must entertain the doubts of paternity and thus of identity (as encoded in a name)—doubts that patriarchy tries to banish. The confrontation with illegitimacy and doubt does not mean that the son ought now to divest himself of his parents. On the contrary, he has to acknowledge and affirm both of them. Hawthorne needs Hester, the woman-mother, to break the force of traditional authoritarianism, which causes the sterility of tradition. "The Custom-House" is the patriarchal text that Hawthorne must revise. He affixes to it the text of "the scarlet letter," the text that names sexuality as inextricably part of house and custom.

The Critique of Matriarchy

The question Who is my child? which seems in this novel to express male anxiety, is symmetrical with and intimately intertwined with another question about paternity. The question that preoccupies Pearl throughout the book and that concerns Hawthorne as well in "The Custom-House" sketch, even though it assumes there a more complex form, is Who is my father? which also means for Hawthorne, Who is my mother? (I will return to the second aspect of this question later.) According to Freud and his disciples, the question Who is my father? has important implications for the writing of fiction. Nor is asking the question of parenthood, specifically in terms of paternity, unrelated to the position of women both within male society and within the literary tradition. What is the relation between the question Who is my child? and the question Who is my father? and what kind of family romance does Hawthorne's novel tell?

The Scarlet Letter tells two family romances; and it is by no means clear which is the second story: Pearl's rather conventional family romance concerning the discovery of the father or Hawthorne's unique revision of this romance concerning the mother. In the conjunction of the two romances in Hawthorne's imagination of himself as the female child of an unwed mother, Hawthorne produces the special kind of skepticist fiction that we have come to call American romance. This skepticist romance has directly to do with the two-way acknowledgments of the parent-child relationship and the implications of that process for the community as a whole.

Like philosophical skepticism understood in relation to questions of parental knowledge, Freud's theory of the family romance may constitute anything from a fact about human psychological development to a social construct to a convenient fiction. To the extent that it helps locate certain features of Hawthorne's text, it is useful to employ in reading Hawthorne's novel. According to Freud's theory, all children, moving along the necessary path of acquiring self-identity and self-authorization, initially fantasize about themselves as being the children of other, more distinguished parents. Then, however, as the child "comes to know the difference in the parts played by fathers and mothers in their sexual relations, and realizes that *'pater semper incertus est,'* while the mother is *'certissima,'* the family romance contents itself with exalting the child's father but no longer casts any doubts on his maternal origin."[14] Such a scenario neatly fits the plot of *The Scarlet Letter*. Here the child, highly identified with the mother, searches for her father, finally locating Arthur Dimmesdale, the minister and hence the most elevated figure that her society has to offer, as her father. Hawthorne's novel already represents a significant wrinkle in the Freudian plot: Dimmesdale is Pearl's father, and Roger Chillingworth, the legal father under whose shadow her investigation for the noble father proceeds and hence the father whom, under normal circumstances, the child might reject, is not her father at all. I will consider the implications of this difference from the Freudian plot later.

Freud's family romance has distinct implications for women, both as the subjects of fiction (whether by men or by women) and as themselves the writers of fiction. According to Christine van Boheemen, the novel, as genre, may well represent the narrating of just Freud's story of the search for the father. It may, therefore, be, by definition, characterized by what we would have to call male discourse. Novels, she suggests, "articulate the progress toward selfhood and maturity of their protagonists (both male and female) as the transcendent rejection of the qualities of the mother as symbol of otherness. In thus eliminating the threat of supplementarity, which questions patriarchal self-identity, the plots argue, demonstrate, and reconfirm the notion that meaning depends on the relationship to a single principle of origin, which in Western discourse is conceived of as the father." The novel, she concludes, "is the instrument of patriarchy, giving presence to its predominance in the act of utterance."[15]

This pattern of family romance affects both the depiction of the mother in the family romances of men and women and the position of the woman in family romances by female authors. Because the identity of the mother is never placed in question, Marianne Hirsch argues, the mother can become subject only to minor, manipulative fantasies, subordinate to the primary fantasy concerning the father. Thus the place of the mother within the family suffers devaluation, the mother often being depicted as an adulterer (as in Hawthorne's novel) in order to facilitate the fantasy of the discovery of the heretofore unknown father. At the same time, the situation for the female child is as devastating as the situation for the mother: "If these daydreams and fantasies are the bases for creativity, what are the implications of this shift in the family romance for the girl? . . . If the mother is *certissima,* then according to this model the girl lacks the important opportunity to replace imaginatively the same-sex parent, a process on which imagination and creativity depend. The father's presence, since his identity is *semper incertus,* does not preclude fantasies of illegitimacy, fantasies which can constitute a new self, free from familial constraints. The mother's presence, however, makes such fantasies impossible; therefore, we might extrapolate, in order to make possible the 'opposition between successive generations' and to free the girl's imaginative play, the mother must be eliminated from the fiction."[16]

This problem of the family romance vis-à-vis the female child is related to a second implication of Freudian theory, which Hirsch also develops and to which I have alluded. Quoting Margaret Homans's *Bearing the Word,* Hirsch explains that, according to the "'myth of language' prevalent during the Victorian period and later theorized by Freud and Lacan . . . 'language and culture depend on the death or absence of the mother and on the quest for substitutes for her.'"[17] In the Freudian-Lacanian account, in other words, the birth into symbolic consciousness depends upon the absence and displacement of the mother. According to Hirsch, not only is the mother absent in much nineteenth-century fiction by women, but, where present, she is often silent, as she is in fiction by men.

We have to look no further than Pearl's story for fictional confirmation of many of van Boheemen's, Hirsch's, and Homans's hypotheses. As James M. Mellard has pointed out (developing some earlier work by John Irwin), *The Scarlet Letter* records the story of Pearl's birth into a symbolic and language-based consciousness of the world.[18] As Hirsch's study might predict, in this scenario the mother does not speak. If one were to tell the rest of the story of the strongly imaginative female child leaving her mother behind in New England, Pearl's mother might well be represented as both absent and silent. Very possibly Henry James sets out to tell this story in *The Portrait of a Lady,* where Isabel Archer, as a latter-day Pearl, comes back to the land of her fathers. In James's story Isabel's mother is painfully absent, with dire consequences for the imaginative daughter.[19] Similarly, Isabel's marriage to the typically paternal husband (a pattern that characterizes Hester's own marriage to Chillingworth, not to mention her relationship with Dimmesdale) anticipates elements of Freud's family romance.[20]

The story of Pearl, her mother, and her two fathers would seem, then, to replicate closely the antipatriarchal critique of "The Custom-House." By insisting on answering the unanswerable question of genetic connection, male society forces men and women constantly to reenact and renarrate a single story: the family romance of patriarchy itself. Is there no way out of this psychological, sociological, narratological determinism?

In both of the scenes that Mellard and Irwin interpret as testifying to the child's linguistic development—scenes that, whatever our system of reference, certainly have to do with Pearl's relation to Hester's letter—the mother is not so much silenced as she is shown to render herself silent. Hester refuses to speak, in direct defiance of her daughter's pleas to tell her what the letter (and thereby language itself) means. "My little Pearl, . . . the green letter, and on thy childish bosom, has no purport. But dost thou know . . . what this letter means which thy mother is doomed to wear?" Hester repeats the question a few sentences later (178) and once more refuses to answer it. In a single stroke, the mother discredits the child's experience. She also delegitimizes her desire to speak, either through material shapes (like the green seaweed letter) or through more fully symbolic letters and words. Hester senses that the child is "seeking to approach her with childlike confidence, and . . . establish a meeting-point of sympathy" (179). This sympathy extends beyond a simple sympathy with her mother. On it depends her whole sympathy with the created universe. And yet when Pearl asks her question "a third time," Hester not only evades but lies: "Silly Pearl, . . . what questions are these? There are many things in this world that a child must not ask about. . . . As for the scarlet letter, I wear it for the sake of its gold thread." When Pearl repeats the question one last time at home Hester responds with unusual "asperity": "Hold thy tongue, naughty child! . . . else I shall shut thee into the dark closet!" (180–81). In refusing to speak, Hester withholds not only symbolic meaning but sympathy and love.[21] She silences Pearl, condemns her to hold her tongue.

The extent of Hester's unwillingness to instruct Pearl in speech of any kind is even more vividly dramatized in the second scene, when Dimmesdale and Hester make the decision that amounts to Pearl's banishment, not only from the world of self-conscious sympathy and participation but from the world itself. Hester decides to start "anew" (198, 202) with Pearl's biological father. She casts away the A to undo the past and "make it as it had never been" (202). In so doing, she again refuses the child entry into the world of symbolic consciousness. But she does more. To undo the symbolic world, she throws away the letter, which is not only a symbol but—like Pearl's seaweed letter, like Pearl herself—a physical object. In other words, to deny what the letter has come to mean, Hester denies the letter itself; she denies the child who originates in the world of the biological and sexual relationships between men and women that the letter recalls. Thus Hester repeats the major gesture of patriarchal society. She denies the origins of her daughter in the uncertainties of sexual union and replicates another principal pattern of action in the story: the failure of Pearl's two fathers to acknowledge their daughter.

Hester's act conspires with Pearl's disinheritance. It eventually leads to what must be one of the oddest turns of plot in fiction: Pearl's inheritance, not of the moral and theological estate of her biological father, but of the literal estate of her legal father. By refusing Pearl entry into what Lacanians call the Law of the Father, Hester also refuses Pearl entry into the biological world, which might well be associated with the mother. She forces Pearl to embrace a paternal law totally devoid of biological, which is to say maternal, content. Chillingworth emerges as the father; and insofar as Pearl lives out her life in Europe as wife and mother, supported by her father's money and far away from her mother, she is rendered motherless, like so many nineteenth-century female heroes. But it is Hester who is largely responsible for bringing about this turn of events.

What is going on here?

Before I explore Hester's failings as a mother (which she herself comes to realize and correct), let me hasten to note that, as the book presents her, Hester is a far better mother than either Chillingworth or Dimmesdale is a father. To emphasize this fact and to reinforce our sense of the possible relation between the biological and the symbolic (which the A and therefore, in Hawthorne's view, all language represent), Hawthorne plays out both of the tableaux of language acquisition in the presence of the father, as well as the mother. The first scene occurs simultaneously with Hester's long interview with Pearl's legal father, Chillingworth; the second occurs during Hester's conversation with Pearl's biological father, Dimmesdale. Either father or mother, Hawthorne suggests, might help this child grow into adulthood. Neither one, at this stage, does.

But by including both parents in these moments when the child struggles for identity and language, Hawthorne also evokes the primal scene, to which the child therefore also becomes witness. In other words, in these two Lacanian scenes of language acquisition, Hawthorne recalls the family romance. By identifying the birth into symbolic consciousness with the simultaneous advent of the family romance, the scenes suggest the double disadvantaging of the mother and intensify our sense of the inevitability of her remaining silent and her motives in so remaining. At the same time, these scenes also suggest how denying the birth into symbolic consciousness (at least in the androcentric world as we know it) may similarly silence the woman. For the mother to refuse her daughter entry into the world of symbolic consciousness may not return her to a world unmarred by the Law of the Father. Rather, it may deliver her out of the world altogether, back into some prelinguistic, prenatal world of unconsciousness and nonbeing. This is silence as death. Such a silence is not unrelated to the final warning issued on the tombstone at the end of Hawthorne's novel.

Uncannily, Hawthorne seems to have anticipated much contemporary thinking on the existence of what some feminist critics have called a mother tongue and on the problems that such a mother tongue might present. Hester's embroidered letter, before Hester's return to New England, is one figure for such a presymbolic, material, literal mother-daughter language, such as Margaret Homans has described in *Bearing the Word*. Pearl's seaweed letter is another. Both of these letters would communicate without recourse to symbolic signification through "gold" (181) and "green" (178) threads and filaments of maternal-filial bonding. Both, therefore, in Hawthorne's view, could easily render communication nonexistent. What Hawthorne recognizes about what Margaret Homans calls the "reproduction of the literal," which Hester and Pearl's language of material letters seems to represent, is what, according to Homans, various nineteenth-century women writers also seem to have realized about this mother tongue: that it "endangers a text's place within what we are calling the symbolic order."[22] But Hawthorne, I suggest, understands even more. He sees that—as Sandra Gilbert and Susan Gubar have indicated in relation to some of Nancy Chodorow's conceptions of language formation—"the interidentification [between mother and daughter] could be said to deny girls the space language negotiates."[23] Speaking a mother-daughter language, in other words, might leave women as silent as the Freudian and Lacanian theories of language development that Chodorow's and Homans's theories work to replace.

By focusing on the mother-daughter relationship in *The Scarlet Letter* Hawthorne examines more than the social or political consequences for women of the institutions of patriarchal society. He explores as well the implications of an all-female world that refuses symbolic consciousness. "Speak, woman! . . . Speak; and give your child a father!" the magistrates instruct Hester. But Hester "will not speak! . . . 'My child must seek a heavenly Father; she shall never know an earthly one!'" (68). The result of Hester's refusal to name the father is that Pearl remains her "mother's child" (110). It is as if Pearl were produced by something other than heterosexual progeneration, as if she were a clone of her mother, identical in every way. "The child is yours,—she is none of mine," Chillingworth informs Hester, reinforcing our sense of Pearl's origins outside the normal relations of father and mother or of man and woman; "neither will she recognize my voice or aspect as a father's" (72). If the male response to the uncertainties posed by sexual progeneration is to elevate the symbolic over the biological facts of reproduction and if, therefore, men institute names as the legal conveyors of relationships, Hester will withhold that name. She will undo patriarchy by privileging biology over custom. The immediate result of Hester's refusal to enter patriarchy and its symbolic system of naming is to reinscribe patriarchy as matriarchy, with all of the worst problems of patriarchy still intact.

Some of this maternal reinscription of the patriarchal is trivial and even humorous. For example, although Prynne is the name that Hester takes in marriage and therefore represents Hester's submission to male authority, for the reader Prynne is the name that Hester gives to the otherwise nameless Chillingworth. That is, we know Chillingworth's real name (Prynne) only through Hester. "Have I her name rightly," Chillingworth asks one the Puritan community, unintentionally alluding to Hester's power to name him. "Truly, friend," his interlocutor responds (62), answering more than he knows. And later Prynne's name is "announced as Roger Chillingworth" (71; compare 118–19): only through Hester's consent not to reveal his real name can Prynne assume his pseudonym.

Some of the consequences of matriarchy are, however, dire in the extreme. The following moment is typical of many in the novel: "Hester [is] looking at her own image in [Pearl's eyes], as mothers are fond of doing [when] suddenly . . . she fancied that she beheld, not her own miniature portrait, but another face in the small black mirror of Pearl's eye. It was a face, fiend-like, full of smiling malice, yet bearing the semblance of features that she had known full well . . . . Many a time afterwards had Hester been tortured, though less vividly, by the same illusion" (97). For Hawthorne, to seek one's image in someone else is the devil's work. But the form of Hester's self-(non)-reflection, as the semblance of the betrayed husband, the canceled father, is equally crucial. Hawthorne's point is not that, just as the A externalizes Hester's guilt, so does Pearl; and that Hester therefore sees her guilt reflected everywhere. Rather, for Hester, Pearl is not a separate person. She is a miniature self, reflecting the entirety of the mother's world, including her act of adultery. By projecting into Pearl's eyes the image of Chillingworth, who now functions also as an image of self, Hester in a way posits a new law of genetics. In this new biology, the mother imparts to her daughter the genetic materials of her nonbiological father, who is now converted into a reflection of the mother as well. This illusory violation of nature to some extent replicates or, more precisely, interprets a dominant feature of patriarchy: the desire to settle doubts by thinking the father back into the child through the patrinomial that gives the child an identity through the father's name. By seeing Chillingworth in Pearl's eyes, Hester, as it were, reinstitutes her marriage to Chillingworth, albeit by instituting a new law of biology and genetics.

Hester's "own" Pearl is the focus of the exploration of the laws of matriarchy in the text. Matriarchy, in Hawthorne's view, threatens not only to render mother and child as something like a natural landscape, silently occupying the outskirts of the civilized world, but to reduce the child to a miniature reflection of the female parent. Another scene that the moment carries with it is the view of Hester as the Virgin Mother, with Pearl the Christ child. This image of Hester contributes to Hawthorne's critique of the attempt of patriarchy, especially Christian patriarchy, to bypass sexual generation. And yet this Madonna is no innocent victim. Hester is an adulterer. She expressly conspires, moreover, in the myth of the virgin birth: Pearl, according to Hester's own account, has only a heavenly father, she has no earthly one. When Hester rethinks Chillingworth back into his illegitimate daughter, she replicates an important feature of the original Christian paradigm: even though Jesus is the Messiah by right of his descent from the house of David through Joseph, which is to say through history and genealogy, he can in no way reconstitute that line, for Joseph is *not* his father. At the same time that the Christian paradigm would posit some supernatural birth bypassing both man and woman, it strives to maintain the sanctity and legitimacy of marriage and history by preserving the myth of Christ's human genealogy. By seeing Chillingworth in Pearl, Hester would seem to be doing the same thing: declaring birth a fact of exclusively female biology and, at the same time, repairing her broken marriage to Chillingworth. Hester would reestablish the child's legitimacy by fantasizing a new law of reproduction, which, bypassing the human father, also incorporates him.

To appropriate the language of one of Dimmesdale's sermons, it is as if Hester imagines the possibility of planting a community in the wilderness. The rosebush at the "threshold" of *The Scarlet Letter*, which is said to have sprung from the "footsteps of the sainted Ann Hutchinson" (48), conveys the link for the woman between virgin birth and botanical reproduction. Pearl is not only her "mother's child" by the miracle of immaculate conception. She is also, by another account she gives, "plucked by her mother off the bush of wild roses, that grew by the prison door" (112; the governor calls Pearl "Rose Red"—110).

Whether her birth is sacred or demonic, involving a god or some method of self-fertilization, Pearl is her mother's child by the miracle of asexual partheno-genesis.[24] No wonder, then, that Pearl seems more like a text than a person. She has been fashioned by her mother in her own image: "The mother herself . . . had carefully wrought out the similitude [between Pearl and the letter]; lavishing many hours of morbid ingenuity, to create an analogy between the object of her affection, and the emblem of her guilt and torture." More than just "the likeness of the scarlet letter running along . . . side" her mother (102), Pearl is the mother tongue incarnate. And her mother would render her as silent as the letter itself.

The Cogito and the Imp of the Perverse

What is this powerful and even painful critique of matriarchy doing in a book that seems unequivocally to announce itself, both in "The Custom-House" and in the story itself, as a critique of patriarchy? Does the novelist, as some critics have argued, find himself unable to make good on his insights into the abuses of patriarchy, withdrawing the punch of his argument before he hits his target?

I have said that Hawthorne's critique of patriarchy is centered on the question Who is Pearl's father? the question that means, for the father and for patri-archal society as a whole "who is my child?"—the question that for the child emerges in the question Who is my father? For neither father nor child is the question susceptible to the answer of biological evidence. It must therefore in Hawthorne's view, lead not to knowledge but to acknowledgment. What a man doubts about his children, what his children (both male and female) doubt about him, must become for Hawthorne a part of a skepticist commitment to family and community. It is this skepticist commitment that Hawthorne's somewhat bastard historical romance attempts to convey. But what does a mother doubt, and what do her children (male and female) doubt about her? "Art thou my child, in very truth?" Hester asks Pearl, echoing the central ques-tion of the text. "Nor," Hawthorne adds, "did she put the question altogether idly" (98). What does or can this question mean to Hester?

The question Whose child is Pearl? can legitimately express the community's skepticism. For this reason Hawthorne can use it to explore the problem of philosophical doubt in patriarchal societies. The question of Pearl's parentage is the one question that Hester, as mother, may not be able to ask. Hester might suffer doubt (92, 96, 98, 99) about her child's essential nature. She might even doubt Pearl's paternity (though she does not). Nonetheless, for Hester there may be a logical, biologically determined discontinuity between the two questions What kind of being is Pearl? and Whose child is Pearl? Hester knows beyond the shadow of a doubt, as perhaps only a mother can, whose child Pearl is.[25] The early scene of Hester in the public square with her baby daughter in her arms, thinking about her parents and discovering that, compared to her present reality, the world of her ancestral past is tenuous and doubtful (as is Hawthorne's in "The Custom-House"), points, I think, to a difference between maternal doubt and all other forms of skepticism. What, then, does it mean for Hawthorne to have Hester ask these particular questions?

One answer might be simply that Hawthorne can imagine no doubt that is not identical to his own (male) doubt. Hawthorne, to his credit, would have Hester emerge as the heroic skeptic of this book, even if it means transforming her in some way into a man. But whatever the force of Hawthorne's imputation to Hester of the male skepticist question, whatever the inevitability that a male writer will perceive even his female characters in a masculinist light, the major drama of the novel lies in the portrayal of Hester as struggling with the problem, not of doubt, but of certainty. Pearl is her Pearl, her very own child, a diminutive Hester reincarnate in the world. How, then, can Hester escape the fatality of biological knowledge? How can she, as mother, acknowledge Pearl as her daughter?

How, for that matter, might any daughter or son acknowledge her or his mother? If doubting the birth connection is not somehow natural to the mother-child bond, how might mothers and their children (that is, all of us) come to skepticist acknowledgment after all—only by ignoring the mother in our search for suitable fathers? Or might it be possible to think of skeptical exploration, not as being inevitable or automatic, but as constituting a relation to the world that human beings manufacture to define their relationships in terms other than those of genetics, biology, and nature? And, if so, might not embroidering doubt constitute an achievement of human consciousness far greater than merely entertaining or permitting it?

To become more than a "tolerably good Surveyor of the Customs" (38) and "go forth a man" (39–40), Hawthorne must end his "term" of confinement (42) in the patriarchal Custom-House. His novel begins at the moment that Hester, having reached the end of one term and given birth to her baby daughter, is about to reach the end of another "term of confinement" (78), her prison sentence. The ending of Hawthorne's term and of Hester's coincide. It is as if both of them emerge from prison at the same moment and as if Hawthorne and Pearl are born at the same moment and to the same mother. Many critics have noted that Hawthorne replicates himself in Hester as an imprisoned artist emerging into expressive freedom.[26] He also reproduces himself in Hester's child. His emergence as an artist is intimately related to what Hester, as mother-artist, teaches her daughter about the responsibilities of parenthood and speech.

As striking as the affinities linking Hester and Hawthorne are those linking Hawthorne and Pearl. Like Pearl, Hawthorne is, by his ancestors' lights, "degenerate," "worthless," and "disgraceful" (10). Unlike the father of the Custom-House, Hawthorne is not "a legitimate son of the revenue system, dyed in the wool, or rather, born in the purple" (16). Rather, like Pearl, he is the illegitimate child, perhaps even the noninheriting female child, of the unaffiliated, unmarried mother, cut from the cloth that is scarlet in hue. "'What is he?' murmurs one gray shadow of my forefathers to the other" (10). The question echoes the central inquiry of the text: Whose child is Pearl, and what is she, devil or saint? One curious aspect of Hawthorne's tale is this substitution of himself for the child of Hester's adulterous union—the child of doubtful origins who, as the letter's double, raises the problem of social inheritance and naming, the child who leaves New England, never to return. As a writer, Hawthorne traces his origins to the illicit union between an official surveyor of the customs and an adulterer. Why? And what does Pearl's departure have to do with Hawthorne's own return via his "mother" to the New England of his fathers?

To rephrase the question: How does a child like Pearl, a forceful, imaginative female, become a fully autonomous adult person? How does she break the force of the mother's impositions and of her father's restrictions in order to learn to act and, finally, to speak? And what might Pearl's experience reveal about a male offspring like Hawthorne? Let us look at one more scene in which Hester is false both to the letter and to the child. In this scene, the child, persevering in her quest for autonomy, begins the quest that takes her to her two lakeside moments of confrontation with symbolic consciousness and with the dynamics of patriarchal culture. Hester and Pearl are in the governor's mansion, a bastion of patriarchal authority, when they catch a glimpse of themselves in the "polished mirror of a breastplate." "Owing to the peculiar effect of this convex mirror," which is associated with images of militarism and political authority, "the scarlet letter [is] represented in exaggerated and gigantic proportions" (106). This exaggeration of the letter reflects the distorting authority of the male world. It also, however, accurately conveys an element of the letter's meaning—which Hester refuses to recognize. She will not see that her own embroidery of the letter, with its metallic threads, has converted her bosom into a militant breastplate not so very different from one in the male world.[27]

Hester, then, refuses to look at the letter and see what at the end of the novel she will, in fact, consent to see and what she will also dramatize the seeing of. At this moment in the story, Hester is no aversive thinker. Under penalty of the Law of the Father, she will not consider that the issues between her and Puritan society may be joined in unending argument. Even more problematic, and consequent to her refusal to consent to a public process of vision and revision, she will not agree to look at what is "likewise reflected in the mirror." Pearl, we are told, is reflected "with so much breadth and intensity of effect, that it made Hester Prynne feel as if it could not be the image of her own child, but of an imp who was seeking to mould itself into Pearl's shape." "Look! Look!" the child implores (106). But the mother will not look. Just as later she will refuse to answer the child's questions about language or to read or hear the language in which the child attempts to communicate with her, here she will not consent to look at the child and see her for what she is. Hester not only refuses to see herself as the community sees her; she also refuses to see Pearl either as the community sees her or as Pearl wishes herself to be seen.

Revealed in this scene are the dire consequences for the child of the mother's unwillingness to facilitate the separation between them, of her refusal to entertain the world of symbolic meanings and reflections that mark the daughter's separateness from the mother. Pearl's request that her mother look, like her insistence later on that she speak, drives her mother away and silences her. It produces her retreat back into the botanical world of the female. "'Come along, Pearl'! said she, drawing her away. 'Come and look into this fair garden'" (106). As we earlier observed, for Hester the world of nature opens up the possibility of a nonpaternal law of genetics through which the child might be rendered truly her mother's child. The scene suggests what it would mean to return to a time before language and symbolic consciousness, to return, as it were, to the Garden, before sexuality and before the Fall (earlier Pearl is likened to an "infant . . . worthy to have been brought forth in Eden"—90). We might think of Hester's retreat as the return to a woman's world of a pure maternal relationship. In Hawthorne's view, the Puritan patriarchy had erred in positing American history as the fulfillment of the Scripture, culminating in a new promised land in New England. But naturalism and romanticism, Hawthorne understood, in no way solved the problem of the patriarchal imperatives of Puritanism. In Hawthorne's view, later generations of Americans, rejecting the Puritan idea of America as a new Israel governed by Old Testament law, had reconstituted the problem of parental coercion by trying to begin anew. Hawthorne's story of Hester and Pearl, like the even more extensive rewriting of the Eden myth in his "Rappaccini's Daughter," powerfully reveals that to conceive America as Eden was to plant nature's nation, not humankind's.[28] "Native grace" (90) is only a variant of divine grace. It ascribes parentage to something outside the human community. Such natural grace can no more speak to the duality of human nature, to the bipartite lineage of mother and father, nature and God, self and other, than can the grace that proceeds through other kinds of immaculate conceptions. Nor can it become an instrument of our speaking to and within the community of human beings.

The garden to which Hester leads Pearl does not prevent Pearl from seeming impish. It just prompts one form of perversity rather than another. Crying for a red rose (107), Pearl finally asserts that she is a red rose (112). Pearl will seek her identity everywhere and anywhere, even in a garden. Pearl's statement carries Hester's fantasy of botanical relations to absurd lengths. In the process, Pearl disowns Hester as surely as Hester is inadvertently disowning Pearl. Pearl is no more Hester's own child than is Hester the community's own type and symbol. And Pearl, through her impishness, will make this fact known.

Stanley Cavell has analyzed the Poe story to which this reference to Pearl as imp may be alluding (see also 93, 98, 106, 134; on page 92 Hawthorne identifies Pearl as perverse). Cavell has argued that, like Ralph Waldo Emerson's "Self-Reliance," Poe's "imp of the perverse" revolves around the need of the self to claim its existence. For Cavell, Poe, like Emerson, takes upon himself "the problematic of the cogito." According to Cavell, Emerson does this "by denying or negating it, Poe by perverting or subverting it." Emerson and Poe share "the perception that authoring—philosophical writing, anyway, writing as thinking—is such that to exist it must assume, or acknowledge, the proof of its own existence." If I am the devil's child, Emerson declares in "Self-Reliance," then let me live according to the devil. According to Cavell, "The Imp of the Perverse" dramatizes the need for self-affirmation, the necessity for proving one's existence, even at the cost of destroying it.[29] Pearl is an imp in this sense. Pearl insists that her mother look at their reflections as if to say to her, "See me as I really am," not your own Pearl but my own Pearl. This Pearl may be anything from a grotesque distortion of the mother to an image of one or another of her fathers to a completely alien, unrelated individual, as demonic as the townsfolk say she is. Whatever, whoever, she is, Pearl insists, she is Pearl. This is a declaration no more impish than Hawthorne's in "The Custom-House" when he takes upon himself, as illegitimate son, custody of New England's customs and traditions. But whereas Hawthorne's impishness makes him a progenitor of American culture, Pearl's takes her out of the New World altogether.

Hawthorne and the Lettered Intercourse of History

For a time Hawthorne insinuates himself into the all-female, botanical-matriarchal line created by Hester and Pearl. "Finding [the rose-bush] so directly on the threshold of our narrative, which is now about to issue from that inauspicious portal, we could hardly do otherwise than pluck one of its flowers and present it to the reader" (48). Hawthorne might well have found roses an appropriate alternative to his own thorn(e)y past. As many critics have commented, Hawthorne does seem to entertain the romantic idea that nature contains redemptive power. For this reason perhaps, he names one of his own daughters Rose. Given, however, what Hawthorne dramatizes about Pearl and Hester's relationship, it is clear than this romantic world is no alternative to civilized life. The "virgin soil" (47) and "unadulterated sunshine" (65), he realizes, only reproduce the problem of self-duplication, the endless expression of self, that characterizes patriarchy as well.

At the conclusion of the book, when the rose reappears, written into Hester and Dimmesdale's tombstone legend as the A, it has earned the right to relieve a tale of sin and sorrow because by then it has entered into the realm of civil rather than natural or supernatural law (or lore). This is the realm that produces sexual and social intercourse, procreation and language. It depends on the acquisition of symbolic consciousness alongside biological knowledge. The refusal of Hawthorne's Salem forefathers to tell Hawthorne about his biological link to his mother produces one kind of sterility. Hawthorne addresses this problem by rediscovering his sexual origins in his mother. He locates in Surveyor Pue a father willing to acknowledge a mother. Hester's refusal to name the father, to grant the importance of the name of the surveyor of customs, does little to promote the real interests of either family or children. It creates sterility of another kind. The world of symbolic consciousness created by the father at the expense of the mother complicates but does not totally prohibit

the son's search for his biological origins: Hawthorne can still find the purloined letter within the sterile Custom-House of patriarchal society. The world
of botanical and parthenogenic law, however, as created by the mother, may
leave daughters (or, for that matter, sons) no place at all in which to discover
their identity within the human community. If there is a discernible male bias
in Hawthorne's text, it is in Hawthorne's insistence that matriarchy is more per-
ilous than patriarchy—both for the individual and for the community. Pearl
will eventually outgrow her fantasy that she is Rose Red. When she does so, she
will have forever left the land of her forefathers and foremothers. A woman's
world of nonfigural language, as feminists have suggested, may offer women
(or men) no more freedom of expression than the world of symbolic presence
that it replaces.

For this reason, Hawthorne inscribes in *The Scarlet Letter* two family romances,
two laws of parental descent, two kinds of language—each of which throws
the other into doubt, each of which demands a conscious choice to acknowledge and accept a discourse and a way of being in the world that cannot be verified through knowledge and experience alone. We now realize that a kind of
bilingualism is present in the letter from the moment that Hawthorne discovers
it in the Custom-House. This same bilingualism characterizes the tombstone
inscription at the end. "Subtly communicating itself to my sensibilities, but
evading the analysis of my mind," the cloth *A*, "three inches and a quarter in
length" and fiery hot, represents the same mother-daughter language of "gold"
and "glitter" through which Pearl and Hester communicate (31–32). Only
through Pue's accompanying manuscript, however, as through Hester's willingness finally to talk to her daughter, can the letter make full intellectual and
moral sense. What constitutes the *A* in its fullness, the *A* as the literary text
entitled *The Scarlet Letter,* is "the original papers, together with the scarlet letter
itself" (32–33)—the "legend," as Hawthorne calls it at the end of the novel, as
both heraldic pictograph and story (261). No wonder, then, that the tombstone
that reembodies the intercourse of the male and the female, without which the
A would be rendered meaningless, is also a sort of marriage certificate for the
two lovers, one headstone serving for both of them.

By searching for his mother, Hawthorne, himself a surveyor of customs (in
both senses of the word), does discover a father as well as an official ancestor in
Pue, with whom he shares a name and therefore tradition, custom, and story—
Surveyor Hawthorne and Surveyor Pue. In fact, Hawthorne discovers multiple
male ancestors. Playing as he is with letters and names, invoking such stories as

"The Purloined Letter" and "The Imp of the Perverse," Hawthorne might not have missed the convenient similarity between the names Pue and Poe. The emphasis in the text on Pue's "mental part, and the internal operations of his head" (30), and the "hundredfold repetition" and "remembering" (34) to which Hawthorne's discovery of the story leads him hints that another of Hawthorne's ancestors, Edgar Allan Poe, the master of doubling and duplication, may not have been far from his mind. If the death of Hawthorne's mother in 1848 prompted his desire to rediscover the mother, perhaps Poe's death in 1849, while Hawthorne was composing *The Scarlet Letter*, activated his search for an appropriate literary father. This father would admittedly be linked to the son by cultural rather than biological lines. He would be an official ancestor, a conveyor of a relationship to the past defined according to tradition. And Hawthorne would be his somewhat illegitimate son.

This father would also, however, acknowledge and give Hawthorne a mother. Pue-Poe is different from the other Custom-House officials in that he is willing to acquaint Hawthorne with his maternal predecessor. He even exhorts him to do his "filial duty" (34) by taking up her forgotten, purloined letter and making it speak once more. Hester Prynne, Surveyor Pue-Poe, and Surveyor Hawthorne constitute a peculiar family. But this reconstruction of the family suggests the critical importance for Hawthorne of family itself, of two-parent, heterosexual descent: a father who determines the official lines of inheritance (by providing a name) and a mother who will ensure that the official will never depart from the fictitious, from the doubts that names cannot dissolve any more than language can.

In the same essay in which Cavell discusses Poe's and Emerson's relations to the cogito, he also analyzes

> the connection . . . between Emerson's ecstasies (together with Thoreau's) and Poe's horrors (together with Hawthorne's). The connection must be some function of the fact that Poe's and Hawthorne's worlds . . . have other people in them, typically marriages, and typically show these people's violent shunning, whereas Emerson's and Thoreau's worlds begin with or after the shunning of others . . . and typically depict the "I" just beside itself. The interest of the connection is that all undertake to imagine domestication or inhabitation. . . . For Emerson and Thoreau you must learn to sit at home or to sit still in some attractive spot in the woods, as if to marry the world, before, if ever, you take on the burden of

others; for Poe and Hawthorne even America came too late, or perhaps too close, for that priority.[30]

In the midst of history, Hawthorne acted to redomesticate the country, to teach it how to inhabit its home. In Cavell's terms, Hawthorne recognized that our moral relation to the world depended upon domestic relationships. Through home and family evolved history, and through history evolved the moral conscience of the nation. Throughout the book Hawthorne experiments with various family structures, but all fail to break the cycle of patriarchal or matriarchal sterility and historical repetition. There is, for example, the three-parent, four-member family formed by Hester, Chillingworth, Dimmesdale, and Pearl (the four of them appear together at several key moments). In this family the two fathers, one representing biological origination, the other social legality, mutually exclude one another and thus cancel each other out. Then there is the family of the childlike Dimmesdale, Chillingworth, and the "motherly . . . widow" with whom they live, a family structure that excludes Pearl and all children (126). This family includes the couple composed of Chillingworth and Dimmesdale (that their relationship is potentially homoerotic is clearly suggested in the passage that records their reunion in heaven).[31] For Hawthorne this family grouping is the image of sterility, the end of history. It parallels the family structure composed of Pearl and Hester and duplicates the problems of the single-sex family. Finally, there are two other families: the legal family of Hester, Chillingworth, and Pearl, which Hester has violated through her relationship with Dimmesdale, and the biological family of Dimmesdale, Hester, and Pearl, which Hester and Dimmesdale refuse to constitute and which betrays and belies social institutionalization. All of these family structures fail because they cannot provide Pearl with an access to the past that might facilitate her emergence into the future. So Hawthorne constructs a fictional family, consisting of Hester, Pue-Poe, and himself. This family reintegrates the mother and preserves the doubts that she initiates. It also creates a historical, cultural tradition able to survive. This family is the one named by the scarlet letter and monumentalized on Dimmesdale and Hester's tomb; its name is the one that Hawthorne the son inherits and makes his own, with the scarlet letter as the noble emblem and title of his book.[32]

Peggy Kamuf has suggested that

Hester's art—the embroidery of the letter—may be read as a necessary difference which exceeds the law of the same. It is a speculation she embroiders on the position of the symbol of the guilty subject—the subject of nonidentity, the "woman" presented in social spectacle. This speculation of the letter overturns in its movement the narcissistic grounds of interpretation in the self-identical subject. . . . This "speculation" cannot be specular, since the movement from the position of the thinking subject through "the whole system of society" back to itself does not close a circle but opens the possibility to thought of a woman who is essentially not a woman, as well as a man who is essentially not a man. If we may call such speculation feminist, then clearly it is only as a place to begin: a place at which to begin to think about both woman and man as other than guilty subjects which phallic law represses in its own midst.[33]

I have already expressed my reservations about Hester's A during the largest part of the book, where—Hawthorne tells us and the action of the story confirms—the letter does not do its office. Through most of the novel Hester's letter does not embroider speculative or specular difference. It wavers unproductively between embellishing ideological statement and withdrawing itself altogether from symbolic or linguistic meaning. The A that does express such "feminist" consciousness as Kamuf describes (consciousness of nonessentialism or of difference) is Hawthorne's A, not Hester's, until the end of the novel. Ironically, this letter depends for its power on its return to ideology, even if this ideology is aversively defined; it depends on specifying meaning and assuming responsibility for it in the face of the immense doubts that it also incorporates. It demands acknowledging that, just as the sexual intercourse between men and women is the only way to produce children and thus to reproduce ourselves, so only true intercourse between the mother's way of speaking and the father's can produce history and tradition.

According to the logic of this novel, a woman must embroider a skepticism that does not naturally exist for her. Then she must, like a man, work through that skepticism to affirmations and acknowledgments of a more symbolic form. The letter, which is both nonfigural (physical) and symbolic, must submit itself to the cultural conversation—male and female—in which it exists and aversively acknowledge this submission, which it reaffirms. It must also make itself available to future generations; it must participate in creating a future that is not only private but public as well. When Hester's scarlet letter declares itself in relation to doubt, when it takes a position in relation to family, community, and history, as it does at the end of the novel, then Hester becomes a mother who has moved beyond the biology of mothering and accepted the philosophical and moral challenges. For the mother the challenge of parenting may be not (as it is, perhaps, for the father) to establish intimacy with her child. Such intimacy may be inherent in her organic link to the child. Rather, for the mother the challenge might be to reestablish such intimacy, on some other, nonbiological grounds. Hester's transatlantic correspondence with her daughter might signify just this reestablishing of intimacy, a completion of the movement toward sympathy that Hester recognized in Pearl's seaweed letter and in her questions about Hester's scarlet one, but to which she could not then respond.

Thus, the mother, in Hawthorne's view, is much like the artist. She communicates in letters that fabricate doubt. She creates words that reflect needs. Perhaps what is most agonizing about language is not the way it can never quite say what we mean but the way it does, in fact, convey meaning. And this may be another way of thinking about a parent's relationship to the child: not that the child will not reflect the parent but that (impish and perverse) the child will do just that. The relationship of a mother and a son might provide the best paradigm for what it means to be a good parent and a good writer: knowing the child to be hers, the mother must let the child express himself in a way that is not the mother's. That Hester learns that her life is not the child's, that she allows Pearl to discover her own life in Europe, makes her the hero of the story Hawthorne tells. That she herself returns to New England makes her a mother capable of producing a nation. For Hawthorne, as for Hester, there is more "real life" (262) in Salem, Massachusetts, than in England, because of the lettered intercourse that Hawthorne (because of Hester) discovers there.

Hawthorne achieves the specified future of historical relationships that Pearl does not because of what he chooses to affirm. Hawthorne replaces impish perversity (in which he also initially indulges) with aversive consent. He does not accept the legalities of patrimony but instead acknowledges the uncertainties of sexual reproduction. Hawthorne's father does not convey name and property biologically. As Pue-Pue, he only surveys the customs. He bestows the family name uncertainly, illegitimately. Like Dimmesdale, he stands vigil over customs he neither institutes nor inherits. But the son, in discovering his father and his relationship to his mother, inherits both his father's legal estate and the maternally derived power to keep that estate open to reinheritance on continually shifting terms in future generations. He does this through the discovery to which the knowledge of his parents moves him, the discovery of himself. Hawthorne thus inserts himself as a writer between past, present, and future, all of which must be acknowledged though none can be possessed. And like the w he inserts into his patrinomial, he finds his unique, personal signature in the lettered intercourse that, raising our doubts, generates our hopes as well.[34]

2

A Portrait of Female Skepticism

Henry James

Like Hawthorne's *Scarlet Letter,* Henry James's *Portrait of a Lady* concludes with a return. Unlike Hester, however, Isabel Archer returns not to America but to Europe, to a home far more narrow and dismal than Hester's cottage on the outskirts of Salem. Although there is sadness in Hester's returning alone, there is anguish in Isabel's returning to a tyrannical husband and a loveless marriage. Whether Isabel's return represents her capitulation to a grim fate (either of her own or of society's making) or whether it signals her final freedom to live by moral choices she herself has made—that debate I will not put to rest.[1] Nor will I explain once and for all why Isabel marries Gilbert Osmond. I do, however, want to explore Isabel's marriage and her return home in terms of the thinking in the book about women, specifically about the relation between sexual and maternal desire and the requirements and responsibilities of parenthood.

Isabel's return—prompted by a sexual encounter with a man who is not her husband—is not only to a house and a husband but to a daughter as well. This daughter is poised on the verge of womanhood, about to enter into the story of courtship, marriage, and parenthood, from which Isabel herself is just emerging. Pansy Osmond is the surprise in this novel—the apparently meek, sexless little bloom of a child who, startlingly, knows her own desire and works toward its achievement. There is more Pearl in Pansy than at first meets the eye (James twice calls Pansy a pearl).[2] In Hawthorne's novel, Pearl, despite her impishness, ultimately submits, in Europe, to a conventional patriarchal marriage with an armorial seal of approval. The hope in the *Portrait* is that Pansy, who, however obliging and obedient, knows her own mind and who has her stepmother at her side, may make a marriage of a different sort.

Like *The Scarlet Letter, The Portrait of a Lady* has come in for some sharp feminist criticism.[3] Yet it, too, is a sternly antipatriarchal novel. Gilbert Osmond is the chief villain, although Daniel Touchett, Ralph Touchett, and Caspar Goodwood also conspire in Isabel's victimization. Nonetheless, it is Isabel herself who is largely responsible for the tragic circumstances of her life. In some readings of the novel this assigned culpability has made James the misogynist culprit. I will explain in more detail later why I reject this criticism of the novel. Let me suggest now that, like the *Letter*, the *Portrait* is fully committed to the strength and power of its female protagonist. It charts the growth of its hero's self-confidence from childish, naive, and rebellious to profoundly moral and philosophically deep in order to suggest this woman's difference from all the other individuals with whom her life intersects. Isabel's skepticism, in James's view, allows her to become the parent whose daughter may succeed in doing what she herself cannot do. Her skepticism may have to do with coming to terms with her own sexuality—an idea of skepticism that James receives from Hawthorne. As he incorporates it into his novel, he strengthens the tradition of skepticist, antipatriarchal critique, which later women writers inherit.

James's Portrait of Mother and Child

Of the many affinities linking Hawthorne's novel and James's, the most profound may be the focus (not typical of nineteenth-century fiction by men) on a woman, who is also (even more atypically) a mother. In the depiction of the complex requirements of motherhood, James outdoes Hawthorne. Isabel mothers a daughter not her own; and when she returns to her place in society, she does so to assume responsibility for that daughter. "I won't desert you," Isabel promises Pansy, who has become, by the end of the novel, "my child" (455). "She's very nice, in spite of her deplorable origin," Isabel's sister-in-law remarks, as she reveals to Isabel who Pansy's real mother is; "I myself have liked Pansy; not, naturally, because she was *hers,* but because she had become yours." "Yes," Isabel replies, "she has become mine" (447).

Nor is Isabel the only mother in this text. However much we dislike Madame Merle, we are obliged to recognize that she is motivated, neither by hope of personal gain nor even by passion for her former lover, but by her maternal aspirations for her daughter. Isabel comes to share these aspirations so closely that Isabel and Madame Merle become virtual doubles of each other.[4] "Has she any children?" Isabel asks Ralph upon seeing Madame Merle the first time, to which Ralph erroneously answers, "Not the very least little child" (153). "If I could only begin again," Madame Merle laments to Isabel, "what have I got? Neither husband, nor child; nor fortune, nor position, nor the traces of a beauty that I never had" (171). "Ah, . . . if I had a child," she complains to Osmond (429)—a complaint that Isabel herself might voice after the early death of her baby son.

These statements do more than make us think about Madame Merle as mother. They suggest, first of all, the failure of society to always identify the woman's maternal role. Thus, Ralph asserts that Madame Merle has no children, an error that is echoed by his mother, Lydia Touchett, when, forgetting that Isabel has borne and lost a son, she says to her, upon Ralph's death, "Go and thank God you've no child" (472). Second, they point us to the way Isabel takes up the maternal role that Madame Merle has abandoned. "Shall you miss mother Catherine?" Madame Merle asks Pansy. "Perhaps some day . . . you'll have another mother" (200). By the end of the novel, Madame Merle has come to sympathize with Isabel over Osmond, while Isabel so closely takes on Madame Merle's anguish at having lost her place as Pansy's mother that she admonishes Pansy never again to say that she does not like Madame Merle (455; compare Isabel's comment to her sister-in-law ten pages earlier, "Poor woman—and Pansy who doesn't like her"). Henrietta Stackpole is an adoptive mother (even before she is a wife), and Isabel's Aunt Lydia, so unemotional throughout the novel, suffers deep pangs of loss when her son dies. Aunt Lydia's statement to Isabel, "Go and thank God you've no child," coming as it does so close to the climactic moment of the novel, when Isabel decides to return home to Pansy, also reminds us that Isabel still has a child.

This emphasis on the mother-child relationship is associated with the subject of patriarchal authoritarianism.[5] Like Hawthorne, James is interested in the powerlessness of women, especially of mothers, who are themselves treated like children in the male world. Even though Pansy has been raised by "more than thirty mothers at the convent" (200), whom she duly addresses as "*mam-man*," Pansy is a victim of male power. All of these mothers serve the F/father and H/his desire that his daughter be, in Osmond's words, "fresh and fair . . . innocent and gentle" (434). The effect of all this mothering, then, is only to "impregnate" the female child "with the idea of submission" (199). The legacy of mothering within the institution of the Church is female passivity, and it causes women to bequeath similar passivity to their daughters. Like Hawthorne, James examines the implications of a matriarchal alternative while critiquing patriarchy. He is also exploring one of the major myths of the mother in Western culture. *The Portrait of a Lady*, like *The Scarlet Letter*, evokes the woman as the Virgin Mother (Isabel is called a Madonna on page 385).[6] The crisis between Osmond and Isabel, which sends Pansy back into the convent, is precipitated by Osmond's disapproval of Pansy's love for a man. Osmond would control the passion in Pansy, as he does in his wife and her stepmother—that is to say, both her sexuality and, more critically, the progeny whom she will produce in his name.

Like Hawthorne in the *Letter*, James in the *Portrait* would make parenting a matter of acknowledgment rather than of knowledge and power. Like Pearl, Pansy marks the mystery that the mother (like the father) must acknowledge. Whose child is Pansy?—the question galvanizes the action of the book. That the question is not spoken gives it additional power and makes it the unacknowledged question organizing patriarchal society. Like Hawthorne, James (perhaps erroneously) imagines the mother as asking the father's question. "Art thou my child, in very truth?" Hester asked Pearl. "Nor did she put the question altogether idly." In the *Portrait* the imputation of doubt to the woman is even more powerful and complete. Isabel does not know the answer to this question, except that the father is the father and that she is not the mother, although she feels, exquisitely, that she has "deceived" her husband (356). "Pansy's not my husband's child then?" Isabel asks the Countess Gemini when first acquainted with the facts of Pansy's birth, to which the countess answers, "Your husband's—in perfection" (442). Pansy is "his daughter, not mine," Isabel tells Ralph, recalling Chillingworth's words to Hester.

In *The Scarlet Letter*, Hawthorne portrays the shadowy conditions of birth that seem to prompt patriarchal societies to institute measures to control the terms of reproduction. In *The Portrait of a Lady*, James outdoes Hawthorne. He creates a birth far more mysterious than Pearl's, depicting the fantasy of birth as men might have it: not only is the child born in a "virgin" birth (the mother contributes no complicating biological features of her own), but the (step)mother herself does not know who the mother is (though she knows who the father is). In this way, the father virtually succeeds in achieving what many men might wish to achieve: certain knowledge of paternity. He achieves as well a kind of parthenogenic replication, in which the child replicates the father and only the father. In the *Portrait,* the father firms up his knowledge and control by dividing the mother into her various, partial functions. There is the biological mother (Madame Merle), who is not his wife; the social mother (his dead first wife), who gives the child legitimacy; and the stepmother (Isabel), whose wealth enables him to marry his daughter to the man of his choosing, thus perpetuating his control into succeeding generations. Finally, as the father gives over the child's education to the thirty convent nuns who raise Pansy, he makes childrearing a female enterprise while simultaneously taking the legality and biology of birth out of female hands.

James, in other words, graphically realizes what is only suggestively imagined in Hawthorne's novel. But his purposes and Hawthorne's are largely the same. He depicts the circumstances of uncertainty that may, in his view, account for the social institutions and traditions of society; and he tries to initiate his protagonist into these circumstances the only way he (as a man) knows: through a double recognition of the impossibility of sweeping doubt away and of the cruelty in trying to do just that. Like Hawthorne's Hester, James's Isabel must come to acknowledge, despite her doubts that the child is hers. And Isabel does so, making her the central skepticist, that is, the central moral consciousness of the book. But also like Hawthorne, James has Isabel enact a kinship to doubt that may be more female than male.

In Hawthorne's view, skepticism for women seems to have to do with the apparently simple but emotionally complex realization that children have fathers as well as mothers. To allow the child its independence, the mother may have to imagine the father's doubt—allow it, grant it, fabricate it. She may, in other words, have to permit the child to accede to a symbolic consciousness of the world that is somehow antimaternal. In the *Portrait,* James pursues a different route. To grant the unknowability of the child, the woman may have to come to terms with her essentially unknowable, sexual desire for the child's father. What a mother (in the view of this novel) might have to be willing to recognize about her child in order to simultaneously grant that child its autonomy and independence and yet fulfill her function as nurturer may be the way motherhood is not dictated by something as simple and straightforward and morally easy as the desire to have and care for children.

This idea about the relation between sexual desire and the capacity to mother seems to motivate the particular connections brought to bear in Isabel's major meditation in chapter 42. It is no accident that the impetus for what I would like to describe as the scene of Isabel's instruction in philosophical skepticism—her coming to terms with a sense of her "mistrust" and "distrust" (349) and "doubt" (343), seeing half her husband's nature and half the nature of things (349–50)—is the prior scene of Osmond's intimacy with Madame Merle. Insofar as Madame Merle stands in this story for an aspect of Isabel, this intimacy stands for Isabel's own heretofore unacknowledged sexual desire for her husband. The scene concerns as well, therefore, Isabel's suspicions about Lord Warburton's continuing attraction to her, alongside her dawning consciousness of her stepdaughter's sexual feelings for Ned Rossier.

What, in this text, does sexual desire have to do with philosophical skepticism, and what does sexual skepticism have to do with mothering?

Skepticism, Sexuality, and Motherhood

Like *The Scarlet Letter, The Portrait of a Lady,* I maintain, is largely about the conditions of doubt in human life. As a young woman, Isabel lacks more than some general, encyclopedic knowledge of the world. She also lacks a philosophical consciousness of life. Such a consciousness—what we call skepticism—is associated in James's mind, as in Hawthorne's, with Emerson. Emerson defines an American form of skepticist consciousness, which James would not at all like to surrender to the more history- and tradition-oriented consciousness of Europe. Knowledge of the world and of its history and institutions is important to James, which is why James moves in his fiction toward literary realism. But James, as an American author, imagines historical consciousness, not as an instrument of knowing, but as a reinforcement of our sense of what we do not know and what, therefore, we must come to acknowledge on some grounds other than those of fact and proof. Sexual intimacy, which not only puts us into direct, intensive relationships with other people but produces other people— and thus history and society—is, for James, one figure for the kind of knowing that depends on and produces acknowledgment.

As an American, Isabel is already a product of an Emersonian upbringing, but she has a lot to learn about Emerson. Her "theory," early in the novel, "that it was only under this provision life was worth living; that one should be one of the best, should be conscious of a fine organisation . . . , should move in a realm of light, of natural wisdom, of happy impulse, of inspiration gracefully chronic," contains all of the right Emersonian categories, including "a certain nobleness of imagination," feelings about "beauty and bravery and magnanimity," and "infinite hope" (53). But her Emersonianism is hardly sufficient to direct her growth into adult maturity. Her misreading of Emerson (Isabel is neither the first nor the last American protagonist to so misread him) lacks the one major caution without which Emerson's own transcendentalism would degenerate into mindless optimism and egotism. This is Emerson's "noble doubt," in its two, mutually skeptical directions: the self doubting the world and, equally, the world casting doubt on the self.

James's long description of Isabel early in the novel glosses the kind of simplistic and erroneous interpretation of Emerson that will characterize such widely diverse American characters as Kate Chopin's Edna Pontellier and F. Scott Fitzgerald's Jay Gatsby. Isabel believes that "it was almost as unnecessary to cultivate doubt of one's self as to cultivate doubt of one's best friend: one should try to be one's own best friend and to give one's self, in this manner, distinguished company. . . . She had a fixed determination to regard the world as a place of brightness, of free expansion, of irresistible action. . . . She was in no uncertainty about the things that were wrong" (53). Isabel has all of Emerson's criteria but none of his philosophical depth. She resists, for example, "inconsistency," which is perhaps a hallmark of Emerson's philosophy, one of many of Emerson's words for the mutual opposition and interdependence of self and other out of which the relationship between the self and the other is established (54). Self-consistent, Isabel is solipsist and conformist both.

Part of what Isabel's idealism precludes is other people. In Isabel's view "her life should always be in harmony with the more pleasing impression she should produce; she would be what she appeared, and she would appear what she was" (54). Idea and reality would be one; and that oneness, in which the self is the self's own best friend, would be a self-containedness that would exclude the rest of the world. Like Madame Merle—who is the "cleverest woman" Ralph knows, "not excepting" Isabel—Isabel is "complete," to use Ralph's word for Merle (153). Isabel "never called it the state of solitude" (54) because—unlike Emerson's solitude (or Thoreau's)—it has less to do with a momentary retreat from the world than with an eclipsing of it. Like Gilbert Osmond's "indifference" (354), Isabel's "independence" (54; the word is used to describe Osmond as well—354) is not a self-confessed position in relation to the world, a vantage point from which one views difference and dependence. It is an escape, a repression of relationships. Like Fitzgerald's Gatsby forty years later, Isabel imagines herself a "neoplatonic conception" of self.

Isabel's escape from human relationships is specifically an escape from sexual relations—from family and futurity. Like Gatsby, or even like William Faulkner's Thomas Sutpen, Isabel conceives of herself (and in a way conceives herself) as the product of an autoerotic, self-willed, immaculate conception. "Her nature had . . . a certain garden-like quality, a suggestion of perfume and murmuring boughs, of shady bowers and lengthening vistas, which made her feel that introspection was, after all, an exercise in the open air, and that a visit to the recesses of one's spirit was harmless when one returned from it with a lapful of roses" (55). What could possibly be wrong with such an affecting romantic conceit of oneself as natural and flowerlike, chaste and decent, especially in view of its opposite? Isabel, James tells us, "was not a daughter of the Puritans, but for all that she believed in such a thing as chastity and even as decency. . . . Some of his traditions made her push back her skirts. Did all women have lovers? Did they all lie and even the best have their price? Were there only three or four that didn't deceive their husbands?" (355). Isn't Isabel's innocence, like Pansy's, preferable to the rampant sexual infidelity that seems to surround them?

Our thinking about Isabel's romantic image of herself as a garden is influenced by Osmond's image of both his daughter and his wife as flowers (355, 434; whenever the adult conversation turns to sexual matters, Osmond sends Pansy out into the garden to pick flowers). Osmond would "attach" Isabel to himself "like a small garden-plot to a deer-park. He would rake the soil gently and water the flowers; he would weed the beds and gather an occasional nosegay" (355). In the same way that Hawthorne's Rappaccini cultivates Beatrice (there is much in these passages to make us think of Hawthorne's story), so Osmond cultivates Isabel, converting her from a sexual partner into an asexual object. What is equally important to see here, however, is that Osmond's imagining of Isabel as a garden mirrors Isabel's own imagining of herself. Nor is Osmond alone in envisioning his daughter as being, like her stepmother, a "nosegay" of flowers. The stepmother, too (not to mention the natural mother), would like nothing better than to deny, not only the child's origins in sexual desire, but the child's own budding sexuality.

James's reference to Isabel as not being a daughter of the Puritans makes it inevitable that our thinking about the issue of mothers and daughters and sexual conduct will keep the image of Hester Prynne and Pearl at the forefront of our consciousness. Like Hester, Isabel prefers the roses without the thorns, especially for her daughter. But Isabel is no more innocent of sexuality than that genuine daughter of the Puritans, Hester, and her daughter is no less the product of a sexual union (adulterous at that) than is Pearl. And like the roses in Hawthorne's text, Isabel's (especially the ones in her lap) conceal just what it is about human beings that is not gardenlike. This is not just the set of (thorny) social traditions that accrue to human experience (the linkage between nature and society implied in the name Gardencourt, for example) but the (no less thorny) sexuality of human beings—fathers, mothers, daughters, and sons. The story of Pansy's birth—like the story of Pearl's—makes it abundantly clear that human children do not originate in beds of flowers but in beds of a wholly different kind.

Isabel's garden conceit, like Hester's retreat to nature, evidences her evasion of sexuality. It is her response to her belief that she can do without the "society of a more or less coarse-minded person of another sex," that she can "[plan] out her own development, [desire] her perfection, [observe] her progress" unaided, unpolluted, by male hands (55). Osmond's conceit is similarly prompted. He fears Isabel's procreative power (James passes lightly over the loss of Osmond and Isabel's son, perhaps in reflection of this fear) and sees her "infidelity" as having nothing to do with the possibility of sexual misconduct. It shows instead "that she could after all dispense with him," that having "a mind of her own," she might have desires all her own and the bodily capacity to realize those desires in the flesh. Osmond and Isabel, in other words, share—in relation to each other and especially in relation to Pansy—a fantasy of asexual reproduction, in which the self might reproduce itself without the complicating interference of another. For this reason, Osmond employs his daughter to seduce Isabel. "My daughter," he says to Isabel, "would be so glad" if you would come visit, "or rather, for she's too young to have strong emotions, I should be so glad—so very glad . . . I should be so happy if you could know my daughter" (209). "Go and see my little daughter before you leave Florence," Osmond bids her; "tell her she must love her poor father very much." "It will be a great pleasure to me to go," responds Isabel (260), whose feelings for Osmond are similarly "maternal" (351). Like Osmond, Isabel would cultivate children—plant them and reproduce them—without all the messiness of sexual relations. Osmond never outgrows his avoidance of procreative sexuality. Isabel, because of Pansy, does.[7]

More than one critic has noted the way James's novel takes up certain con-

ventions of nineteenth-century fiction, in particular the marriage of the motherless young woman to a man who is more nearly a father figure than a lover.[8]
In marrying Osmond, Isabel manages not only the feat of recovering the father
and thus preserving herself as the eternally virginal daughter but also, by
becoming a mother to Osmond's daughter (not to mention to Osmond himself), the feat of becoming a mother without becoming a sexually mature
woman. Isabel's admiration for Henrietta Stackpole, who "without parents and
without property had adopted three of the children of an infirm and widowed
sister" (54), is related to her objectives in marrying Osmond. So is Pansy's
innocently expressed desire to avoid marriage—"If he were not my papa I
should like to marry him; I would rather be his daughter than the wife of—of
some strange person" (263)—as is Isabel's way of becoming a daughter and a
sister in the Touchett household. Isabel would remain innocent of sexual
knowledge. "Let [Pansy] stay please," Isabel says to her sister-in-law, who wants
to tell her all about Osmond, including, presumably, the facts she later reveals
to Isabel about his affair with Madame Merle. "I would rather hear nothing that
Pansy may not" (295). That Isabel has given birth to and lost a son reinforces
our sense of the potential costs of biological mothering.

   The novel forces us to ask whether there is any way to become a mother—
biologically, emotionally, or spiritually—without accepting the terms of sexual
intimacy. Isabel's perception of Pansy as "a sheet of blank paper" that, as much
by her hand as by that of anyone else, might become an "edifying text" (233)
restates the problem of Isabel's own avoidance of the sexual in terms that recall
Hester's relationship to Pearl. Without sexual knowledge or at least without the
acceptance of such knowledge, the mother not only refuses the child's origins
in someone other than herself but also denies the child's own desire. In imagining Pansy a blank page Isabel repeats Hester's error in seeing Pearl as a text.
She also replicates her own error in relation to Osmond. For Isabel has as much
tried to create Osmond in her own image as he has attempted to create Pansy
and now Isabel in his. "It was wonderfully characteristic of her that, having
invented a fine theory about Gilbert Osmond, she loved him not for what he
really possessed, but for his very poverties dressed out as honours. Ralph
remembered what he had said to his father about wishing to put it into her
power to meet the requirements of her imagination. He had done so, and the
girl had taken full advantage of the luxury" (288). For Isabel, as for her husband, meeting the requirements of her imagination means converting lovers
and children into objects of that imagination. Fortunately people are more

stubborn—impish and perverse—than either flowers or books. There is in Pansy more hard and polished pearl than the reader at first imagines.

Osmond is the "manly organism" (352) that "stepped forth and stood erect [and] made her push back her skirts" (355). He introduces Isabel to the world of heterosexual relations. Before she can become a mother to her daughter, Isabel has to understand this world. It is crucial to the novel that what sets Isabel on her final odyssey to philosophical and social, which is to say parental-maternal, maturity—an odyssey that moves away from Osmond and Pansy and then, through her sexual encounter with Caspar Goodwood, back to them again—is her discovery of the sexual relationship of which Pansy is the product, the relationship between Osmond and Madame Merle, or, in other words, between Osmond and herself. The intimation of sexual intimacy frames and penetrates the whole of chapter 42. Early on in the meditation we are told that "what had suddenly set [her thoughts and terrors] into livelier motion she hardly knew, unless it were the strange impression she had received in the afternoon of her husband's being in more direct communication with Madame Merle than she suspected. That impression came back to her from time to time, and now she wondered it had never come before" (348–49). And the chapter concludes: "When the clock struck four she got up; she was going to bed at last . . . . But even then she stopped again in the middle of the room and stood there gazing at a remembered vision—that of her husband and Madame Merle unconsciously and familiarly associated" (358). Isabel's evolving skepticist consciousness, which will eventually return her to Pansy as a mother on the side of her daughter's desire, has to do with a sudden intimation of the sexual dimension of human experience.[9] This awareness causes Isabel to "distrust" or "mistrust" her husband (349). Her emerging "doubt" (343) causes her to begin not to "trust herself" (347), either. Without such skepticism Isabel cannot become wholly a woman, nor can she help Pansy to become one.

Just before this burst of budding consciousness Isabel had decided on a very different course: she had decided to become (like so many other women in Osmond's life) an agent of the father's wish that his daughter marry the man whom he has selected for her. James chooses his language here carefully. Isabel, we are told, has been "trying to persuade herself that there was no reason why Pansy shouldn't be married as you would put a letter in the post-office" (358). In Isabel's view, the issue to be decided by her intervention is whether Pansy will or will not become "a perfect little pearl of a peeress," like her ancestor in the romance tradition. Isabel is not taking Pansy's "tenacity" (342) fully into account; neither is Osmond. Isabel suggests to Osmond that "perhaps" Pansy will not "sit perfectly still" (346) and marry whomever he chooses. Perhaps she will insist on her desire as opposed to his. Like her predecessor, Pansy may be more insistent than anyone has heretofore imagined.

Still, Isabel knows, as does Pansy, that the mother has a crucial role to play in the daughter's future, especially if the daughter is to become something more than a letter, something more than a pearl of a peeress. The question that Isabel knows she must pose to herself and answer to the best of her ability is whether the man in question, Lord Warburton, genuinely loves Pansy and Pansy him. To put this in the more explicit terms that Isabel herself shuns, she must decide whether this man and woman desire each other in a sexual way. To confront this puzzle, Isabel must wrestle with the prior mystery of her own sexuality and its place in her relationship with Lord Warburton. The focus of her investigation is the question, rather oddly put, "Was [Lord Warburton] in love with Gilbert Osmond's wife?"

The form of the question is important. By referring to herself as Osmond's wife and by wondering whether Warburton is in love with that wife, Isabel reveals an element of what is going wrong here: a large-scale confusion of sexual and parental roles. Like Isabel herself marrying Osmond in order to become a mother to Osmond and Pansy and, in addition, a daughter to her husband, Warburton's marrying Pansy out of desire for Isabel is to make him the same kind of father-husband to Pansy that Osmond is to Isabel. The question, however, also stands for the question that Isabel would most especially not like to examine, the question that she must in the end confront and that she does confront through another surrogate for Osmond, Caspar Goodwood. The question is whether or not Gilbert Osmond is (or once was) in love with Gilbert Osmond's wife and, equally important, whether Osmond's wife did or does return that passion, either to Osmond or to some other man. Isabel does not yet understand the power of sexual desire. Nor does she recognize sexual desire as having motivated her own decisions, especially in marrying Osmond.

Perhaps it is for this reason that what so appalls Isabel about her friend Henrietta's engagement to Mr. Bantling is that it reveals Henrietta to be "after all" not only "human" but "feminine." The rub is not that the marriage contradicts the idea (of which Henrietta seems to be living "proof") "that a woman might suffice to herself and be happy" (55). Rather, the decision to marry Mr. Bantling reveals Henrietta to be a sexual being. Bantling, Henrietta tells Isabel, is not an intellectual; their relationship is based on something other than what she now considers the exaggerated claims for the intellect, the infatuation with brain-power that, in Henrietta's view, characterizes the American mind-set (462). Bantling and Henrietta want, in Henrietta's words, to discover the "mystery and the proportions of it" (463). The mystery, I suggest, is as much about sexual intimacy as anything else.

Isabel's immediate response to the question Was Lord Warburton in love with Gilbert Osmond's wife? mirrors her consistent repression of her sexual feelings for Osmond as well as for Warburton and Goodwood. Her response is typical of her reactions to everything that she does not immediately understand and control. She puts aside her doubts: "Isabel wandered among these ugly possibilities until she had completely lost her way; some of them, as she suddenly encountered them, seemed ugly enough. Then she broke out of the labyrinth, rubbing her eyes, and declared that her imagination surely did her little honour and that her husband's did him even less. Lord Warburton was as disinterested as he need be, and she was no more to him than she need wish. She would rest upon this till the contrary should be proved; proved more effectually than by a cynical intimation of Osmond's" (348). But because the matter pertains so directly to Pansy, it is not so easily set aside. How disinterested, we might ask, need Warburton be? How much is "no more . . . than she need wish," or, for that matter, how much need she wish? The same questions could be put concerning Osmond. As in most things, Isabel wants proof about issues that cannot be proven, about feelings that depend on needs and wishes that can be defined only subjectively. Warburton's feelings for Isabel and for Pansy are no more straightforward and easily interpretable than Osmond's feelings for Madame Merle, which is to say for Gilbert Osmond's wife herself. Her "resolution" of the question of Warburton's affections leads directly to her "impression" of Osmond and Madame Merle's sexual relationship. The doubts and anxieties engendered by sexual feelings are not so easily set aside.

What, according to James's novel, does the sexual intimacy of adult human beings look like? The description of Isabel and Osmond's marriage, which constitutes most of chapter 42, is hardly what one would want to put forward as a paradigm of male-female relationships. The evil of Osmond's nature and the wreck of his marriage to Isabel are too profound, too deep, to serve as a model of anything. The language of James's description nonetheless suggests the usual state of marriage — before it has taken the dive into disaster.

To Isabel, the conflict between herself and Osmond (as between Daisy and Winterbourne in *Daisy Miller*) ostensibly has to do with intellectual matters of tradition and social convention, like those separating European and American culture. Osmond, we are told, is "unable to live without" society; "his ideal was a conception of high prosperity and propriety, of the aristocratic life, which . . . he deemed himself always, in essence at least, to have led." Osmond despises Isabel because "she had no traditions and the moral horizon of a Unitarian minister" (354–56). In Osmond's view, Isabel has "too many ideas and . . . she must get rid of them" (352). Her "real offence, as she ultimately perceived, was her having a mind of her own. . . . Her mind was to be his" (355).

But the case is not so simple as it might at first appear. The whole analysis of Osmond's egocentricity and possessiveness is set within Isabel's dawning awareness of the sexual relationship between Osmond and Madame Merle. Sexual innuendo penetrates the meditation at every point, exposing the vast gap between Osmond's desire for Isabel and Isabel's perception of her desire for Osmond and of Osmond's for her.[10] To put it simply, Osmond's feelings for Isabel express a desire (traditionally associated with male sexuality) to dominate and control and possess. Isabel's feelings for Osmond, in contrast, though no less possessive, consistently repress the physical aspects of her desire. What she thinks she wants of her husband is a pure meeting of minds, wholly unmediated by sexuality. Although I have cited some of these moments let me range over several places where this mismatching of desires occurs. Much of the peculiar implication of the passage depends on the density of its sexual ambience.

Isabel, for example, represents herself as having "taken all the first steps in the purest confidence"—childlike, we might say, and innocently—when "she had suddenly found the infinite vista of a multiplied life to be a dark, narrow alley with a dead wall at the end. Instead of leading to the high places of happiness, from which the world would seem to lie below one, so that one could look down with a sense of exaltation and advantage . . . it led rather downward and earthward," leading, in other words, into the world of the material and the sexual. A multiplied life, I take it, carries with it a sense of a multiplying, that is, reproductively active, life; while the dark, narrow alley and the ideas of downward and earthward conjure images of physical relations and of birth. Such ideas of the physical and earthly do not necessarily contradict what Isabel imagines as the high places of happiness. The physical and the spiritual do, however, come to contradict each other when Isabel misperceives the relation between them, the relation between sexuality and love. In wishing to exempt herself from ordinary human feeling, Isabel expresses a primary egotism, which is at base a fear of sexuality. Isabel's egocentricity is not so very different from Osmond's. It is a reluctance to be like other people (this theme reverberates in American romance fiction, and I will return to it later). It is part of the naïveté of her misconceived Emersonianism. "It was her deep distrust of her husband [that] darkened the world." The shadows that thus emanate from him have particularly to do with a "half" of his nature she had not heretofore glimpsed—the physical, sexual side, leading downward and earthward, to the dark and narrow alley of sexual intercourse and birth (349–50). Isabel's introduction to doubt is a part of her confrontation with sexuality—his and hers. Osmond as the agent of skeptical reflection reduces Emerson's shining apparition to sly malice. But the doubt that Osmond introduces is no less effective an instrument of skepticist education.

Isabel knows that her falling in love with Osmond had to with a feeling of "ardor" that had taken possession of her. She was under his "charm": "the finest . . . manly organism she had ever known had become her property" (351–52). But Isabel denies the sexuality implicit in this. To her, ardor appears rather to be "tenderness," a desire to "launch" Osmond: "As she looked back at the passion of those full weeks she perceived in it a kind of maternal strain—the happiness of a woman who felt that she was a contributor, that she came with charged hands"—charged in her view with some sort of moral or religious fervor rather than with passion. "The recognition of her having but to put out her hands and take [this manly organism for her own] had been originally a sort of act of devotion" (352). No wonder, then, that the bedroom should seem a "house of darkness . . . dumbness [and] suffocation" or that his demands, as he stood forth erect and made her push back her skirts, should be tantamount to rape: "His egotism lay hidden like a serpent in a bank of flowers" (353).

What is sexuality? What is our knowledge of our sexual desire, of someone else's? Are sexual desire and the desire for children the same thing, and how do children change the valence of sexual feeling? James does not provide answers to these questions. To imagine, however, that he is not raising just these issues is to severely diminish the depth and range of his enterprise.

Why shouldn't Pansy be married as you would put a letter in the post office? "But even then she stopped again in the middle of the room and stood there gazing at a remembered vision—that of her husband and Madame Merle unconsciously and familiarly associated" (358). Children are not texts to be written. They are not instruments of the communication between their parents. Nor are they products of an unconscious and familiar communion that precludes the need for communication altogether. In the end Lord Warburton will not mail the letter to Osmond proposing his marriage to Pansy largely because of what Pansy herself manages to communicate to him about what she has undertaken to communicate to Ned Rossier. This is her declaration to Ned that although she will not disobey her father, she will not abandon Ned, either. As I suggested earlier, Pansy is the surprise in this book; she is a lot more like her ancestor Pearl, independent and strong-willed, than anyone (including the reader) expects.

To lend her support to Pansy's decision and help Pansy make a good marriage (not in her father's sense of the word), Isabel has to understand what Pansy already understands about love. This she does at Gardencourt, when Caspar Goodwood reveals to her not only his sexual desire (which her husband also embodies) but hers as well. Isabel's climactic meeting with Caspar seems like one more instance of her flight from sexuality. On some level it is. But James's conclusion wrestles with the fact that both the withdrawal from sexual relations and the indiscriminate indulgence in them may constitute acts of moral violation and escape. The only distinction between flight and commitment is the conscious choice that such a decision embodies. This choice, for James as for Hawthorne, has to do with the idea of family, with taking responsibility for the consequences of a sexual encounter. For neither of these writers is there any consecration outside the social realm. Like Pearl, Pansy evidences why this is so.

Isabel's final meeting with Caspar is set up to recall two earlier scenes in which she confronted male sexuality—when she receives marriage proposals from Lord Warburton and from Caspar himself. "The place had an air of association. Then she remembered that she had been sitting there, six years before, when a servant brought her from the house the letter in which Caspar Goodwood informed her that he had followed her to Europe; and that when she read the letter she looked up to hear Lord Warburton announcing that he should like to marry her. . . . The past came back to her in one of those rushing waves of emotion" (477). The final scene with Caspar reveals once again Isabel's intense fear of male sexuality. But it reveals that fear—to Isabel as well as to the reader—to be not so much of the man's desire for her as of her own desire for him.[11]

Isabel is correct to suspect Caspar's intentions. "He glared at her a moment through the dusk, and the next instant she felt his arms about her and his lips on her own lips. His kiss was like white lightning, a flash that spread, and spread again, and stayed; and it was extraordinarily as if, while she took it, she felt each thing in his hard manhood that had least pleased her, each aggressive fact of his face, his figure, his presence, justified of its intense identity and made one with this act of possession" (482). Isabel may well object to this kiss, which does reveal a lot about Caspar, not to mention Osmond and perhaps (at least in James's view) men in general. But the white lightning is not to be denied. The flash that spread, and spread again, is her own response to that kiss, not what Caspar imposes on her.

The next moment, which occurs "in an extraordinary short time—for the distance was considerable" (482), consolidates the equally considerable, philosophical distance of Isabel's experience into the instant of her confrontation with her own sexuality. What passes through her mind at the moment of the kiss is Goodwood's face and figure, his bodily presence. And so Isabel dies, in the manner of one of the most ancient puns in English literature, within her own sexual orgasm: "So had she heard of those wrecked and under water following a train of images before they sink" (482). What happens next is crucial: "But when darkness returned she was free. She never looked about her; she only darted from the spot. There were lights in the windows of the house; they shone far across the lawn. In an extraordinarily short time—for the distance was considerable—she had moved through the darkness (for she saw nothing) and reached the door. Here only she paused. She looked all about her; she listened a little; then she put her hand on the latch. She had not known where to turn; but she knew now. There was a very straight path" (482).

This straight path is not, I maintain, one more figure for Isabel's perceived sexual frigidity or her asceticism and self-denial. Her moment of sexual ecstasy is anticipated by—and also sharply discriminated from—the moment immediately preceding the embrace, when she feels the world opening out around her, in "the form of a mighty sea, where she floated in fathomless waters. She had wanted help, and here was help; it had come in a rushing torrent. . . . she believed just then that to let him take her in his arms would be the next best thing to her dying. This belief, for a moment, was a kind of rapture, in which she felt herself sink and sink. In the movement she seemed to beat with her feet, in order to catch herself, to feel something to rest on" (481). This moment reconstructs the powerful death wish that Isabel expresses during her train ride to London and that she once again articulates to Ralph at his deathbed. "She envied Ralph his dying, for if one were thinking of rest that was the most perfect of all. To cease utterly, to give it all up and not know anything more—this idea was as sweet as the vision of a cool bath in a marble tank, in a darkened chamber, in a hot land" (457). "I would die if you could live," she tells Ralph; "I would die myself, not to lose you" (469). Like Edna Pontellier in Kate Chopin's *Awakening,* Isabel would escape the life of active sexuality, the life of interpersonal relationships, in which so much is dark, terrifying, and divisive. She would drown herself in the passive unity of a sexual wholeness achieved without sexual relations. "She had moments . . . in her journey from Rome which were almost as good as being dead" (457).

Isabel would like nothing more at this moment in her life than to escape. Dying, whether in literal fact or metaphorically in sexuality, seems to her preferable to enduring the reality of her life with Osmond. This desire for refuge has brought her back to Gardencourt, to the dying Ralph and to the sexually desirous Caspar Goodwood. Isabel's rejection of Caspar, then, represents her rejection of the alternative that he, like Ralph, embodies: dying away from life and commitment and responsibility. This is one thing that sexuality, like death, can represent, and she rejects it. But while experiencing sexual desire, Isabel also recollects what sexual intercourse between men and women can also produce. "In life there's love," Ralph tells Isabel (470).[12] In love there's life, we might add. Pansy is the figure for both of these truths, which bring Isabel back home.

The straight path back that Isabel discovers at the end of the novel is the path back to life and hence back to love, and—although she may never achieve her own passionate fulfillment because of the nature of her relationship to Osmond—back to the daughter's desire. Isabel discovers the path back the moment that she experiences sexuality, not as the denial of life, but as one of its most fundamental expressions. Her orgasm delivers her back to life—not through a sudden revelation or epiphany that illuminates the world but, quite the opposite, through her private and personal confrontation with the darkness, the nothingness, that is at the center of human consciousness and being. The text stresses that all the lights are shining. Nonetheless, Isabel moves in darkness. She sees nothing; she sees *the* nothing, which represents the insubstantiality and immateriality of the world. Seeing the nothing, Isabel comes to understand that all that distinguishes it from the eclipse of consciousness that we call death or unconsciousness is the choice to affirm life despite it. Isabel's ability to see the nothing testifies to the skeptical consciousness that Isabel has acquired over the course of her experience. Putting her hand on the latch, opening the door, Isabel returns home. From the beginning of the book, Isabel has been associated with one house or another. At the end she returns, not so much to a physical home as to the idea of home as a place of sexuality and family. Isabel knows that to escape with Caspar into sexuality (as into death) or to escape from sexuality altogether—as she tried to do when she rejected Caspar to marry Osmond—will not solve the essential crisis of her life. So she returns to her daughter, to the next generation of women, for whom she bears primary responsibility.

In *The Reproduction of Mothering,* Nancy Chodorow disputes the Freudian idea that women develop heterosexual feelings for men because they envy the male penis and want to incorporate it into themselves. In the Freudian view of female sexuality, the child substitutes for the penis: it is what men can give women in its place. Chodorow challenges these ideas by claiming that women are motivated by their own innate sexual feelings and that they desire men because men can satisfy those feelings. One might read the end of James's novel as confirming the Freudian view: Isabel returns to the child who seems a substitute for the hard manliness she both craves and rejects. The case is otherwise. The final scene, which develops directly from the earlier scenes of Isabel's instruction in philosophical skepticism, portrays the woman's realization that her sexuality belongs to her and not to anyone else. Isabel understands that her sexuality is innate and—this is the crucial point—that she cannot know it in any scientific or objective way. To love, Isabel discovers, is not to settle one's doubts about what one does or does not know. To love is to know only in the sense of to acknowledge and affirm, to go back home, to create a home, in the absence of proof and certainty.

The home to which Isabel returns is even more imprisoning than the one that Hester reoccupies on the edge of Puritan society. Freed of her connection to men altogether, Hester will enjoy as well the liberty of living at the margins. But Isabel's decision, like Hester's, throws into prominence the fact that having a home is no more inevitable or natural or easy than having children is. Home is a decision, a choice; it requires a constant process of returning to. In James's novel, with its stepmother-stepdaughter relationship, where the stepmother resumes her role upon her return home, family becomes the most deliberate of human choices. *The Portrait of a Lady* is not, I think, one more male picture of femininity, silently reinscribing the woman into patriarchal society. James's novel, like Hawthorne's, seeks nothing less than to domesticate the nation, to make the world into a home—one with all of the obligations and responsibilities that biology forces upon us. In this home, however, mother, father, and child can reside by principles other than those of psychological or sociological or even biological determinism.

3

Worlds Without Women

Herman Melville

and Edgar Allan Poe

At crucial moments in *The Scarlet Letter* and *The Portrait of a Lady*—and in William Faulkner's *Sound and the Fury* as well—the female protagonists (Caddy Compson in Faulkner) contemplate committing suicide. Hester, in fact, contemplates both suicide and infanticide. James's comments on Isabel may serve to explicate Hester's and Caddy's reasons for persevering with their lives, despite the considerable pain they feel and despite the insolubility of the crises in which they find themselves:

> Deep in her soul—deeper than any appetite for renunciation—was the sense that life would be her business for a long time to come. And at moments there was something inspiring, almost enlivening, in the conviction. It was a proof of strength—it was a proof she should some day be happy again. It couldn't be she was to live only to suffer; she was still young, after all, and a great many things might happen to her yet. To live only to suffer—only to feel the injury of life repeated and enlarged—it seemed to her she was too valuable, too capable, for that.

Then she wondered if it were vain and stupid to think so well of herself. When had it ever been a guarantee to be valuable? Wasn't all history full of the destruction of precious things? Wasn't it much more probable that if one were fine one would suffer? It involved then perhaps an admission that one had a certain grossness; but Isabel recognised, as it passed before her eyes, the quick vague shadow of a long future. She should never escape; she should last to the end.[1]

Isabel's conviction that she will live, that she must live, is, as I have already suggested, given depth by Ralph's statement that in life there's love. Isabel's love for Pansy, like Hester's love for Pearl and Caddy's love for her daughter, Quentin (which recalls her love for her brother, Benjy), constitute in these novels what Hawthorne calls a "woman's strength" and what James calls "proof of strength." This strength is intimately tied in all of these novels to the realities and responsibilities of motherhood.

In two of the major texts in the now-emerging canon of women's fiction, Kate Chopin's *Awakening* and Edith Wharton's *House of Mirth,* suicide is the course of action from which the heroine does not turn aside. A major element of my argument in this book is that at least four of the most important American women writers of the twentieth century—Carson McCullers, Flannery O'Connor, Toni Morrison, and Grace Paley—inherit the romance tradition of Hawthorne, Melville, Poe, James, and Faulkner. They do *not* (as we might suppose or even wish) inherit the women's tradition of Harriet Beecher Stowe, Susan Ann Warner, Maria Cummins, Lydia Maria Child, E. D. E. N. Southworth, Kate Chopin, Edith Wharton, Sarah Orne Jewett, and Mary Wilkins Freeman—to cite only a few of the possible female forebears. The line of inheritance has something to do with the availability of the male romancers when McCullers, O'Connor, Morrison, and Paley were writing. But it also has to do with the kind of skepticist-genderist fiction that the male romancers write. Their fiction provides the basis for a declaration of female identity that sacrifices nothing of the strength of a woman as a sexual, reproductive, philosophical, and sociopolitical being.

Even as we say this, we must immediately acknowledge that imaginings of female strength—an idea immortalized in fiction by Faulkner's comment about Dilsey, that "she endured"—do not necessarily imply a feminist consciousness. The existence of such women as Hester and Isabel does, I think, contradict Judith Fetterley's assertion that in depicting the powerlessness of women in American society male writers like Hawthorne, James, Faulkner, and Ernest Hemingway could not get beyond the image of the woman as helpless. As has also been pointed out, myths of the woman as enduring earth goddesses may not necessarily convert male texts into feminist ones. Such myths are as abundant and as time-honored as myths of the woman as the embodiment of purity, divinity, and self-sacrifice. They may serve to reinstate, not dislodge, the status quo.[2]

The suicides in both Chopin's and Wharton's novels might be read as registering their resistance to just this apparent nonchalance in the male tradition about the political and social disadvantaging of women. As Elizabeth Ammons has argued about the frequently contrasted works of James and Wharton, Wharton's flawed and failing women may directly comment on James's misplaced and somewhat inappropriate confidence in his women's strength.[3] Male-female relationships in American society are inextricable from power structures. Feminist fiction inevitably contains a politics of feminism, even where the text seems not to have much to do with politics in the conventional sense of the word.[4] Chopin and Wharton may have seen a painful lack of such a political dimension not only in the nineteenth-century male romance tradition but in the sentimental female tradition as well.

One complaint against the male tradition, then, might be that despite the authors' awareness of the sexism of patriarchal society, they could imagine no alternative to it. They might, therefore, despite their best efforts, have rein-scribed the terms of gender construct even as they questioned them. This objection forms the basis of the major resistance to Hawthorne and James as "feminist" authors, despite their depictions of recognizably strong female protagonists. Let me put the argument as Alfred Habegger formulates it in *Henry James and the "Woman Business."* Habegger asserts that James's writings appropriate and distort, for complex social, intellectual-historical, and psychological reasons (which Habegger traces in his book), basic themes and images of nineteenth-century fiction by women, which James's contemporary readers would immediately have recognized and understood.[5]

Of particular importance to the construction of James's *Portrait,* according to Habegger, is the "traditional orphan-heroine's story," popular in the writings of nineteenth-century women. Emerging "from a denial of the agonist premise that the heroine truly wishes to be free," the *Portrait* is also "concerned to enclose, sum up, assess this story." The *Portrait* thus comes to be "*about* the treacherous feminine imagination that had created a vast Anglo-American tradition of fiction." It does not so much tell the woman's story as prevent the woman from telling that story for herself. Just as Isabel suffers the fate of being silenced by her tyrannical husband, so, too, argues Habegger, does James's book suppress the female voices that it incorporates (including the voice of James's own beloved cousin Minnie Temple). Habegger concludes that James is not a feminist or even a protofeminist.[6] Nor is Habegger alone in feeling that James produces a striking female consciousness in his major romance fictions, *Daisy Miller, The American,* and *Portrait,* only to make that consciousness a part of the male economy in which his texts function.[7]

One could make very similar arguments about Hawthorne's *Scarlet Letter,* in which the success of the male writer (economically, politically, socially, and historically) derives directly from his appropriation of a woman's artwork. For Hester, the scarlet letter is the painfully wrought expression of her anguish and her desire. For Hawthorne, at least when he first confronts it in the Custom-House, the letter is "worn and faded . . . greatly frayed and defaced, so that none, or very little, of the glitter was left, [a] rag of scarlet cloth,—for time, and wear, and a sacrilegious moth, had reduced it to little other than a rag."[8] Hawthorne would seem to be twice guilty in *The Scarlet Letter.* He reneges on his argument about women's rights, pulling Hester back into the patriarchal world from which she had managed her escape.[9] He also reinscribes Hester within patriarchal society so that he may take up her letter and use it to his own considerable advantage. Hawthorne's apparent exploitation of the letter might stand for what many women feel about the relation of most men to female culture.

I will respond to some of these charges against James's and Hawthorne's fiction at the end of this chapter. For the moment, however, I want only to cite them and to suggest that neither Hawthorne nor James is the arrogant male ventriloquist that some critics have described them as being. What prevents the romancers' telling of the woman's story from becoming a male takeover has to do with the conditions of domesticity that prevail in both the *Letter* and the *Portrait.* These are the conditions of home that dominate the major nineteenth-century women's tradition and that are decidedly not present in the fiction of the two other important nineteenth-century male romancers, Edgar Allan Poe and Herman Melville.

Like the fictions of Hawthorne and James, those of Poe and Melville, and those of William Faulkner as well, are trenchantly antipatriarchal.[10] They figure as important influences on the twentieth-century women's tradition, especially

Southern women's fiction with its decidedly gothic strain. But whereas the absence of the woman from the sociopolitical reality that Hawthorne and James inhabit compels these writers to attempt to reincorporate the woman, this same fact in the lives of Poe, Melville, and Faulkner leads them rather to reinscribe their society's silencing of the woman. Poe and Melville and to a lesser degree Faulkner present worlds without women. (The centrality and the silence of Caddy in *The Sound and the Fury* represents Faulkner's variation on this feature of the gothic romance tradition; I will discuss Faulkner in my next two chapters.) In so doing, Poe and Melville create a world as some men might fantasize it. This is a world (like Hawthorne's Custom-House) largely free of female presence. These writers also demonstrate the sterility of such a world, its sheer gothic horribleness. But in leaving the woman unrepresented, excluding them from male society, Poe and Melville also suggest what it would mean for male writers *not* to represent women speaking in their texts. At first glance, the silence of Poe's and Melville's women might seem an appropriate decorum on the parts of these male writers. In the final analysis, however, it exacerbates rather than resolves the problem of patriarchy. My purpose here is twofold. I want to trace the contours of Poe's and Melville's special variety of antipatriarchal critique. At the same time, I want to consider why Hawthorne's and James's kind of romance fiction might better suit the purposes of later women authors than does the Poe and Melville variety.

The Pregnant Lesson of Moby Dick

One response to my recuperating Melville's *Moby Dick* as an antipatriarchal text might be simply to say, You jest.[11] Surely, as Richard Brodhead has suggested,

> *Moby-Dick* is a novel so outrageously masculine that we scarcely allow ourselves to do justice to the full scope of its masculinism. It is a masculine book in the obvious sense that it is all about men and men's activities. (The feminine sphere as the nineteenth-century described it—the sphere of piety, home, family love and nurture, and general sociability—is the missing element in a novel otherwise so inclusive.) But it is masculine too in its deepest dramatic fantasies: What is the hunt for the enormous sperm male Moby Dick if not a quest for absolute potency, a quest in which the aggressive assertion of masculine strength calls up a fantastically enlarged version of that strength as its imagined nemesis?[12]

And yet isn't Melville's point in *Moby Dick,* as it is Hawthorne's in "The Custom-House" (or, for that matter, Harriet Beecher Stowe's in *Uncle Tom's Cabin* or a host of other nineteenth-century women novelists) that in an America otherwise so inclusive, the feminine sphere is the one place that has been ignored and abandoned, so that men recklessly seek absolute potency, only to discover sterility and death? It seems to me that we resist too much in Melville's novel when we fail to catch the poignancy of its lament throughout its concluding chapters for home and family or when we ignore the devastation of its ending, when Ishmael, riding the coffin, is not reborn into sexuality and procreation but remains floating in uterine waters, in unabating infantile regression. "Let us home!" Starbuck beseeches Ahab just before they embark upon their final, fatal, pursuit of the whale. "Wife and child, too, are Starbuck's—wife and child of his brotherly, sisterly, play-fellow youth; even as thine, Sir, are the wife and child of thy loving, longing, paternal old age! Away! let us away!" (534). The tragedy in this novel is that Ahab will not go home. Peleg assures Ishmael earlier in the story that Ahab "has a wife—not three voyages wedded—a sweet, resigned girl. Think of that; by that sweet girl that old man has a child: hold ye then there can be any utter, hopeless harm in Ahab? No, no, my lad; stricken, blasted, if he be, Ahab has his humanities!" (80).

But Ahab refuses to assume the responsibilities of husband and father. He will not resist the "nameless, inscrutable, unearthly thing . . . [the] cozening, hidden lord and master, and cruel, remorseless emperor [that] commands [him]; that against all natural lovings and longings . . . so keep[s him] pushing, and crowding, and jamming . . . all the time" against his "proper, natural heart" (535). Ahab refuses, in other words, to quit his self-consuming, masturbatory quest for self-authorization and self-fulfillment and to return to his "girl-wife," whom he "wedded past fifty, and sailed for Cape Horn the next day, leaving but one dent in my marriage pillow—wife? wife?—rather a widow with her husband alive!" (533). (That Ahab has a girl-wife puts him in the less than illustrious company of Chillingworth and Osmond and raises many of the same issues about marriage with which Hawthorne and James deal.) Starbuck's pleadings with Ahab take place against the background of a search very different from that of Ahab's for the whale—which is to say for the phallus, whether as male organ or as the symbol of symbolic consciousness. This is the search of the *Rachel* for her lost children. When Ahab refuses to return to his wife and child and to search for the lost children, he sets on his final journey toward death.

Nor does Ishmael's scant survival at the end of the novel provide much relief from the pervasive sense of doom. Most critics are agreed that Ahab is a monomaniac of the first order.[13] Many, however, have insisted in seeing Ishmael as an alter-Ahab, who can capitalize on Ahab's legitimate intellectual gifts and designs without losing the human connection. In particular, Ishmael's relationship to Queequeg has been interpreted as a paradigm of human intercourse.[14] That Ishmael alone survives the wreck, buoyed up on Queequeg's coffin, would seem to confirm that whatever salvation exists in the world of this text accrues to those whose souls have reached out to other (male) souls.

But Ishmael's story is little more than Melville's self-conscious rendering of one man's childlike and impotent, grotesque, masturbatory fantasy of self-fulfillment. As many critics have argued, Melville's novel acknowledges the fundamental strangeness of an unknowable universe, as much through the way it tells its story as through the story itself. Ishmael's experience and the story push in the opposite direction, toward deadening certainty and paralyzing self-fulfillment.[15] Ishmael is well placed to tell the story of the egotistical Ahab.[16] Fundamentally, he shares Ahab's drive to render an unknowable universe knowable. For Melville no less than for Hawthorne and James, this desire to settle the skeptical question is gendered. Like Gilbert Osmond in Isabel's early, immature view of him, Ishmael and Ahab only appear to be skepticist voyagers. They are instead seekers of knowledge and certainty and self-replication.

Throughout the novel Melville signals how Ishmael's narrative—which is everywhere marked by the quality of a dream—attempts to resolve doubt:

Some years ago—never mind how long precisely—having little or no money in my purse, and nothing particular to interest me on shore, I thought I would sail about a little and see the watery part of the world. It is a way I have of driving off the spleen, and regulating the circulation. Whenever I find myself growing grim about the mouth; whenever it is a damp, drizzly November in my soul; whenever I find myself involuntarily pausing before coffin warehouses, and bringing up the rear of every funeral I meet; and especially whenever my hypos get such an upper hand of me, that it requires a strong moral principle to prevent me from deliberately stepping into the street, and methodically knocking people's hats off—then, I account it high time to get to sea as soon as I can. This is my substitute for pistol and ball. With a philosophical flourish Cato throws himself upon his sword; I quietly take to the ship.

Except for the famous sentence "Call me Ishmael" (to which I will recur in a moment), this paragraph opens Melville's novel. The desire to sail about to see the watery parts of the world is identified from the beginning as a response to a world of uncertainties and doubts. Whenever his hypos get the better of him, Ishmael starts knocking people's hats off—a response that is as comical as it is menacing and that suggests a connection between violence and skepticism. Fraught with doubts about his own existence, he sets about proving that existence by causing visible consequences in the real world. The scene recalls Pearl's similar ventures into doubt and self-affirmation, when she simultaneously sets little fleets of boats asail and pelts birds with stones. (The scene may also set the stage for Ralph Ellison's *Invisible Man* a century later.) It seems that for Melville, as for Hawthorne, the self will prove itself at whatever cost—even Poe fashion (as Stanley Cavell suggests), by destroying itself or others.[17]

Recognizing his destructive tendencies, Ishmael chooses the less violent of the alternatives. Rather than take up pistol and ball, he takes to sea. But in this book of abundant sexual puns, the pistol and ball, not to mention the sword, also represent male sexuality, for which his trip to sea is a substitute. Pearl fashions for herself a green *A,* emblemizing her budding awareness of where her doubt is leading her—toward progenerative relationships with others. Ishmael's response to skepticism evades sexual knowledge and the options that it provides. His response is suicidal. That he survives the drowning that overtakes the rest of the crew when they pursue the whale, instead of rescuing (or returning to or becoming in engaged in having) their children, may be attributed not so much to Ishmael's superior philosophical wisdom as to awakening from his dream of potency, his fantasy of asexual procreation, which is the story itself: "I was then, but slowly, drawn towards the closing vortex. When I reached it, it had subsided to a creamy pool. Round and round, then, and ever contracting toward the button-like black bubble at the axis of that slowly wheeling circle, like another Ixion I did revolve. Till, gaining that vital centre, the black bubble upward burst; and now, liberated by reason of its cunning spring, and owing to its great buoyancy, rising with great force, the coffin life-buoy shot lengthwise from the sea, fell over, and floated by my side" (566). Like so many other moments in the book, this one reads as a masturbatory wet dream in which the dreamer, entertaining sexual fantasies (suggested by the Ixion reference) but incapable of sexual deeds, is threatened with drowning in his own creamy semen. Ishmael will produce no futurity. Having awoken, Ishmael may, as we may, learn the lessons of his own dream of asexual generation. He also may not learn it.

The conclusion of the book does not present a scene of birth or of rebirth—as many readers have felt. It dramatizes instead a desire for being *unborn*. The desire to return to the womb is related to another fantasy that pervades the book: the imagining of birthing oneself. As Ishmael is being drawn back into the maelstrom of his own masturbatory fantasy (like the sailors in Poe's "Descent into the Maelström" and *Arthur Gordon Pym*), Ishmael searches for a way *not* to be redelivered by this ocean womb, which is also, for this reason, a grave. The association of the life buoy with the coffin, the womb with the grave, is not, I think, some masculinist aggression against women. Rather, it identifies a possible feature of male mentality or male socialization that Melville would resist. Men, according to Melville (at least some men) would like to be unborn, out of the world of women; and they desire this because they desire to rebirth themselves through some wholly male mechanism.

The scene of Ishmael's desire for unbirth and self-contracting rebirth is replicated at several key moments in the text, making the book itself a scene of non-procreative labor. Queequeg's midwifery, for example, does not really deliver Tashtego into life. It only saves him from being unborn when he falls back into the uterine head of the dead whale. The birth is represented as an inverted or breech birth. The Jonah sermon that Ishmael hears earlier anticipates the scene. In the sermon "the whale came breeching up towards the warm and pleasant sun, and all the delights of air and earth; and 'vomited out Jonah upon the dry land' [and] Jonah did the Almighty's bidding . . . to preach the Truth" (47). (The names Tashtego and Tarshish may further yoke these two moments together.) Like Tashtego, Jonah knows an unnatural birth, which may only be the consequence of his desire to be unborn or at least not to be reborn. Although Father Mapple might understand Jonah's delivery by the hand of God to be thus redemptive, our experience in the novel of another "pilot of the living God" (47), who is single-minded in his pursuit of truth, suggests another, more heretical reading of the Jonah story. This second reading is, I suggest, part of the "pregnant lesson" (41) of Melville's text. Like Hawthorne in *The Scarlet Letter,* Melville in *Moby Dick* examines the implications of male-directed virgin births (even when the man is a god), whether the sources of those births are female bodies or their symbolic representation as the bodies of whales.

Ishmael's only recorded memory of his childhood fits directly into the pattern of attempted unbirth and self-birth: Ishmael tries to climb up a chimney and is pulled out again, in the breech position, by someone who, though in this case a woman, is not his natural mother. The succeeding scene is equally important for the pattern that Melville is establishing. Banished to bed, the young Ishmael longs for resurrection; he desires to complete the process begun when he first climbed up the chimney. He discovers instead a deathliness and paralysis that he cannot quite shake off, which culminate in his fantasy of the hand-holding phantom. The "phantom" that Ishmael is seeking to recover when he goes off to sea (3), the phantom that is only a version of the self, originates in the fantasy of self-generation that Ishmael first experienced as a child. He discovers the phantom, or imagines that he discovers it, in Queequeg, who arouses in Ishmael the very same "sensations at feeling the supernatural hand" in his own, minus the "awful fear" that accompanied that first experience (26). Queequeg is less fearful to Ishmael than the phantom of his youth because he is flesh and blood. But to point out that he is a man is only to say that the passion that exists between Ishmael and Queequeg is an attempt on Ishmael's part to discover or rediscover the phantom of self in the world. Homosexuality seems to have served a purpose for Melville similar to that of incest in Faulkner's fiction: it approximated sexual intercourse with and of the self.

Moby Dick, I suggest, is Melville's self-conscious rendering of one man's all-consuming, self-deluding fantasy of self-contained male potency and self-generation. Melville recognizes the allure of this fantasy, but he realizes—and resists—its dangers. The male marriage of Ishmael and Queequeg may appear innocent and quaint in the early chapters of the novel; but tied together by a "monkey-rope," "wedded" as "twin" brothers, Queequeg and Ishmael are caught in a unending repetition of self that can yield nothing but deathly self-duplication (317). In this world of resistance, sexuality does not yield life. Instead, it verges on castrating male rape and self-destruction. "I will dismember my dismemberer," Ahab declares (166), summarizing the book's theme of revenge in precisely the right countersexual terms. Starbuck immediately comprehends the implications of this aspect of Ahab's quest as they pertain not only to the whale but to the entire male community over which Ahab would rule:

> My soul is more than matched; she's overmanned; and by a madman! Insufferable sting, that sanity should ground arms on such a field! But he drilled deep down, and blasted all my reason out of me. . . . Will I, nill I, the ineffable thing has tied me to him; tows me with a cable I have no knife to cut. Horrible old man! . . . Oh, God, to sail with such a heathen crew that have small touch of human mothers in them. Whelped some-

where by the sharkish sea. . . . Methinks it pictures life. Foremost through the sparkling sea shoots on the gay, embattled, bantering bow, but only to drag dark Ahab after it, where he broods within his sternward cabin, builded over the dead water of the wake, and further on, hunted by its wolfish gurglings. (166–67)

In the world here shadowed forth, sexuality is violence. Brooding over dead waters, motherless births produce heathens and orphans, who awaken to death, not life. Overmanned, Starbuck is unmanned. Only by dismembering his dismemberer (by cutting the monkey rope that weds the brothers) would he, like Ahab, be able to cut the umbilical cord–penis, the ineffable cablelike thing that ties him to his mother-father. Melville intends every bit of this grotesqueness. (Further confirmation of the association of umbilicus with penis may be had from the description of the whale umbilicus as resembling a sailor's rope.) As Edgar Allan Poe understood all too well, masturbatory self-impregnation is a serious matter.

Male Economy and Female Speech

Like Hawthorne's "Custom-House" sketch, *Moby Dick* depicts the consequences of the male desire—everywhere dramatized in the fiction of Edgar Allan Poe—to constitute the world as wholly male, wholly symbolic, wholly ideal, and therefore wholly not female, at least not in the biological sense of the word. In a series of Poe stories, including "Ligeia," "Morella," "Berenice," "Eleanora," "The Fall of the House of Usher," and "The Oval Portrait," the attempt on the part of the male narrator to transcendentalize and aetherialize the woman out of existence culminates in his horrific discovery—made too late—that in killing off the flesh, he has stranded himself in a wasteland of sterility, death, and destruction.[18] (Melville may be invoking Poe when he opens *Moby Dick* with a description of "the pale Usher . . . dusting his old lexicons and grammars"—xix.) By the end of the typical Poe story the narrator is as speechless as he is lifeless. The dizzy swoon, for example, that is about to overtake the narrator in "The House of Usher" as he is poised to topple over into the tarn (which has its counterparts in the other Poe stories) is one figure for the same masturbatory wash in which Ishmael also finds himself when, spilling his seed to no purpose, he awakens (or dies) into a world without women.

The sterility of a world engendered by impotent male fantasies of self-reproduction exposes part of what lies behind the famous opening injunction of *Moby Dick*. "Call me Ishmael" has its analogue in the self-declarations with which the typical Poe story also begins. Like many a Poe narrator, Ishmael would birth and name himself. But in so doing, he ensures that even though he may wander like his biblical ancestor, he will not, like that ancestor, father a nation—great or otherwise. What remains at the end of this story about men in an all-male universe is the Ishmael who, like the many narrators of Poe's gothic fiction, is painfully and tenuously caught in the position of being endlessly birthed-unbirthed-rebirthed: it is impossible to say which.

Or perhaps what remains in *Moby Dick,* in addition to Ishmael, is the whale itself and the natural universe that the whale figures forth. Melville, in recommitting his text to the world of nature, parts company with Poe and declares his allegiance to Hawthorne's brand of romance fiction. Poe's fiction culminates in self-annihilation and an absolute, irremediable end to history. Melville's novel comes very close to such an end, as does the fiction of another Poe descendant in the romance tradition, William Faulkner. But Melville imagines the whale, and the whale, like the letter in Hawthorne's novel, returns us to the world of the feminine and the maternal from which Melville's egomaniacal males, like Hawthorne's and James's, would separate it.

Moby Dick is the grand figure of the potent, abundant world of nature that Melville's novel develops in such precise and loving detail—quite in opposition to the mind-set of its major character. This world—the natural universe— is far more powerful, far vaster, far more intensely reproductive than the figurative male world that assaults it. The whale defies the idealism, symbolism, and egocentricity of the male characters. As part of the realm of nature, it does not embody the law of symbolic presence, as Ahab insists—hence its silence, like the silence of the mother in both *The Scarlet Letter* and *The Portrait of a Lady.* Because the whale is a physical presence, it is a figure for the inchoate, nonfigural language (the gurglings and bubbling of the sea itself) that feminist critics have called the mother tongue.

The sperm whale as mother tongue might sound as farfetched as it sounds grotesque (notwithstanding Carson McCullers's representation of the tongue of her mute male protagonist as a whale speaking, in a novel deeply concerned with male and female ways of speaking). But it is no more farfetched and certainly no more grotesque than Ahab's attempt (akin to Hester's and Isabel's— though far more extreme) to transform a living creature into a text. Nor is it any more absurd than trying to read Melville's encyclopedic commentary on the

natural world as an allegory. The whale's biological maleness in no way interferes with its naturalness. Male sexuality, therefore, is not necessarily Melville's
villain in the social construct of gender. The whale is sexually progenerative.
But by transcendentalizing the sperm whale, rendering it symbolic, Ahab dis-
sociates sexuality from genderedness. He replaces potent sexual identity with a
crippling and sterile social construct of gender. As a result, Ahab cannot find
his way back to the source of all language and of all life: the reproductive world
of nature. The offspring of his mad quest for male supremacy in his self-gener-
ated world of symbolic meanings is the infertile, fetal Ishmael, who (if he produces anything at all) will birth nothing but himself.

Speaking the Mother Tongue

Let me add to the letter and the whale the portrait in James's novel—not the
interpretation of Isabel that the major characters of the novel would impose
upon her but her physical self, the embodiment of her living presence. Letter,
whale, and portrait are material objects that express a kind of natural language,
associated in these texts with the maternal. This language, the three authors
insist in their books, has been appropriated to male discourse. Therefore, they
recover these objects and through them the woman and the language she
speaks. Does the recovery constitute its own aggression against the woman?
Does focusing the drama on the great sperm whale—despite the antipatriarchal message of the book and despite the reticence to speak the woman's
words—return the discourse of society and literature to the phallocentric
realm from which the image of Ishmael's infantile, impotent, (self)(un)-
(re)birthing seems at last to deliver it? There is no way out of the bind of power
relations. If women are not permitted to speak and men speak for them, the
status quo is inevitably reinforced. Then, how does a man lend his voice to the
woman's cause? How do any of us, for that matter, if we do not happen to be
the victims, in every sense of the word, speak of gender discrimination *and*
racism *and* class, religious and ethnic persecution, and so on? Can silence be
our only response? And what (and for whom) might be the cost of that silence?

If silence is all that male speech may be permitted in a world already disfig-
ured by male language, then Poe and Melville emerge as more powerfully positive feminist authors than Hawthorne and James. Both Poe and Melville confess the problem of patriarchal society to be its repression of women. Both
represent language as originating as much within women as within men. But

neither goes any further than to depict the consequences of male dominance and the silencing of female speech. In this, Melville (for all his gloominess) is the more hopeful of the two writers: whereas Poe imagines a fatality from which there is no return, Melville imagines the female as persisting within the world of nature and therefore within the human community. (I am reminded here of Hawthorne's discovery of the letter in the Custom-House, which reconfirms that although the tie with the woman has been forgotten, it can still be recovered, even within the world of patriarchy.) The same logic that makes Poe and Melville stronger feminists than Hawthorne and James, however, also makes Poe a stronger feminist than Melville. Poe's vision of patriarchy does not presume for an instant to sidestep the consequences of the silencing of women. For Poe there is no sperm whale who continues to embody, envision, and speak a mother tongue. Like Kate Chopin and Edith Wharton after him (and, we might add, like Faulkner), he can figure forth only the death of the beautiful woman.

There is, from a feminist perspective, much to recommend Poe's and Melville's refusal to imagine a world with women, as if the prisonhouse of patriarchy might simply suddenly be made to vanish (by men, no less) to make room for them. There is power in their refusal to speak in a woman's voice. It may well be that what women need from men is a willingness to recognize the problem of patriarchy and to speak against it without going so far as to put words in their mouths. But do James and Hawthorne in fact convert women into the instruments of their own creative undertaking and make them speak their words?

Here the silence at the end of *The Scarlet Letter,* as at the end of *The Portrait of a Lady*—where the texts refrain from reporting the heroes' words and thoughts—cannot be ignored. This silence is not unrelated to the silence of the whale itself. I have already argued that at the end of the *Letter* Hawthorne attributes to Hester a primary authority over his text. His words are only a paraphrase of hers. Nonetheless, Hawthorne acknowledges that the words thus recorded are to be only his rendering of her words, not a direct quotation. Some kind of silence still characterizes the conclusion of the *Letter,* but it is the silence, not of the woman, but of the author. The author refrains from presuming to say how Hester might herself have explained her return to New England. He refuses to violate the privacy of Hester's mind, just as he protects the contents of her correspondence with her daughter. There is a similar refusal at the end of the *Portrait,* when James refrains from specifying what it is that

Isabel knows that sends her home to Pansy. What a woman knows, what she doubts, how she loves and whom—these are secrets neither Hawthorne nor James presume to tell.

Hawthorne's and James's art might empower later women's writing in one more way. Hawthorne, by placing the letter on his own breast, makes his telling of the woman's story more than a nod in the direction of the marginalized victim of patriarchal society. He does more than entertain a different kind of language or recognize that whatever language has become it may well have originated (either within human history or within the psychosexual history of the individual) in a different kind of nonsymbolic, reality. By incorporating the female letter, Hawthorne acknowledges his own origins within the female body; he graphically demonstrates (in her language) that his story is the extension of hers, that he (and perhaps all men or, for that matter, all women) only edit and retell the stories their mothers tell to them. Such a relationship between child and parent, as between editor and text or surveyor and customs, is not without its aggressions. How could it not be? But for Hawthorne the important thing is not simply the story one embodies or tells but, as I suggested in the Introduction, why and how and from where one *chooses* to tell that story. Hester's position in Hawthorne's novel, only seems to mirror her place in Puritan society. When Hester resumes the letter, begins to speak, and, speaking, becomes the mother of her country, she ceases being a pawn in an all-male economy, whether her job is defined as seamstress (in the service of the great and powerful) or mother.[19]

A similar transformation occurs as Hester moves from her status as authorial device or character or symbol in the text to her status as creator of the story that Hawthorne tells. When Hawthorne puts himself in his mother's line of inheritance and declares himself her heir, he accepts and explicitly acknowledges that his power derives from hers, that he is empowered, even as he is engendered, by his mother. Hawthorne may profit from his mother's craft: as I have already suggested, it is her letter that he sells on the nineteenth-century literary marketplace and that secures his place in the canon of American literature. But his letter is a copy of hers, his language a language he has learned from her. So, I would argue, is James's *Portrait of a Lady* a story of female strength that places the writer in the position, not of the master (either of the text or of the home), but of the son, engendered by and responsible to the mother. His *Portrait,* like Hawthorne's *Letter,* merely reproduces the mother's inscription of herself.

Still, this summation seems a little too tidy, especially given Hawthorne's and James's confessed hostility to the women's movement, recorded by Hawthorne in *The Blithedale Romance* (and in his sketch on Anne Hutchinson) and by James in the novel that revises *Blithedale, The Bostonians*. If Hawthorne and James are as feminist as I am claiming that they are (at least in their two feminist novels), why were they so intolerant of the only women in the nineteenth century who seemed to be willing to speak? What is their grievance against what Hawthorne called the "damn'd mob of scribbling women," who were the dominant literary voices of their day and to whom James, at least, was largely indebted?[20]

Answers to these questions have to do with the difference between Hawthorne's and James's conception of home and the conception that dominated the domestic women's fiction of the day. And this, in turn, has to do with the difference between the aversions of romance fiction and the subversions of the competing traditions of female writing in the nineteenth century—the sentimentalist, domestic, and realist-regionalist traditions. Hawthorne knows and Poe, Melville, and James confirm that a Custom-House may not be a home. But neither may a home, as Harriet Beecher Stowe and others define it, be a place sufficient for sustaining human tenancy, capable of housing the generations to come. Homeward bound, the fiction of Hawthorne and James constructs for women the possibility of a political and economic future in America for which the nineteenth-century women's writings do not allow.

II

The Antiphallocentric Romance

4

The Material

Reproduction of Culture

William Faulkner

William Faulkner is the consummate twentieth-century romancer in the male line of the tradition.[1] Most critical readings of Faulkner have noted his difference from contemporary twentieth-century writers of realistic and naturalistic fiction and his striking continuity with the mid-nineteenth-century romancers—Hawthorne, Poe, and Melville. The eccentricity of his style—with its haunting suspensions of mimetic representation—has featured prominently in the literary criticism of his work, both as a theoretical subject and as a way of understanding what is equally unique about Faulkner: his deep commitment to comprehending the history and contemporary reality of the American South.

The antipatriarchal thrust of Faulkner's major writings is indisputable. According to Faulkner himself, *Absalom, Absalom!* is primarily the "story of a man who wanted a son and got too many . . . the story of a man who wanted sons."[2] Certainly the details of that story, with Thomas Sutpen's brutal disregard for the women with whom he tries to do nothing less than breed a dynasty, confirm Faulkner's reading. Similarly, in *The Sound and the Fury* and *As I Lay Dying* questions of legitimacy play a prominent role: to the question Was Jason Compson a bastard? Faulkner answered, "Not an actual one—only in behavior."[3] Not only are Caddy Compson's brothers obsessed with her virginity (or lack of it) but ·n the third section of the book Jason viciously questions whether Caddy knows who the father of her child is. Like Hester, Caddy refuses to "name the father."[4] Quentin Compson's incestuous desire for his sister, like Jason's for Caddy's daughter or like Benjy's for the young Caddy substitutes whom he mistakenly assaults, all point toward a desire on the part of the Compson men to make reproduction a matter of self-replication. Caroline Compson's neurotic attachment to her brother and her statement to Jason that he is a Compson in name only also point in this direction. As Eric Sundquist has observed, the incestuous desires indicate one of the other major themes of Faulkner's fiction: racism and the fear of miscegenation.[5] This feature of *The Sound and the Fury* resurfaces in *As I Lay Dying,* when Darl Bundren taunts his brother Jewel with Jewel's illegitimacy by accusing him of having a horse for a mother.

In evoking questions of paternal (and even maternal) origin, these texts, like the novels of Hawthorne, James, and Melville, probe what it means to live in a world, not of certainty and knowledge, but of familial and communal acknowledgment—what it means, that is, to live one's skepticism. In Faulkner's fiction, as in the works of his predecessors in the tradition, women are represented as providing what Hawthorne calls a labyrinth of doubt. Hawthorne, Poe, Melville, James, and Faulkner are not primarily concerned with political feminism. Rather, they oppose the desire of male society to convert history into the repetition and reflection of self, to make the world knowable by making it identical with the self. As works of *romance* fiction, the books that I have discussed and the ones that I will now be treating celebrate a history of doubt and uncertainty, a bastard history as it were, that proceeds through and is utterly dependent on women, who have been largely banished from the story they create.

Yet there is an important difference between the nineteenth-century romancers and Faulkner. Feminist critics have usefully distinguished between antipatriarchal and antiphallocentric texts. Antipatriarchal texts oppose the dynamics of male dominance. Antiphallocentric texts oppose not only male society but male language.[6] Poe, Hawthorne, Melville, and James write antipatriarchal fiction. Faulkner, I suggest, moves toward an antiphallocentricism that resists not only the laws of the political fathers but the Law of the symbolic Father as well, the law of symbolic presence. Since the earliest readings of

Faulkner, critics have been aware of what in contemporary critical terminology we call the play of the text. The text, writes John Matthews, resists "a metaphysics of consciousness." In Stephen Ross's terms, it defies the idea of presence. Such play has definite feminist consequences, not to mention implications for race.[7]

As Mimrose Gwin puts it, "Faulkner . . . writes difference by allowing the female subject's capacity for creation to remain open and productive . . . to 'play' without seeking center or boundary."[8] According to Eric Sundquist and James Snead, Faulkner's novels expose a general human intolerance to nonsignification. In Faulkner's view, such intolerance leads to racism and sexism, which represent the attempt to keep signification precise and lucid.[9] In their and others' views as well, therefore, Faulkner resists both mimetic representation and ideological statement. Following these critics, we might say that such voice as speaks in his fictions, such presence as is created, is nothing more than the scene of writing that defers, decenters, and destabilizes meaning. In Faulkner's view of the matter, for human societies to avoid the evils of logocentric ideologies like racism and patriarchy, writing must remain nothing more and nothing less than its own scene of self-composition and deconstruction.

The Faulknerian text revises the romance tradition in ways that are crucial for the female inheritors of that tradition, especially for Carson McCullers, Flannery O'Connor, and Toni Morrison, who write into a Southern literary tradition. The poetics of what we might call the antisymbolic or antiphallocentric text nonetheless create problems for the women writers even as it seems to solve others. The major nineteenth-century male romancers seem not to have grasped that, however inflected toward the feminine, their very mode of symbolic composition constituted a masculinist bias. Similarly, Faulkner, and his immediate predecessor in the tradition, Sherwood Anderson, do not seem to have recognized how the antiphallocentric text might constitute a denial of the materiality and literalness of the woman, especially of the mother.[10] More like foreplay than passionate sexual intercourse, Faulkner's texts produce a frustration not unlike Melville's unsatisfying dream of masturbatory ecstasy. Not for naught was *Moby Dick* one of Faulkner's favorite novels.[11]

Christine van Boheemen discusses some of the problems of the antiphallocentric text in connection with Joyce's *Ulysses* (Joyce is another writer with whom Faulkner feels strong affinities). *Ulysses,* she suggests, "would seem to perversely turn the structure and meaning of what we might call the plot of patriarchy inside out. It flaunts its 'feminine' indeterminacy and celebrates flux and open-endedness." In the final analysis, however, "*Ulysses,* too, proves to hinge on a strategy of doubling which is meant to safeguard patriarchy, however paradoxically, in designating not material reproduction but text productivity as origin. If Western literature has traditionally seen the feminine as emblematic of nature and biological origin, modern thought from Joyce to Derrida rests upon a double dispossession or repression of 'femininity' and the appropriation of otherness as style." Before I explain how the antipatriarchal fiction of Hawthorne and James avoids some of these problems, let me explore how the fiction of Anderson and Faulkner, which, "flaunt[ing] its 'feminine' indeterminacy" (flooding and flowing, in Gwin's terms) simultaneously opens up female textual possibilities and yet creates a text hostile to women.[12] This hostility is ultimately antitextual. The latent sexism of Faulkner's fiction is also related to the latent racism that haunts many of his writings, possibly against the author's own best wishes.

Sound, Fury, and the Male Voice

The masculinist bias of Faulkner's antisymbolic text is a dominant feature of two of Faulkner's later masterpieces, *As I Lay Dying* and *Absalom, Absalom!* He introduces this problem in the first of his major novels, *The Sound and the Fury*, although here it is mediated perhaps by the proximity of this novel to its immediate predecessors in the romance line, *The Scarlet Letter, Moby Dick,* and *The Portrait of a Lady*. In *The Sound and the Fury*, Faulkner creates a woman only slightly less powerful than Hawthorne's Hester and James's Isabel. Caddy Compson is a bossy, independent, and self-willed little girl, much like the young heroines of much nineteenth-century American fiction by women. She later becomes (unlike those other heroines) an unwed but fiercely protective mother. Nor, for all her problems, is Caddy's daughter, Quentin, far behind her in moral courage (or behind Hester's Pearl or Mark Twain's Huckleberry Finn, for that matter). "I dont care," she retorts to the accusation that she is a "nigger wench": "I'm bad and I'm going to hell, and I dont care. I'd rather be in hell than anywhere where you are" (114). Caddy's loss and absence define the Compson tragedy, especially as that tragedy has to do with the patriarchal obsessions of the Compson men.[13] Her presence as woman and mother is at the center of Faulkner's achievement.

For this reason, *The Sound and the Fury* is a perfect place to begin thinking about the feminist implications of Faulkner's aesthetics. Here, early in his career, Faulkner preserves the force of the antipatriarchal critique that he inherits from Hawthorne and James. Later he oversteps that critique when he loses sight of the female presence around which *The Sound and the Fury* is organized. Caddy is replaced by the lesser female lights that illuminate his later fiction (Addie and Dewey Dell Bundren, Rosa Coldfield, and Ellen and Judith Sutpen). What Faulkner imagines to be the failure of *The Sound and the Fury*—its resistance to achieving the total open-endedness of his later fictions—accounts, I believe, for what eventually becomes the equally painful failure of these later novels: their inability to figure forth racially or sexually different others. Faulkner knew that his "most splendid failure" had succeeded where his most magnificent successes had, if not failed, then suffered some serious qualification.[14] Whether he understood the intimate connection between this qualification and the issue of the woman's procreative capacity is another question.

The Sound and the Fury brings the philosophical skepticism of romance fiction to decidedly new depths. The Benjy section in particular seems a veritable transcription of radical doubt: the text unsettles everything—from language to the world to the self. It leaves unanswered and unanswerable the questions How do I know the world? How do I know myself? and How, if I know one or the other, might I move (through language? through some other means?) from one proof to the other? Preserving the unanswerability of these questions is, for Faulkner, as for Hawthorne, a large part of the enterprise of writing. The Benjy section is one of the most open, indeterminate and decentered, sensitive and affecting pieces of writing ever to appear, while the Jason section with its simple, autocratic assumptions about language as signification is one of the most coercive and offensive. It begins: "Once a bitch always a bitch, what I say" (109). A racist, anti-Semitic male chauvinist, Jason in no way doubts what he knows. Nor does he doubt his ability to name it.

The Benjy section offers no model for human language either, or, for that matter, for human behavior. Faulkner rejects the language philosophy of the Benjy section as strenuously as he does that of the Jason section. It is as if Faulkner reconstructs the problem of the antiphallocentric text as itself the mirror of the problem of ideology—a strategy not so different from Hawthorne's in *The Scarlet Letter,* where, as I argued earlier, Hester's A, until its reconstruction at the end of the text, is both ideological and deconstructed symbol, signifying either one thing or everything and therefore meaning almost nothing. In this context, Benjy's object-oriented and often tactile-induced thought processes could be considered reminders of a mother language. Benjy never leaves the world of the literal. Unlike Pearl (to whom he is related through the book's Christ symbolism), Benjy never accedes to symbolic consciousness.

By making first-person narrative the target of Faulkner's criticism, one could circumvent the objection that Benjy and Jason represent polar opposites that reconstruct each other. Jason may be no more egocentric and no less centered in words than his brothers. Certainly what all three first-person narratives emphasize is the organizing power of the self-referential "I," of the "self," even if this "self" (as for Benjy) is nothing more than a perceptual protoplasm where language and world indeterminately intermingle. The first three sections of the book are internal monologues, addressed to no one, intended to communicate nothing. In fact, all three sections embarrass the reader with their raw and revealing contents, turning the reader into a voyeur.

Faulkner's use of multiple, first-person narrators, here as elsewhere in his fiction, could be his way of divesting himself of authority. By depriving himself of omnipresence and omniscience, Faulkner would seem to break his potentially despotic hold on the narrative. Unlike Thomas Sutpen, who declares, "*Be Sutpen's hundred* like the oldentime *Be Light*," and unlike Benjy, Quentin, and Jason, Faulkner will not play God.[15] By using multiple first-person perspectives, Faulkner would seem to resist enslaving totalities and coherence of vision. The problem with this view of the novel, however, is that it does not account for the final section of the book, which is spoken in the voice of a traditional, omniscient, third-person narrator. Most critics remain consistent to their view of the book as decentered by pointing out how little this last section actually resolves. Or they argue that it demonstrates the dangers inherent in a return to order. Nonetheless, as many other critics have argued, this final section, which undoubtedly represents a dramatic shift in the novel—a shift back to a form the novel seems to be rejecting—does seem to achieve some kind of closure.[16] Perhaps the question to ask is what kind of closure? and why, if Faulkner wanted to produce an antiphallocentric text, he would conclude with what seems to be just its opposite? Finally, what might this have to do with the figure of Caddy, the absent center of the novel, who almost bodily figures forth presence?

Faulkner's own comments on the final section of the book support the view that he intended to reach some kind of conclusion there. They also, however, reveal what closure meant to Faulkner, which prevents that section from simply reproducing the hateful fallacies of the Jason section. Faulkner explains:

I wrote Quentin's and Jason's sections, trying to clarify Benjy's. But I saw that I was merely temporising; that I should have to get completely out of the book. I realised that there would be compensations, that in a sense I could then give a final turn to the screw and extract some ultimate distillation. Yet it took me better than a month to take pen and write *The day dawned bleak and chill* . . . . There is a story somewhere about an old Roman who kept at his bedside a Tyrrhenian vase which he loved and the rim of which he wore slowly away with kissing it. I had made myself a vase, but I suppose I knew all the time that I could not live forever inside of it, that perhaps to have it so that I too could lie in bed and look at it would be better; surely so when that day should come when not only the ecstasy of writing would be gone, but the unreluctance and the something worth saying too. It's fine to think that you will leave something behind you when you die. But it's better to have made something you can die with. Much better the muddy bottom of a little doomed girl climbing a blooming pear tree in April to look in the window at the funeral. (224)

In the last section of the novel, Faulkner (like Hawthorne and James) removes himself from the text by explicitly putting himself into it. He releases the text into the world by completing it, rendering it in all its artifactual independence as one might a work of sculpture. Contrary to the impression created by the initial three first-person sections, Faulkner here confesses his hand in the creation of his text. His introduction sexualizes his relation to the book. It expresses his passionate love for the novel, which is both his partner in creativity and—like Caddy, with whom the novel is associated—his progeny. By the end of the introduction Faulkner emerges in the role of father, who makes, not just imagines, something to leave behind him. This something is the child herself, the physically real little girl, who can no more escape reproductive messiness and death than can her father. Faulkner assumes responsibility for her in order to finally grant her independence. Faulkner's final gesture in his introduction clarifies the final gesture in his novel. Faulkner takes responsibility—for his words, for his offspring—even as he lets those words and children go. Faulkner's action in the introduction thus recalls Hawthorne's in the preface to his novel, where he also establishes himself in the role of father and tells us that his children will have birthplaces and destinies different from his own. It also recalls, to resist, the opening image of Sherwood Anderson's *Winesburg*, where a bedridden old writer accepts that he will never do better than to watch the imagined parade of grotesques going through his mind and whose eternal fecundity, therefore, will never yield genuine issue.

In other words, like Hawthorne in *The Scarlet Letter,* Faulkner in *The Sound and the Fury* speaks; and for him this speaking is related to the responsibilities and requirements of parenthood, which is to say of community and history. As language has increasingly come under the scrutiny of philosophical thinking about perception and symbolic consciousness, it has begun to seem synonymous with the human capacity for abstraction and representation. Language both responds to and occasions the loss of our presence to the world (and the world's presence to us). These are important insights into human language acquisition crucial to understanding Faulkner's fiction. But thinking about language this way may marginalize another facet of language—its role, perhaps its primary role, as an instrument of communication and feeling. Faulkner represents just this function of language in the final section of *The Sound and the Fury,* whose major character is the "mammy" Dilsey.

The Mother's Voice

The first three sections of the novel dwell on the coerciveness and egocentricity of voice. These qualities of voice implicate Faulkner's own voice throughout the novel, however much he tries to disguise it by assigning it to other characters. When Faulkner returns to the convention of the omniscient narrative voice in the fourth and final section, he acknowledges that, no matter how fragmentary, how internally self-fractured and apologetic a voice is, to speak is to enter the realm of egocentric self-impositions—which is precisely what Faulkner's novel as a whole would have us resist. Furthermore, placing one's words in someone else's mouth also has a cost. For three-quarters of the novel Faulkner represents language as anything but a means of communication between individuals or expression of genuine feeling. Benjy's inability to speak can stand for Quentin's and Jason's (and potentially Faulkner's) equally palpable unwillingness to speak: it represents the termination of language in acts of noncommunication, like Quentin's interrupted and incomplete sentences.

The topic of the final section, then, is speaking: how we achieve meaning in a universe that, on the one hand, defies meaning and, on the other, tempts us to impose meanings that are merely subjective reflections of self. As in *The Scarlet Letter,* this feat of moral meaning-making has to do with the assumption of responsibility, especially familial responsibility. *The Sound and the Fury* is a story about family within the context (in the fourth section) of the larger community and finally in the context of the human family itself—black and white. The Compson characteristic that comes most brilliantly to the fore in the Dilsey section is the family's unwillingness to assume responsibility in the multivalenced, complex sense that Faulkner intends it. The responsibility is not simply one of assuming a particular burden. Caroline Compson and her son Jason are more than willing to suffer. In fact, they see their whole lives as martyrdom. "I know it's my fault," Caroline says to Jason about the servants' day off. "I know you blame me" (167). "You're not the one who has to bear it," she says to Dilsey about Benjy. "It's not your responsibility" (162). Caroline would like nothing better than to be what Jason also imagines himself to be: Christ on the cross. The fantasy of self-crucifixion obsesses the son Quentin as well.

The solution to such destructive and false fantasies of self-martyrdom is not the denial of responsibility. "Dese funny folk," says Luster. "Glad I aint none of em" (165). "'Twarn't none o my business," he says later (171). Rather, the solution lies in the genuinely Christ-like assumption of the responsibility of love— the responsibility of acknowledging, nurturing, and speaking, not to possess but to release others into independence and freedom. There is an alternative to the silence represented by the three major characters' internal monologues, all of which represent, like Benjy's speech—or nonspeech—so many wordless expressions of sound and fury, signifying nothing ("It was nothing. Just sound," the text says of Benjy's bellow—172). That alternative is Dilsey's kind of speaking—everything from the expressions of love and commitment, which Dilsey everywhere articulates, to the simple human niceties that she also expresses ("From the doors negroes spoke to them as they passed, to Dilsey usually: 'Sis' Gibson! How you dis mawnin?' 'I'm well. Is you well?' 'I'm right well, I thank you'"—173–74).

Dilsey's kind of speaking finds its fullest expression in the revivalist sermon of the minister: "And the congregation seemed to watch with its own eyes while the voice consumed him, until he was nothing and they were nothing and there was not even a voice but instead their hearts were speaking to one another in chanting measures beyond the need for words, so that when he came to rest against the reading desk, his monkey face lifted and his whole attitude was that of a serene, tortured crucifix that transcended its shabbiness and insignificance and made it of no moment, a long moaning expulsion of breath rose from them and a woman's single soprano: 'Yes, Jesus!'" (175–76). The minister's moaning and wailing, which transcend words, might seem to duplicate Benjy's inarticulate sound and fury. But the minister's sermon produces affirmation ("Yes, Jesus," is a refrain throughout the scene). It reinforces community: "brethren" (175, 176)—indeed, "breddren en sistuhn (176–77). As if reinforcing the heterosexual context of its address, the text of the minister's sermon is not Christ but Christ's mother. At first this focus on Mary might seem to reinforce some of the other potentially racist and sexist stereotypes that seem to inform this scene: African American, child, idiot, and woman all seem somehow associated with each other and with the realm of feeling and affection. Nonetheless, the focus on the mother is crucial. It leads directly back to Dilsey and through Dilsey to Caddy. Both as mothers and as mother substitutes, Dilsey and Caddy take on the responsibilities of parenting. They assume the responsibilities of love and relationship. "Ef I dont worry about y'all, I dont know who is," Dilsey says to Frony and Luster (173). There is nothing self-consciously heroic in Dilsey's words. They simply confess a necessity, which one is willing to accept because of a bond of flesh or of love.

Through Caddy, Faulkner adds to the Hawthorne-James line of strong mother protagonists. As the novel's absent presence or present absence, Caddy has proved central to most interpretations of the novel, including those that stress the idea of language as Faulkner's central subject. Thus, in the Benjy section she represents language as both what attempts (and fails) to substitute for loss and as what occasions loss. As she is recalled and relost to Benjy's world by the word *caddie,* we might well feel that Faulkner is primarily a theorist of semiotics, especially regarding the arbitrariness of words and the relation between language acquisition and the mother—important subjects in *As I Lay Dying* as well. The Quentin and Jason sections reinforce our sense of this. What such an interpretation of the novel does not take into account is what this theoretical dimension of the lost Caddy has to do with what readers of the novel have always registered as one of its central themes: the unwillingness of any one of the three brothers to let Caddy become a sexually mature, procreative woman. The problem with the Faulkner's flirtation with indeterminacy is that it fixes Caddy exactly where Benjy, Quentin, and Jason would have her: in the eternally nonreproductive place of virginity. This is the place in which the specificity and materiality of a meaning (as the specificity and materiality of a child) is prevented from coming into being. The problem with the idea of an indeterminate, virginal text is that it not only substitutes textual for sexual reproduction (as in van Boheemen's comments on Joyce) but goes against the idea of textual reproduction as well.

In *The Sound and the Fury*, Faulkner imagines, in order to resist it, a condition of virginity preceding all violation—physical, linguistic, social. As Quentin's father puts it, virginity is a concept invented by men. It goes against nature; women must resist it in order to survive as women. Even though Caddy represents loss for Benjy, Quentin, and Jason (the loss of love, of family, even of money—as for Jason), in her own person, for herself, she represents presence, life, including the life she creates through her daughter. For Faulkner in this novel, woman is no virgin, nor ought to be.

The triumph of *The Sound and the Fury*, which Faulkner achieves through the radical doubt that is a vital component of his antipatriarchal, antiracist politics, is the acknowledgment and affirmation, through Caddy, of human relatedness and of the function of language in creating this relatedness. For all its indeterminacy and decenteredness, at the center of *The Sound and the Fury* is Caddy, with her muddy drawers in the pear tree—the same pear tree through which her daughter, Quentin, will escape the tyranny of the last Compson male. "It's much better to have made something you can die with," Faulkner writes. "Much better the muddy bottom of a little doomed girl climbing a blooming pear tree in April to look in the window at the funeral." Sexuality pervades *The Sound and the Fury*. And it is an expressly procreative sexuality.

This is not to convert *The Sound and the Fury* into a story with a happy ending. As Faulkner writes of Jason in his appendix to the novel, Jason is a "childless bachelor," the "last" Compson (233). He confirms our sense of the novel as a tragedy: with one Quentin dead, the other vanished, Benjy a castrated idiot, Caddy the mistress of a Nazi, the Compsons, like Melville's Ishmael, come into no futurity, familial or otherwise. Quentin does escape, though; and Caddy, not to mention Dilsey, exist—as images of the reproductive and emotional capacities of the human world, however complicated and awkward those capacities may be.

In this context we better understand Faulkner's revivalist minister. His description of the minister cannot but make us feel uncomfortable. "Undersized, in a shabby alpaca coat," with a "wizened black face like a small, aged monkey" (175), the minister seems a racist caricature. The description of the service reads like a parody of our worst (racist) imaginings of revivalist, especially black revivalist, religion. But Faulkner's description of the African American church is no simple, even grotesque, attack against religion.[17] It is intended, I believe, to put something at risk: namely, Faulkner's own ambivalence about the sentimental and rhetorical excesses of language—excesses that many would claim characterize his own writing. Were it not for the emotionless vacuum of the rest of the novel, the Dilsey section might well seem discredited by its oversentimentality. But, as I will be arguing later, on some level romance fiction is sentimental fiction, and this equation holds no less for Faulkner than for Hawthorne and James before him (or, I might add, for Carson McCullers and Flannery O'Connor after him). When Dilsey says to Jason, "You's a cold man, Jason, if man you is . . . I thank de Lawd I got mo heart dan dat, even ef hit is black" (125), she speaks an important truth. For all the sophisticated strategies of this novel, Faulkner embraces the minister, as he does Dilsey and Caddy, because of the way they speak and live, unembarrassed by what others may think or say. "Dilsey made no sound, her face did not quiver as the tears took their sunken and devious courses . . . . 'Whyn't you quit dat, mammy? . . . Wid all dese people lookin. . . . 'Never you mind me. . . . Never you mind'" (177). Dilsey's willingness to cry in public, even in front of white people, is matched in courage only by Caddy's willingness to beg Jason for the privilege of seeing her daughter (122–23). Perhaps the capacity to endure humiliation (something that Hester and Isabel come to know all too well) is not the ultimate achievement of human existence. But as many a woman writer in the nineteenth and twentieth centuries have understood, such is a woman's strength. This strength is not to be underestimated in the universe of human affairs. Faulkner himself achieves it within the sentimental rhetoric of his own novel. It is a strength that ultimately issues in creative and procreative power both.

5

Textual Indeterminacy and

the Death of the Mother

William Faulkner

and Sherwood Anderson

Nowhere in his work does Faulkner better fulfill the conditions of his own aesthetic of authorial self-divestment and deferral than in *As I Lay Dying*. This rambling and at times almost uninterpretable jumble of first-person monologues, with its moments of impossible clairvoyance and mind reading, constitutes a text that is not only emphatically decentered but that raises directly the issue of what constitutes voice. In the Addie section of the text, Faulkner creates a narrative production even more complex than that of the Benjy section in *The Sound and the Fury*. The character who speaks in this section is (presumably) already dead. Her voice is not simply that of someone whom we assume to possess no powers of intellection or consciousness but that of one who no longer even possesses the physiological apparatus of speaking. This placement of some of the most important and affecting lines in the book in the mouth of a dead woman has generated some of the best investigations to date of Faulkner's art. Indeed, insofar as it is a woman and mother who voices Faulkner's poetics of language as loss, it might well seem that intrinsic to Faulkner's larger linguistic undertaking is the desire to write not only an antipatriarchal but an antiphallocentric, even a feminine, text.[1]

As I Lay Dying carries forward the antipatriarchal critique that Faulkner first inherits in The Sound and the Fury. Like its predecessors in the romance tradition, it suggests that within patriarchal cultures husbands desire and demand from their wives verification of their authority to name and control reality. In the Addie section Faulkner identifies the issue between Addie and Anse Bundren as what she perceives as his desire to use her as a reproductive vehicle. Addie wants to "kill Anse" for getting her pregnant a second time (165–66).[2] And when, after her second son is born, she asks Anse to take her back to Jefferson after she dies, so that she can be among her own folk, his response confirms her suspicions about his motives in marrying her: "Nonsense," Anse says, "you and me ain't nigh done chapping yet, with just two" (165), where chapping suggests the production of male as opposed to female children, a suspicion about male reproductive desire that is at the center of Absalom as well. That Anse marries again immediately after Addie's burial reconfirms her suspicions. Faulkner's novel, in other words, like a group of antipatriarchal romances before it, highlights an important link between skepticism, sexism, and social authoritarianism. Men would control women in order to compensate for a kind of knowledge that women seem to possess, which men cannot possess: knowledge of the biological connection between sire and offspring.

Nor does Faulkner's retelling of the story of patriarchal society ignore one typical female response to the tyranny of patriarchy. Addie commits adultery. Furthermore, with Anse already "dead" in her view (she repeats the word several times), her adulterous pregnancy is something of a virgin birth. This idea is strengthened in the text by another happenstance: the biological father of her next child is a man of God, the minister Whitfield. Together Addie and Whitfield produce her Jewel (her pearl, her Christ). Addie Bundren is not the first of Faulkner's characters to produce an illegitimate child. Nor is she the first American protagonist to produce such a child by way of committing adultery with her minister.[3] Addie's illegitimate child asserts the link to the natural-maternal as opposed to the symbolic-paternal (whereas Pearl is associated with birds and roses, Jewel is associated with horses). Like Hester's Pearl, this Jewel is "her" child and hers alone, the child who is "my cross and . . . my salvation. He will save me from the water and from the fire. Even though I have laid down my life, he will save me" (160).⁴ This is just what happens in the course of the novel, when Jewel drags the coffin containing Addie's body over the flooding river and out of the burning barn. (Addie's relationship to Jewel, we might note, also reproduces Caroline Compson's relationship with her son Jason. If Jason is a Compson in name only, then he is, as it were, the product of a quasi-parthenogenic birth such as Hester and Addie and Isabel Archer fantasize about.)

Addie, in other words, like Hester before her, subverts patriarchy by making the production of children as much as possible a female affair. Thus is her Jewel removed from the political and social implications of patriarchy, which render both mother and daughter the property of the father, either literally or symbolically. Even more important, the link between her and the child remains purely physical: the child is hers, not by virtue of the name they share, but because of an incontestable bond of flesh that unites them.

Repetition, Reproduction, and the Nonterminating Pregnancy

Addie's production of Jewel without benefit of husband replicates an aspect of Addie's expectations in relation to her first child, Cash, and this is where Faulkner's thinking about women and the antiphallocentric text takes its fatal swerve away from the woman and, finally, away from textuality itself. In Addie's view, childbearing promises to put her in touch with a dimension of experience that words and symbols can in no way capture. In her monologue she discusses the difficulty of making words mean what we want them to mean, which is to say the difficulty of discovering the connection (inevitable, arbitrary, or otherwise) between the quotidian and linguistic worlds. Addie articulates what could well constitute a theory of an antiphallocentric language or even a mother tongue:⁵

And when I knew that I had Cash, I knew that living was terrible and that this was the answer to it. That was when I learned that words are no good; that words don't ever fit even what they are trying to say at. When he was born I knew that motherhood was invented by someone who had to have a word for it because the ones that had the children didn't care whether there was a word for it or not. I knew that fear was invented by someone that had never had the fear; pride, who never had the pride. I knew . . . that we had had to use one another by words like spiders dangling by their mouths from a beam, swinging and twisting and never touching, and that only through the blows of the switch could my blood and their blood flow as one stream. . . . And so when Cora Tull would tell me I was not a true mother, I would think how words go straight up in a thin line, quick and harmless, and how terribly doing goes along the earth, clinging to it, so that after a while the two lines are too far apart for the same person to straddle from one to the other; and that sin and love and fear are just sounds that people who never sinned or loved or feared have for what they never had and cannot have until they forget the words. (163–66)

We might well be tempted to applaud Faulkner here and to read the novel as itself an expression of the feminine were it not for two facts. The first and simpler is that the woman-mother who expresses her contempt of phallocentric language (which goes straight up in a thin line) is dead. The second has to do with Addie and her daughter as mothers or potential mothers. Let me begin with the first.

For Addie to speak in this text (even to speak her own nonfigural female language) she must yield to the male world of symbolic, nonliteral discourse. Lying in her coffin, stretched out horizontally, Addie occupies what Anse identifies as a nonhuman direction (the human direction, Anse explains, is vertical, as in walking). The woman, then, can exceed the vertical direction of male discourse and become more than human only by occupying a position that also makes her less than human, less than alive. That horizontal position is also the position of sexual surrender. It is no accident that her sons alternate riding her coffin, accentuating the sexual domination that sons, as well as fathers, have over women.

The "death" of this woman-mother is intended only metaphorically. She is, after all, speaking in this text. The implications of the scene about the relationship between women and language are nonetheless disturbing. For all his distrust of the conventions of the patriarchal tradition, Faulkner seems to be buying into a myth about language and the woman that is as old as poetry and as new as Freud, Lacan, and their psychoanalytic, psycholinguistic restatement of it: the death of a beautiful woman is one of the most poetical of subjects, in the words of one of Faulkner's important predecessors, Edgar Allan Poe. Faulkner's placement of his linguistic philosophy within the consciousness of a dead woman is no more comforting that his placing it within the consciousness of an idiot.

Another way of putting this is that, even though Faulkner credits Addie's statements about the literal language of the mother as having an important power and force, Faulkner's own style of composition is anything but literal. If the critical reading of Faulkner is any indication, his language throughout his writings much more closely replicates his placement of Addie at the site of language as loss and absence than it reproduces the philosophy of language that Addie articulates. Addie is thus a vehicle of Faulkner's discourse rather than an embodiment of her own. Addie's sons, we might say, are not the only men who ride the coffin of the dead mother. As a writer, Faulkner is released into consciousness by Addie's dying. The way Addie does not simply die but keeps on dying throughout the novel, even after she is literally dead (hence the title), makes perfect sense. Faulkner, like his characters, produces language only by the perpetual reenactment of the loss of the mother. Indeed, if we attend closely to the implications of Faulkner's text, he would seem to prefer that women not become mothers in the first place.

In his provocative *Doubling and Incest / Repetition and Revenge: A Speculative Reading,* John Irwin asks the question "Is there no virgin space in which one can be first, in which one can have authority through originality?"[6] This question, Irwin suggests, has special relevance to problems of narration. It also, as Faulkner understands, has relevance to the simple facts of human reproduction. For Faulkner, symbolic language (the father tongue) and literal, nonfigural language (the mother tongue) are not alternative forms of language. They are versions of each other. They replicate the basic problem of language that his own texts are attempting to escape: the problem of repetition. Faulkner resists the physical literalness of the woman with her powerful capacity to reproduce. The only other important subplot in *As I Lay Dying* involving a female character is the story of the daughter's journey to Jefferson to terminate her unwanted pregnancy. Here is a bizarre and discomforting paralleling of the processes of female gestation and dying. One way to understand this paralleling is to understand Faulkner as ascribing to women a primary linguistic power that is part and parcel of their ability to contain presence and absence in the same site. Women, in Faulkner's view, are sources of creativity and language. They may express absence and loss, but they are themselves present and real. But—and this is the problem—women lose their privileged position as containers of absence the moment they realize their potentiality and produce a living body. According to Faulkner's trope, language can remain creative only on its way to its first articulation. Pregnancy thus figures creativity only until the moment that an offspring is produced, or a second offspring, who thus immediately enters into the chain of human reproduction (repetition). Every child, even first children, reproduces its parents and becomes part of this chain. But the fact of repetition becomes more vivid and more problematic with every additional birth. To apply certain ideas expressed by Irwin in *Doubling and Incest,* each additional birth redefines the just-born child as first born, one of a series. This notion is exactly what Addie is responding to when she becomes pregnant a second time.

The problem with the pregnancy that comes to term, which becomes a term, is the problem of the repetitions and imitations of which language consists. Addie is fleeing this problem when she marries Anse. She rediscovers it in the world of the literal to which her flight takes her. For Addie, pregnancy and birth—the first time around—represent what she calls the violation of her aloneness. Aloneness was the consequence of words, which, repeating and endlessly circulating, prevented the direct contact of one human being with another. Addie's experience as a teacher is not unlike that of another teacher in American fiction, Sherwood Anderson's Wing Biddlebaum, who can only "carry [his] dream in the young minds" of his students by caressing them.[7] Although Wing's caressing his students would seem totally unlike Addie's whipping them, both acts serve the same purpose: they make human contact. Wing's hands are just as much instruments of violation as love. They imply their own threat of violence. Pregnancy and birth seem to Addie to offer a solution to her aloneness. And so they do—but only the first time around. Thereafter, pregnancy and birth become like language, endlessly circulating and repeating markers no longer fixed to the tangibility of doing. They reinstate the aloneness that they initially assuaged. Like the language for which pregnancy and birth are figures, they rewrite loss. They become instruments of patriarchy, which asserts, now in more ways than one, the Law of the Father.[8]

Addie's four births after Cash (except for the birth of Jewel) reconstruct the conditions of language that the nonfigural experience of birth initially seemed to avoid (Cash, the firstborn, is represented as a carpenter, who does much and speaks little). Darl is the child she most resents because he first proves the inevitability of repetition (for this reason, Darl is an artist, an unrepentant user of words). Nor does Dewey Dell manage to solve the problem of the chain of repetition or reproduction. As the only female offspring and therefore as a potential emblem of a female consciousness, opposed to a male consciousness, Dewey Dell might have reinforced her mother's sense of the womanly or literal. And yet Dewey Dell, Addie realizes, is also the father's child: "I gave Anse

Dewey Dell to negative Jewel," she says (168). Negative language, Addie realizes, still belongs to the realm of linguistic discourse. So does the law of substitution, which Vardaman represents: "Then I gave him Vardaman to replace the child I had robbed him of" (168). Addie continues: "And now he has three children that are his and not mine. And then I could get ready to die" (168). As Darl says, "*Are* is too many for one woman to foal" (95). Multiple offspring reproduce the problems of figuration.

The only two of Addie's children who do not belong to Anse are the firstborn and the first born illegitimately. According to this novel, after the first pregnancy and the (first) illegitimate pregnancy, the only way to avoid rendering the child the property of the father—to prevent the child from entering into the nonliteral law of repetition, reproduction, representation—is to prevent life from coming into being, hence the paralleling of Addie's dying and Dewey Dell's pregnancy. Faulkner's antiphallocentricism is nonterminating, like Dewey Dell's pregnancy. Its fecundity consists in its quality of always-about-to-become.

Sherwood Anderson's *Winesburg, Ohio* stands closely behind Faulkner's text. It opens with the same image of a nonterminating pregnancy that figures for Faulkner as an image of art itself. For Anderson, too, this nonterminating pregnancy is neither young nor old, male nor female. He explains that "the thing inside" the old writer "was not a baby but a youth. No, it wasn't a youth, it was a woman, young, and wearing a coat of mail like a knight. It is absurd, you see, to try to tell what was inside the old writer." (22). The female male is here represented as pregnant with a male female (a female wearing a coat of mail/male), who is not even a baby but a youth. Even this complex, ageless image of bisexuality is, however, inadequate to Anderson's purposes, and so he gives up definition altogether. It is absurd, he says, to define this "thing" going on in the old writer. Meaning, to remain meaningful, must constantly defy definition; it is always about to be born, always metamorphosing into something else in the uninterrupted process of being birthed.

Linked as it is, both here and throughout *Winesburg,* with an assortment of images of androgyny, bisexuality, and homosexuality, this figure of the nonterminating pregnancy might seem to offer everything for which a feminist, deconstructionist critic might hope. Androgyny provides one important solution to gender conflict.[9] But images of androgyny, homosexuality, and ambiguous sexual definition point immediately to a potential problem of the antiphallocentric text as both Anderson and Faulkner conceive it. In failing to come to term, both the text and the nonterminating pregnancy can as easily lead to sterility, loss, and death as to some kind of new conception or creativity. Anderson's novel stresses a fecundity that is fecund only when it fails to come to any kind of term at all—biological, linguistic, or otherwise. It is concerned with how the seed of conception might be prevented from coming to maturity, how it might remain in an eternal state of gestation. For Anderson abortion is preferable to birth.

In the introductory "Book of the Grotesque," Anderson provides the most direct statement of his poetics of indeterminacy: "In the beginning when the world was young there were a great many thoughts but no such thing as a truth. Man made the truths himself and each truth was a composite of a great many vague thoughts. All about in the world were the truths and they were all beautiful. . . . And then the people came along. Each as he appeared snatched up one of the truths and some who were quite strong snatched up a dozen of them. It was the truths that made the people grotesques" (24). In "Paper Pills" he repeats his theory no fewer than three times: "In Doctor Reefy there were the seeds of something very fine. . . . Little pyramids of truth he erected and after erecting knocked them down again that he might have the truths to erect other pyramids. . . . One by one the mind of Doctor Reefy had made the thoughts. Out of many of them he formed a truth that arose gigantic in his mind. The truth clouded the world. It became terrible and then faded away and the little thoughts began again. . . . During the winter he read to [his wife] all of the odds and ends of thoughts he had scribbled on the bits of paper. After he had read them he laughed and stuffed them away in his pockets to become round hard balls" (35–38). Doctor Reefy is one of the most sympathetic characters in the book, a man who contains the seed of something fine. And his practice of continuously decomposing his own truths is very appealing—until one begins to consider this habit in the context of the story in which it is embedded. That story is about Reefy's marriage to "a girl who had money [and] had been left a large fertile farm when her father died. . . . Within a year after the marriage she died" (35).[10]

The story of this girl (who is given no name in the text) is itself an exposition of Anderson's theory of the grotesque. A victim of everyone's truth about virginity, she is finally seduced and made pregnant by one of her boyfriends. Her pregnancy brings her to Reefy. "For several weeks the tall dark girl and the doctor were together almost every day. The condition that had brought her to him passed in an illness, but she was like one who has discovered the sweetness of the twisted apples . . . . In the fall . . . she married Doctor Reefy and in the following spring she died" (38). Somehow the sweetness of the twisted apples, which represents Reefy and his perpetual dismantling of potentially distorting truths, is not life producing. Even if Reefy is not directly responsible for the abortion that terminates the girl's pregnancy, his exposition of his philosophy uncomfortably plots the same course as the loss of his wife's pregnancy and her subsequent demise. Like Addie Bundren, the dying and dead Mrs. Reefy, who is, in the first lines of the story, associated with the fertile farm that she inherits, functions to link poetic beauty with the death of the beautiful woman. She is a reminder that the absence of the woman may be a condition of language. Reefy succeeds in undoing the grotesque truth of virginity that has made his wife pregnant only by substituting an equally grotesque truth of his own: the truth of indeterminacy. This truth, paralleling and inverting the truth of virginity, transfers gestation from the world of female reproduction to the male-authored text, where it produces only an endlessly gestating, endlessly deferred procreation. Working ceaselessly to erect little pyramids of truth that he immediately knocks down to create new erections containing the "seeds of something very fine," Reefy indulges in a masturbatory sexuality that reconstructs the truth of virginity as the truth of literary indeterminacy. Even his literary productions do not remain at the end of the story. They are aborted as surely as his wife's pregnancy.

Reefy's medical role is inseparable from his role as (non)writer and (non)lover: "In the office of the doctor there was a woman, the wife of the man who kept the bookstore in Winesburg. Like all old-fashioned country practitioners, Doctor Reefy pulled teeth, and the woman who waited held a handkerchief to her teeth and groaned. Her husband was with her and when the tooth was taken out they both screamed and blood ran down on the woman's white dress. The tall dark girl did not pay any attention. When the woman and the man had gone the doctor smiled. 'I will take you driving into the country with me,' he said" (38). The hand of the doctor, which throughout the story is associated with writing small notes and squeezing them into tiny paper pills, here writes in blood on the white sheet of the woman's being (the woman is expressly associated with books) in an act that also figures the piercing of the woman's hymen. But Reefy violates this woman's virginity only to ignore and leave her. The ending of the tall, dark girl's pregnancy is a fitting conclusion to Reefy's intellectual, artistic (non)relation to sexuality and textuality both.[11]

As they push time back to the moment before, Anderson and Faulkner escape some of the potentially antifemale bias of nonliteral, symbolic discourse. What they fail to realize in their texts, however, is that even if the woman may be the other whom the male writer can only suggestively invoke, to herself she is no other but her self, with all of her procreative specificity. Anderson's and Faulkner's problems with the reproductive woman are related to Faulkner's problem with race in *Light in August, Absalom, Absalom!* and *Go Down, Moses.*

Indeterminacy, Racism, and the Definition of the Human

Concerning issues of gender, *The Sound and the Fury* marks a singular achievement in Faulkner's writing. At one moment early in his career, at a time when he perhaps stood closest to his progenitors in the romance tradition, Faulkner glimpsed the connection between the uncertainty of the woman and the necessity that it generated, not for a surrender to the impossibility of knowing but for a commitment to thinking through the dilemma of skepticism. Unintimidated by his own feelings of fatherly affection and fully committed to the biological, sexual, and procreative woman, Faulkner created in Caddy (and in Dilsey as well) a fully gendered image of female power. Through Dilsey, Faulkner further linked his concern with female strength to the power of the African American, who, like the woman, was a victim of Southern patriarchy. Not until *Go Down, Moses* and *Intruder in the Dust* did Faulkner make good on the implications of his incipient African Americanism (and even then, not perfectly). But the rudiments are already present in Dilsey and in the revivalist preacher who delivers the stinging sermon of the fourth section of *The Sound and the Fury.* What prevents Faulkner earlier in his career from achieving a fully adequate representation of the American black (as he does brilliantly, for example, in "Pantaloon in Black") is what also prevents him from portraying the woman: not his being neither female nor black but the identity-dissolving, gender- and race-effacing effects of his aesthetics of the antiphallocentric text.

Parallel to Faulkner's attempt to write an ungendered text is his effort to create a nonracial text. His racially sensitive texts do not, however, represent the power of integration. Rather, they de-create both races in a mutual horror of annihilation. This annihilation is figured at the end of *Absalom, Absalom!* both in the image of the idiot Jim Bond—"the scion, the last of his race"—and in the penultimate words of Quentin's and Shreve McCannon's reconstruction of what becomes, finally, the story of "his" race, which is to say of the race of all human beings, whatever their color: "In time the Jim Bonds are going to conquer the western hemisphere. Of course it won't quite be in our time and of course as they spread toward the poles they will bleach out again like the rabbits and the birds do, so they won't show up so sharp against the snow. But it will still be Jim Bond; and so in a few thousand years, I who regard you will also have sprung from the loins of African kings."[12]

Despite the fierce critique of racism and patriarchy in *Absalom* and despite the subversion of both sexism and racism in the antimimetic, antiphallocentric style of the novel, the book concludes with an image of amalgamation as degeneracy. Why? Is the fear of miscegenation Faulkner's, as well as Quentin's and Shreve's? Or does Faulkner, in the final moment of the book, recognize something about the problem of miscegenation to which the poetics of the book may unwittingly contribute?

According to Eric Sundquist, miscegenation constitutes a deep and powerful subtext in almost all of Faulkner's best works.[13] He suggests that Faulkner crystallizes a bizarre fact about American racism: its way of "defining race as . . . subject to reproductive, not ocular, laws."[14] In other words, for Faulkner, racism, like sexism, has something to do with doubt and with the desire of white men to know the world as a self-replicating extension of the self.[15]

To the large subject of patriarchal society, Faulkner adds his stunning insight into racism as a particular response to radical doubt. If male society generally wanted guaranteed paternity, Southern white male society wanted further to ensure that the perfect familial resemblance provided by children would exclude any admixture of "tainted" racial elements. In reading *Absalom* as a family romance, one critic has argued that "Sutpen is seeking, through his Design, to be autonomous."[16] Sutpen's horror at discovering that his firstborn son contains African blood does more than threaten Sutpen's design to found a dynasty. It threatens his dream of self-perpetuating autonomy. It reveals that the child can never wholly reproduce the father: even the same-sex child contains elements that do not originate in the male progenitor. In Sundquist's reading, the incest theme follows: through incest the white male line would preserve both its whiteness and its maleness.

A large question that Faulkner's novels of the South raise is, What constitutes family? What constitutes community or nation or humankind? Is family a matter of bloodlines, faithfully transmitted (preferably from father to son), or is family a decision undertaken to establish ties that do not necessarily originate in the blood? The problem with a certain reading of the miscegenation issue is that it suggests that the problem of racism is a failure to recognize bonds of shared blood. The issue of racism, however, as Faulkner presents it, has less to do with coming to accept the sharing of genetic features than with the need to acknowledge and accept differences among human beings. Even the question What constitutes the human? begs the central question of racism, because for many Southern racists (though not all) the issue is not whether black people are human beings (they know that they are) but whether their humanness is to be acknowledged and acted on. The issue of family in Faulkner's fiction has to do with how individuals create a family feeling that is not simply a celebration of the family gene pool.

Faulkner seems little concerned with race in As I Lay Dying, but it contains the basis of the contemplation of racism that is central to Light in August, Absalom, Absalom! and Go Down, Moses and even (albeit in subtle ways) The Sound and the Fury. Race as such seems to enter As I Lay Dying casually, if at all, as in the unpleasant confrontation between the Bundrens and the three Negroes they meet on their way to Jefferson (219–20) or in the names Jewel and Vardaman, which together recall the name of a famous white supremacist, Jules Kimble Vardaman (there is also the odd fact that both Jewel and Cash seem to metamorphose into blacks in the course of the story: Cash when he breaks his leg and it turns black, Jewel when he suffers burns that turn his back black). Yet the subject of racism is intrinsic to this book in a form directly expressive of the skeptical issue. Racism appears in a form so unique as to expose a further feature of the skepticist's dilemma that pertains particularly to racism: the pretense of asking a question, the answer to which cannot be proven and yet to which the individual already knows the answer. The question is, How do I know that another human being is a human being?

In As I Lay Dying the question Whose child is Jewel? quickly metamorphoses into a contemplation of the definition of the human. Darl, who is one of the few characters in the novel who seems to know of Jewel's illegitimacy (129), taunts Jewel with a bizarre form of the question of paternity: "Jewel, . . . whose son are you? . . . Your mother was a horse, but who was your father, Jewel? . . . Jewel, I say, who was your father?" (202–3). Paternity is not here simply a matter of genealogy. Nor does it locate itself in a straightforward assumption of maternal identity, as in Freud's model of the family romance. For Faulkner the illegitimate birth raises a question of human definition itself. Faulkner inherits the question from Hawthorne and his consideration of Pearl's demonism, as well as from Anderson. In "Hands" Anderson worries in the same breath about Wing Biddlebaum's sexual identity and about his ontological status: Is Wing a "bird" or a "fish" or a human being? Because hands define the human, Anderson will query that definition by representing Wing Biddlebaum as not knowing what his hands are for. Faulkner accomplishes the same questioning of the human when Darl claims that Jewel's mother is a horse, which produces in Vardaman the analogous claim that his own mother is a fish. The claim raises the problem that such laws of biology might produce:

> "Jewel's mother is a horse," Darl said.
>
> "Then mine can be a fish, cant it, Darl?" I said.
>
> Jewel is my brother.
>
> "Then mine will have to be a horse, too," I said.
>
> "Why?" Darl said. "If pa is your pa, why does your ma have to be a horse just because Jewel's is?" (95)

Is Pearl the devil's child? Is Wing Biddlebaum nonhuman because he will not use his hands? Does Wing's sexual preference render him not a man? Is Jewel, in Darl's view, really the son of a horse and therefore not human? These are reasonable questions, given how little we can ascertain about the world. But in all three texts these questions also represent perverse and willful denials of the human. Is there any character in *The Scarlet Letter* more human than Pearl? Who in *Winesburg* is more fully evocative of the human situation than Wing? The problem of racism is not, in Faulkner's view, one of accepting ties of blood, as if black people have become part of the human family *because* of acts of miscegenation. Rather, the abolition of racism depends on a willingness to publicly act on what people know to be the case: that black people and white people are and always have been and always will be human in the same way, whether their blood intermingles or not. Pinning the brotherhood and sisterhood of black people and white people on miscegenation makes the challenge too easy, even too sentimental. (One could make an analogous case for gender.)

Race, explains James Snead, is a system of binary divisions through which one defines the self by its difference from clearly marked others.[17] Joe Christmas "break[s] all the semiotic codes of society: he is both masculine and feminine, both black and white." The problem he thus exposes is the general human discomfort with nonsignification.[18] In Faulkner's thinking about race—as in his thinking about gender—in such books as *Absalom, Absalom!*, *The Sound and the Fury*, and *Go Down, Moses*, as well as *Light in August*, he educates his reader to the kind of fluidity that social institutions, like racism and patriarchy, close down and control. I propose that in the case of race, as in the case of gender, this move toward nonspecificity produces as many problems as it initially seems to solve. To dissolve racial difference is too much like realizing the intentions of incest. It renders the other knowable by discovering its likeness to the self. It dissolves or "bleaches" the other into a version of the self.

In subverting racism and sexism through narrative indeterminacy, Faulkner neither grants nor acknowledges sexual and racial differences. As he portrays two white males constructing or reconstructing the story of sexism and racism, we begin to realize why women and blacks will have to tell their own stories for those stories to have any significant relation to the real world of men and women, blacks and whites. For all white men to have sprung from the loins of African kings may be no more desirable for the African kings, who are thus bleached away into oblivion, than for the white racist, who imagines his own empowerment now compromised by the infusion of black blood into the white race. In Faulkner's strange reversal of the usual process of racial transformation, the dominance of white over black genes suggests the power of Faulkner's own dominating literary force. In exposing power Faulkner reasserts it; for all his opposition to Thomas Sutpen, he banishes blackness and femaleness as powerfully as his racist, misogynist villains do.

John Matthews describes Faulkner's writing in terms of "interpenetrations of voices" and "intimacies of telling."[19] Intimacy and interpenetration sound appealing. Intimacy as interpenetration conjures the images of androgyny, bisexuality, nonterminating pregnancy, and miscegenation in such a way as to raise an issue fundamental to Hawthorne and James earlier in the romance tradition. This issue is the preservation of personal responsibility and commitment in the moment of entering into relationship and communication with others to create relatedness rather than false unities or communion. In Hawthornean romance, as in Stanley Cavell's literary philosophy, intimacy is achieved, not by acts of interpenetration, but by the preservation of mutually respecting autonomies—male and female, black, white, Asian, other.[20]

When Vardaman in As I Lay Daying imagines his mother to be a fish, he, like Benjy in The Sound and the Fury, figures the violation of individuality. Through the archetypal linkage of fish and fetus, Vardaman expresses a desire to reenter and reintegrate with the mother. This desire is expressed as well when he eats the fish, which figures the possibility of intimacy as transubstantiation.[21] When Benjy, Quentin, and Jason Compson wish their sister eternally virgin, they express something similar. The point is not, as Quentin misunderstands it, that they will know their sister in the sexual sense but that they will know her as a version or extension—in the flesh—of themselves. What motivates the incest theme in Faulkner is this desire to prevent the woman from entering into the reproductive chain—that is, the chain of difference and differentiation, which destroys self-knowledge. This desire has direct implications for the issue of race. To prevent the generation of difference, in other words, is both sexist and racist. And yet Faulkner's style, with its rambling, unending sentences and interactive, interpenetrating consciousnesses, defies differentiation. It represents intimacy as communion—an apparently noble response to the politics of gender and race. In the final analysis, however, it replicates the desire for undifferentiated wholeness that, in Faulkner's view, marks the racist patriarchy of the South.

Faulkner undeniably contributes much to the subsequent writing of American romance fiction, especially Southern fiction, by white and black writers, women and men. But female writers and black writers—and the female black writer in particular—will have to capitalize on the benefits of Faulkner's style without forfeiting their right to sexual and racial identity. The reproductive (as opposed to ocular) definition of race will function for twentieth-century African American women writers as the source of their power, which will be the power to mark their children as racially theirs. This marking, by the black woman of her child, especially the female child, is a critical feature in a range of fictions, from Gayl Jones's *Corregidora* to Gloria Naylor's *Mama Day* to Toni Morrison's *Beloved*. It is related to the skeptical issue underlying both sexism and racism. African American women, not doubting that their children reproduce them, will have an easier time accepting their racially different children than black men will (I think, for example, of Harriet Jacobs in the autobiographical *Incidents in the Life of a Slave Girl* and the slave mother in the introduction to Ralph Ellison's *Invisible Man*).

In inheriting and transforming Faulkner, the female romancers return to the antipatriarchal romance tradition of Hawthorne and James. The final sentence of *The Scarlet Letter* is important here. It enacts a relationship between open-endedness (process) and closure that is tied to the special features of femaleness that Faulkner ignores: "On a field sable, the letter A, gules" (264).[22] These words combine pictorial image (the *A* as object, as mother tongue) and discursive sentence (symbolic language). The letter flows on, femininely, almost menstrually; but on the field sable it also leaves its mark: it writes in order to specify, making language and reproduction inextricably linked functions.[23] For this reason, the *A* that concludes a book titled by the *A* is both a tombstone and a marriage certificate. Its function is to give legitimate birth, to Hawthorne and to the text, on terms other than those of either biology or custom.

In dispossessing themselves of the phallocentric symbolism (letter, portrait, whale), that keeps Hawthorne's, James's and Melville's novels tied to a world of male and female discourse, Anderson, in *Winesburg, Ohio,* and Faulkner, in *As I Lay Dying,* problematize the female engendering that the earlier male romancers more boldly acknowledged. They turn the mother-and-child-oriented, history-oriented fiction of Hawthorne and James away from the reproductive future that it promises and back to the sterility and barrenness of the male-dominated Custom-House. If James's qualified optimism is informed by Hawthorne's, then Faulkner's deep and abiding pessimism originates in Melville and Poe. Melville's and Poe's fiction culminates in an end to history, in an impotent, all-male universe. When Faulkner tries to escape into a wholly antiphallocentric language, he discovers himself (at least in *As I Lay Dying*) stranded in the same place outside history where *Moby Dick* and so many of Poe's short stories conclude. Only the twentieth-century women romancers can deliver romance fiction from the dead end to which Anderson and Faulkner (unwittingly perhaps) bring it. And although they learn much from Anderson and Faulkner, their midwives in this endeavor are Hawthorne and James.

III

Nineteenth-Century

Women's Fiction

6

Sentimentalism and

Human Rights

Harriet Beecher Stowe and

Herman Melville

Uncle Tom's Cabin, a text written by a woman in a form no longer revered by today's literary establishment and reflecting an earlier cultural ethos, has become a cause célèbre in the rewriting of the literary canon. Its displacement by the nineteenth-century canon of American literary texts (works by Poe, Hawthorne, Melville, Twain, and James) was not, as critics have argued, the result of some illegitimate use of power and influence through which the dominant canon sought to extinguish a fictional form that, for whatever reasons (including reasons of gender and race anxiety), the male writers found problematic. Rather, taking sentimental fiction like Stowe's both for a cultural base and for an object of revision, the nineteenth-century romance tradition specifically defined itself through and against the sentimental tradition. That romance had a case to mount against sentimentalism can be glimpsed from the signs of fracture within Stowe criticism itself. Even as scholars from the 1970s into the 1980s have attempted to explain why the modern literary sensibility failed to appreciate *Uncle Tom's Cabin* properly, so more recent critics feel obliged to confess some compromising weaknesses in the novel. These are weaknesses, I suggest, to which the romance writers were already responding. The question that the romance writers raised about sentimental fiction is whether its sentimentalism might not prove most dangerous in the area of its most intensive concern: in directing the moral activity of the reader. In the view of the romance writers, the sentimental tradition lacked the skepticism whereby feeling might be translated into significant political action.

To understand the relation between nineteenth-century romance fiction and the sentimental tradition, the first thing to observe is that the romance tradition did not reject the values of sentimentalism outright. Hawthorne, Melville, and Mark Twain—the three male writers who concern me in this chapter—are all sentimental writers. Hawthorne, in his famous preface to *The House of the Seven Gables,* defines romance as "sin[ning] unpardonably, so far as it may swerve aside from the truth of the human heart."[1] Most nineteenth-century romance is sentimental. But the romance writers link sentimentality to something that would seem to be its very opposite: law, or what we might call the body politic. Hawthorne states unequivocally in the same preface that the work of art "must rigidly subject itself to laws."[2] By *law* Hawthorne does not simply mean formal aesthetic principles. Nor is he applying to a law of metaphysics or some eternal truth. For him, law has specifically to do with the legal institutions by which any society governs itself. Hawthorne's most famous full-length romances, *The Scarlet Letter* and *The House of the Seven Gables,* deal explicitly with judiciary matters (trial and punishment, in the first case; land rights, in the other). So do Melville's "Benito Cereno," *Billy Budd,* and "Bartleby, the Scrivener," as well as Mark Twain's *Adventures of Huckleberry Finn.*

Brook Thomas has dealt extensively with the relation between literature and law in the works of Hawthorne, Melville, and Stowe. Reading through an exquisitely developed background of historical data, Thomas demonstrates how neither literature nor law can escape fundamental problems of uninterpretability. By invoking and implicating each other, both literature and law reflect the way certain human issues—such as the slave issue—cannot easily be resolved.[3] I suggest that the difference between Stowe's novel and the fictions of Hawthorne, Melville, and Twain is the degree to which the author selfconsciously incorporates and stresses this fact about law and literature into the text. In Fred See's terminology, the romance tradition "scandalizes" sentimentality. It exposes the fallacy at the heart of the law of presence that sentimentalism asserts.[4] To invoke Philip Fisher's key term, it reveals the way what a culture assumes to be the "hard facts" of its existence are only social constructs and not eternal, universal, or essential truths.[5] The romance tradition separates between feeling and law. It asserts that whereas all human laws inevitably incorporate some level of sentiment or feeling and are therefore to be as firmly resisted as sentimentality itself, there is one law that guarantees feeling and law both. The law of human rights separates emotion from legal institutions, the home from the body politic. In preserving the autonomy of feeling and politics, it enables feeling and politics to each arrive at a proper functioning that serves the interests of both the individual and society.

Racism, Sexism, and the Ideology of Sentimentalism

Harriet Beecher Stowe's Uncle Tom's Cabin exhibits as sentimentalism all the problems of ideology that romance writers resist. It is no accident that recent defenders of the book, including Jane Tompkins, Philip Fisher, Elizabeth Ammons, and Gillian Brown, have chosen to counter earlier devaluations of the book by locating its strong ideological center. Sentimentalism, they contend, is not a neutral expression of some kind of naive intellectual contentment. In their view, it is forceful engagement of the emotions, geared to effect political and social change. Sentimentalism, then, is a form of political radicalism. It aims at nothing less than the subversion of consensus and the replacement of the status quo. Elizabeth Ammons's claims about Stowe can stand for the force and direction of many recent revaluations: "In the tradition that Stowe heads, if we look at it seriously and on its own terms, there exists an important and radical challenge to the emerging industrial-based definition of community in the nineteenth century as something organized by work, ruled by men, and measured by productivity." By stirring the emotions of readers, Uncle Tom's Cabin intends to convert readers to a more humane and Christian way of being in the world and through individual conversion to transform the entire sociopolitical configuration of the nation.[6]

Part of the problem with this defense of sentimentalism as political force is that time and again in the novel and at its most emotional peaks—when Tom and Eliza's child are sold from the Shelbys and when the moment of Tom's sale is reenacted at St. Clare's—Stowe's novel dramatizes the impotence of sentiment to effect significant change. Sentimental feeling, the book shows, cannot protect individuals against enslavement. Even more troubling, it does little to move individuals to change the system. "This is God's curse on slavery," exclaims Mrs. Shelby early in the novel, when she discovers that her husband has sold Tom and Eliza's son. "I was a fool to think I could make anything good out of such a deadly evil."[7] "Talk of the *abuses* of slavery!" exclaims Augustine St. Clare. "The *thing itself* is the essence of all abuse!" (228; see also 282–83, 315–16; compare Stowe's own statement in her "Concluding Remarks": "Is *man* ever a creature to be trusted with wholly irresponsible power?"—452). Stowe recounts these moments to induce the reader to feel strongly enough to force a change in the law about slavery. But the scenes show human feeling to be inadequate to secure human rights, and they do so not only within the context of the bad law of slavery, which is so powerful that it paralyzes the effects of right feeling, but also with the conception of feeling as an instrument of subversion. Neither Arthur Shelby nor St. Clare is moved to change the legal system, even though St. Clare is finally persuaded to change the legal status of a few individuals, as is Shelby's son, George. Even if feeling effects certain changes in the status quo, it does so slowly and unevenly, in a way that is horrendously complicitous with the real and present suffering of human beings.[8]

Nowhere is this complicity more in evidence than in the concluding chapter of Stowe's novel; and because that is the moment when Stowe reaches out of the world of fiction and points her finger directly at the nation, the failure of the sentimental strategies to produce even in its author a clear political directive is extraordinarily telling. Stowe's "Concluding Remarks" exposes the severe limitations of sentimentalism. The remarks also indicate a further problem that sentimentalism generates and that is of major concern to the romance writers: it closes the gap between the subjectivity of feeling and the distance and otherness of external reality so convincingly that it threatens to replace one ideological consensus with another equally restrictive and problematic one. Even more compromising than the self-paralyzing philosophy of inaction is the racist and sexist cultural bias the novel puts into play.

Given the apparent political objectives of *Uncle Tom's Cabin,* one of its most startling aspects must surely be what the novelist refuses to say in her "Concluding Remarks": that the redress demanded by the legal institution of slavery is a change in the law. "But, what can any individual do?" she asks.

Of that, every individual can judge. There is one thing that every individual can do,—they can see to it that *they feel right.* . . . See, then, to your sympathies in this matter! Are they in harmony with the sympathies of

Christ? or are they swayed and perverted by the sophistries of worldly policy? . . . Christian men and women of the North! still further,—you have another power; you can *pray!* . . . But, still more. On the shores of our free states are emerging the poor, shattered, broken remnants of families,—men and women, escaped, by miraculous providence, from the surges of slavery,—feeble in knowledge, and, in many cases, infirm in moral constitution, from a system which confounds and confuses every principle of Christianity and morality. They come to seek a refuge among you; they come to seek education, knowledge, Christianity. (454–55)

Stowe mentions every solution to the problem of slavery except the legal one. This omission is especially troubling because earlier in the novel St. Clare delivers a speech very similar to Stowe's concluding harangue. There he makes the same important point that so long as human beings are placed at the mercy of other human beings, most of whom are mediocre at best, they are bound to suffer:

Here is a whole class—debased, uneducated, indolent, provoking,—put, without any sort of terms or conditions, entirely into the hands of such people as the majority in our world are; people who have neither consideration nor self-control, who haven't even an enlightened regard to their own interest,—for that's the case with the largest half of mankind. Of course, in a community so organized, what can a man of honorable and humane feelings do, but shut his eyes all he can, and harden his heart? (225)

St. Clare's passivity, his inability to act, exposes the weakness of Stowe's own argument. Just as St. Clare's hard-heartedness casts the shadow of a pharaoh over his otherwise saintly character, making him as much slave driver as potential emancipator, so, too, does his imagination fail: he cannot conceive of fulfilling the one divine commandment that is demanded of him, to "let my people go." Neither can Stowe go the whole distance to emancipation.

The one thing that this abolitionist novel does not directly advocate is the legal abolition of slavery. Even more strangely, it does not consider whether the legislation of the terms of human rights is not itself the problem. In other words, at the end of the novel Stowe substitutes one realm of law for another, the law of Christianity for the law of the land. Stowe cannot get behind the bad law of slavery to the idea that what must be rendered into law is *not* the law of

Christianity (or some contemporary version thereof) but rather the legal separation of feeling from human rights. Surely one of the most unsettling aspects
of Stowe's novel, especially from a current perspective, is its unacknowledged
expression of racism and sexism. What troubles St. Clare about his power over
people is not power in and of itself but how "ignorant and weak" they are over
whom he exercises such power (227) and therefore how incapable of resisting
him. Stowe mirrors this attitude herself when she notes that recently escaped
blacks are "feeble in knowledge" and "infirm in moral constitution" (455). The
history of the term Uncle Tom, culminating in Richard Wright's subversive
rewriting of Stowe's title in *Uncle Tom's Children,* itself tells the story. Although
Stowe's intentions in associating both the feminine and the African American
with the best moral feelings may be admirable, the consequences of this kind
of sexual and racial prejudice are deplorable.

Eliza's husband George is a perfect example of the paradoxical offense delivered by Stowe's sentimentality. What is most heroic about George is linked to his
white (and therefore masculine-aggressive) blood; worse, by the end of the
novel Stowe has to defuse George's (and Eliza's) black power. Stowe ships
George and Eliza and their family back to Africa, where they do not even continue in their radical militarism but become missionaries for the Protestant
church. Only years later does Alice Walker in *The Color Purple* reverse the course
of the black missionary, to effect, not a Christian revolution in Africa, but an
African revolution in America. Stowe, however, can imagine no moral system
aside from Christianity; nor can she allow for the possibility of political alternatives that differ from her own. In the final analysis it is violence, in the form of
the Civil War, that frees the slaves. Violence is probably no one's favored method
for effecting civil change. But when the rights of individuals are concerned, we
may have to be willing to sanction violence—something that Melville is not
beyond doing in "Benito Cereno."

The problem with Stowe's sexism and racism is not that they exist, for she is
only reflecting the cultural consensus of her time. As critics like Thomas,
Fisher, and Tompkins rightly point out, Stowe is a nineteenth-century Christian woman, the product of a certain cultural, economic, social, and religious
milieu. The problem is, rather, her lack of self-skepticism, her unwillingness to
imagine that her own point of view—however politically correct concerning
slavery, for example—may contain elements of bias that make it inadequate or
even dangerous concerning other, perhaps unimaginable political realities.
From Stowe's point of view, Christianity and love distinguish good laws from

bad ones. But to assert this, Stowe has to imagine that Christianity's support of slavery, which she readily acknowledges, represents just an institutional problem. Stowe believes that the church, along with the political institutions of the country, have simply misunderstood and distorted the divine word. If politicians and churchgoers can be made to feel what Christ would have them feel, they will set law and religion aright. Stowe cannot fathom how leaving the question of human rights to interpretation is itself part of the problem. If the "ruffian, the brutal, the debased" (453) may prevail in public law, what is to prevent them from determining the interpretation of divine law? Isn't this what has occurred? Stowe cannot see that the reason for the inability of Christianity to change the slave system, the reason that it could be used to defend the system in the first place, has to do with the place of interpretation in determining the moral meaning of Scripture. Stowe's attempt to change her audience's understanding of Christianity does not address the basic problem of interpretive abuse that her novel exposes—the problem of what it means for the rights of individuals to depend on the personal feelings and morality of other individuals.

Stowe's sanctification of Christianity defeats the project of sanctification that her book is written to promote. She does not see that what may be required to end slavery may not be the recognition that all men and women are brothers and sisters in Christ. It might instead be the realization that all human beings are equally entitled to freedom and independence, whether in Christ or outside him.[9] Stowe is happy to imagine Uncle Tom as Christian, even as Christ himself. She is less ready to acknowledge that he is a whole and entire human being. (In *Billy Budd*, Melville reverses Stowe's logic and claims that whether or not Billy is Christ, he is human.) Although some critics have defended Stowe's novel by suggesting that the revolution that *Uncle Tom* effects is to convert the public view of blacks from objects to people, Stowe does not treat the black characters as wholly human, even though she, like her characters, knows that African slaves are as human as anyone else.

Sentimentalism, Allegory, and Legal Fictions

In a scene in "Benito Cereno," in which the white American sea captain Amasa Delano first confronts African slavery, Melville exposes the fallacy of Stowe's novel, which is the flaw of sentimentalism itself:

His attention had been drawn to a slumbering Negress, partly disclosed through the lace-work of some rigging, lying, with youthful limbs carelessly disposed, under the lee of the bulwarks, like a doe in the shade of a woodland rock. Sprawling at her lapped breasts was her wide-awake fawn stark naked, its black little body half lifted from the deck, crosswise with its dam's; its hands, like two paws, clambering upon her; its mouth and nose ineffectually rooting to get at the mark; and meantime giving a vexatious half-grunt, blending with the composed snore of the Negress.

The uncommon vigor of the child at length roused the mother. She started up, at a distance facing Captain Delano. But as if not at all concerned at the attitude in which she had been caught, delighted she caught the child up, with maternal transports, covering it with kisses.

There's naked nature, now, pure tenderness and love, thought Captain Delano, well pleased.

This incident prompted him to remark the other Negresses more particularly than before. He was gratified with their manners; like most uncivilized women, they seemed at once tender of heart and tough of constitution, equally ready to die for their infants or fight for them. Unsophisticated as leopardesses, loving as doves. Ah! thought Captain Delano, these, perhaps, are some of the very women whom Ledyard saw in Africa, and gave such a noble account of.

These natural sights somehow insensibly deepened his confidence and ease.[10]

The point of this passage exceeds the obvious point that Captain Delano is an extremely poor interpreter of the world around him. Represented here is the process of sentimental imagination itself, the way, with the best intentions in the world, sympathetic seeing voyeuristically transgresses the distance between self and other, converting others into self-serving allegories of love and affection and human nature. The passage reveals sentimental seeing to be a form of ideological persuasion: it enslaves. It makes the world a confirmation of the presumed hard facts of consensus and the status quo. Melville's story exposes the way the structure of ideology and the structure of sentimentalism are the same, the way the cult of feeling serves the needs of the self-serving process of telling oneself a story that one wants to hear.[11]

Melville's story reveals the inadequacies of sentimentality to deal with the problem of slavery. It exposes the impossibility that the crucifixion of either blacks (like Babo) or whites (like Cereno or his predecessor aboard ship, Don Alexandro), whether at the hands of others or by their own hand, will make any difference to the life of the slave. (One might recall here the inefficacy of Billy Budd's crucifixion in that story.) For Melville sentimentality, especially Christian sentimentality, stands in the way of emancipation. "Benito Cereno" reads Stowe's novel, as it were, and finds it seriously lacking just where it meant to do the most good.

"Benito Cereno" evidences the unbridgeable gap between sentimentalism and allegory, on the one hand, and social justice, on the other. There is the allegory (however sentimental) that we write and that, if we are sensitive interpreters, we read within our own texts or, if we are more naive, we expose for other more sensitive interpreters to read. Then there is the political step that allows us to actualize fantasies of possession by disenfranchising the rights of other individuals. The lack of agreement between the allegorical implications of the story and its moral message has led critics to conclude that Melville (as a kind of Benito Cereno) shared the basic assumptions of his society, so his allegory simply materializes those prejudices, or that (like Delano) he could not, because of his own unstated racism, move beyond complicity in the national sin. But the lack of agreement between allegory and law is Melville's subject, not his offense. Wolfgang Iser has argued that a text cannot correspond to anything outside itself.[12] "Benito Cereno" reproduces neither the conditions of slavery nor the author's or reader's totalizing representations of those conditions. It is only an instrument for bringing a new world into being, a world that exceeds anyone's attempts to control it. The story, then, is a conduit for considering these issues in their relation and disrelation. Even though Melville risks being misunderstood in this bewildering allegory of black and white, even though he might seem to assert the racism he would condemn, he can do no less than take this chance, for the guarantee of human rights depends on leaving interpretive acts open, even to misinterpretation.

Remaining open to interpretation means insisting on the difference between textuality and contextuality, the word and the world. Either interpretation or politics can close the gap between the text and its meaning. But interpretation without political power, however reductive, can do nothing except generate other texts. Like allegory, interpretation can possess meaning, enslave it, but only in other words. Political power, however, with or without interpretation, can create slavery. Melville's text demonstrates that there is no way out of the allegorical perception of reality. There is, however, a way to avoid acting as if those perceptions meant everything we would have them mean. The moment that we credit other human beings with equal rights under the law, it does not matter how we see them. That is a personal matter, between us and our analysts or between our texts and our readers.

Still, one objection to my criticism of Stowe's novel surely remains. Even if we depend on a society of law to protect individuals from the uncensored feelings and beliefs of other individuals, we must have a definition of human being that includes everyone and not just one racial group. Stowe's novel might still be defended on the grounds that, in Philip Fisher's terms, it effects upon the public imagination a transformation of blacks from "things" to people.[13] But Stowe's novel reveals that even Southern plantation owners who defended the system of slavery, such as St. Clare's father and wife, knew that slaves were human beings. "Don't you think they've got immortal souls?" Ophelia St. Clare asks Marie St. Clare. "'O, well,' said Marie, yawning, "that, of course—nobody doubts that. But as to putting them on any sort of equality with us, you know, as if we could be compared, why, it's impossible!" (178). Later St. Clare says about his father, "I suppose, to be sure, if anybody had asked him, plump and fair, whether they [blacks] had human immortal souls, he might have hemmed and hawed, and said yes. But my father was not a man much troubled by spiritualism; religious sentiment he had none, beyond a veneration for God, as decidedly the head of the upper classes" (230). Stowe's sentimental rhetoric, at least in her own view of things, does *not* have to convert the reader to an unawareness of the humanness of blacks. Even her slave owners know this. The point is that they act in defiance of this knowledge.

Stanley Cavell has argued that we simplify rather than complicate the issue of slavery when we understand it as the denial of someone else's humanness. The statement that slave owners do not see their slaves as human beings conceals what is most profoundly horrific about slavery: that many slave owners did see their slaves as human beings and still denied them fundamental human rights.

So what is this about "not human beings"? How would our more or less mythical slaveowner mean this? . . . He means, indefinitely, that they are not *purely* human. He means, indefinitely, that there are *kinds* of humans. . . . He means, indefinitely, that slaves are different, primarily different from him, secondarily perhaps different from you and me. . . . In the end he will appeal to history, to a form, or rather to a way, of life: this is what

he does. He believes exactly what justice denies, that history and indefi-
nite difference can justify his social difference of position. He need not
deny the supremacy of justice . . . He need deny only that certain others
are to be acknowledged as falling within its realm. It could be said that
what he denies is that the slave is "other," i.e., other to his one. . . . . He
may acknowledge everything about them. I mean reveal his true feelings
to them, about everything from their suffering to their sense of rhythm,
with the sole exception of their existence in the realm of justice.[14]

This insight into slavery informs Melville's "Benito Cereno." In Delano's allegory of the black mother, for example, Delano is responding to her humanness, not failing to do so. Indeed, he is celebrating it, romanticizing it. The passage reveals Delano's ability to act toward blacks and women in a certain way
despite his knowledge that they are human beings. It is vital to Delano's
romantic allegory of the black mother that she is a woman, perhaps even, as he
suggests, a noble woman, and not literally a doe or a leopardess. Only her
humanness makes her available to gratify his desire to possess her. Only as a
human being can she satisfy the needs of his projection. What Delano must
deny is his violation of another human being. He must put the black woman
outside the laws of civilization, imagine her as uncivilized.[15] When, for example, she catches his glance and turns her face away, he must quickly dissipate
any discomfort that he might feel at this accusation of voyeurism. He concludes
that she looks "as if" she is "not at all concerned at the attitude in which she
had been caught[;] delighted she caught the child up, with maternal transports,
covering it with kisses." Delano must imagine the black mother delighted not
only by her child but by having been caught by Delano's eyes. In some perverse
way, Delano shares the child with her, as if he has fathered that child and is
now entitled to participate in the woman's delight. Given the incidence of rape
among slave owners, the suggestion is ominous.

Being caught by another's sight or feeling is, according to the logic of the
passage, the condition by which we are all seen and through which we create
the network of human relatedness in which we exist. Delano sees the black
woman through the lacework of the ship's rigging, and presumably she sees
him through that same lacework (the designation of the rigging as lacework
suggests a feminine as well as a masculine viewpoint). The mother, who is
caught by Delano's eyes, catches up her child. What makes catching another
individual bad is when it is done against another's will, when the need to make

human contact turns into voyeurism, rape, and enslavement. Delano's language betrays what his psyche would deny: what he sees is only a condition of "as if." And what controls that "as if" is the fact that the black woman is literally caught. She is a slave; and Delano's slave mentality is rigging the meaning of what he sees.

In Melville's view, America did not need a redefinition of the human being or a new recognition of it. It required a law that protected people from other people's retreat from what they already knew about humanness. This need for law motivates Melville's text. It also produces Henry David Thoreau's like-minded and similarly controversial comments on slavery in *Walden*: "I sometimes wonder that we can be so frivolous, I may almost say, as to attend to the gross but somewhat foreign form of servitude called Negro Slavery, there are so many keen and subtle masters that enslave both North and South. It is hard to have a Southern overseer; it is worse to have a Northern one; but worst of all when you are the slave-driver of yourself. Talk of divinity in man! Look at the teamster on the highway, wending to market by day or night; does any divinity stir within him? His highest duty to fodder and water his horses! What is his destiny to him compared with the shipping interests?"[16] Like Melville, Thoreau recognizes that human beings are driven to act in immoral ways against their better judgment because of the economic and social pressures under which they place themselves. Thoreau's focus on the economics of slavery, like his discussion of "economy" generally, does not ignore the issue of ethics. Rather, it radically exposes ethics to be a matter of willfully ignoring for the sake of material gain what we know to be true about other human beings. The last cover for slavery, which is that the slave owner did not understand or consciously acknowledge the humanness of the slave, slides away, to reveal a more repulsive aspect of the evil of slavery: that it existed despite the knowledge of slave owners that it constituted a violation of human rights.

For Melville and Thoreau, American society required a single law (a law that existed in the Constitution only to be ignored), which protected the inviolable rights of all human beings—regardless of race or gender—against exploitation and disenfranchisement and enslavement. Melville's "Benito" has seemed less emotional than Stowe's *Uncle Tom* and therefore less humane. But Melville's purpose is to separate feeling from the definition of the human and to assert that human rights must be protected irrespective of how any one feels in this matter. Racial prejudice, according to Melville's logic, is no more than feeling gone wrong—which is what the story of Miss Ophelia's relationship to Topsy painfully dramatizes. Given this equivalence, given the reality of racism, indeed, given the possibility that even an anti-slavery writer like Stowe or Melville can be racist, Melville will not prefer sentiment to law. He will not, because he cannot, trust even his own feelings.

The danger of sentimentalism is also Mark Twain's subject in *The Adventures of Huckleberry Finn*. Like *Moby Dick* and "Benito Cereno," *Huck Finn* does not celebrate two males striking out for social independence. The story is a highly sentimental one reminiscent of many nineteenth-century sentimental fictions by women. The two main protagonists are a child and a black man, outcasts to whom we might not immediately extend our sympathy. As in Stowe's novel, the black man is a figure of humane Christianity, who converts a nominal Christian (Huck) to the faith, enabling him to resist the distortions of organized religion (such as slavery). The book is family oriented (take, for example, Jim's story about his deaf daughter or his comments on King Solomon), and it focuses on a rare and compelling intimacy between two characters across racial barriers.[17] Furthermore, like other sentimental fictions, it seems to want to return the reader (in Thomas Joswick's words) to a "primary language of human character."[18] As Jim vividly points out, cows and cats may speak differently from human beings and differently from each other, but human beings cannot afford to speak differently from themselves. Huck and Jim discover on the raft that they do in fact speak the same language, which is to say that they share the same definition of the human. Given the power of Jim's and Huck's experiences and the affection that they establish with one another, it is more than disturbing that at the end of the novel Huck is incapable of either recognizing or respecting Jim's freedom. The final child's play at the end of the book, which occurs when Huck does not yet know that Jim is legally free, suggests where sentimentality must end and law intervene. In the world of Mark Twain, sentiments, no matter how enlightened, right directed, or Christian, are no place to deposit another being's human rights. Even the most loving of friends may lapse.

I make my point about male romance fiction's argument with sentimentalism in connection with "Benito Cereno" and *The Adventures of Huckleberry Finn* because both texts relate directly to the same issues that inform Stowe's novel. But I could as well allude to a number of other nineteenth-century fictions by men. *The Scarlet Letter,* for example, fulfills many of the conditions of sentimental fiction. We have again the outcast-criminal (Hester), this time a woman, and the child, also female, who redirect the reader's sympathies. As Carol Bensick has argued, *The Scarlet Letter* is extraordinary in that the adulterous woman is not only forgiven but allowed to survive with her child.[19] But sentimentality is what Hester, like the novel, must resist. In the forest scene, when Hester tries to recapture with Dimmesdale the passion that initiates the tale in the first place, Hester flings away the letter that represents the rational impositions of a society over personal feelings. In so doing, she makes her daughter an outsider in the most intimate of spaces, where she most has a right to feel at home: the family. In the end, Hester must forsake consecrations of private manufacture ("our love," she says to Dimmesdale, "had a consecration all its own") for the responsibilities of parenthood, that is, for the responsibilities of social obligation.[20] Hester's return to New England nationalizes the responsibilities of parenting. It brings them to bear on the heart of Hawthorne's subject: the founding of a nation strong enough to support a home. Similarly, in *The House of the Seven Gables,* the feeling that binds together two feuding families is not allowed to stand alone. Documents must be produced and legalities must be met before the family can establish in peaceable harmony the new homestead that will further both domestic and national interests.

Even in *Billy Budd,* which seems a clear attack against law in favor of feeling, Melville places the judicial—in the sense of the one law of human rights—over the sentimental. As I have argued at greater length elsewhere, Vere's violation of the law involves more than his decision to bypass naval procedure when he tries and sentences Billy: it involves his putting himself in the place of God the Father, determining the welfare of no less than the whole of humankind through the sacrifice of his son. Vere, in other words, like Stowe, imports into his definition of the legal a religious sentiment that then determines the course of his judicial decisions. Had Vere understood the difference between the human and the divine, the difference between himself as a human father, however patriarchal, and his misconception of himself as God, then Billy might have lived to continue the relationship between God and man, state and citizen, that Vere had hoped to ensure. As it is, Billy dies a Christlike but graceless, nonredemptive death.[21]

Billy Budd returns us to the problem of the weak, self-sacrificing, religious protagonists of sentimental fiction, who—as opposed to strong, independent heroines like Hester and Isabel—because they do not resist society, are crucified. Like Tom and Eva, Billy is the lamb, or child, feminized as Christ often is. The connection between the crucifixion of Billy under the law of naval conscription and the crucifixion of Tom under the law of enslavement might help account for the odd opening description of the prototype of the handsome sailor, whom Billy is about to become. The "African of the unadulterate blood of Ham" links Billy, and therefore the issue of the text, directly to the issue of race and slavery.[22] The "Rights of Man" (and woman) according to *Billy Budd,* depend upon one thing and one thing alone: the legal guarantee of those rights.[23] The moment the rights of man and woman are violated, as when the feminine and (by association) racially different Billy is pressed into military service, it no longer matters how much we love or care. Even children must be protected against their fathers (and mothers), lest their fathers (or mothers), with the best intentions in the world, sacrifice their rights to what they believe to be a greater good. In the views of these writers, only self-skepticism can produce a parent. Only a social contract predicated on the rights of man and woman can build a home, let alone a nation.

7

Literary Realism and

a Woman's Strength

Edith Wharton and

Kate Chopin

In Kate Chopin's *Awakening* and Edith Wharton's *House of Mirth* the protagonists choose the path that Hester, Isabel, and Caddy, not to mention countless other heroines in nineteenth-century fiction, resist (the example of Harriet Jacobs, in *Incidents in the Life of a Slave Girl,* immediately comes to mind); Wharton writes of Lily Bart:

> She stirred once, and turned on her side, and as she did so, she suddenly understood why she did not feel herself alone. It was odd—but Nettie Struther's child was lying on her arm: she felt the pressure of its little head against her shoulder. . . . She settled herself into an easier position, hollowing her arm to pillow the round downy head, and holding her breath lest a sound should disturb the sleeping child. . . . She struggled . . . feeling that she ought to keep awake on account of the baby . . . for a moment she seemed to have lost her hold of the child. But no—she was mistaken—the tender pressure of its body was still close to hers: the recovered

warmth flowed through her once more, she yielded to it, sank into it, and slept.[1]

Chopin and Wharton do not simply present feminist alternatives to the fiction of Hawthorne, Melville, and James. They provide as well a critique of Harriet Beecher Stowe's brand of sentimentalism, with its weak, self-sacrificing women and feminized men. At the same time, they take on the dominant tradition of nineteenth-century domestic fiction by women.

Like Stowe's *Uncle Tom,* the recently recovered novels of such writers as E. D. E. N. Southworth, Susan Ann Warner, Fanny Fern, Maria Cummins, Catherine Sedgwick, and Lydia Maria Child promote the idea that proper Christian feeling is fundamental to a moral society and that such feeling more usually resides in women and in nonwhites than in Anglo-Saxon males. Unlike Stowe's novel, however, these books feature independent female protagonists who succeed in the world through their own resourcefulness; they marry and become strong wives and mothers.[2] This last turn of plot, when the heroines rejoin the status quo, possibly exerts pressure on turn-of-the-century writers like Chopin and Wharton and like-minded regionalist writers (including Mary Wilkins Freeman, Sarah Orne Jewett, and Ellen Glasgow) to provide scenarios that explicitly reject marriage (and children).[3] In *The Awakening* and *The House of Mirth,* Chopin and Wharton take this rejection of patriarchal society to its ultimate expression. Rather than in any way accommodating to patriarchal society, their protagonists take their own lives.

More accurately, Edna Pontellier and Lily Bart do not resist society: they passively, passionlessly, dissolve and disappear. In both Chopin's and Wharton's novels the temptation to suicide is represented in sensual, water-related imagery such as James and Faulkner also employ. Chopin's hero drowns in an ecstasy of sexual sensation. Lily Bart, in Wharton's novel, submerges herself in a "bath of oblivion" (374), recalling Isabel Archer's association of death with a cool bath. Their deaths seem to have been intended to portray the only kind of fulfillment—sexual, spiritual, emotional, or otherwise—available to these women. The scenes describing Edna's and Lily's deaths nonetheless do little to suggest that the deaths constitute acts of defiance in any way commensurate with (even if antithetical to) the vivid power of the life-affirming decisions made by Hester, Isabel, and Caddy and by their strong female-created sisters (black and white). In *The Awakening* and *The House of Mirth,* the female protagonists fade away as if even their deaths could not rouse them from inertness. It is not even clear that Edna dies; we are told only that her strength—that woman's strength perhaps—gives out. Whether Lily intended to take a fatal dose of sleeping potion or did so accidentally is left unresolved. For her a "woman's courage" depends on a "man's faith" (372). It is not an independent resource. In a scene reminiscent of Isabel on the train to Gardencourt, Lily looks into the "emptiness of renunciation" (373) and can summon "strength" only to meet her troubles "tomorrow" (375).

Neither Edna's nor Lily's deaths, in other words, reflect the hero's break with her helplessness but, instead, her final, fatal, surrender to it. In both cases the hero's suicide is positioned against her complex (negative) relation to her role as mother: Edna's rejection (however ambivalent) of the responsibilities of motherhood, and Lily's paralysis before the haunting realization that children are absent from her life. Explicitly (in *The Awakening*) or implicitly (in *The House of Mirth*), the surrender to death simultaneously involves reneging on the rights, privileges, and responsibilities of motherhood.

What is curious about Chopin's and Wharton's political radicalism, including the way it is played out in these scenes of suicide, is that it ignores the similar radicalism of Hawthorne's *Scarlet Letter* and James's *Portrait*. This is so even though Wharton (at least) has James's novel in mind when she writes *The House of Mirth*, even as Hawthorne's novel about a house, *The House of the Seven Gables*, is not far from her thinking. As we shall see, Lily's self-portraiture in the *tableau vivant* scene (155–61) forms a direct commentary on both these novels, while the early scene with Laurence Selden at the Trenors' home constitutes a potent echo of Hawthorne's *Seven Gables*. But neither Hawthorne's *Scarlet Letter* nor his *Seven Gables*, nor James's *Portrait*, portrays weak women who must forfeit motherhood along with sexuality and marriage. None of these texts culminate (as in the somewhat different fictions of Freeman, Jewett, and other turn-of-the-century regionalists) in the decision to remain celibate. In *The Scarlet Letter* and *The Portrait of a Lady* (as later in *The Sound and the Fury*) strong and powerful women (who are biologically as well as psychologically potent) also refuse to reenter the dominant society as happily married wives. They do not, however, remain childless and celibate. Nor do they take their own lives.

Whatever the male fictions may appear to be evading in terms of political realism, they do provide an image of female strength that is not easily set aside. The idea of realism is important here: the difference between Chopin's and Wharton's fiction, on the one hand, and Hawthorne's and James's, on the other, may be the difference between realism and romance, between the subversion of society and its aversion, and, finally (to pick up the language of Wharton's novel), between fate and freedom. Romance fiction, I suggested earlier, transgresses boundaries between literature and philosophy, between the self and the other, between the imaginary and the real. Like the Emersonianism that it incorporates, romance fiction lives within and through contradiction. What characterizes novels like *The Awakening* and *The House of Mirth* and a whole series of women's texts before them and what therefore determines what I see as the fatality of their endings is their resistance to such contradiction. As politically and socially realistic accounts of the problems of women, they would define and resolve problems clearly. The mid-nineteenth-century women's novels endeavor to overthrow the dominant, oppressive patriarchy and to replace it with a different, presumably less oppressive ideology—one defined by the values of Christianity, charity, and domesticity. To subvert the status quo, the novels melodramatically display the corrupting features of patriarchal society. But to ensure the efficacy of the new ideology that they introduce, the authors naturalize their claims. They represent them as obviously, universally, and eternally true. In so doing, the nineteenth-century women's novels return literature to its ideological function. In spite of their differences from mid-nineteenth-century fiction, so do the novels of Chopin and Wharton.

Let me put the problem this way: although on one level the women's books are politically radical (primarily feminist, occasionally—as in Lydia Maria Child's or Stowe's fiction—antiracist as well), on another level they all too quickly return to the consensus that they initially seem to disturb, or they create an equally troubling new consensus. Joseph Boone has argued (via Bakhtin) for the basically protean qualities of the novel as a genre. For Boone the novel is "potentially noncanonical, inherently multivocal, and profoundly invested in the ideological dismantling of a unitary world view." At the same time, it promotes a "restrictive sexual-marital ideology," which, emphasizing the opposition of the sexes, renders their reconciliation to each other a function of marital union. The novel, Boone suggests, "subvert[s] what (and while) it conserves."[4] Romance fiction is not subversive in Boone's terms. It does not offer a different and better ideology to take the place of the ideology that it calls into question. Rather, it defines a relation to consensus having to do with the free and unhindered activity of consenting. In the particular way Chopin's and Wharton's novels depict the deaths of their heroines, they seem to have less to do with either consent or its opposite than with an ineluctable movement away from life that leaves nothing in its wake.

Subversion and the Ideological Function of Literature

For Wharton the "custom of the country" that dooms a woman like Undine
Spragg to an insatiable restlessness—much like that of Edna Pontellier or Lily
Bart or, for that matter, Theodore Dreiser's Carrie Meeber—originates in social
conditions. These social conditions are intimately connected to the institutions
of patriarchy, particularly to the American institution of capitalism:

> Why haven't we taught our women to take an interest in our work? Sim-
> ply because we don't take enough interest in *them.* . . . Why does the
> European woman interest herself so much more in what the men are
> doing? Because she's so important to them that they make it worth her
> while! She's not a parenthesis, as she is here—she's in the very middle of
> the picture. I'm not implying that Ralph [Undine's husband] isn't inter-
> ested in his wife—he's a passionate, a pathetic exception. But even he has
> to conform to an environment where all the romantic values are reversed.
> Where does the real life of most American men lie? In some woman's
> drawing-room or in their offices? The answer's obvious . . . . In America
> the real *crime passionnel* is a "big steal"—there's more excitement in
> wrecking railways than homes.[5]

In Wharton's social analysis America is faulted more with a lack of romanticism than with a generalized patriarchal oppressiveness. And this lack is
directly related to the market economy in which women constitute only so
many commercial objects.

This description fits Wharton's portrayal of Lily Bart's situation in *The House
of Mirth.* When Rosedale proposes marriage to Lily, it is as a means of buying
his way into respectability. Lily is the currency with which he can acquire certain goods and services. Women are complicit in their circulation as currency.
Lily in no way resists the objectification of herself. In fact, she repeats it when
she makes herself into a tableau vivant. Lily's self-transformation into an art
object represents the more problematic of the two forms of objectification and
commercialization. In the tableau scene, Lily is internalizing the principles of
the market economy.[6] Such self-portraiture expresses Undine Spragg's egocentricity as well; this egocentricity is directly related to her lack of parental feeling
for her child. Undine abhors being pregnant because it interferes with her perfect, artful beauty. She willfully, painfully, neglects her son, using him only to
secure money for herself. The neglect is figured forth most powerfully, in all its

consumer-oriented selfishness, when she forgets her son's birthday party and goes to have her portrait painted instead.

Wharton's women buy into the capitalist economy, nor is Wharton herself exempt from this failing. Although Wharton shows the tragic consequences of her characters' capitalistic ventures, her texts for the most part reconstruct the problems that her protagonists' experiences dramatize. As realistic fictions, Wharton's novels almost inevitably, fatally, discover only death and destruction at the end of the capitalist highway. Perhaps the discovery is inevitable. In a brilliant reading of a group of realist-naturalist writers, Walter Benn Michaels argues that Wharton reflects the psychosexual, social economy of turn-of-the-century capitalism, which itself reflects a far more fundamental and philosophical theory of production and writing.[7] Lily's exhibitionism, in other words—her commercialization of herself—corresponds to Wharton's own self-display as a writer, her own participation in the commercial marketplace. And the commercial marketplace, in Michaels's view, far from being a crassly materialistic realm of human corruption, which writers like Dreiser and Wharton would have their readers resist, represents instead nothing less than the core of human energy and creativity.

For this reason Michaels associates the Hawthornean romance tradition, in its apparent refusal to enter into commerce with the world, with deathliness rather than vitality (as with Dreiser and Wharton). This deathliness is emblematized for Michaels in the daguerreotype of the dead Judge Pyncheon in *The House of the Seven Gables.*[8] Michaels's observations are useful, and his example from Hawthorne apt. But his conclusions seem to me oddly to misstate the consequences of the opposition between romance and realism, which is to say between aversion and subversion as literary strategies. Although Wharton and her characters are willing to gamble financially or materially, they cannot put anything at risk spiritually. Both for the author and for the society that she presents in her fiction, the world is irrefutably material, real. As up-and-coming capitalists, therefore, Wharton and the people she represents are willing to take risks within the realm of big business and commercial enterprise. They are not, however, prepared to question the existence of the world itself or the relation between the real and the unreal. In particular, they will not risk the venture of skepticism. For the writers in the romance tradition, this may be the only venture worth taking.

Lily's tableau vivant is a perfect example of the nonskepticist philosophy of art that informs the novel. The "picture," we are told, is "simply and undisguisedly the portrait of Miss Bart. . . . She had shown her artistic intelligence in selecting a type so like her own that she could embody the person represented without ceasing to be herself." Predictably her art makes her audience feel that "for the first time . . . the real Lily Bart" is being presented to them. "It makes her look like the real Lily," says Gerty Farish, "the Lily I know." "The Lily we know," Selden adds (156–57). So grounded in the real is Lily's art that not only does she produce in her audience no doubts as to what is real and what they know, but Lily herself as artist is under no illusions.

> Lily had not an instant's doubt as to the meaning of the murmur greeting her appearance. No other *tableau* had been received with that precise note of approval: it had obviously been called forth by herself, and not by the picture she impersonated. She had feared at the last moment that she was risking too much in dispensing with the advantages of a more sumptuous setting, and the completeness of her triumph gave her an intoxicating sense of recovered power. Not caring to diminish the impression she had produced, she held herself aloof from the audience till the movement of dispersal before supper, and thus had a second opportunity of showing herself to advantage, as the throng poured slowly into the empty drawing-room where she was standing. (158)

The consequence of Lily's "banishing the phantom of [the] dead beauty [of Reynolds's painting] by the beams of her living grace" (156) is a death-dealing vitality. Not only do artist and audience respond to the work of art with overweening pride and self-confidence, but the portrait tempts George Trenor to seduce Lily. His attempt begins a series of tragic seductions that unself-consciously confound the boundaries between the imaginary and the real. Selden and Trenor leave the party together, pointedly coupling characters and events. With the world become a drawing-room, Lily's aloofness from her audience is matched only by the desire of Trenor and Selden to possess her. All three of them are caught moving away from rather than toward a human relationship. Selden will never find his way back to Lily again, at least not while she is alive.

For all her gambles, Lily Bart will not risk the one thing that she must risk in order to realize her relationship with Selden, to become, not the person she is or thinks she is (or that he thinks she is), but the person she might become. Michael Gilmore has suggested in connection with *The Awakening* that Chopin's feminist narrative makes a turn toward the anti-naturalist, self-referential agenda of modernism as a liberating mode of behavior in life and art. Yet neither Edna nor Chopin achieves such liberation. . . . Both women remain trapped in habits of thought they oppose, conceptual systems that prove so pertinacious that they saturate the very act of opposition. Edna, who struggles to free herself from her society's ideal of feminine identity, never relinquishes a limiting Victorian notion of what constitutes a "real" self. And Chopin, in her quest for escape from representation, reverts to nature as a pattern to be imitated. She unwittingly makes clear that Edna's sense of selfhood as an awakened being paradoxically rests on the same ideology of likeness that she and the heroine reject as antithetical to genuine individuality.

Realism and the imaginary, Gilmore notes later in his essay, coincide in the idea of "being like oneself."[9]

Similar statements could be made about Wharton's *House of Mirth,* in particular the tableau scene. The idea of being like oneself, of having a fixed, immutable self that one can realize defines Chopin's and Wharton's characters and their texts. Hawthorne and James resist this idea in their romance fictions. So do Emerson and Thoreau when they speak of a self as a "becoming," where what one becomes cannot be specified or predicted. The early Isabel Archer with her immature Emersonianism has the same resistance to living in and through contradiction that characterizes Lily and Edna throughout their experiences. Like her, like Melville's Ahab, like Faulkner's Sutpen or Fitzgerald's Gatsby, like Hester midway through *The Scarlet Letter* (speaking anachronistically), Edna Pontellier and Lily Bart are bad readers of Emerson . They misunderstand the lessons of self-reliance. Isabel and Hester (largely because of their daughters) outgrow their early misunderstanding of self-reliance. Lily and Edna do not. They will not learn what Hester and Isabel learn, that the self exists only by sustaining its relationships to others, that it achieves selfhood only by affirming its responsibilities to others, including the responsibilities of children and family.

For this reason, Hester and Isabel (and Phoebe Pyncheon and Caddy Compson) not only survive but reproduce. Embracing shadows and dead phantoms (like the daguerreotype of the dead Judge Pyncheon), they, and not Edna and Lily, continue on in the ebb and flow of human events, realizing the vitality that comes not out of the imitation of life (as in a tableau vivant) but out of the self-divestiture, the deadness, of art. All four of these women, in fact, come into possession of very real real estate with all the problems of commercialization that that implies (Hester is certainly one of the earliest entrepreneurs and homeowners in American literature). Romance writers do not withdraw from the marketplace. They resist it, or rather, avert it, redefining, like Thoreau in *Walden*, the meaning of the word *economy*, adding spirituality to what was purely material. Hester, Phoebe, Isabel, and Caddy will risk the transformation of the world. Edna and Lily will not, so their escape from the real can be an escape only into death, a transformation of a wholly other kind. As Judith Fetterley has put it, "Lily's value ultimately derives from her self-hatred; her beauty is finally located in her unwillingness to survive."[10]

Motherhood and Self-Reliance

Critics have hardly been oblivious to the Emersonian, or romance, context in which *The Awakening* might be read. As Elaine Showalter has written: "*The Awakening*, which Chopin subtitled 'A Solitary Soul,' may be read as an account of Edna Pontellier's evolution from romantic fantasies of fusion with another person to self-definition and self-reliance."[11] As soon as Edna is freed of her domestic responsibilities—her husband is in New York, her father recently departed, her children visiting their grandmother—Edna sits in the library and, in a pose highly reminiscent of Isabel sitting with her book in Albany, reads Emerson (190).[12] It is not inconceivable that Chopin modeled Edna on the early Isabel. The echoes of Emerson, and through Emerson of James (his novel appeared almost twenty years earlier), are sufficiently plentiful to warrant such a claim. Note, for example, the following statements: "Mrs. Pontellier was beginning to realize her position in the universe as a human being, and to recognize her relations as an individual to the world within and about her" (33). "The past was nothing to her; offered no lesson which she was willing to heed. The future was a mystery which she never attempted to penetrate. The present alone was significant" (116). She feels that Mr. Pontellier "could not see that she was becoming herself and daily casting aside that fictitious self which we assume like a garment with which to appear before the world" (148). "I don't want anything but my own way. That is wanting a good deal, of course, when you have to trample upon the lives, the hearts, the prejudices of others—but no matter" (292–93). Naked, "some new-born creature, opening its eyes in a familiar world that it had never known" (301), Edna reconstructs Isabel's early philosophical immaturity.

Like Emerson and the early Isabel, Edna shuns father and mother and husband and child when her genius calls her.[13] For her, self-reliance is the aversion of conformity.[14] By aversion, however, Edna intends nothing so sophisticated as what Emerson has in mind. As her experience unfolds, she more and more assumes the pose of the individual whose brand of self-reliance does not engage society but rejects it. We might not want to go so far as to reiterate early responses to the novel that saw Edna as "weak, selfish, and immoral."[15] Nor might we decide to identify Edna's problem as being primarily psychological.[16] But we might well fault Edna for seriously misunderstanding the philosophical grounds on which she locates her newly found self-reliance. We cannot ignore the result of her philosophy of self-reliance: she not only kills herself but abandons her two small children.

To say of Chopin, as did an early reviewer, that she "fail[s] to perceive that the relation of a mother to her children is far more important than the gratification of passion" is to put the case crudely.[17] Still, Edna's abandoning of her children remains a problem for readers of the novel. To moderate some of the ambivalence that the reader feels at the end, Sandra Gilbert and Susan Gubar read the suicide as more mythic than realistic.[18] In interpreting the novel this way, Gilbert and Gubar follow Chopin's lead. Chopin knows that the moral complexity in her novel is neither Edna's adultery nor her sexual passion. For both adultery and passion there were important literary precedents, including Hawthorne's *Scarlet Letter* (Theodore Dreiser's *Sister Carrie* comes out only one year after Chopin's novel). The genuine moral offense is Edna's abandonment of her sons. Therefore, Chopin portrays Edna again and again as struggling with the issue of her children: "I'm not going to be forced into doing things," she tells Doctor Mandelet. "Nobody has any right—except children, perhaps—and even then, it seems to me—or it did seem— . . . I don't want anything but my own way. That is wanting a good deal, of course, when you have to trample upon the lives, the hearts, the prejudices of others—but no matter—still, I shouldn't want to trample upon the little lives. Oh! I don't know what I'm saying, Doctor. Good night. Don't blame me for anything" (291–93). Edna asks the doctor not to blame her for anything, because she already knows what she will stand accountable for at the end of the novel. "It doesn't matter about Léonce Pontellier," Edna thinks to herself as she approaches her decision, "but Raoul and Etienne! . . . The children appeared before her like antagonists who had overcome her; who had overpowered and sought to drag her into the soul's slavery for the rest of her days. But she knew a way to elude them" (299–300).

"Edna had once told Madame Ratignolle that she would never sacrifice herself for her children, or for anyone. . . . 'I would give up the unessential; I would give my money, I would give my life for my children; but I wouldn't give myself'" (121–22). This idea is now repeated, when Edna begins her walk into the sea: "She would give up the unessential, but she would never sacrifice herself for her children" (300). "Léonce and the children . . . were part of her life. But they need not have thought that they could possess her, body and soul" (302). The problem with Edna's attractive declarations of independence is that self and life, soul and body, are inextricably intertwined. Edna cannot give up the unessential, including, presumably, her life, without simultaneously giving up something of her self.

Gilbert and Gubar differentiate Edna's death from Lily Bart's. Her suicide, they argue, is a "willed voyage out from the shores of a culture," whereas "Lily's accidental suicide results from a desire for the cessation of consciousness."[19] But the two suicides are more similar than not. Edna surrenders to the ocean as passively as Lily surrenders to the "bath of oblivion." Edna's death by drowning might, in the context of so thoroughly feminist a novel, seem to reverse the narcissistic implications of such a death.[20] In fact, it heightens those implications. Like Ishmael's escape from death in a watery grave, Edna's drowning constitutes something of the same masturbatory, egocentric, narcissistic fantasy of self-sufficiency.[21] From the moment of her dinner party, which is the ceremony of her unmarrying herself, first from the world of marriage, then from the world of men and sexuality, Edna begins her de-creation. She moves further and further back into a state, first of naked childishness and finally of fetal dissolution. Not only is Edna incapable of sustaining the claims of her procreative being, but in denying those claims she causes her own reproductive reversal. In death Edna does not arrive at what Gilbert and Gubar identify as the openness of childhood, with its potential for growth and development.[22] Rather she delivers herself (perhaps like Ishmael) into the nonexistence of prenatal nonbeing.

Like the efforts of other critics to read Chopin's novel as mythic, Gilbert and Gubar's interpretation has much to recommend it. Chopin's novel is not romance but realism, however. Edna's fantasy of liberation, which, according to Gilbert and Gubar, patterns itself on the myth of Aphrodite, is, finally, an escape from life rather than a recommitment to it. The only real defense for Edna's actions may derive from the arguments of social realism that cite extenuating social and personal circumstances (including, for example, her own lack of good mothering; bad mothering is an important element in Wharton's *House of Mirth* as well). Still, in the final analysis Edna can and must be held accountable for her actions. Isabel Archer walks back into a marriage far more restrictive than Edna's. And the child whom Isabel comes back to is not even her own flesh and blood. Isabel returns. Edna does not.

Lily Bart and the Avoidance of Romance

Like Chopin's Edna, Wharton's Lily embodies the Emersonian principles of James's Isabel without reproducing her capacity for survival and moral commitment. The relationship between Wharton and James, specifically between such characters as Wharton's Lily Bart and Newland Archer (in *The Age of Innocence*) and James's Isabel Archer and Christopher Newman (Newland Archer's name virtually reconstructs the Jamesian American), has not gone unnoticed.[23] And critics have been sensitive to Lily's failings. But the contrast between James and Wharton is not so simple as blithe male optimism versus legitimate female pessimism.[24] Throughout *The House of Mirth*, Wharton resists the possibilities (dominant in romance fiction) of internal contradictions, eruptions out of and against external reality. For Hawthorne, James, and Faulkner these forces constitute the strength not only of writing but of the woman as well.

The following description of Lily and Selden looks forward to the climax of the novel, when Lily takes the fatal dose of sleeping medicine. It also anticipates the scene of the tableau vivant: "They stood silent for a while after this, smiling at each other like adventurous children who have climbed to a forbidden height from which they discover a new world. The actual world at their feet was veiling itself in dimness, and across the valley a clear moon rose in the denser blue. . . . Suddenly they heard a remote sound, like the hum of a giant insect, and following the high-road, which wound whiter through the surrounding twilight, a black object rushed across their vision" (85–86).

This is the Hawthornean moment of ambiguity and doubt and no small measure of fear. Through the reconstruction of a kind of Eden and especially through the odd reference to the giant insect, the description recollects the scene of Judge Pyncheon's death in *The House of the Seven Gables* (just as the title of Wharton's novel points to its predecessor text). The death scene is behind the tableaux vivants as well. It is the scene of the "phantom" (156) that Holgrave records on film and that transforms both Phoebe's and Holgrave's perceptions of reality and their relationship to each other. Like Phoebe and

Holgrave, Lily and Selden can either seize this moment or not. To realize their love for each other, Lily and Selden must "risk" more than social success (85). They must entertain even more than the "risk" of death (375). They must risk nothing less than the dissolution of the world as they know it. They must be willing to discover a new world, veiled in twilight (what Hawthorne calls in *The House of the Seven Gables* a "heavy earth-dream"), which is not reality at all.[25]

But so committed to "safety" is Lily, so much given to "premeditation," that for her even "mental vagrancy" constitutes an enormous psychological and emotional threat (78). Nor is Selden any more of an emotional gambler: "My idea of success . . . is personal freedom . . . from everything—from money, from poverty, from ease and anxiety, from all the material accidents" (79). Yet what attracts each to the other is the "danger-point" of "spontaneity," of the "unforeseen" (80), of losing self-control, so that one might not remain, in Selden's word, "amphibious" (81). Selden and Lily play at making love only until it threatens to dissolve, not just their social positions, but their sense of reality. After the tableau vivant, when Selden and Lily come again to occupy a "magic place," they repeat the move away from "the unreality of the scene" (159), even though they know, and the scene makes clear, that their love for each other depends on the solitude and unreality in which they find themselves.

The journey to separation and death becomes inevitable. "She had never hung so near the dizzy brink of the unreal": these words toward the end recall Lily's position earlier on the "forbidden height" of passion and her moment of unreality with Selden. "Sleep was what she wanted," "darkness was what she must have at any cost" (374). The alternative to the perils of the unreal is death. Selden and Lily resist the ultimate risk of world transformation, of relocation between the imaginary and the real, where the gamble (to appropriate Michaels's term) is not simply accident versus action or chance versus freedom but their very ability to verify their perceptions of the world. Wharton resists the gamble, too. Her conclusion flirts with the fairy-tale ending that she has created for Nettie Struther and her Prince Charming—marriage and children—which characterizes much nineteenth-century women's fiction. But, in Lily's case, Wharton entertains the possibility only to dismiss it as itself a phantom of death.

Lily's virgin death, while she is haunted by the image of the absent child, reminds us that the giant insect that rushes in on Lily and Selden represents more than the undefined horrors of a world transformed. The threat is specifically sexual. In the moment of reaching out toward one another, almost risking everything, Lily and Selden are represented as children, as is Lily after the tableau vivant scene. But Lily and Selden will not be the kind of children who venture the forbidden. Neither, however, will they allow themselves to outgrow childhood, to enter a forbidden world (as do Hawthorne's Adam and Eve: Phoebe and Holgrave), discover a new world, and, creating, procreating, populate it. The final scene of the novel, in which Lily is portrayed as never becoming a mother, evokes this earlier scene of Lily as eternal child. A failure of parenthood pervades the novel. Not one of the parents presented is willing to assume the attendant responsibilities.

Lily Bart perishes, the casualty of her own incapacity for romance—in both the literary and amorous senses of the word. Lily's death realizes the fatality of both Lily's and Wharton's brand of realism. For Lily, as for Edna before her, the sleep she sleeps is a regression back into infancy, denying the possibilities of motherhood. Like Edna, Lily struggles with the feeling that she ought to keep awake (alive) for the sake of the child that, in Lily's case, she does not have but only imagines. Finally, Lily yields to a self-created warmth that denies nurture to anything outside herself. Her unwillingness to survive is directly linked to her refusal of motherhood.

Female Realism and the Barren Ground

We might say Edna Pontellier, like Melville's Ahab, will not go back home. Lily Bart, like Mark Twain's Huckleberry Finn, refuses to create and maintain a home. In refusing family and motherhood, Lily is not unique in turn-of-the-century fiction by women. Mary Wilkin Freeman's New England nun, for example, like other of Freeman's characters, as well as many of the unmarried or widowed women in Sarah Orne Jewett's fiction, achieves freedom only at the price of giving up sexuality and family. To cultivate a self without running into the inevitable biological consequences of sexuality, which often compromise that self, these women—Dorinda Oakley in Ellen Glasgow's novel, for example—must turn themselves into "barren ground." Dorinda's development in Glasgow's *Barren Ground* can stand for that of several late nineteenth-century and early twentieth-century female protagonists, including Joanna in Jewett's *Country of the Pointed Firs,* who punishes herself for an aborted love affair by incarcerating herself on an island. Illegitimately pregnant, Dorinda runs away, only to miscarry. The loss of the unborn child is eclipsed in the narrative, as if this portion of her reality, of her procreative desire, disappears. When the text resumes, Dorinda has given up on her reproductive function and on her desire for men. When she finally does marry—a widower, whom she loves more for his children than for himself—the marriage is sexless. Instead of giving herself to a man, Dorinda gives herself to the land and to a man's children, thus (like a man perhaps) realizing her fertility by tilling the barren ground, not of herself, but of someone or something else.

The relation between Dorinda and the land makes us reconsider Annette Kolodny's thesis that nineteenth-century attitudes toward the landscape represented male fantasies of domination.[26] Dorinda's cultivation of the land, like Isabel's early attitudes toward herself as a garden, suggest the way women might imagine themselves and nature as continuous and interchangeable media of intercourse and reproduction. Unlike some of her less fortunate comrades, Dorinda (like Isabel) does attain the condition of motherhood, though by marrying a widower she bypasses natural process. She becomes a mother by benefiting from some other woman's yielding to what she herself would resist. Dorinda's reconstitution of the family without herself producing children is repeated throughout these texts: in Jewett's *Country of the Pointed Firs*, for example, the narrator is adopted into a largely female community, thus presenting the possibility of family without involving the problems of sexuality. The family grouping that emerges in another of Wharton's novels, *Ethan Frome*, can stand for the social disfigurement that Wharton attributes to both male and female romanticism: Maddie Silver and Ethan permanently disable themselves in their mutual suicide attempt, thus remaining childless and childlike; the family that emerges at the end consists of the somewhat grotesque trio of Ethan and Zeena Frome and Maddie.

As I suggested in my reading of Hawthorne's *Scarlet Letter*, the reconstitution of the family on nonpatriarchal terms is a major concern of his novel, as it is of James's. The theme recurs in the fiction of many contemporary American women writers, including Carson McCullers, Grace Paley, Toni Morrison, Gloria Naylor, and Alice Walker. But whereas Hawthorne and his descents maintain at least the illusion of heterosexual relationships and hence preserve the options of familial and historical continuity, Jewett's *Country of the Pointed Firs* and Wharton's *Ethan Frome* represent a dead stop to history, such as Melville and Faulkner also imagine. The contemporary feminist-realist tradition, which inherits Chopin, Wharton, Jewett, and Freeman, runs into a similar dead end and surmounts it in much the same way. In Marilyn French's *Woman's Room* and *My Mother's Daughter,* for example, the female protagonists escape the tyranny of marriage and heterosexual relationships into lesbian relationships only after they have parented children and are therefore already mothers.

What is curious about this group of turn-of-the-century women's novels is that the writers, in resisting the happy endings, in marriage, of nineteenth-century domestic fiction, fail to imagine what Hawthorne, James, and Faulkner (or Dreiser, for that matter) clearly saw as one direction that female sexuality might go. For the male writers, female sexuality did not necessarily have to find its home in marriage. Dreiser is not a romancer; he buys into many clichés about women. But even Dreiser's *Sister Carrie* seems a stronger portrayal of a woman's options than the female fictions coetaneous with it. Like so many late nineteenth-century and early twentieth-century heroines, Carrie Meeber, by the end of the novel, seems to reject both marriage and motherhood. Rocking in her rocking chair with no infant in her arms, Carrie, like Edna and Lily, is her own self-nurturing child. But Carrie survives, and she survives sexually active—something that heroines like Glasgow's Dorinda cannot do. "Why, you may marry again," one of the characters says to Dorinda after the death of her husband. "Dorinda smiled, and her smile was pensive, ironic, and infinitely wise. 'Oh, I've finished with all that,' she rejoined. 'I am thankful to have finished with all that.'"[27]

Works like *The Awakening* and *The House of Mirth* cannot be read outside the context of the male and female fiction that they oppose. Nonetheless, their subversive function so overtakes them that, to invoke an old cliché, they literally throw out the baby with the bathwater. Charlotte Perkins Gilman's short story "The Yellow Wallpaper" seems to me another example of this phenomenon in turn-of-the-century women's writing. According to Walter Benn Michaels (who is following through on the logic of Gilman's *Women and Economics*), Gilman here discovers a fatal discrepancy in the nineteenth-century construct of female gender. Society fails to allow women to express the natural need of all human beings to produce and, by entering into production, mark and identify themselves as individuals. The story, in Michaels's reading, neither endorses nor resists culture; it "*exemplifies*" it:

The desire to mark—to maintain the self by producing the self and to produce the self by consuming the self—is the primitive like [that is, desire] that makes the institution of selfhood possible. This very desire produces modern production and consumption; it produces, above all, the dissemination of subjectivity intrinsic to naturalism as a mode of writing. For what Gilman's child wants is to *mark*. His means of inscription into consumer culture is the desire for inscription itself, as if the very category of subjectivity—the possibility of being a subject—were an effect of writing, as indeed, in "The Yellow Wallpaper," it is. Hence the impossibility of conceiving the desire to mark as simply the desire of a preexisting subject. And hence the point of the question, what kind of work is writing. Gilman's own answer is production, and in insisting on herself as a writer she means, as we have seen, to insist on the possibility of women transforming themselves from consumers into producers. . . . What kind of work is writing? It is the work of at once producing and consuming the self.[28]

What Gilman forgets about her heroine and what Michaels ignores in his reading of her is her position as a mother. Biological reproduction begins as the inseparability of consumption and production. It can therefore be understood as endorsing Michaels's description of writing as a dissemination of subjectivity, always more and less than what it seems to be.[29] But what birth produces can never be reappropriated back into the self.

This notion returns us to Hester Prynne and the tradition that she inaugurates. Hester becomes a mother-artist when she acknowledges the difference between her productive and reproductive functions, the two different kinds of productivity that the child and the letter constitute . In Hawthorne's view, Hester can enter into the marketplace and also be a mother. (Hester is, after all, economically independent throughout the novel: a single parent and a working mother.) She can write and she can reproduce, and in doing both she can create a home and a history for the nation. In "The Yellow Wallpaper," the house—more paper than walls—is a temporary dwelling that by the end of the story has been defaced from within and emptied of all its human possessions and possessors. Like Poe's House of Usher or like the Sutpen estate in Faulkner's *Absalom, Absalom!* this house will never become a home.

"The Yellow Wallpaper" is a very powerful story about a woman driven mad (in some readings) by the economy of exchange in which she finds herself, or at least realizing the implications of the marketplace (in Michaels's reading) with a kind of fanatical literalism. There is no blaming the narrator or her author—or the characters and authors of such novels as *The Awakening* and *The House of Mirth*—for what they do or say or for what they do not say or do.

The literary event, like the human lives that it puts into play, is what it is, not what we want it to be. Let me suggest, however, that the one thing that the tradition of novels extending from Stowe's *Uncle Tom's Cabin* through a series of nineteenth-century and early twentieth-century works by women does *not* provide for a particular group of modern and contemporary women writers is a model of female strength.

Like Chopin and Wharton, the women writers who achieve artistic prominence in the last quarter of the twentieth century—Grace Paley and Toni Morrison, to name the two who will most basically concern me in this book—resist simple gender definitions and social conformity. At the same time, they acknowledge the primary claims of sexual desire and familial responsibility. They portray survival as a strength capable of supporting both nurture and self-realization, and finally home building. The difference between the male romancers and their female descendants on the one hand and the fictional tradition that they resist on the other is the difference between Hawthorne's and Wharton's ideas of customs, the difference between romance and realism. For Wharton customs are social forms that individuals can accept, subvert, embody. For Hawthorne, and for James and Faulkner, customs are duties. They do not represent essential or universal truths. But they must be paid. Payment need not imply total obedience to the system, as if we were the currency of our exchange. It can incorporate resistance at the same time that it acknowledges and affirms community and relationship. This is the economy, not of the marketplace, but, as in Thoreau's writing, of human relatedness.

The titles of Wharton's novels and Hawthorne's *House of Seven Gables* and "Custom-House" can stand for one major difference between feminist realism and male romance, which accounts for the subsequent inheritability of the male tradition by women writers. *The Custom of the Country* naturalizes and extends consensus. This drama is also played out in *The House of Mirth*. "The Custom-House," in contrast, legislates duties that in no way reflect universal or biological or even immutable social truths but instead insist on social obligations as what creating a home and living in it demand. But because these duties are formal and legalistic, as opposed to essentialist and natural, they need never impinge upon the heart of the matter. Individuals are also free, as in *The House of the Seven Gables,* to seek each other out and establish relationships. Relationships of aversive consent, within community and within marriage, are what many of the fictions of Hawthorne, Melville, Twain, James, and Faulkner are about. They constitute the subject in a major tradition of the female romance as well.

IV

The Female Romance

8

The Mother Tongue

Carson McCullers

Like her predecessors in the romance tradition,
Carson McCullers, in *The Heart Is a Lonely Hunter,*
renders a portrait of reality more suggestive than
mimetic. As with *The Scarlet Letter* and *The House
of the Seven Gables* (and the tradition of sentimental
fiction to which these texts are related), its subject
is the truth of the human heart, and its fundamental message has to do with what the text specifies
as "one word—love."[1] At the end of Wharton's
House of Mirth, Lily is trying to remember this single word, and Selden in on his way to Lily to say it.
The word is never stated in Wharton's novel, but it
is spoken in McCullers's. A central concern in *The
Heart Is a Lonely Hunter* (as in the *Letter*) is what it
means to risk speaking the word *love,* which is to
say what it means to risk not speaking it. Through
her female protagonists Mick Kelly and Portia—
and through the bisexual Biff Brannon—McCullers
discovers a language of the heart that, like
Faulkner's antiphallocentric discourse, transcends
the limitations of symbolic, representational, ideological discourse.[2] But because she is as much
invested in the *word* love as in love itself, her text
does not, like the sentimental novels of the nineteenth century, dissolve into pure emotionality,
beyond language; nor does it, like Faulkner's fiction,
resist the material, maternal, symbolic universe.

Stanley Cavell has written of the reader-writer relationship that "the reader's position [is] that of the stranger. To write to him is to acknowledge that he is outside the words, at a bent arm's length, and alone with the book; that his presence to these words is perfectly contingent, and the choice to stay with them continuously his own; that they are his points of departure and origin. The conditions of meeting upon the word are that we—writer and reader—learn how to depart from them, leave them where they are; and then return to them, finding ourselves there again." In McCullers's novel, speaking requires the same autonomy of speaker and listener, the same necessity for what Cavell elsewhere imagines as letting words go and finding them again.[3] *The Heart Is a Lonely Hunter* has to do with the requirements of both verbal and sexual intercourse, as well as with taking responsibility for what such intercourse produces.

The Law of the Father

In *The Heart Is a Lonely Hunter* four lonely characters seek to escape isolation and open intercourse with the world through their conversation with a deaf person who cannot hear them and refuses to speak to them. This pattern of nonconversation, in which the individual chooses as the recipient of communication a person who cannot or will not respond, is poignantly reinforced by John Singer's own choice of dialogic partner: the deaf and dumb, mentally retarded Spiros Antonapoulos. There is no mistaking McCullers's sympathy for her isolated individuals—no ignoring, either, the complaint about lonely hearts who ruthlessly hunt companionship, only to use the other as a sounding board for the self. As if anticipating the poststructuralist accusation against new formalist criticism—that it reads out texts as mirrors of the designs that the reader places on them—the characters of McCullers's novel seem to speak only to hear their own voices. They convert each other into self-reflections, allegorical mirrors of the self, which permit them to engage in endlessly self-referential monologues. "Each man described the mute as he wished him to be" (197), writes McCullers. The monologic structure of Faulkner's *Sound and the Fury* and *As I Lay Dying* stands close behind McCullers's montage of voices, in which the many consciousnesses in the book remain painfully stranded outside the community of human exchange.

Causing this failure to establish intercourse is the individuals' self-absorption, which prompts them to choose as the object of their communication someone who cannot or will not hear or respond. McCullers suggests, however, that the silent listener is as much victimizer as victim. The silent Singer seduces the other characters into choosing him as their listener, their god. From the beginning of the book McCullers leaves us in no doubt that Singer chooses to remain voiceless; he is not innately mute. Might we not think of Singer—who, when he does communicate, does so through written words, engraved symbols, and signs—as being like a text, which, in its unresponsive, nonconversational mode of transcription, leaves the interpreter free to imagine everything and anything? The problem that Singer, both as character and as text, raises is, What does it mean not to say or not to say clearly? What are the consequences to others of a refusal to enter into the two-way process of conversation? What does it mean in a human relationship to be made the interpreter of a static, silent object (person or text) as opposed to a partner in the mutual (and mutually responsible) production of meaning?

For McCullers the alternative to the silent text is not political discourse. The book explicitly rejects the language employed by Benedict Mady Copeland, the black doctor and activist, and Jake Blount, the radical labor organizer. "Talk—talk—talk" is the way Biff describes Blount (19). Like the other major figures in the story, Blount, according to Singer, is "always talking" (85). Nor is this talk—talk—talk idle or innocent. It is focused obsessively on the idea of an exclusive unitary "truth" (141)—a "true purpose" in the case of Copeland (125)—which the individual is convinced he or she can articulate. Like Anderson's greedy grotesques (and Flannery O'Connor's), Carson McCullers's "freaks" (23) want to possess the beautiful, multiple truths of the world. In possessing them, they distort the truths and themselves alike. They render the truth false and themselves grotesque. The consequences of this obsession with truth and with the ideological speech through which one imagines one can express truth are devastating, as in *Winesburg, Ohio,* both for family and for community. Copeland loses his wife and alienates his children, while Blount roams aimlessly throughout the country, (not)husband and (not)father (to formulate the problem in the terms of another of McCullers's important precursors, William Faulkner).

The painfulness of conversation turned ideological argument is stunningly portrayed in the quarrel between Blount and Copeland, which occurs toward the end of the novel. The confrontation—not unlike that in Ralph Ellison's *Invisible Man* (published a few years later)—is between an American white political activist and an American black. It exposes the limitations of white political thought about African Americans along the lines of Ellison's and Richard Wright's conclusions concerning the exploitation of the race problem by the Communist party. The conversation begins as a discussion between two like-minded and socially engaged individuals but quickly degenerates into childish accusations and name-calling: "Oh, the Hell with it! . . . Balls!" "Blasphemer! . . . Foul blasphemer!" "Short-sighted bigot!" "White . . . Fiend!" (268). By the end of the novel, Blount, beaten down and running for his life, realizes that what separates him from Copeland is only words. "On some points they might be able to work together . . . if they didn't talk too much" (298). As in Hawthorne's *Scarlet Letter,* ideological discourse replicates the problem of the silent text: it repels and attracts, in effect silencing itself, regardless of all its apparent wordiness and noise. Sitting in the presence of his family, Copeland finally falls "dumb" (131, 132): "If he could not speak the whole long truth no other word would come to him," not even the word "farewell" as he leaves the family gathering and goes out the door (133). By the time Blount reaches Copeland, it is too late for both of them.

For all her concern with issues of sexism, racism, anti-Semitism, and economic exploitation, McCullers, like her predecessors in the romance tradition, refuses to write a directly political text. Copeland and Blount are both given their say in this book. But for McCullers morality is more a way of seeing the world than a set of political objectives. For this reason, perhaps, she has Copeland articulate a political philosophy that directly misstates the romance politics of Thoreau and Emerson. "If I could just find ten Negroes," he says to Portia, "—ten of my own people—with spine and brains and courage . . . only four Negroes" (71–72). Here is the text from Thoreau's "Civil Disobedience" (itself a gloss on an Old Testament passage) that Copeland misunderstands: "I know this well, that if one thousand, if one hundred, if ten men whom I could name—if ten *honest* men only—ay, if *one* HONEST man, in this State of Massachusetts, *ceasing to hold slaves,* were actually to withdraw from this copartnership, and be locked up in the county jail therefore, it would be the abolition of slavery in America."[4] The difference between Copeland's formulation and Thoreau's is that Copeland has bred, raised, and groomed (even named) four specific individuals (his own children) for this particular task of saving the black people, whereas Thoreau has no one man in particular but any man, and therefore potentially every man, coming to this moral perception on his own. Thoreau's idea carries forward the biblical idea that it inherits. When Abraham pleads for Sodom on the basis of the ten honest men, he has no ten in particular in mind but any and therefore potentially all who might exist within the city. Portia's response to her father that "Willie and Highboy and me have backbone. This here is a hard world and it seem to me us three struggles along pretty well" (72) understands what Thoreau understands: that moral courage is not political and public so much as individual and private.

But if McCullers sides with Emerson and Thoreau against Copeland and Blount, she does so fully aware of the dangers of Emerson's and Thoreau's way of turning aside from direct confrontation with sociopolitical issues. McCullers is tortured by the possibility that writers, artists, and musicians, in avoiding politics, do little to correct either social problems or the problem of ideology itself. The language of the writer, she realizes, may even intensify tendencies in language to express human egocentricity, producing a text that becomes everyone else's mirror of self. Not surprisingly, this self is also an embodiment of a transcendent perfection. Singer's dream midway through the novel, which foreshadows the painful denouement of the book, is a virtual diagram of a hierarchical transcendentalization of reality. The pyramid of world order, in which the self celebrates itself, depends on the silence of the god or text or idea at the pinnacle—a silence that allows the self to endow itself with divine qualities.

Out of the blackness of sleep a dream formed. There were dull yellow lanterns lighting up a dark flight of stone steps. Antonapoulos kneeled at the top of these steps. He was naked and he fumbled with something that he held above his head and gazed at it as though in prayer. He himself knelt half-way down the steps. He was naked and cold and he could not take his eyes from Antonapoulos and the thing he held above him. Behind him on the ground he felt the one with the moustache and the girl and the black man and the last one. They knelt naked and he felt their eyes on him. And behind them there were uncounted crowds of kneeling people in the darkness. His own hands were huge windmills and he stared fascinated at the unknown thing that Antonapoulos held. The yellow lanterns swayed to and fro in the darkness and all else was motionless. Then suddenly there was a ferment. In the upheaval the steps collapsed and he felt himself falling downwards. He awoke with a jerk. The early light whitened the window. He felt afraid. (192)

The central figure in the scene is the something, the thing, the unknown thing, that Antonapoulos holds in his hands. Singer refuses to identify it, even though it is as naked and in view as the crowds of kneeling people who compose the scene. Nor will Singer—his hands like windmills incapable of signing and therefore incapable of speech—name the one with the moustache and the girl and the black man and the last one or count the uncounted but not countless crowds. There are two ways of understanding Singer's unwillingness, or inability, to articulate what is represented in his dream. Insofar as the thing represents something mysterious, not easily given over to a name, his silence can be understood as an appropriate restraint from the excesses of verbalization. Certain details—the cathedral-like setting of the dream, with all of the characters kneeling, and that the one object Antonapoulos possesses is a crucifix and that in the very next scene he is represented as majestic and godlike (194–96)—suggest that the thing is a cross. What is a cross, the text implies, to be so lightly named? What does the name tell us about what a crucifix is or means? Singer's silence, then, might seem a prudent response to the dangers of mindless talk—talk—talk.

But the interpretation is not so simple. Although one of the few ways in which Antonapoulos uses his hands is to sign the words "'Holy Jesus,' or 'God,' or 'Darling Mary,'" another is to indulge in his "solitary secret pleasure," masturbation (8). Awaking with a jerk, Singer might well feel afraid of what he has witnessed in his dream of raw and naked desire. He may have very good reasons for refusing to say what thing he has seen.

Is the thing a cross—or a penis? Does it stand for the divine or the purely human? the purely human as divine? McCullers's text owes something here to Melville's *Moby Dick*. Like the great white whale for Ahab, the thing (whatever it is) is, for Singer, a transcendent object of worship. Deification of the unknown and mysterious thing (which may be no more than a figure for one's own sexual desire) extends down through the pyramid of worshipers. For Singer, Antonapoulos is God. Singer himself is God for Biff, Blount, Copeland, and Mick. McCullers's text illuminates a tendency within human beings to construct a universe of divine meanings, in which discovering the divine in someone or something else is both a cover for confronting the physical and the sexual within oneself and a way of converting the merely biological and human into the transcendent and spiritual. But insofar as the author refuses to write what the thing in Antonapoulos's hand is, she conspires in this process of deification. She makes the text into the seductive god who commands the worship of the reader.

The failure to specify what the thing is mimetically reproduces the silence of dreams: the text replicates an aspect of the everyday experience of the world in which language-as-clarification is naturally withheld. Dreams do not represent reality in a transparent symbolic script. As often as not, they withhold the terms of identification through which the dreamer might interpret the dream. One might say that Singer never achieves self-knowledge of his tragic attachment to Antonapoulos because he is a poor interpreter of dreams. But he is a poor interpreter of dreams (that is, of himself) because dreams do not say what they mean. They are dreams and they exist because they say without saying. Dreams are an expression of human resistance to self-clarification. They remind us that there are things we simply do not want to know about ourselves. And there are things that we do not want others to know about us. In many ways, Singer, who speaks with silent signs and symbols, embodies the language of dreams. By speaking with and to him, Mick, Biff, Blount, and Copeland confront a dreamlike language that they can choose not to understand.

But Singer does not refuse the role that he plays for the other characters. Like a god, Singer speaks in the language of dreams—through signs and symbols; he speaks in silence, and he speaks in order *not* to be understood. McCullers's text, like perhaps all literary texts, similarly threatens self-deification and mystification. But the consequences of leaving the world uninterpreted, the text makes clear, are terrifying. Naked and cold and gradually metamorphosing into a monster with windmills for hands, Singer is understandably frightened by his dream. Later, when Antonapoulos's fumbling for his cross makes Singer recall the dream and he tries and once again cannot sign the dream (196), Singer falls prey to impulses that he can neither understand nor control. Singer cannot convert the dream into speech. As the bitter climax of the novel approaches, Singer "surrender[s] himself wholly to thoughts of his friend. . . . Behind each waking moment there had always been his friend. And this submerged communion with Antonapoulos had grown and changed as though they were together in the flesh. Sometimes he thought of Antonapoulos with awe and self-abasement, sometimes with pride—always with love unchecked by criticism, freed of will. When he dreamed at night the face of his friend was always before him, massive and wise and gentle. And in his waking thoughts they were eternally united" (282). The failure to interpret is a fantasy of union, in which self and other respect no distance and exist outside the differentiations and disintegrations of language. Its consequence is the collapse into nothingness that the fiction of Edgar Allan Poe vividly records.

Singer's suicide is one of many figures in the book for the identification of unity with death. To achieve total union with the other is to kill off the other.

No sooner has the author articulated Singer's feelings of oneness with Anton-apoulos than we discover that Antonapoulos is dead. In this book even think-ing about unity can be murderous. And this brings the text to another aspect of totalizing desire: to achieve union with the other and hence with oneself is to destroy the other and oneself. With the death of Antonapoulos, Singer commits suicide, and with Singer's suicide the whole chain of human community breaks apart: Blount is routed out of town after the murderous riot at the fair; Copeland, sick and defeated, is taken to the farm of his father-in-law to die; Mick takes a job at Woolworth's, which puts to an end her artistic ambitions; and Biff is left alone tending the shop. Were it not for a certain prospect for the future that the author deftly constructs (to which I shall return in a moment), the novel would end, as do the fictions of Faulkner and Anderson, Melville and Poe, with a sterility and deathliness, signaling the end of family, community, and history—the end of literature itself.

According to McCullers's novel, the cause of suicidal-murderous sterility is the tendency toward transcendental, symbolic thought. As I have already sug-gested, the thing that Antonapoulos holds in his hand is not only the crucifix (which figures the Law of the Father) but (by implication) his penis, which is the Law of the Father in its biological form. What makes Singer voiceless in the first place and what keeps him voiceless until the end is his fear of being exposed as merely human, a biological and sexual creature, neither divine nor transcendent.

There was one particular fact that he remembered [about his childhood], but it was not at all important to him. Singer recalled that, although he had been deaf since he was an infant, he had not always been a real mute. He was left an orphan very young and placed in an institution for the deaf. He had learned to talk with his hands and to read. Before he was nine years old he could talk with one hand in the American way—and also could employ both of his hands after the method of Europeans. He had learned to follow the movements of people's lips and to understand what they said. Then finally he had been taught to speak. . . . But he could never become used to speaking with his lips. It was not natural to him, and his tongue felt like a whale in his mouth. From the blank expression on people's faces to whom he talked in this way he felt that his voice must be like the sound of some animal or that there was something disgusting in his speech. It was painful for him to try to talk with his mouth, but his hands were always ready to try to shape the words he wished to say. When he was twenty-two he had come South to this town from Chicago and he met Antonapoulos immediately. Since that time he had never spoken with his mouth again, because with his friend there was no need for this. (13–14)

Singer's silence is foremost a response to his particular handicap, which is deafness. But his response carries with it the force of a more general and pervasive human response to the problematics of speaking. Immediately after Singer's discovery of Antonapoulos's death, a strange thing happens that suggests that Singer's flight from speech may not be from the possibility of not being understood or being thought of as less than human. On the contrary, it might represent a flight from the possibility that he may well be understood, not as a brilliant, multilingual student but as a mere mortal, who gropes for and stumbles over words that may not only express what he wants to say but that may expose all his human frailty.

Singer meets "three mutes . . . talking with their hands together. All three of them were coatless. They wore bowler hats and bright ties. Each of them held a glass of beer in his left hand. There was a certain brotherly resemblance between them. . . . He was clapped on the shoulder. A cold drink was ordered. They surrounded him and the fingers of their hands shot out like pistons as they questioned him." After a few awkward efforts to communicate with them, Singer abandons communication for the last time, "his hands dangling loose . . . his head . . . inclined to one side and his glance . . . oblique" (285). Singer's choice not to communicate with these friendly, brotherly mute people, who—unlike everyone else in the novel, including Antonapoulos—could understand him, suggests that Singer cannot face the possibility that he is like other human beings, absurdly, comically identical with them (as they are identical with each other), that speech reduces him, not to the animalistic or subhuman, but to the human. Singer will not seek out his brothers for to do so would be to discover he is one of them.

That his tongue in his mouth feels like a whale prompts us to think of Melville's novel. So does Biff's denial of his sexuality (29). Like Ahab, Biff and Singer prefer to imagine themselves as not limited by biology. In McCullers's novel, speaking silently (which is to say speaking not to be understood) is associated with a withdrawal from sexual relations. Phallocentricism, the author suggests, does not necessarily place the penis in the position of power. Rather, in denying that the penis is potent sexual agent, it may be substituting a feeble and ineffectual law of abstract, intellectually derived symbols of the world for the procreative, phallicly reproduced biohistorical world itself. McCullers's male characters (excluding Biff) are not feminized males or androgynous human beings, realizing the fusion of male and female principles. They are self-castrated men, who relinquish male potency and deny procreative power.

The relation between the assertion of phallocentric law and the denial of phallic biology in self-canceling males characterizes another important precursor of McCullers's art. Like Jay Gatsby in F. Scott Fitzgerald's *Great Gatsby,* the men who populate the world of McCullers's text desire to be Platonic conceptions of self. The case of Gatsby is instructive, both for McCullers's novel and for Flannery O'Connor's *The Violent Bear It Away.* Not only does Gatsby (in true Freudian romance fashion) disown his parents ("his imagination had never really accepted them as his parents at all"), but he rejects reconciliation with the biological terms of human birth altogether: "He was the son of God—a phrase which, if it means anything, means just that—and he must be about His Father's business, the service of a vast, vulgar, and meretricious beauty. So he invented just the sort of Jay Gatsby that a seventeen-year-old boy would be likely to invent, and to this conception he was faithful to the end." Gatsby's Platonic conception of himself rejects the biological woman: "He knew women early, and . . . he became contemptuous of them, of young virgins because they were ignorant, of the others because they were hysterical about things which in his overwhelming self-absorption he took for granted."[5] When he falls in love with Daisy he knows that "when he kissed this girl, and forever wed his unutterable visions to her perishable breath, his mind would never romp again like the mind of God. . . . At his lips' touch she blossomed for him like a flower and the incarnation was complete." Gatsby's desire, moments earlier, to mount to a "secret place above the trees" where "he could suck on the pap of life, gulp down the incomparable milk of wonder" is fulfilled only in the birth of self that his relationship to Daisy produces (112).

Gatsby culminates in a uterine birthing motion (as opposed to a phallic thrust) reminiscent of *Moby Dick.* But this birthing can only be endured; it cannot itself give birth: "So we beat on, boats against the current, borne back ceaseless into the past." Male "brooding" produces only Platonic conception and incarnation (182). It does not bear life. Fitzgerald's novel reveals what emerges as a problem in Faulkner's and Anderson's writings as well: that male imaginings of the female, for all their generosity and goodwill, may not be able to move beyond gestation (brooding) to birth. Because Gatsby will not be a man ready to assume the responsibilities of the phallus, he dies, stillborn after his self-inseminated virgin birth. McCullers's silent Singer, orphan and bachelor, embodies similar problems.

The Lawless Woman Speaks

Much has been made in recent feminist criticism of the multivocalism, authorial decenteredness, and indeterminate open-endedness of novels by women. All are understood to be antiphallocentric strategies. All to some degree characterize McCullers's novel, as they also characterize the fiction of McCullers's two major literary predecessors, William Faulkner and Sherwood Anderson. *The Heart is a Lonely Hunter* flows uninterruptedly from consciousness to consciousness, weaving together the community that does not exist within the world of the novel. But like Anderson's and Faulkner's strategies of antiphallocentricism, McCullers's threaten to produce a non-progenerative and perhaps antifemale sterility. Not only are Blount and Singer confirmed bachelors but Biff and Copeland are widowers (Biff's wife dies of a tumor as big as a baby). Portia, the strongest female presence in the book, is childless. At the close of the novel only Mick, on the verge of adulthood, remains to create a future. Mick's position at the end of the novel and her nurturing nature throughout are important for McCullers's idea of family. The figure who will enable her mothering is Portia.

Early in the novel McCullers presents an extended conversation between Portia and her father that pits Portia's female, African American discourse against her father's white-inspired intellectual ideology, his language of law against her language of the biological and reproductive: "All his life he had told and explained and exhorted. . . . It is not more children we need but more chances for the ones already on the earth" (69). Not only does Copeland's statement appear (indecorously) in the center of a conversation with his own daughter, but his thinking on this matter proceeds directly from a painful and equally blind conversation with Portia on her childlessness: "So you and your husband and your brother have your own cooperative plan," he says to her. "Do you intend to plan for children?" The text continues: "Portia did not look at her father. Angrily she sloshed the water from the pan of collards. 'There be some things,' she said, 'that seem to me to depend entirely upon God'" (68).

Copeland cannot understand—either about his daughter's communal living arrangements or about the many children produced by the black community—the positive and creative nature of these affirmations of life. For all his concern with the "Negro people" (as his interjections into Blount's Marxist discourse remind us—259–68), Copeland adopts a political philosophy as white as that of Blount. Copeland's rejection of Christianity might have constituted a part of a necessary turn away from white institutions to African American culture. It represents instead Copeland's decidedly masculinist rejection of the unknowable and the uncertain in human experience—his rejection both of women and of the African past of black Americans. "I am not interested in subterfuges," he says. "I am interested only in real truths" (72). These real truths contain no space for "hell and heaven" or for the "ghosts" and "haunted places" of African legend (75). Therefore, Copeland turns to Marx for his politics, Spinoza for his philosophy, and Shakespeare for his literature. In resisting what he calls his wife Daisy's stubborn meekness—her insistence on teaching her children both Christianity and African Americanism—he resists as well his wife's sexuality.

The question that McCullers's novel raises, both in the conversation between Dr. Copeland and Portia and in the story as a whole, is, What does it mean to know by heart? McCullers writes: "Eugenic Parenthood for the Negro Race was what he would exhort them to. He would tell them in simple words, always the same way, and with the years it came to be a sort of angry poem which he had always known by heart" (69). The question is inseparable from the issue of parenthood. To know by heart certainly does not mean what Copeland means: to memorize by rote and recite in anger, unwilling to wait for a reply, unyielding to the demands of conversation. To know by heart is something else entirely. "Hamilton or Buddy or Willie or me—none of us ever cares to talk like you," explains Portia. "Us talk like our own Mama and her peoples and their peoples before them. You think out everything in your brain. While us rather talk from something in our hearts that has been there for a long time" (72–73).

The mother tongue that Portia speaks, when, for example, she tells her father about the amputation of Willie's feet, is the "low song" of "grief" (specifically African American grief) to which her father is "deaf." Copeland cannot hear and understand what Portia says any better than he could Daisy. "The sounds were distinct in his ear, but they had no shape or meaning" (223). Like Mick, listening to the music of Beethoven, Copeland must discover the relation, not between words and meanings (he understands that well enough), but between words and feelings. Jake Blount's response to Willie's pain ("the terrible misery down in my toes . . . where my feets should be if they were on my l-l-legs"—254) is political. So is his father's. But the response to loss cannot simply be an imagination of recovery and restitution. It must involve the pain that loss occasions. When the "black, terrible anger" does not come, the "feeling of a song" within Copeland (225) finally takes shape and expresses itself:

> He spoke no word and let them do with him as they would. He waited for the terrible anger and felt it arise in him. Rage made him weak, so that he stumbled. . . . It was only when they had entered the jail that the strength of his rage came to him. . . . A glorious strength was in him and he heard himself laughing aloud as he fought. He sobbed and laughed . . . . They dragged him foot by foot through the hall of the jail. . . . He fell to his knees on the floor. . . . . [He] swayed to and fro. . . . He swayed, . . . and from his throat there came a singing moan. He could not think of William. Nor could he even cogitate upon the strong, true purpose and draw strength from that. He could only feel the misery in him. Then the tide of his fever turned. A warmth spread through him. He lay back, and it seemed he sank down into a place warm and red and full of comfort. (230–31)

By giving up on words, Copeland experiences his son's pain, even losing the use of his legs as he is dragged into the prison. And by experiencing that pain, he regains the language of misery, which expresses itself, not in words but in the almost maternal rocking and warmth of his body. The language of misery is the mother tongue, which his daughter and his wife have always spoken (or, sung) to him but which he cannot hear and speak until he experiences loss and misery bodily. For Copeland, however, it is too late to be husband, father, or community leader. He will not be able to convert feeling back into words, even the single word—love.

It is not, however, too late for Mick Kelly.

The mother tongue that Portia speaks is no less verbal, no less rational and conceptual, than the father tongue that her father inherits from Shakespeare and Marx. But in it words have less to do with exchanging information than with establishing relationship and mutuality. This language is affective rather than discursive; it nurtures, expresses, and evokes feelings and produces family, community, nation. "A person can't pick up they children and just squeeze them to which-a-way they wants them to be," Portia says to her father. "Whether it hurt them or not. Whether it right or wrong. You done tried that hard as any man could try. And now I the only one of us that would come in this here house and sit with you like this" (73). Portia is able to accept people as they are. Childless, she can envision herself the mother of racially, culturally, sexually different others. "Them three little children is just like some of my own kinfolks," she says of Mick, Bubber, and the baby. "I feel like I done really raised Bubber and the baby. And although Mick and me is always getting into some kind of quarrel together, I has a real close fondness for her too. . . . Mick now . . . she a real case. Not a soul know how to manage that child. She just as biggity and headstrong as she can be. . . . Mick puzzles me sometimes. But still I really fond of her" (77).

Like the commune that she builds with her husband and brother, Portia's extended family reconceptualizes the idea of kinship. (We might recall Blount's claims to be Negro, Jew, and Indian [199] and the continuing refrain that Singer is a Jew [77, 177].) Mick benefits directly from the mothering that Portia provides. As in many of the novels discussed in Marianne Hirsch's *Mother/Daughter Plot,* the mother in Carson McCullers's novel is strangely silent, as are Mick's two older sisters, Hazel and Etta.[6] It is as if Mick can become a strongly motivated, artistic, and imaginative female only by silencing the women who precede and create her. Like Frankie Addams in McCullers's other novel about a female adolescent, *The Member of the Wedding,* Mick is a self-declared tomboy, who, on more than one occasion, expresses her preference for maleness (41, 94, 216); the names Mick and Frankie capture this feature of the girls' personalities. But Mick is not motherless, either literally or figuratively. Like Frankie and (we might add) like Caddy in Faulkner's *Sound and the Fury,* Mick enjoys the mothering of a loving and wise black woman.

In the Lacanian model language not only responds to the loss and absence of objects in the world but occasions loss and absence. In McCullers's novel, language, in responding to the primary painfulness of loss, keeps feeling (especially the feeling of maternal love) alive. Portia does not educate Mick in the Law of the Father—in language as a substitute for and repetition of loss (language, in other words, as symbolic consciousness). Rather, she instructs her in the affect of the mother: language as the expression of and reproduction of pain, the pain of the separation from and loss of the mother. As a surrogate mother, Portia is both mother and not-mother. She reconstructs the mother in a lost relationship *and* in an uninterrupted and unmitigated love, which does not cease simply because the mother-child bond has moved from its initial phase of total interdependence. She also suggests a relationship between mother and child that does not depend on the biological link between them. Herself motherless, Portia continues to feel the influence of her mother's love, which she incorporates into everything from her mode of being to her way of speaking. Childless, she transmits that love to genetically and racially different others.

In almost everybody's reading of the novel, Mick is the primary figure of the artist. "Empty" and confused, not a "feeling or thought in her" (106), Mick seeks more than an idea in her art, whether an idea of God or even (as in the case of Singer) an idea of love: she searches for feeling. She pursues the language that transcribes feeling, that renders feeling an instrument of human relatedness. The following scene provides the countermoment to Singer's transcendental vision. Both scenes proceed through dream to mystical, religious vision; and both are violent. But whereas Singer's dream culminates in an aphasic collapse into suicide and death, Mick's initiates her into the responsibilities of living, speaking, and loving in a human world.

> The music started. Mick raised her head and her fist went up to her throat. How did it come? For a minute the opening balanced from one side to the other. Like a walk or march. Like God, strutting in the night.
> . . . It didn't have anything to do with God. This was her, Mick Kelly, walking in the day-time and by herself at night. . . . This music was her— the real plain her. . . . Wonderful music like this was the worst hurt there could be. The whole world was this symphony, and there was not enough of her to listen. . . . She put her fingers in her ears. The music left only this bad hurt in her and a blankness. . . . Suddenly Mick began hitting her thigh with her fists. She pounded the same muscle with all her strength until the tears came down her face. But she could not feel this hard enough. The rocks under the bush were sharp. She grabbed a handful of them and began scraping them up and down on the same spot until her hand was bloody. . . . With the fiery hurt in her leg she felt better. She was limp on the wet grass, and after a while her breath came slow and easy again. . . . The night was quiet. . . . She was not trying to think of the music at all when it came back to her. . . . She could see the shape of the sounds very clear and she would not forget them.
> Now she felt good. (107–8)

Blending the sexual and the religious, the passage initially suggests a displacement of meaning along a transcendental pyramid reminiscent of Singer's dream. Art almost transports Mick beyond language, where one need not specify what a thing is. But beyond language is unconsciousness. To regain life, Mick must regain language. Only when the sounds come back to her as material shapes, formed letters, does she feel good. Unlike Singer, who cannot convert the dream back into signs, Mick is restored to language. She is returned to family, to her parents, whom she knows must by this time be worried. Whereas Mick's brother Bill is always poring over words in a book, her own "pictures [are] full of people" (42). The shapes of the musical notes, like the shapes of words and the drawings of people, preserve for Mick the materiality of art, with which the men in the novel (including Bill and Singer and Blount and Copeland) are willing to dispense. McCullers thus deftly picks up the threads of Hester's lawless embroidery and weaves them into a new musical and pictorial speaking of the mother tongue. By weaving together Mick and Singer, McCullers reminds us of what we tend to forget about the written or engraved word: its essentially material form. Through the relationship between Mick and Portia, McCullers remembers that language originates in the mother, not the father. That Singer is an orphan may have some bearing on his never having learned how to speak. Learning to speak has to do with more than the acquisition of a vocabulary of words.

The book ends with a vision of historical continuity and procreative possibility. What stands between the silence that divests us of world and self, and the images or words that are only the imposition of self on the world is "one word—love."

> The silence in the room was deep as the night itself. Biff stood transfixed, lost in his meditations. Then suddenly he felt a quickening in him. His heart turned and he leaned his back against the counter for support. For in a swift radiance of illumination he saw a glimpse of human struggle and of valour. Of the endless fluid passage of humanity through endless time. And of those who labour and of those who—one word—love. His soul expanded. But for a moment only. For in him he felt a warning, a shaft of terror. Between the two worlds he was suspended. He saw that he was looking at his own face in the counter glass before him. Sweat glistened on his temples and his face was contorted. One eye was opened wider than the other. The left eye delved narrowly into the past while the right gazed wide and affrighted into a future of blackness, error, and ruin. And he was suspended between radiance and darkness. Between bitter

irony and faith. Sharply he turned away. . . . he composed himself soberly
to await the morning sun. (312)

Throughout the novel Biff has presented a unique image of male-female gender
distinction. Sexually inadequate, perhaps even impotent (like Singer, Antonapoulos, Copeland, and even Blount), Biff is not a sexual male. But unlike these
other characters (and like Mick's more adolescent self), Biff's androgyny does
not stand opposed either to women or to procreation.

His eyes closed he began to sing in a doleful voice:

I went to the animal fair,
The birds and the beasts were there,
And the old baboon by the light of the moon
Was combing his auburn hair.

He finished with a chord from the strings and the last sounds shivered to
silence in the cold air.

To adopt a couple of little children. A boy and a girl. About three or
four years old so they would always feel like he was their own father.
Their Dad. Our Father. The little girl like Mick (or Baby?) at that age.
Round cheeks and grey eyes and flaxen hair. And the clothes he would
make for her . . . . The boy was dark and black-haired. The little boy
walked behind him and copied the things he did. . . . And then they
would bloom as he grew old. Our Father. And they would come to him
with questions and he would answer them. (207)

Biff dreams of the nurturing, self-sacrificing, interactive responsibilities, not of
fathering as opposed to mothering, but of parenting. Nor is parenting necessarily biological. Biff will adopt these children, not produce them biologically,
and he will perform for them the function of mother and father both. Like Portia, Biff is not restricted by convention. He has a similarly expansive vision of
procreative possibility, which is what his final vision represents. He speaks the
language of rhyme and limerick, the language of the nursery.

Love in McCullers's novel is thus both creative and procreative. It is word.
But it is also a quickening and a labor. Like Hawthorne and Melville, McCullers
creates a neutral ground between the imaginary and the real, between radiance
and darkness and irony and faith, where anyone may well end up alone, shut
away from private hopes and expectations (like Mick at Woolworth's), staring
into one's own face. The maternal function, so prevalent in the nineteenth-cen-

tury women's tradition, is nonetheless here brought to bear with powerful force. For one can, like Biff, choose to turn away from despair and to compose oneself, not merely submitting to the condition of the human but responding to and perpetuating that condition. Just as Biff pulls himself together (in an almost Thoreauvian fashion) to meet the morning sun, so Mick is also at the end poised on the path to a future of responsibility and human commitment. The love of family (277) that sends her out of the private room of her fantasies of artistic self-fulfillment (a self-fulfillment associated throughout the book with a withdrawal from family and society) is the promise of a future.

To say this is not to deny Mick's anger and frustration at the end of the book, any more than it is to deny Biff's definite pain. Taking responsibility for the remaining payments on Singer's radio, Mick knows both that "it was good to have something that had belonged to him" and that it is only a remote possibility that "maybe one of these days she might be able to set aside a little for a second-hand piano."

> Maybe it would be true about the piano and turn out O.K. Maybe she would get a chance soon. Else what the hell good had it all been—the way she felt about music and the plans she had made in the inside room? It has to be some good if anything made sense. And it was too and it was too and it was too and it was too. It was some good.
> All right!
> O.K.!
> Some good. (307–8)

The lines are ambiguous. There is no saying with certainty how to read the final "Some good." Every realistic assessment tells us that Mick will suffer the same disappointments that everyone else in the world of the novel has suffered. Yet the text is not realistic. The word *good* resounding through the passage sets up a condition of affirmation that is not so easily ignored. Set as it is against the argument in the novel about the problems of political and literary discourse, the phrase "some good" represents the only kind of affirmation that matters: affirmation in the face of doubt, in the midst of pain, affirmation of life in the midst of living and producing life.

This is the affirmation that Biff achieves at the end of the novel. The optimism of *The Heart Is a Lonely Hunter* derives finally from a faith in words wedded to feeling and to the desire, which such language embodies, to communicate with love. In spite of the sharp criticism of words—words—words, the book gives us all of those words, quoted and unexpurgated. And in spite of its equivalent distrust of the dissolution of literary language into silence, *The Heart Is a Lonely Hunter* is a work of literature. But it is a female romance, in which the direction of human creativity is the direction of procreation as well. Its direction, in other words, is toward family and community, reconstructed and redefined. Like Biff, the author chooses to turn away not only from any one language but from the impasse to which the competition between languages can take us and which would yield silence in one form or another. It composes itself as a multiphonic, many-voiced text, representing not an indeterminate or decentered text but a multifaceted consciousness. The novel is committed to speaking. It enters into a community of voices. In this community every voice, like every person, is equally entitled and permitted and finally encouraged to speak. Speaking even one word becomes the source of community. To speak is, for McCullers, to be willing to make oneself understood and, understood, to be willing to understand what somebody else is saying; equally important, to speak is to be willing to feel and, feeling, to enter into the lives of others and to produce other lives. The human condition is to exist between impossible alternatives. What mediates between them, what makes them bearable, and what is itself a figure for the torment that is also salvation is the single word—love.

9

Art and the Female Spirit

Flannery O'Connor

Flannery O'Connor repeatedly and emphatically declares herself part of the romance tradition. She frequently refers to Hawthorne, James, and Faulkner in her letters and essays and has commented that she felt "more of a kinship with Hawthorne than with any other American writer."[1] Even without such authorial confirmation, however, the author's indebtedness to the classical tradition of American fiction would be evident. The echoes of Hawthorne, Poe, and Faulkner are pervasive. And as long as we think of romance fiction as primarily symbolic and allegorical (O'Connor read and admired Richard Chase's *American Novel and Its Tradition*), there is no difficulty in squaring O'Connor's presumably analogical poetics with the designs and methods of the romancers' more secular but still Christian art.[2]

In the view of most critics, O'Connor's writings comprise an obvious, sometimes even simplistic rendering of the contours of the divine presence in the world. They verify the truth of Christian history and dogma. What happens, then, if we redefine the art of romance fiction as skepticist? Is there any way an endeavor as religious as O'Connor defines her own enterprise as being can be understood as questioning how and what we know and what it means that we know the world this way? And if O'Connor's work can be understood as skepticist, what exactly does that mean about O'Connor as a Roman Catholic and as a woman? Does she resist the tradition of theological patriarchy only to place herself within a more secular but equally oppressive patriarchal tradition, or does she discover within both the religious and the literary traditions places of skeptical consciousness into which she can write and to which she can commit her belief?

Take, for example, her novella *The Violent Bear It Away*. According to one critical line, the story reads out as follows: The young protagonist, Francis Marion Tarwater, is caught between the bizarre and excessive religious orthodoxy of his granduncle Mason Tarwater and the hysterical anti-Christian secularism of his uncle Rayber. He is finally brought to recognize the truth (for all its apparent absurdity and grotesqueness) of his granduncle's position; and through several acts of violence (perpetrated both by him and against him) he is converted to his proper mission, which is to propagate the word of God in the world. Although, as one critic has put it, there is some question whether Tarwater will succeed in his mission, there is, for many critics, no doubt what his decision is and means.[3]

Reading O'Connor this way has met with much resistance; and where critics are persuaded that this reading is valid, they do not accept O'Connor's writings as first-rate.[4] A good number of O'Connor's best critics are nonetheless convinced of the essentially orthodox Christian affirmation informing her work. As O'Connor herself puts it, "Redemption is meaningless unless there is a cause of it in the actual life we live"; or, "The Catholic writer, insofar as he had the mind of the Church, will feel life from the standpoint of the central Christian mystery: that it has, for all its horror, been found by God to be worth dying for."[5] O'Connor's work, by bearing down on its subject most violently, reproduces with an intensity not unlike that of grace itself the central experience that her fiction records. In such a view, the homosexual rape of Tarwater, which leads directly to his transfiguration, becomes a singularly appropriate metaphor for the infusion of grace. It realizes the plea of a poet like John Donne for the three-personed God to batter his heart. The violence in O'Connor's fiction, then, seems to be an extension of the violence that abounds in her world. It appears to be the medium whereby fiction and God transform one kind of violence into another.[6] It would not be inappropriate to dub O'Connor's writing a kind of crucifiction.

Yet there is something too grotesque, too violent, too painful, in O'Connor's fiction for us not to feel uneasy with such unifying, even celebratory readings.

It seems immoral, even anti-Christian, to make rape and murder instruments of the divine will, even, if the stories are to be read symbolically and allegorically—as transparent representations of the processes of grace—leaving the odd possibility that we are intended to conform our own lives to the configurations recorded in them. Does a story like *The Violent Bear It Away* mean for us to understand that only through acts of violence, which pierce the secularist complacency of a godless world, can we achieve our own salvation or effect it for others? Could such a meaning in any way correspond to a religious vision?

The Tree of Man and the Fatality It Bears

The human story that O'Connor's novel is certainly also telling concerns two equally grotesque, equally unbalanced characters, who are, for all their apparent differences, mirrors of each other. These characters, Rayber and old Tarwater, are pitched in deadly battle over the souls of two other characters—both children—who are as grotesque and unbalanced as the men who compete for them. This feature of the obsessive doubling and redoubling of characters and events is so insistent that it exerts a pressure difficult to resist.[7] Is it one more expression of the story's powerful and unyielding drive toward the depiction of a unitary Christian truth, or does the story stand outside this doubling and redoubling in order to expose in the characters some more human, psychosexual impulse that accounts for the self-destructive and mutually destructive processes of duplication?

Whatever else the pattern of replication represents, it must be noted that the conflict among the three generations of Tarwater men proceeds largely in the absence of women. Old Tarwater teaches his grandnephew (young Tarwater) "two complete histories"—each typically masculinist. One is "the history of the world, beginning with Adam," "Adam expelled from the Garden and going on down through the presidents to Herbert Hoover and on in speculation toward the Second Coming and the Day of Judgment."[8] This is the history that for old Tarwater culminates in his own salvation and in that of his grandnephew, who, in his view, has been rescued from the womb of his dying mother in order to participate in this history, not of woman, but of man. The other history is "the history of the schoolteacher, beginning with his mother, old Tarwater's own and only sister who had run away from Powderhead when she was eighteen years old and had become—the old man said he would mince no words, even with a child—a whore, until she had found a man by the name of Rayber who was willing to marry one" (337). Although old Tarwater was at one time as interested in the salvation of the schoolteacher as he is now in the salvation of the schoolteacher's son and nephew, he is never interested in saving the schoolteacher's sister, young Tarwater's mother—further confirmation of his masculinist view of history.

Rayber's attitude toward women would seem to be totally different from that of old Tarwater, but in fact it replicates the sexism of his uncle. Rayber secures for his sister the lover with whom she conceives young Tarwater. He does so for many of the same reasons of self-reproduction that pertain to Henry Sutpen in Faulkner's *Absalom, Absalom!*—"The old man had a great deal to say about Tarwater's conception, for the schoolteacher himself had told him that he had got his sister this first (and last) lover because he thought it would contribute to her *self-confidence*. . . . The lover had shot himself after the accident [in which his wife dies and the baby is born], which was a relief to the schoolteacher for he wanted to bring up the baby himself" (337). Old Tarwater's accusation against Rayber, that having "no child of his own at the time[, he] wanted this one of his dead sister's to raise according to his own ideas" (305), receives authorial confirmation later in the text when Tarwater arrives at his uncle Rayber's home: "His nephew looked enough like him to be his son. . . . He thought of his poor sister. The only real pleasure she had had in her life was the time she had had the lover who had given her this child, the hollow-cheeked boy who had come from the country to study divinity but whose mind Rayber (a graduate student at the time) had seen at once was too good for that. He had befriended him, and helped him to discover himself and then to discover her. He had engineered their meeting purposely . . . [and] after the calamity he had killed himself, a prey to morbid guilt" (363–64). Because old Tarwater believes that the carnal corrupts the spiritual, he wants a genealogy culminating in a virgin birth (young Tarwater is snatched from the womb of his dead mother—327). Rayber indulges an incestuous desire, which performs the same function. Each would reproduce an offspring who is as nearly as possible a self-replication.

In both cases the male protagonists imagine perfection in terms of self-replication without benefit of women. From the very first night of Tarwater's arrival, with his wife finally out of the picture—she is the mother of his retarded son, who, to his mind, does not reproduce him—Rayber fantasizes that "at last he had a son with a future" (421). "You have a father," he announces to Tarwater, as if the child has sprung, godlike, from his loins (368). "Now you belong to someone who can help you and understand you. . . . It's not too late for me to make a man of you" (357). To bear, in this book, is not, as in ordinary human sexuality, a female function, producing life out of the conditions of fertility and love. It is an act of violence against nature. Because it proceeds through a consummately hubristic and egocentric pattern of self-replication, it can only bear things away.

This pattern of bearing away punctuates the novel. Tarwater thinks that Rayber's "interest in his forebears would bear fruit, but what it bore, what it bore, stench and shame, were dead words. What it bore was a dry and seedless fruit . . . dead from the beginning" (314). The reference is to a scientific analysis that Rayber has written up on old Tarwater. It could, however, as easily be to Rayber's idiot son. (He could get only one child out of the social worker, old Tarwater says contemptuously of Rayber's decision to marry Bishop's mother.) Old Tarwater's words may refer as well to that other fruit of male self-conception, the child Tarwater, who is "rescued . . . out of the womb of a whore" (327). In the climactic moment of the story, young Tarwater is the victim of a homosexual rape. At the end he sets off, still a child, to wake the sleeping children of God—never, we feel, to produce any offspring of his own. This strange scene of annunciation augurs only the cessation of procreation and generation. Annunciation may not even culminate in the replication of the male line, as did the original virgin birth of young Tarwater.

Truth to tell, the Tarwaters do seem to achieve something very like the parthenogenic reproduction of self imagined earlier in the tradition by Hawthorne, Melville, James, and Faulkner. Young Tarwater strikingly resembles his uncle Rayber, as Rayber does old Tarwater, and Bishop all of them. It is as if these fathers succeeded, godlike, in fathering sons in their own image.[9] It is not surprising that inbreeding should produce the idiot child Bishop, who like Jim Bond at the end of *Absalom* (and recalling Benjy of *The Sound and the Fury* as well) can do nothing more than "bellow" (422) at the sterility and meaninglessness of their lives (Tarwater, both at the beginning of the novel and at the end, sets both house and woods afire, in an echo of the blaze at the finale of *Absalom*). "Idiocy" is what the three generations of Tarwaters reincarnate (337, 358). O'Connor goes out of her way to have old Tarwater, Rayber, and young Tarwater each play the role of the idiot: young Tarwater when his uncle makes him deceive the truant officer who would enroll him in school (313–14); old Tarwater when he is "so shocked by the likeness and the unlikeness [between himself and Bishop] that the time he and Tarwater had gone there, he had only stood in the door, staring at the little boy and rolling his tongue around outside his mouth as if he had no sense himself" (316; I'm not an idiot, he hysterically declares elsewhere); and Rayber when Tarwater pushes Bishop away, and the "schoolteacher's face was red and pained. The child might have been a deformed part of himself that had been accidentally revealed" (358). Nor do the characters refrain from referring to each other as idiots or imbeciles (337, 358, 391)

But O'Connor's representation of all the Tarwater men as veritable idiots (who are often imagined as deaf and blind as well—see page 369, for example) is no simple comment on the problem of genetic inbreeding or even of asexual reproduction—although O'Connor herself lived on a farm and bred animals, which may well have contributed to her choice of metaphor. (The metaphor recalls the Pyncheon chickens in Hawthorne's *House of the Seven Gables*; O'Connor may be explicitly evoking Hawthorne's novel in the passage that describes Tarwater's desire to kill off his uncle's "worthless . . . bantams"—317.) Given both old Tarwater's and Rayber's compelling desire for self-reproduction and given the profound family resemblances that are achieved despite the messy interference of women in the progenerative process, what is surprising is how unwilling the three generations of uncles and nephews are to recognize themselves in each other. Old Tarwater, Rayber, and young Tarwater refuse to acknowledge their mutual kinship for the same reason that Singer, at the end of *The Heart Is a Lonely Hunter*, refuses to speak with the only characters with whom he might communicate. The three Tarwater men dread to discover in the reflection of themselves in each other that they are only human.

As in McCullers's novel, the characters in *The Violent Bear It Away* struggle to reproduce a replica of themselves, not as men but as gods. They wish (like Gatsby in Fitzgerald's novel) to declare themselves to be of autonomous self-generation, each created in total disrelation to any thing but his own self, which is then in a position to (asexually) perpetuate itself in pure disrelation to the material and physical universe. Tarwater's first words to his cousin Bishop are in keeping with the family pattern, as are the words that he scrawls on the motel ledger and the sentiments that he expresses to his uncle: "Before you was here, I was here," he snarls at Bishop (322); "Francis Marion Tarwater . . . Powderhead, Tennessee. NOT HIS SON" (397); "it's nothing about me like you" (418). The Tarwaters will not confess their humanness, which is also their connection to other human beings, including the mothers who bear them or the women who would bear their children.

Like many of Poe's fictions or like Melville's *Moby Dick,* O'Connor's novel reveals what her male protagonists would not like to discover: that the world of the purely intellectual and spiritual, in disrelation to the world of biology, sexuality, and women, cannot produce viable offspring. Even more problematic, in imagining themselves God (whether in religious or secular terms), the Tarwaters prevent themselves from discovering God. The figure of Christ in this novel is Bishop, whom they reject.

In the character of Bishop the religious argument of this novel intersects with its more human and psychological concerns. Old Tarwater and Rayber only seem to represent diametrically opposed attitudes toward Christianity, with young Tarwater caught between them, articulating to himself in an internal monologue the opposing attitudes of both uncles. In fact, both of them, and Tarwater, too, suffer from the same sin of arrogance and pride. Each of them imagines himself his own Christ. Each forgets not only that Christ has already been crucified in order to gain human salvation (including their own) but that Christ himself was a human child of a human mother. As Leo Steinberg has pointed out, the iconographic depictions of the Christ child emphasize the humanness of Christ.[10] Might we not argue that pictures of the mature Christ, which emphasize his suffering and gentleness, remind us that this humanness has more than a little to do with his maternal origins? The femininity of Christ is not a new idea (it functions prominently in Stowe's *Uncle Tom's Cabin*). Nor is the idea that what binds together the Father and the Son is a feminine Holy Spirit. Looked at slightly differently, the virgin birth, which seems so troubling in its apparent bypassing of female sexuality, produces a child that (like the Christlike Pearl of another story) is more female than male. In one sense, Christ has no father. He certainly has no biological father. He may therefore be thought of as a purely maternal creation. This possibility is recalled in O'Connor's novel in the name of her Christ child. Although Bishop abides with the father, he carries only the name of his mother. And, like Pearl, he seems to have no earthly father: Rayber "did not believe that he himself was formed in the image and likeness of God but that Bishop was he had no doubt" (372). The father's feelings of revulsion toward his son, like those of old and young Tarwater as well, are related to his problems with sexuality and women, which is to say, his problems with the human.

The Sacrifice of the Son and the Crucifixion of Christ

David Eggenschwiler has aptly summed up O'Connor's Christian thesis: "As a Christian humanist with an intense concern for art as well as for faith, [O'Connor] presents man in his relationships to God, to himself, and to other men, and she reveals that all of these relationships are indivisible aspects of his being."[11] It is not surprising that the Tarwaters' desire to eliminate sexuality and women from their world coincides with their desire to be their own purely masculine Christs, securing their own salvation and promoting the salvation of other men.[12] In *Fiction and Historical Consciousness* I discussed a recurring motif in a group of American fictions, the sacrifice of the son, and dubbed the fictions in which it reappears akedian romances (in the Old Testament, Abraham's binding of Isaac is called the *akedah*). The texts discussed there (which include O'Connor's "View of the Woods") present fathers or father figures sacrificing their sons (or children or grandchildren) to bring salvation into the world. In each story the author reveals that the protagonist's impulse is misguided. Each of the sacrificing fathers forgets that Christ has already been crucified and redemption already achieved. Each of them, representing Abraham as well as God, violates the type of the original sacrifice, when the son was released from the divine injunction to await the coming of the divine son, who would indeed be sacrificed.[13]

The Violent Bear It Away is an important member text in this subtradition of akedian romances. Like earlier texts in the tradition, it discriminates between a literalist, blindly repetitious relation to Old and New Testament and a fully Christian, which is to say fully redemptive relation to Christ. Also like the other texts in the tradition, it constructs the scene of the sacrifice twice, reproducing the typological dimensions of the Old-New Testament relation. In fact, O'Connor's novel doubles this doubling: Rayber recalls the first scene of the sacrifice moments before Tarwater performs his own aborted duplication of this same scene. The climactic moment in this progression of scenes, when Tarwater does finally drown/baptize Bishop, is preceded by two types, each characterized by the same failure to implement the sacrifice. These scenes reveal in their interrelations the same desire within both Rayber and Tarwater to be their own Christs and, in being their own Christs, perform the role of both father and son in an act of self-sacrifice that denies not only divine grace (the act is murder, after all, and suicide) but human mortality.

In the first scene

[Rayber] had taken [Bishop] to the beach . . . intending to effect the accident as quickly as possible . . . . He had taken him out on his shoulders
and when he was chest deep in the water, had lifted him off, swung the
delighted child high in the air and then plunged him swiftly below . . . . A
fierce surging pressure had begun upward beneath his hands and grimly
he had exerted more and more force downward. In a second, he felt he
was trying to hold a giant under. Astonished, he let himself look. The face
under the water was wrathfully contorted, twisted by some primeval rage
to save itself. . . . He stood sweating in the water, his own mouth as slack
as the child's had been. . . . Then as he looked at it, he had a moment of
complete terror in which he envisioned his life without the child. He
began to shout frantically. . . . The next day there had been a picture in the
paper . . . . OVERJOYED FATHER SEES SON REVIVED. (388–89)

By killing Bishop, Rayber wishes to kill the part of himself that he associates
with the idiocy of Christian love:

For the most part Rayber lived with [Bishop] without being painfully aware
of his presence but the moments would still come when, rushing from some
inexplicable part of himself, he would experience a love for the child so outrageous that he would be left shocked and depressed for days, and trem-
bling for his sanity. It was only a touch of the curse that lay in his blood.

His normal way of looking on Bishop was as an x signifying the general
hideousness of fate. . . . The little boy was part of a simple equation that
required no further solution, except at the moments when with little or no
warning he would feel himself overwhelmed by the horrifying love. Anything he looked at too long could bring it on. Bishop did not have to be
around. It could be a stick or a stone, the line of a shadow, the absurd old
man's walk of a starling crossing the sidewalk. If, without thinking, he
lent himself to it, he would feel suddenly a morbid surge of the love that
terrified him—powerful enough to throw him to the ground in an act of
idiot praise. It was completely irrational and abnormal. . . . It was love
without reason, love for something futureless, love that appeared to exist
only to be itself, imperious and all demanding, the kind that would cause
him to make a fool of himself in an instant. (372)

"He's just a mistake of nature," Rayber tells Tarwater. "Try not even to be aware
of him" (374).

But Rayber can no more ignore Bishop than can Tarwater or than Tarwater and Rayber can ignore each other. To Rayber, Tarwater represents the child that he can, godlike, save according to his own principles of anti-Christian rationalism. Rayber represents to Tarwater the force that he must escape in order (Christlike) to save himself according to his granduncle's fundamentalist precepts. For both of them, however, Bishop represents no other than Christ himself, whom they must both, therefore, resist, in order to discover themselves to be all the Christ there is. Just before Tarwater attempts to drown/baptize Bishop for the first time, when Rayber is recalling his own akedian moment, Rayber metamorphoses into a Christ, "nailed to the bench," his "forehead . . . beady with sweat," an image of what a rationalist, non-Christian Christ might look like (388).

By declaring himself his own Christ, Rayber also effects his revenge against the omnipotent father on whom his salvation would seem to depend. The biblical scenes of the sacrifice of the son (in both the New and Old Testaments) have been interpreted in terms of the father's revenge against his own father, whom he sees reincarnated in the son.[14] In O'Connor's staging of the scene, this fact of revenge becomes doubly powerful, for Bishop stands in for old Tarwater (whom he specifically recalls) and for Rayber himself. In other words, the father would sacrifice both his father and his son; and insofar as he is identical with his father and with his son, he would sacrifice himself. He would become his own savior, and he would die in the process. Rayber is nailed to the bench in the scene in which he recalls the earlier scene of sacrifice; and in the scene that he recalls, his face becomes an imitation of his son's, that is, an imitation of Christ's. In the passage about his love for Bishop (372), the words *surge* and *undertow* suggest an internal link between his desire to drown the son and his desire to drown the love that the son induces. As these scenes collapse into each other, the scene of the sacrifice itself reduces to a wholly self-contained, self-generating, and self-referential experience of crucifixion as suicide.

In the first scene of the sacrifice (388–89), Rayber does not drown Bishop. This failure does not, however, reverse the implications of the scene as a whole. Rayber does not achieve salvation either for Bishop or for himself. He does not *save* Bishop; he only revives him, to await his sacrifice later on (as in one interpretation of the original akedah). But this second, New Testament–oriented scene of sacrifice is no less self-serving and graceless than the first. The final drowning occurs at the hands of Rayber's other son, who is also, according to the logic of O'Connor's text, Bishop's other father. (Tarwater is explicitly placed in the position of the father, both in his statement to Bishop that "before you was here, I was here" and in Rayber's vision of the final drowning, when Rayber sees "the two of them together" drowning the child—322, 422; at the same time, Tarwater's drowning repeats his uncle's earlier action, thus identifying the two figures with each other.) Like the scene of Rayber's almost drowning Bishop, the scene of the baptism/drowning is both murderous and suicidal for Rayber and for young Tarwater alike: "[Rayber] did not move. He remained absolutely still, wooden, expressionless, as the machine picked up the sounds of some fierce sustained struggle in the distance. The bellow stopped and came again, then it began steadily, swelling. The machine made the sounds seem to come from inside him as if something in him were tearing itself free. . . . No cry must escape him. . . . no cry must escape him. . . . He continued to feel nothing. He stood light-headed at the window and it was not until he realized there would be no pain that he collapsed" (422–23). As the experience of the son is again relocated to a place within the father, where something is tearing itself free, Rayber stands, as he has always stood, on the verge of salvation. The task for Rayber is to recognize grace. But he refuses to see the Christ within him, for which his love of the child is the chief figure. Instead, he chooses to remain voiceless; he chooses to feel nothing. Rayber collapses the literal into the divine and experiences a purely human loss of consciousness.

Are the consequences for the religious Tarwater any different?

Freedom, Fate, and the Recognition of Salvation

Like the other Tarwaters, Rayber desires autonomy and self-sufficiency. He would effect his own salvation. He would be his own Christ. He would be free. A desire for freedom obsesses the characters of this book. "Now I can do anything I want to," Tarwater announces after the death of his granduncle (317). Tarwater's boast seems like that of any fourteen-year-old. But Tarwater is no ordinary boy, and the idea of freedom in this book is no simple concept. "[Young Tarwater]'s going to be his own savior," Rayber announces to old Tarwater. "He's going to be free. . . . You've got to be born again, Uncle . . . by your own efforts, back to the real world where there's no savior but yourself" (345–48). "I saved you to be free, your own self," old Tarwater tells his grandnephew (312). "I'm free," Tarwater says to Rayber. "I'm outside your head. I ain't in it" (371).

One way of formulating the central investigation in this text is to ask the question What does it mean to be free? Is freedom something one can gain for oneself? Is it something one can effect for others? As I have already suggested, O'Connor's novel presses with almost crushing weight in the direction of fatal determinism. Characters repeat characters, and plots, words, and images replicate themselves and each other. The story itself seems to collapse into a heavy-handed allegorical, symbolic retelling of the Christ story, which is itself the antitype of another story—the story of the akedah—which it also repeats. This feature of the text is reproduced by much O'Connor criticism. Is there any way to escape the cycle of deadening repetition?

Most readers of *The Violent Bear It Away* are willing to concede that the arch-rationalist Rayber does not achieve salvation. Readers have been less willing to grant the failure of Tarwater to achieve salvation, even though the text hints strongly in this direction. As he approaches Powderhead at the end of the book, vividly recalling his uncle looking like "Moses glimpsing the promised land" (443), Tarwater reconstructs a scene that subtly evokes another scene recorded earlier in American literature: a scene in Nathaniel Hawthorne's "Roger Malvin's Burial," which itself reaches back into a passage in James Fenimore Cooper's *Prairie*.[15] The following passage is from O'Connor's novel: "He remained motionless except for his hands. They clenched and unclenched. What he saw was what he had expected to see, an empty clearing. The old man's body was no longer there. . . . The clearing was burned free of all that had ever oppressed him. No cross was there to say that this was ground that the Lord still held. What he looked out upon was the sign of a broken covenant. The place was forsaken and his own. . . . He felt a breeze on his neck as light as a breath and he half-turned, sensing that someone stood behind him. A sibilant shifting of air dropped like a sigh into his ear. The boy turned white" (444).

Like Hawthorne's Reuben Bourne, O'Connor's Tarwater is forced relentlessly back by some internal compulsion to the place of his broken covenant. He comes to redeem a vow, the fulfillment of which he has lied about. This vow has to do both with personal redemption and, as the author carefully reminds us, with the redemption of the land. But where Reuben kills his son, Tarwater, only a boy himself, does not. Or does he? Insofar as Bishop is Tarwater's son, Tarwater, too, completes the sacrificial act that concludes Hawthorne's story— the act that, originating with the patriarch of Hawthorne's story, Roger Malvin, leaves the son-in-law Reuben also childless. Reuben, Roger, the Tarwaters (young and old)—none achieves what the Old Testament patriarch achieved when he did not sacrifice the son: the creation of a nation.

O'Connor's novel concludes in sterility and barrenness, reminiscent of Hawthorne's story. Just as Rayber internalizes the scene of Bishop's drowning, which is also the scene of his (and therefore their joint) crucifixion, so does Tarwater: "Sitting upright and rigid in the cab of the truck, his muscles began to jerk, his arms flailed, his mouth opened to make way for cries that would not come. His pale face twitched and grimaced. He might have been Jonah clinging wildly to the whale's tongue. . . . He grappled with the air as if he had been flung like a fish on the shores of the dead without lungs to breathe there" (432). The homosexual rape that forms a bitterly ironic version of the annunciation not only reverses the chronological order of crucifixion and conception (tracing Tarwater's de-creation) but replicates the baptismal/drowning scene, which is itself a scene of suicide.

Devastating sterility continues to hover over the final paragraphs of the book: "He knew that this was the fire that had encircled Daniel, that had raised Elijah from the earth, that had spoken to Moses and would in the instant speak to him. He threw himself to the ground and with his face against the dirt of the grave, he heard the command. GO WARN THE CHILDREN OF GOD OF THE TERRIBLE SPEED OF MERCY. The words were as silent as seeds opening one at a time in his blood. . . . His singed eyes, black in their deep sockets, seemed already to envision the fate that awaited him but he moved steadily on, his face set toward the dark city, where the children of God lay sleeping" (447) The scene is double-edged. Although Tarwater's divine call is contextualized within a recognized tradition of such callings—from Moses to Jonah and from Daniel to Elijah—the command is also represented as issuing first from the grave of a mere mortal and then from within seeds bursting in his own blood. (Both features are echoes of "Roger Malvin's Burial"—that Roger Malvin is the patriarch who commands Reuben to bury him and that the voice calling Roger onward to kill Cyrus comes from within and not from without.) The autonomous, internal, self-generating seeds are, in other words, another version of the desire for self-sufficiency and parthenogenic self-reproductive capacity that has characterized the Tarwaters throughout their history, beginning with old Tarwater himself. That Tarwater is at the end of the story moving steadily onward to where the children of God lay sleeping makes even more sinister the designs of Tarwater's sterile maleness. (Re)born through an act of male rape and thus borne away by violence, Tarwater's passion—such as it is—is anything but divine.

The case is even more complex. The silent seeds opening in his blood recall the seeds within Rayber—the seeds of Christian love. "Good blood flows in his veins," old Tarwater concedes about Rayber. "And good blood knows the Lord and there ain't a thing he can do about having it. There ain't a way in the world he can get rid of it" (338). But Rayber denies the seeds of the divine within him: "It was love without reason . . . . The longing was like an undertow in his blood dragging him backwards to what he knew to be madness. The affliction was in the family. It lay hidden in the line of blood" (372). Just as the same seeds drive Tarwater forward, they drive him backward, into the mystery that he is powerless to resist any more than his uncle can. O'Connor's point is that both Rayber and Tarwater enact the plot of grace and salvation, because both of them contain the seeds of the divine. Neither of them, however, can become what no man can ever become: Christ or God. Nor is either of them a genuine prophet—of secularism or of God. Tarwater's willingness to allow himself to be used as the vehicle of the Lord, which he already is and always has been, is more apparent than real, for Rayber—though resisting to the end the tow backward into the family affliction (the affliction of love)—is also an instrument of the divine to any who are willing to see the Christian mystery that his story contains. But neither Rayber nor Tarwater can recognize that, without any particular effort their part, they are instruments of the divine.

Like old Tarwater, both Rayber and Tarwater are prevented from being truly religious by their resistance to recognizing in the Christ story the way the story itself resists simple repetition and unilinear development. True, God the Father creates and sacrifices Christ the Son, and this plot repeats (with the one crucial difference) the story of Abraham and Isaac. But the Christ story depends on a third element: the Holy Ghost, the principle of love and compassion, which (from the Hebrew *shekhinah*) is also the female principle. The female spirit, the mother, is what the Tarwaters try to exclude from their world. It is what O'Connor, like Hawthorne before her, would restore.

In "Roger Malvin's Burial," to which O'Connor's *The Violent Bear It Away* owes so much, the mother—marginalized, ignored, excluded—presides over the final scene. She voices the emotional impact of the story when she shrieks and falls over her son's grave. In O'Connor's version of the sacrifice story, the "Negro" Munsons (328, 445–46) supply this role. "It's owing to me he's resting there," explains Buford Munson; "I buried him while you were laid out drunk. It's owing to me his corn has been plowed. It's owing to me the sign of his Saviour is over his head" (446). Dorcas Bourne in Hawthorne's story and "the woman, tall and Indianlike" (328), in O'Connor's provide the emotionality that the white male protagonists of these stories resist. "Tell her to shut up that," Tarwater admonishes Buford. "I don't want no nigger-mourning" (328). Like Rayber, Tarwater has no need of and no place for the love that is part and parcel of Christ's being.[16]

Love is the dimension that the self-repeating pattern of male inheritance would deny. Denying it, the male world dooms itself to sterility and death. At the end of the novel, Tarwater moves forward into a future that is a fate already envisioned, already transcribed. Searching for freedom, striving to save himself and others, Tarwater fails to recognize that he is already saved and thus already free. With no consciousness of his freedom, which is to say, without consciously choosing what it is that he will be and say, Tarwater reduces prophecy to what McCullers calls, in *The Heart Is a Lonely Hunter,* an angry poem that one knows by heart. O'Connor lifts her story up out of the flatness of redundancy with her inclusion of the single word none of her characters will utter, McCullers's single word—love. For O'Connor love is the essence of Christianity, of the Law of the Father, not in its reductive and impotent form, as symbolic consciousness, but as an instrument of grace, as the law of the heart. Although both Tarwater and Rayber enact salvation, neither recognizes and chooses it. Neither is therefore capable of what we might call O'Connor's crucifiction. Crucifiction is the fiction that, by creating sympathy and love for her broken and twisted characters as they enact the basic Christian plot of suffering and redemption, restores to the story of the Father and the Son what subsequent fathers and sons have attempted to eliminate from it: the third member of the Trinity, the feminine Holy Ghost, which is the heart itself. Freedom, in O'Connor's view, does not consist in changing the contours of a Christian universe. It means, rather, the possibility of recognizing those contours to be informed by an act of love that renders superfluous any desire that we might have to remake the universe on our own terms.

Conversion, Conversation, and Romance Fiction

Rayber would try to achieve Christlike powers to show his love for his nephew: "I must have infinite patience, I must have infinite patience, Rayber [keeps] repeating to himself" as he plans the rescue of Tarwater's soul (387). "[Tarwater's] irrational fears and impulses would burst out and his uncle—sympathetic, knowing, uniquely able to understand—would be there to explain them to him" (393). But all Rayber ever had to do was reach out his hand and in a purely human gesture express his love for Tarwater: "At any point along the way, he could have put his hand on the shoulder next to his and it would not have been withdrawn, but he made no gesture. His head was churning with old rages" (386).

Evoking such a gesture is not sentimentalism, in which the simple power of human love, or divine love, conquers all.[17] There are strong affinities between a work like O'Connor's and Harriet Beecher Stowe's *Uncle Tom's Cabin,* not least of which is the figure of the black, feminized Christ, which is reproduced in O'Connor's novel in the Bufords. More important perhaps, both books intend to convert the reader and to effect this conversion through the emotions rather than through rational discourse. But O'Connor's novel inherits the romance tradition and not the tradition of sentimental fiction. Love in this story does not mean overwhelming the self with rapturous emotions. It means a recognition of and response to one's freedom (as it does in Hawthorne and James). Although the Tarwaters are all prophetic figures in that they embody divine messages, their prophecy is not the same as the novelist's prophecy. The characters of the novel repeat a dogma (either religious or secular) that they do not fully comprehend. The novelist takes upon herself a responsibility to urge upon us a responsibility of our own.

To bear responsibility rather than to be borne away by violence is the urgent message of O'Connor's text. "From the days of John the Baptist until now, the kingdom of Heaven suffereth violence, and the violent bear it away." The quotation from Matthew 11:12 carries with it the double entendre of O'Connor's own text. The Kingdom of Heaven both suffers from violence and allows violence to persist. The violent, therefore, bear it away in the sense that they carry it, support it, and also in the sense that they overwhelm it, destroy it. The paradox does not make the inflicting of violence less damnable. Suffering is suffering, and if the violent bear away both the Kingdom of Heaven and the Kingdom of Earth, their violence is not to be condoned, even if it occasions grace. What is needed is an idea of bearing—bearing responsibility, bearing a future—that is predicated on an idea of freedom, not fate.

To provide this idea is, I suggest, the challenge that O'Connor's undertakes in her novel. On this point it is worth quoting her at length.

Today novels are considered to be entirely concerned with the social or economic or psychological forces that they will of necessity exhibit, or with those details of daily life that are for the good novelist only means to some deeper end.

Hawthorne knew his own problem and perhaps anticipated ours when he said he did not write novels, he wrote romances. Today many readers and critics have set up for the novel a kind of orthodoxy. They demand a realism of fact which may, in the end, limit rather than broaden the novel's scope. . . .

All novelists are fundamentally seekers and describers of the real, but the realism of each novelist will depend on his view of the ultimate reaches of reality. . . .

. . . If the writer believes that our life is and will remain essentially mysterious, if he looks upon us as beings existing in a created order to whose laws we freely respond, then what he sees on the surface will be of interest to him only as he can go through it into an experience of mystery itself. His kind of fiction will always be pushing its own limits outward toward the limits of mystery, because for this kind of writer, the meaning of a story does not begin except at a depth where the adequate motivation and the adequate psychology and the various determinations have been exhausted. Such a writer will be interested in what we don't understand rather than in what we do. He will be interested in possibility rather than probability. He will be interested in characters who are forced out to meet evil and grace and who act on a trust beyond themselves—whether they know very clearly what it is they act upon or not.

. . . When Hawthorne said that he wrote romances, he was attempting, in effect, to keep for fiction some of its freedom from social determinisms and to steer it in the direction of poetry.[18]

Nor is the Roman Catholic Church, for O'Connor, immune from the forms of realism and determinism that her own art resists: "The Catholic press is constantly broken out in a rash of articles on the failure of the Catholic novelist. The Catholic novelist is failing to reflect the virtue of hope, failing to show the Church's interest in social justice, failing to show life as a positive good, failing to portray our beliefs in a light that will make them desirable to others. He occasionally writes well, but he always writes wrong. . . . 'Why not a positive novel based on the Church's fight for social justice, or the liturgical revival, or life in the seminary?' "[19]

For O'Connor a major issue of the fictional text, as in the scriptures, is human freedom—not necessarily the freedom to rewrite or reconstruct God's universe, but the freedom to turn toward Christ. In her view, turning toward Christ is to turn toward other people. As Wolfgang Iser has pointed out, the Calvinist doctrine of predestination may well have set the stage for the flourishing of fiction in the eighteenth century because once the ending is determined by forces outside the control of the individual, the individual is free to turn his or her thoughts to contemplating the life lived.[20] When O'Connor writes, in her essays, that "Christian dogma" is not "a hindrance to the writer" but instead "frees the storyteller," she is thinking of this paradoxical status of freedom in Christian thinking.[21] For O'Connor there is only one plot: the plot of redemption. The plot is inevitable, predetermined. But we can choose to recognize that plot or not; and our freedom consists in this possibility of choosing: to read the text, to hear the word, to see ourselves reflected in the lives and stories of other human beings—or not.

The work of fiction, therefore, is one of "communication," of "talking inside a community.[22] "There is something in us, as story-tellers and as listeners to stories," O'Connor explains, "that demands the redemptive act."[23] The modus vivendi of this redemptive act is the avenue of communication that is opened up between writer and reader through the text. Like Hawthorne's *Scarlet Letter* and like romance fiction generally, O'Connor's *The Violent Bear It Away* establishes a relationship between an autonomous and free writer and an equally independent and free reader. This relationship is predicated on the recognition of each one's freedom to turn to or away from the other and thus to consent or refuse to consent to the communion (human or divine) that the story offers. By producing love, the story does not necessarily produce grace—which is the objective of Stowe's sentimental aesthetic. Rather, by restoring love to a process from which it has been amputated, the story provides the arena in which a reader can come to recognize what grace is and how one might experience it.

Literature, then, is a conversation between a reader and a writer predicated on the freedom of each and therefore on the willingness of each to enter into a relationship that, no way hampering that freedom, allows it to find its Christian and humanistic direction. This freedom differentiates the stories that O'Connor records from the stories that she creates. Old Tarwater, Rayber, and young Tarwater all want to effect their own freedom or to procure the freedom of someone else. None of them realizes that they are already free and that to attempt to secure salvation, either for themselves or for others, violates the terms of grace. O'Connor knows that fiction cannot save anyone. But by making human beings conscious of their freedom, by allowing them to experience their freedom as a part of the reading experience, her fiction sets the terms for the reader's free recognition of the facts of salvation.

Although the methods of O'Connor's crucifiction go far beyond the kind of discomforting aversions that characterize the writings of Emerson or Thoreau, exceeding even the painful sense of human tragedy in Hawthorne, James, and Faulkner, nonetheless, like the other writers in the tradition, O'Connor turns away from the human world only to return to it again. "Fiction begins where human knowledge begins—with the senses," O'Connor writes.[24] To move beyond the economic, the social, and the psychological is not, therefore, to reject the world or to defy the limitations of knowledge. It is, rather, to recognize that because we are bound by our sense experience, acts of faith and trust and belief must represent unbounded, free experiences. This is not simple or sloppy mysticism. It repeats the move that Descartes made when he questioned the existence of the world and discovered that in keeping doubt alive he kept faith alive as well.[25]

What is the power of O'Connor's fiction? What is the mystery of old Tarwater's influence over his nephew and his grandnephew? What is the undertow of faith that even the most rational human being may persist in feeling, if not in religion, then in literature or art? O'Connor once commented that old Tarwater was the hero of her book.[26] This is so, I suggest, in the same way that young Tarwater and Rayber are anti-Christs who incorporate Christ within them and who enact the paradigm of Christian redemption without recognizing the full meaning of the mystery that their being in the world unfolds. Like Rayber and young Tarwater, indeed, like O'Connor herself, old Tarwater is an instrument of divine revelation. The difference between O'Connor and her characters is nonetheless crucial. By struggling to attain to a freedom that they already possess, the Tarwaters make themselves resisting and therefore violently self-crucifying instruments of the divine. O'Connor, on the other hand, recognizes that as a writer, a Christian, and one of God's children, she is necessarily free, so does not struggle to assert her freedom or to secure it for others. She writes a crucifiction capable of converting a reader as free as she is, a reader who is therefore as susceptible of recognizing and choosing the experience of grace.

V

The Feminist Romance

10

Absence, Loss, and

the Space of History

Toni Morrison

Flannery O'Connor's *The Violent Bear It Away* is a
work of skepticist romance fiction despite its
strong Christian meaning or perhaps because of it.
The novel raises questions about how and what we
know in order to move toward affirmations and
acknowledgments that do not depend on impossible epistemological verifications. In O'Connor's
fiction, affirmations and acknowledgments have
particular Christian meanings; still, they are human
gestures in a human world, in which individuals
must assume responsibility for their words and
deeds. Like Carson McCullers, Flannery O'Connor
recognizes the patriarchal implications of the tradition into which she writes, but for her these
patriarchal implications go beyond a law of symbolic discourse. The father that O'Connor sees at
the head of her tradition is the Father himself. Yet
O'Connor chooses to place herself in this tradition
because she understands that tradition is more
capacious and multivalenced than any one of its
interpretations. Accepting tradition does not necessarily mean sacrificing oneself to the beliefs of
others. It can constitute the choice to relate to
those beliefs, to inherit, revise, and transmit them.

Because of the pervasiveness of patriarchy, the

relation to tradition will be more difficult for the female writer than for the male writer. Because of the masculinist bias of most religion, it will be even more difficult for the religious female writer and more difficult still for the African American woman writer, who must confront the institutional constraints not only of gender and religion but of race as well. The idea that African American fiction might be thought of in terms of romance is prevalent in African American literary criticism. Whether the designation *romance* has more to do with what Bernard Bell calls the "double consciousness" of the African American novel or whether it identifies traditions of African legend and magic as a major source of black writing, the term seems to have proved as useful to black scholars as to white.[1] I want to suggest that African American romance fiction shares with the white romance tradition a skepticist argument. Like the romance tradition generally, the African American romance raises fundamental questions about perception. It proposes as a response to doubt the acknowledgment and affirmation of family and community, in spite of doubt and through it. In the African American romance tradition, this thinking about doubt and affirmation has distinct implications for contemplating gender as well as race. My major focus in this chapter is Toni Morrison. I begin, however, with two of Morrison's precursors, who set the stage for the specifically African American romance that Morrison writes.

Skepticism, Gender, and Race

Zora Neale Hurston's "Gilded Six-Bits" contains one of the most extraordinary investigations in modern fiction of the link between gender and radical doubt; it also weaves together suggestive insights into the relevance of male-female sexual relationships to black-white relationships in American society. Hurston establishes philosophical doubt to be internal to African American culture. In her view, as in Emerson's and Thoreau's before her, the everyday activities of human life pose the most profound philosophical dilemmas. As critics have recognized, Hurston inherits and passes on to subsequent African American writers an idea of cultural autonomy. This autonomy may well account for the anxieties that white people have felt about black culture, which they preferred to see as subordinate and dependent. Hurston also provides a sense of the seeming autonomy of the woman, whose apparent self-sufficiency generates the same kind of anxiety in males (whether black or white), making racial fear only one particularly pernicious response to radical doubt.

The story in "The Gilded Six-Bits" is quaint enough. It begins: "It was a Negro yard around a Negro house in a Negro settlement that looked to the payroll of the G and G Fertilizer works for its support. But there was something happy about the place."[2] What follows is a story poignant, like Faulkner's "Pantaloon in Black," in its description of love and pain, although here love is regained, unlike in Faulkner's story, with the happy addition of what the story tenderly calls "little feet for shoes" (61, 66). By the end of the story Missie May and Joe seem to have regained the innocent playfulness of their love for one another as Joe resumes their weekly game of "chunkin' money in [the] do'way" (55, 68). But what has been lost cannot so easily be regained. At the beginning of the story Missie May is as aggressive, vital, and energetic as her husband (54–55). By the end she is debilitated by the emotional strain of her adultery and by the birth of her baby. Missie May no longer "run[s] to the door": "she cre[eps] there as quickly as she could" (68).

We might want to understand the financial metaphor in the story in New Historicist terms, as participating in an early twentieth-century capitalistic fervor. Or, given Hurston's deep interest in anthropology and folk culture, we could understand the economic imagery as critiquing a corruption of black society brought about by (white) capitalistic values. However we choose to relate economics to sexuality in the story, Missie May is both seduced by and made sexually dependent on male money. In a long line of works presenting similar concerns, including Henry James's *Portrait of a Lady* and Edith Wharton's *House of Mirth*, Missie May is for her husband a valuable possession whose value is inextricably linked to her appeal to other men. "He talkin' 'bout his pritty womens—Ah want 'im to see *mine*," Joe says to Missie May when he is about to take her to the ice cream parlor to meet the man who will become her lover. By the end of the story, her value, because of her adultery, has increased: whereas at the beginning of the story Joe chucks nine silver dollars against the door, by the end he's got fifteen coins with which to woo her. But the cost of the profit to the woman is appalling.

The story, then, contains a large economic argument about sexual relationships, which is related to a parallel message about black-white relationships in America. The Negro yard and Negro house may be in a Negro community, but the community looks to the payroll of the G and G Fertilizer company for its support. The capitalism that infects Missie May and Joe's relationship originates in economic realities created by white culture. Otis D. Slemmon's seduction of both Missie May and her husband (for Joe is as much seduced as his wife) occurs not only because of his wealth but because of his likeness to a white man and his appeal to white women.[3]

The economic message of the story, however, is less stunning than the even more sophisticated insight into the problem of sexual reproduction, of which the economic issues, as well as the racial ones, are only distant reminders. The story does not dwell on the emotional betrayal of the husband by his wife (as, for example, in Richard Wright's "Long Black Song," although this story, too, registers the problem of paternal knowledge).[4] Rather, the central issue is one of paternity. "Creation obsessed [Joe]. He thought about children. They had been married for more than a year now. They had money put away. They ought to be making little feet for shoes. A little boy child would be about right" (61). These are Joe's thoughts as he enters his home to discover his wife in bed with another man. The text then goes on to stress, not the emotional repercussions of this discovery, but its physical consequences: the prolonged period in which Missie May and Joe do not have sexual relations and, with repeated emphasis, the question of paternity raised when they resume sexual intercourse.

The question of paternity enters the text as radically and abruptly as pregnancy itself, wordlessly and without transition, totally transforming the reality in which it intervenes:

> One morning as Joe came in from work, he found Missie May chopping wood. Without a word he took the ax and chopped a huge pile before he stopped.
> "You ain't got no business choppin' wood, and you know it."
> "How come? Ah been choppin' it for de last longest." . . .
> "You know dat 'thout astin' me."
> "Iss gointer be a boy chile and de very spit of you."
> "You reckon, Missie May?"
> "Who else could it look lak?"
> Joe said nothing, but he thrust his hand deep into his pocket and fingered something there. (66)

The text's concern with the issue of paternity is reinforced a few sentences later at the baby's birth when Joe's mother says to him: "You ain't ast 'bout de baby, Joe. . . . You oughter be mighty proud cause he sho' is de spittin' image of yuh, son. Dat's yourn all right, if you never git another one, dat un is yourn. And you know Ah'm mighty proud too, son, cause Ah never thought well of you marryin' Missie May cause her ma used tuh fan her foot 'round right smart and

Ah been mighty skeered dat Missie May wuz gointer git misput on her road"
(67).

Joe's mother's statement about Missie May's mother reinforces the ostensible
problem with which the text deals: how adultery complicates for fathers the
knowledge of their paternity. The hesitations of Missie May's mother-in-law
suggest further how the laws of marriage and family function—as much for
women as for men—to secure the community against such doubts. But the
form of Joe and Missie May's conversation, coupled with his fingering something in his pocket, which is not identified as the gold coin that Missie May has
placed there, suggests that the doubt Joe experiences is as much the natural
consequence of male sexuality as it is the result of any social institution. Earlier
in the story Joe and Missie May's game of foreplay involves her going through
his pockets: "Move yo' hand. Woman ain't got no business in a man's clothes
nohow. Go 'way.' Missie May gouged way down and gave an upward jerk and
triumphed" (56). Deeper in his pocket than money is the source of his procreative potential, and of his doubt.

Joe can know Missie May's pregnancy and later the child it produces only
through physical manifestations divorced from knowledge of his own body:
resemblances, hints of similarity, reassurances by women like his wife and his
mother. His knowledge, he knows, may not correspond to Missie May's knowledge: You know it, he tells her twice, the second time adding, "thout astin' me."
Immediately thereafter he asks, "You reckon, Missie May?" Joe's question ostensibly refers to Missie May's assertion that "Iss gointer be a boy chile and de very
spit of you." The woman, no more than the man, cannot know either of these
things. But what Missie May may know and may be telling him is that the child
is his. As the word *reckon* suggests, her knowledge also has to do with access to
an internal biological clock. The story emphasizes the three-month period
when they do not have sex and then the ten-day intervals when they do. The
rhythm of Missie May and Joe's relationship is broken, true; but, more important, what happens in the sexual relationship between men and women, its
consequence or issue, depends, elusively, on timing. Missie May's adultery is
thus described as causing the "great belt on the wheel of Time [to] slip and
eternity [to stand] still" (62). What is suspended is birth itself and hence history and the future. The sun "that beams as brightly on death as on birth"
becomes an "impersonal old man" (64). Without the female body to give time
measure and substance in the form of a child, sun time (male time) leads
nowhere (the son-sun pun is here; Joe thinks a male child would be just right).

Without female reckoning, male time produces nothing; it is as much deathly as life-sustaining, incalculable, beyond reckoning.

The obvious relation between the economic subject and the sexual one is that for men women are a means of production, which must be kept under control. Missie May creeps to the coins at the end of the story, signaling her appropriate contrition. She has betrayed a very good and loving husband. But given the evolution of the economic metaphor, the conclusion makes us ask, How much and for what must the woman repent? Is it the woman's fault that she alone contains the source of a man's future, his link to time and to physical reality? Does this quirk of biology justify the dependency and childlikeness to which women are reduced? In "Modernization as Adultery," in which Werner Sollors reads Hurston's story against Richard Wright's "Long Black Song" (another story about adultery), the author has described both works as responses to modernization, which he understands as introducing into rural black society a different relation to time itself. Sollors reads both Hurston and Wright as positing a certain capacity for recovery within folk culture, specifically within women, who may be seduced by modernization but who nonetheless survive it. Sollors's essay powerfully puts into play an opposition between sociological readings of twentieth-century black society and anthropological ones, which address the difference between male and female sensibilities concerning these issues. But the end of neither Wright's story nor Hurston's seems to me as optimistic as Sollors suggests. Hurston presents an awareness of what Wright almost presents an awareness of (although he cannot quite conceptualize it): men and women will both pay the price of modernization, but they will pay that price unequally. Hurston's story presents this asymmetry directly; Wright's recognizes it despite itself, for the author imagines the woman's adultery to cause tragedy, not so much to her and her baby (although to women readers these may well seem the victims) as to her husband.

Hurston's story confronts the institutionalization of patriarchy as a response to the circumstances of human reproduction. That Joe and Missie May are black is almost irrelevant, although the story implies that white values have played more than their fair share in corrupting their relationship. The story goes further. White society enters at two points only, though it is implied in the G and G Fertilizer company. The first is in connection with Slemmons, who is more white than black. The second comes toward the end of the story when the white clerk from whom Joe has purchased, with his counterfeit gold coin, candy kisses for his wife remarks to his next customer: "Wisht I could be like these darkies. Laughin' all the time. Nothin' worries 'em" (68). The comment has an impact similar to that of the statements of the white characters in Faulkner's "Pantaloon in Black." Black humanity is invisible to whites, to adapt Ralph Ellison's metaphor. The notion that black worries duplicate white worries is beyond the intellectual or emotional capacity of the white clerk.

But in the context of a story in which sexuality is represented as creating worry (doubt), the white clerk's comment may suggest an inherent link between racism and sexism: the need to secure knowledge against doubt, to control the other to achieve power over the threat of otherness. White racism originates at least in part in a fear of otherness, which takes the form of a fear of pollution or infection, of being drawn back into what whites see as a primitiveness, from which, according to racist theories, the white race has already evolved to some higher form. Racism is also a response to the guilt of miscegenation, which has already irreversibly altered the genetic landscape, posing the constant "threat" to whites that the white man's genetic code will one day stare back at him from the face of a black person (one thinks here of the two faces, one black and one white, peering down from Sutpen's loft, half sisters bearing the same features, utterly transformed into unbridgeable difference). Hurston's story reveals that the fear of the other may be the fear of discovering through a sudden genetic flash—like that of seeing one's wife's lover in one's wife's child (something of Chillingworth's situation in *The Scarlet Letter*)—a connection with someone or something outside oneself or one's carefully constructed conception of self. A man doesn't want any surprises in progeneration, whether on the familial or societal level, especially when the surprises might, in revealing his lack of knowledge about his past, demonstrate his lack of control over his future.

The paternal fear emerges in Hurston's text as the fear of difference, which is to a large extent the fear motivating white racism in America. Racism presented as sexism moves us away from the simple sociological idea of a ladder of oppression, in which black women are the rung (except perhaps for black children, especially black female children) at the bottom of a ladder: white men oppress white women and black men, causing white women and black men to exploit black women. The story substitutes instead a sense that black society and white society struggle with the same issue: securing the future against incursions of accident and doubt. What both societies must recognize is the importance, not of eradicating doubt, but of sustaining it. At stake, finally, is one of the ultimate questions created by the skeptical dilemma: how we know and are related to physical reality and, beyond that, how we know and are related to other human beings.

The race issue and the gender issue merge in the fact of children, who are the human beings that we create and who therefore present the most intense test case of our capacity to love and accept other human beings as other. According to the romance writers, we must accept children, not because we know them to be ours, but because we must love them despite the doubts that inevitably attend their births. The fear of illegitimacy exposes the desire on the part of the father and on the part of white society for the virgin birth of the child who will embody absolutely and without adulteration the father and only the father or, in the case of white society, who will embody the Law of the Father, which is the law of white, male, Western civilization.

"This Is the Place I Am"

At the very beginning of Ralph Ellison's *Invisible Man,* the protagonist "enter[s] into the music of his race" and "descend[s]" into its depths. There he meets an old black slave woman, an "old singer of spirituals," who mourns the death of her master as her sons, "laughing upstairs," rejoice. "He gave me several sons," she explains to the narrator, "and because I loved my sons I learned to love their father though I hated him too. . . . I loved him . . . but I loved something else even more . . . Freedom. . . . I loved him and give him the poison and he withered away like a frost-bit apple." The narrator then asks: "Old woman, what is this freedom you love so well?" After looking "surprised, then thoughtful, then baffled," she replies: "I done forgot, son. It's all mixed up. First, I think it's one thing, then I think it's another. It gits my head to spinning. I guess now it ain't nothing but knowing how to say what I got up in my head."[5]

In this opening image of the slave mother, Ellison captures an important feature of much African American women's thinking about the asymmetry of male and female orientations to white society. Like Harriet Jacobs in *Incidents in the Life of a Slave Girl,* Gayl Jones in *Corregidora,* Alice Walker in *The Color Purple,* and Gloria Naylor in *Linden Hills,* Ellison seems to perceive women as more capable than men of sustaining the painful paradoxes of African American history. In these books women manage what men cannot: the acceptance of their children, whether those children are genetically and racially similar or not. The unique features of the female relation to human reproduction are for Ellison the beginning of the empowerment of black community: its children are its children, just as its culture is its culture, however white culture has abused and violated and insinuated itself into that culture.

Like the protofeminism of Hawthorne, James, and Faulkner, however, Ellison's cannot go the whole way to rendering a female perspective. Michael Awkward has objected to what he sees as the masculinist bias of Ellison's book, specifically in the Trueblood incident. What troubles Awkward, both in Ellison's novel and in Houston Baker's reading of it, is that the story is told wholly from the man's point of view, although it is not true to say, as Awkward claims, that the women remain silent. In fact, the story gives powerful expression to the mother's outrage about the incestuous rape of her daughter.[6] Even more to the point, in Ellison's novel the true blood of the race is entrusted to its women, who will not let it die out, however complicated the bloodlines have become, either in the direction of incest or miscegenation.

What Ellison cannot fully register is that the definition of self to which African American men and women arrive as a result of the experiences of slavery and racism may not be identical. Toward the middle of the novel Ellison's invisible narrator constructs his own African American version of the cogito, which Ralph Waldo Ellison's namesake, Ralph Waldo Emerson, had earlier adapted in "Self-Reliance." Emerson revises Descartes's famous formulation from "I think, therefore I am" to "I think, I am"; for the "thinker-tinker" in the "great American tradition of tinkers" in Ellison's novel this comes out as the painfully whimsical "I yam what I am." This statement stakes out the philosophical terrain of the novel. If the conventional skepticist move is from the affirmation of self to the affirmation of world, Ellison's formulation recognizes that for the former slave affirmation begins with the impositions of an irrefutably material world. Only at some later stage can the self realize itself and come back to the world again (11, 231).

This recognition is contained as well in the opening lines of the novel: "I am an invisible man. No, I am not a spook like those who haunted Edgar Allan Poe; nor am I one of your Hollywood-movie ectoplasms. I am a man of substance, of flesh and bone, fiber and liquids—and I might even be said to possess a mind. I am invisible, understand, simply because people refuse to see me. . . . You often doubt if you really exist. You wonder whether you aren't simply a phantom in other people's minds. Say, a figure in a nightmare. . . . You ache with the need to convince yourself that you do exist in the real world, that you're a part of all the sound and anguish" (7). For Ellison there is no doubt that the world exists. His doubt, rather, is whether or not he exists in that world, as if his existence depended not on his own thinking of himself into existence but on the world's acknowledging or mirroring of that thought. "I think, therefore I am destroyed" is Stanley Cavell's formulation of Poe's reformulation of Descartes, of Poe's gothic alternative to Emerson's inheritance of the skeptical tradition.[7] Just as Ellison's text invokes Emerson, it also echoes Poe (as it echoes Melville's equally gothic "Benito Cereno"). Like Poe, as Cavell reads him, and like Emerson, Ellison affirms the need for a self to declare itself in order for it to exist. And Ellison knows what Poe knows: that the price of declaration, which is to say the price of existence, may be self-destruction.

The similar case of Richard Wright's *Native Son* is instructive. Wright's novel is also Poesque, and although its cat may be white rather than black, the confession forced out of the protagonist serves the same function as in such Poe stories as "The Imp of the Perverse," "The Tell-Tale Heart," and "The Black Cat." It shows self-assertion to contain the threat of self-destruction. And what makes self-assertion and self-destruction dangerous doubles in Wright's novel is what makes them dangerous doubles in Poe's fiction: the activities of speaking, writing, and doing, on which the making-visible-of-self depends, establish the self's existence only at the cost of making it vulnerable to being seen. This is what Ellison also understands about the Poesque implications of self-assertion. To remain invisible may be to remain nonexistent, but to become visible may mean to risk being destroyed.

Ellison's *Invisible Man* inherits the philosophical gender- and race-inflected insights of Zora Neale Hurston's "Gilded Six-Bits," alongside its equally powerful inheritance of Emerson's "Self-Reliance," Poe's gothic alternative to "Self-Reliance," and the re-revision of Emerson's and Poe's cogito in novels like Faulkner's *Absalom, Absalom!* American romance writers speak from a place of doubt. They affirm in spite of what they do not know. They exert their presence, make themselves visible, in their texts through an aversive turning away that implies (in Cavell's words) not an attained but an attainable self—even if such a turn puts the self at risk.[8] I take the following passage to contain the essence of Ellison's revision of Emerson:

> Until some gang succeeds in putting the world in a strait jacket, its definition is possibility. Step outside the narrow borders of what men call reality and you step into chaos . . . or imagination. . . . No indeed, the world is just as concrete, ornery, vile and sublimely wonderful as before, only now I better understand my relation to it and it to me. I've come a long

way from those days when, full of illusion, I lived a public life and attempted to function under the assumption that the world was solid and all the relationships therein. Now I know men are different and that all life is divided and that only in division is there true health. Hence again I have stayed in my hole, because up above there's an increasing passion to make men conform to a pattern. . . . Whence all this passion toward conformity anyway?—diversity is the word. Let man keep his many parts and you'll have no tyrant states. . . . Life is to be lived, not controlled; and humanity is won by continuing to play in the face of certain defeat. Our fate is to become one, and yet many—This is not prophecy, but description. (498–99)

What prevents Ellison's faith, as expressed in this veritable transcript of Emersonian ideas, from being naive optimism is, as in the case of Emerson, the place from which this statement is spoken, the "relation" (to quote Ellison and Emerson both) which the individual discovers to his or her society and from which he or she therefore speaks. Ellison's invisible man speaks (temporarily, we are told) from a place of withdrawal under the city, a place of nextness to (as Cavell calls it), where he denies his voice to society in order to consent to society once more, indeed, to make his speaking to society the speech act without which consent and therefore community cannot exist.

Writing into this already biracial, bisexual tradition, Toni Morrison realizes that the African American male writer's idea of self-reliance, with all the implications of that term as Stanley Cavell develops them,[9] might not convey the specific forms of acknowledgment and consent that an African American woman might intend. *Selfishness* is Morrison's word for self-reliance.[10] In *Beloved* her cogito takes the form of the following statements: "This is where I am" (93); "This the place I am" (152); and "I was looking for this place I could be in" (80). She writes: "I got us all out. Without Halle too. Up till then it was the only thing I ever did on my own. . . . We was here. Each and every one of my babies and me too. . . . It was a kind of selfishness I never knew nothing about before. It felt good. Good and right. I was big, Paul D, and deep and wide and when I stretched out my arms all my children could get in between. I was *that* wide. . . . I loved em more after I got here" (198–99). One lesson that slavery taught was that to exist a self must own itself. It must exist existentially and physically. Another lesson, to which women were particularly sensitive, was that the self must be able to reproduce itself. The slave mother in *Beloved,* to realize her self-reliance, therefore, must become big, deep, and wide; she must become a place where she and her children can "be." "We was here" connotes more than arrival; it defines the terms of existence and identity as inseparable from place. "Home" is Morrison's word for family. Even though Sweet Home "wasn't sweet and it sure wasn't home" because of slavery, it is the only home she knows; as Sethe puts it, "It's where we were . . . all together" (17). Nonetheless, the house at 124 is Baby Suggs and Sethe's real hope for a home, a home in freedom where the "scattered" children of Baby Suggs (177), including Sethe's husband, Halle, may be gathered together again in a big, deep, wide place.

Morrison's insight into black female self-reliance is that self depends equally on a past and a future in order to realize itself in the present. As in the tradition of African American writing stretching from early slave narratives through more contemporary writings, Morrison recognizes that a major trauma of slavery is the nonownership of self. "What does a sixty-odd-year-old slavewoman who walks like a three-legged dog need freedom for?" Baby Suggs asks herself after her son Halle has bought her out of slavery. But "when she stepped foot on free ground she could not believe that Halle knew what she didn't; that Halle, who had never drawn one free breath, knew that there was nothing like it in this world. . . . Suddenly she saw her hands and thought with clarity as simple as it was dazzling, 'These hands belong to me. These *my* hands.' Next she felt a knocking in her chest and discovered something else new: her own heartbeat? Had it been there all along?" (173–74). After her escape, Sethe undergoes a similar realization: "That's how she got through the waiting for Halle. Bit by bit, at 124 and in the Clearing, along with the others, she had claimed herself. Freeing yourself was one thing; claiming ownership of that freed self was another" (116).

For Morrison, claiming possession of oneself requires more than mere existential ownership. In a capitalistic society like America it also means, as Houston Baker has argued, taking control of the sources of profit: Halle asks plaintively, realizing that he will never be able to buy his wife and children out of slavery as he had his mother, "If all my labor is Sweet Home, including the extra, what I got left to sell?" (241). And claiming possession of oneself means even more. Like the slave mother in *Invisible Man,* Morrison understands that African America's most crucial capital is its children, not because of the financial value of children (although a son is defined as a somebody who buys his mother out of slavery—29) but because children ensure both procreative continuity and self-definition.[11]

Without such continuity, Morrison realizes, there can be no verification of self, and without verification of self, no true access to the world. Baby Suggs knows that although it's better at Sweet Home than on any other slaveholding homestead she has known, she is not: she is not better, she is even nonexistent, because of the issue of children. "The Garners, it seemed to her, ran a special kind of slavery, treating them like paid labor, listening to what they said, teaching what they wanted known. And he didn't stud his boys. Never brought them to her cabin with directions to 'lay down with her,' like they did in Carolina, or rented their sex out on other farms. It surprised and pleased her, but worried her too. Would he pick women for them or what did he think was going to happen when those boys ran smack into their nature?" (173)

Even "benevolent" slavery, which did not force the issue of sex, could not escape the problem of sexual desire and, with it, the problem of progeneration. The Garners do not tear child from mother (Baby Suggs is deprived of seven of her children by previous owners; her daughter-in-law Sethe has been allowed by the Garners to keep all three of hers). Nor do they force their slaves to reproduce—either by raping them or studding them out. But by keeping their slaves slaves, the Garners cannot but threaten self-definition, which is as much dependent on procreative freedom as on self-ownership. Immediately following Halle's realization that if Sweet Home owns all of his labor and he therefore has nothing left to sell, Sethe understands the threat to her children implied in such economic, which is to say familial, powerlessness: "Say it don't pay to have my labor somewhere else while the boys is small," Halle says to Sethe, explaining about the schoolteacher's unwillingness to let him work off the farm. Halle's comment haunts Sethe: "I couldn't get out of my head the thing that woke me up: 'While the boys is small.' That's what he said and it snapped me awake. . . . That's when we should have begun to plan. But we didn't" (241–42).

Sethe is propelled to act on her realization that what the schoolteacher threatens her with is the loss of her children when she is physically molested. The rape of Sethe's breast dramatizes as an ordinary rape scene could not that more than the woman's body is at stake. An ordinary rape scene might have returned Morrison to the complex emotions about children portrayed in the opening scene of Ellison's book. The issue-less rape of Sethe's breast vividly reminds us of the invisibility of slave children to their white fathers. It also reminds us that black female slaves nursed the slave owners' legitimate children, who were thus made to replace the slave women's own offspring (Sethe specifically tells us that even though her mother was on the same plantation as she was, her mother was not permitted to nurse her). The rape scene in Morrison's novel throws into prominence the de-creation not only of self but of the futurity of self in children—a de-creation in which rape, like slavery, culminates. Slavery figured as the rape of the mother-child bond violates the very terms of the relationship of mother and child on which the identity of each and the future of both depend. It threatens the entire construct of human intercourse—biological and philosophical—on which the life of the people, as well as the lives of individuals, depend. Baby Suggs intuits this threat when she insists on taking the name Baby Suggs. The name suggests more than the tie with her husband, from whom she takes the name (175). It suggests as well the idea of maternity, which is both part of their bond with each other and part of her self-definition (Paul D affectionately calls Sethe "girl"—8 and 334, for example). The name Baby also recalls each and every one of her seven babies, whom she will never see again. It remembers herself as a baby, deprived of a mother and never to fully realize motherhood and hence herself. Baby is the word that, near the end of the novel, "inaugurated [Denver's] life into the world as a woman" (305).

In *Beloved,* Morrison examines with excruciatingly painful thoroughness the way the idea of a self, on which one's relation to the world must be based, must include the idea of not only a present self but a future self, that is, the existence of a full and fully self-possessing reproductive future. Like other of Morrison's texts and like the books of other contemporary African American women writers, such as Gayl Jones, Gloria Naylor, Paule Marshall, Ntozake Shange, and Alice Walker, *Beloved* dwells on the recovery and possession of the past as a prerequisite for the creation of a self. But *Beloved* also concerns the self's need to possess a future. The future, according to the novel, is the mirror by which the self, through its offspring, knows itself, although this kind of knowing must maintain certain gaps, which are equally important to Morrison's romantic skepticism. Of Baby Suggs we read: "Sadness was at her center, the desolated center where the self that was no self made its home. Sad as it was that she did not know where her children were buried and what they looked like if alive, fact was she knew more about them than she knew about herself, having never had the map to discover what she was like" (172). In the Lacanian model that seems to inform texts like Hawthorne's *Scarlet Letter,* the identity of self depends on the original mirror provided to the child by the mother. In *Beloved,* Morrison indicates how such a mirror cannot complete its function without the second mirror that the child reflects back on the parent. *Beloved* explores slavery's shattering of the two mirrors on which the primary identity of self depends.

Beloved will recover these two mirrors, though to make the world thus reflected a home, it will have to exorcise the ghosts that, in the first instance, must be called in to recover the lost dynamics of mirroring. *Beloved* is about the recovery of home. It is about making America into a home, primarily for black people, but for white people as well. Home, Morrison realizes, is first of all a place where people can be. It is a place that enables people to affirm and acknowledge and recognize themselves. Home is also, however, the place from which one enters a world in order to make that world into a home as well. *Beloved* is the story of how a young black woman named Denver learns to take her first steps out of a Negro yard around a Negro house in a Negro settlement (to recall Hurston's story) into the world. Beloved is the invisible woman of Morrison's text, who, in the tradition of Hawthorne, James, and Ellison, gives Denver the nudge that she needs to assume the responsibilities of womanhood and full membership in the human community.

Heterosexual Denial and the Death of History

Macon ("Milkman") Dead, on his long journey back to his cultural origins in the African American community of Shalimar, Virginia, has to take a shorter, more personal excursion back to the history of his own conception and birth. Like the confrontation with the past recorded in *Beloved,* this journey back infuses present realities with past horrors. Like other African American fictions, the story that *Song of Solomon* tells about Milkman's familial past is just the kind of story that we would imagine a black writer had best avoid telling her multiracial, potentially racist audience. Undoubtedly Morrison tells this story for some of the same reasons that other African American novelists tell such stories. She wishes to expose the disruptions in black family life that slavery and white oppression have induced. Even more important, she wants to insist on the right of black novelists to tell any story they choose. But the particular story that she tells reveals another purpose. The relationship between Milkman's mother and father (as in the incidents of incest and rape in other African American novels) can be understood as constituting a consequence of the distortion of African American culture by white racist culture. But the pain and madness recorded in Milkman's past claim for African American history its own self-generating, cosmically encompassing, autonomous existence. In other words, following in the tradition of Zora Neale Hurston's writings, *Song of Solomon* creates a self-referential and self-contained black world, which has all the elements, from the psychological to the philosophical, that define the human. Milkman's private past issues a direct imperative to Milkman to assume personal responsibility for the world in which he lives.[12]

The story that Macon tells his son Milkman about his family past concerns Ruth Foster's apparently sexual love for her father. According to her husband, Ruth never loved Macon at all. From the beginning of their marriage until— even after—the death of her father, Ruth adored no one but the elegant, accomplished, more-white-than-black Dr. Foster. Macon's perception of his wife may represent everything from jealousy to salacious fantasy. Nonetheless, it conforms too closely to evidence provided elsewhere in the book for us to dismiss it (see, for example, Ruth's own version of the story, as well as the narrator's comments and Milkman's own memories of his mother's attachment to him).[13] Macon's story gives full play to one Oedipal story, the telling of which was hardly confined to male authors, even if its predominance in Western society may be inseparable from masculinist bias in that society.

Why does Morrison tell this particular story, even crediting it with a much larger measure of truth than it perhaps needs within the context of the story? Before I attempt to answer this question, let me note a few further elements in Macon's telling of his wife's sexual (necrophiliac) passion for her father. As important to Macon as his wife's unnatural attachment to her father (and what he perceives as the father's equally unnatural attachment to her) is the black doctor's antiblack racism. Almost the first thing that Macon tells his son is, "Your mother's father never liked me." This lack of affection is directly related, in Macon's view, to the color of Macon's skin, and the doctor's racism is inextricably linked, for Macon, to his perverse sexuality: "He didn't give a damn about [the Negroes]. Called them cannibals. He delivered both your sisters himself and each time all he was interested in was the color of their skin. He would have disowned you. I didn't like the notion of his being his own daughter's doctor . . . . Well, we had some words between us about it, and I ended up telling him that nothing could be nastier than a father delivering his own daughter's baby. That stamped it" (71).

When Macon discovers his wife naked in bed with her dead father (Ruth refutes at least part of the story), he immediately experiences the kind of doubts that might naturally arise in such a situation. "I started thinking all sorts of things," he explains, "if Lena and Corinthians were my children" (73). This doubt is recalled when Macon's sister Pilate helps Ruth to become pregnant, commenting that the son she bears might as well be her husband's. But Macon's doubt carries with it the special force of miscegenation, which, as we have seen, Faulkner also brings to bear on the substance of paternal skepticism and which has special meaning for American society. "I come to know pretty quick they were," Macon goes on, "cause it was clear that bastard couldn't fuck nothing. . . . And he wouldn't have been so worried about what color skin they had unless they were coming from me" (73–74).

The bizarre intrusion of the fear of miscegenation into the already peculiar revelation about Ruth's sexuality serves several purposes. Like the introduction of the skeptical issue itself, it transforms the black world from an imitation of or response to white America into a self-contained and autonomous entity in which all manners of perversion and fear (including those that pertain to racism) enjoy their own origination. The idea that black people, as much as white, might fear racial contamination, even in the odd direction of replicating white fears about black blood, demands that we credit African Americans with every possible range of human emotion, even the ones that white Americans would most specifically imagine black people as incapable of experiencing. Foster's fear of black, cannibal blood can represent the infection of black culture by white culture. But it can stand as well for the capacity of black people, like white, to worry about issues of racial purity. Such concern for the preservation of the bloodline is also represented in the book, albeit in the direction of black blood rather than white, by Guitar and the Seven Days. The militant activism of Guitar and his fellow radicals is not geared to overthrowing white America. It is, rather, an attempt to preserve the black gene pool. Its purpose relates directly to the idea of racial purity, or at least the maintenance of race.

This purpose is replicated by Pilate Dead's miraculous birth. Among other things, this birth symbolizes a conception of black people wholly discontinuous with white and male blood alike. Not only does Pilate lack a navel, but she is born after her mother's death. Pilate's unnatural birth (to be repeated in *Beloved* in the birth of the ghost daughter) creates an absolutely black, absolutely matriarchal line. The female lineage of Pilate's subsequent family, with Pilate's explicit rejection of her daughter Reba's father and Reba's unwillingness to attach herself to any male companion (Sing's mother is also unmarried, and Jake, too, is rendered fatherless by Solomon's desertion—325) signals the move from the world of heterosexual relations into a world of sexual (female) autonomy. Morrison may here be playing with a fact about black racial identity to which I have alluded before. In white patriarchal society men determine lineage through a name. In black society women, because of the terms and conditions of slavery, including slave rape, transmit the cultural marker through their blood.[14] Pilate is the founding black matriarch. She originates nowhere unless in something like absolute racial and sexual purity, and she produces and raises two daughters without benefit of male assistance (it is significant that her granddaughter also calls her "Mama"). Even more startling perhaps, she is also responsible, miraculously, for the birth of her nephew, who is born, as it were, through a surrogate mother (Ruth) who sleeps with Pilate's closest genetic double (her brother). "Pilate was the one brought you here in the first place," Ruth explains to Milkman (124). "[Macon] ought to have a son," Pilate says to Ruth. "Otherwise this be the end of us" (125).

The vague hint of (unrealized) incest behind Milkman's birth would be almost not worth noting were it not reinforced by an array of similar suggestions about unusual sexual couplings, most of them also decidedly understated. These intimations of incestuous desire, if not actual sexual union, recall Faulkner's interest in incest (Morrison wrote part of her master's thesis on Faulkner). In novels like *The Sound and the Fury, As I Lay Dying,* and *Absalom, Absalom!* incest figures for Faulkner a drive for individualist, autonomous self-reproduction, which would enable the individual to bypass problems of sexual maturity and racial admixture. Not only are Sing and Jake "stepbrother" and "stepsister" (Jake is adopted as an infant by Sing's mother), but Pilate's granddaughter Hagar and Milkman replicate this originating relationship in their mutual pasts. (Hagar and Sing are further associated with each other in being one-man women.) "This here's your brother," says Pilate, introducing Milkman to Hagar (43). Setting aside Reba's protests that they are "cousins," not siblings, Pilate persists: "They ain't no difference," and "you have to act the same way to both" (43–44). This point about their familial relationship and therefore the potentially incestuous implications of their sexual consummation is recalled later when one member of the community remarks to another, with contempt, that Hagar and Milkman "ought to be shamed, the two of them. *Cousins*" (316).

All this emphasis on racial purity and endogamy—within a racially clean, even sexually homogeneous union—might contain a strongly positive African-Americanist and feminist message were it not that Milkman's recovery of his cultural origins does not lead to either personal or communal renewal, at least not directly. On the contrary, the consequences of Milkman's journey home to Shalimar seem to resemble what we expected of his earlier discoveries in his parents' rather bizarre relationship to each other and to him. The final moment of the story leaves Milkman poised between death and flight. Pilate's decision to reject both white society and men is also called into question by the conclusion of the novel. By the end of the story Pilate, the most consummately vital of human beings (the very opposite of her name Dead), is dead. So is her granddaughter, Hagar, who is made dead as surely as if she had gained her ambition of being married (or rather remarried) into the Dead family. (Because the name of Hagar's father is unknown, her own name is, by default, Hagar Dead.)[15]

What does Morrison intend by all this unadulterated deathliness in her novel, the outrageous pun on the name Dead running rampant throughout the book? Why is it that the journey back to Shalimar, so poignant, so immediately restorative, does not undo the journey back to immediate family origins that precedes it? Like her predecessors in the American romance tradition, from Hawthorne through Faulkner and Ellison, Morrison understands that the concerns of race and gender that drive her work, like the white supremacist and patriarchal impulses that they would resist, might deliver the individual and the community to the same sterility implicit in all such impulses to self-reproduction. Hagar, we are told, "needed what most colored girls needed: a chorus of mamas, grandmamas, aunts, cousins, sisters, neighbors, Sunday school teachers, best girl friends, and what all to give her the strength life demanded of her—and the humor with which to live it" (311).[16] That Pilate is her "mama" rather than her grandmama, so that her mother becomes her sister, reduces rather than enlarges the range of human family. Her love affair with her "brother" narrows the circle even further.

For all the hopefulness conveyed by Milkman's discovery of Shalimar, *Song of Solomon* ends within nearly the same world of barrenness and sterility from which the recovery of Shalimar seemed to offer some escape. Out of all the major and minor characters in the book no progeny remain to carry on the line that Pilate had hoped to preserve by bringing Milkman into the world. This list of potential but ultimately barren progenitors includes all the characters, from the vengeful Guitar and the other Seven Days, who are proscribed by oath from having children, to the hopelessly pathetic Corinthians and Lena, who have had that choice made for them (the relationship between the middle-aged Corinthians and the Seven Days Porter is a powerful figure for the union that will produce no offspring), to the major protagonists, Pilate and Milkman. In recovering essences and restoring power relationships, racial purity, like sexual purity, is shown to be incapable of promoting historical generation. For Morrison, as for Hawthorne, Melville, and Faulkner before her, the future depends on the messiness of heterosexual and (for Faulkner and Ellison) interracial human relationships.

Family, History, Rememory, and Desire

Given the wrenching poignancy of the story that precedes the conclusion of *Beloved* (condensed in the final word of the text: "Beloved") and given the tremendous importance in this story, as in *Song of Solomon* and other recent African American fiction and criticism, of remembering, the endorsement of oblivion in the novel, indeed, the almost hypnotic descent into oblivion, in the final pages, can hardly represent any simple encapsulation of the wisdom of the text.[17] "It was not a story to pass on," Morrison writes in the final chapter of *Beloved*; and she repeats, "It was not a story to pass on." "This is not a story to pass on" (336–38). The insistent forgetting at the end is deeply chilling. The almost lilting quality of the language, with its repetition of words like *disremembered* and *unaccounted for,* creates a ghostly presence all its own. It is as if, in the very denial of the "breath" and "clamor" of the now-to-be "disremembered" and "unaccounted for" ghost, the novel breathes its very own ghostly clamor (336–37). Is this, then, or is this not, a story to pass on? And if it is, what and why and, in particular, how are we to remember the past? The way of remembering that the book dramatizes is not the way of remembering, which, as text, it embodies. This difference between modes of historical recollection is related to another major issue in the text: how men and women might manage the relationship between them to produce not only the story of the past but history itself.

In *Beloved* Sethe calls memory "rememory": "Some things go. Pass on. Some things just stay," Sethe explains to Denver. "Places, places are still there. If a house burns down, it's gone, but the place—the picture of it—stays, and not just in my rememory, but out there, in the world. . . . Someday you be walking down the road and you hear something or see something going on. So clear. And you think it's you thinking it up. A thought picture. But no. It's when you bump into a rememory that belongs to somebody else. . . . Nothing ever dies" (44–45). Rememory is the relocation of the mind's pictures of the past out there to the physical world. It is the concrete and corporeal resurrection of the past in the present, as if time did not exist (compare 226).

Given this definition of rememory (which some critics have understood as a specifically female form of remembering) and given the dangers of disremembering recorded at the end of the novel, Beloved's function in the story seems clear.[18] Whether, as most critics have assumed, she is a literal "resurrection" (128) of Sethe's dead daughter or whether, as one critic has recently suggested, she represents her own and Sethe's fantasies of recovering the lost mother and the lost child, Beloved serves to install the past within the present.[19] She is, in other words, a vivid and vital—perhaps even maternal—rememory of the past. This past is not simply the private, personal past of Sethe, Denver, and Paul D, but, insofar as Beloved figures slavery itself, the history of the entire African American nation.

Nor is Beloved the only attempt at rememory that this book depicts. At the beginning of the story Denver is waiting for the return of her father: "I always knew he was coming. . . . Then Paul D came in here. I heard his voice downstairs, and Ma'am laughing, so I thought it was him, my daddy. . . . But when I got downstairs it was Paul D and he didn't come for me; he wanted my mother" (255). Denver's mother shares the desire to recover the lost Halle. She shares as well her daughter's disappointment that Paul D is not Halle. In response to Paul D's statement that she "must think he's still alive," Sethe responds: "No. I think he's dead. It's not being sure that keeps him alive" (9). Paul D brings inconclusive news of Halle's death, thereby almost killing Halle off and leaving him half-buried. The uncertainty allows Paul D nearly, though not quite, to take Halle's place as Denver's stepfather and Sethe's husband or lover—a position that Paul D willingly assumes for perhaps the same reasons that motivate Denver and Sethe to see him as a potential rememory of the past. As he and Sethe mount the stairs to make love for the first time, "Paul D dropped twenty-five years from his recent memory. A stair step before him was Baby Suggs' replacement, the new girl they dreamed of at night and fucked cows for at dawn while waiting for her to choose" (25).[20]

Whatever else is going on in these passages, it is clear that past losses weigh heavily on present desires. When Sethe thinks about the relationship between Denver, Beloved, Paul D, and herself, musing that "they were a family somehow" (163), we are meant to understand this family as a desperate attempt on the parts of these individuals not so much to create family as to recover it. The problem of rememory—of what and why and how one remembers the past—takes on the contours of a family crisis for specific historical reasons. The complication of family relationships—when husbands and wives, parents and children, were separated from one another and had to go to extraordinary lengths to preserve the continuity of family—was an immediate consequence of slavery.[21] The recovery of lost numbers of the race, who perished before or during enslavement or who vanished into the dominant white majority might well constitute a continuing pressure on African Americans, especially on women, who might feel it incumbent upon them to re-member the people.

Is it, then, in the least surprising that the arrival of the most vivid rememory of the past should attend so directly upon Paul D and Sethe's desire to create a family, a life? It is as if Beloved enters the text as the child of Paul D and Sethe's sexual (re)union. "One night and they were talking like a couple" (52) when suddenly Sethe recognized "how barren 124 really was" (49). "We can make a life, girl. A life," Paul D encourages her. And Sethe agrees to "leave it to [him]" (57). Their "handholding shadows" (58; compare 59 and 61) suggest to Sethe that it "could be. A life" (59). No sooner have these thoughts been entertained than, coming back from their first venture out as a family, they discover this life on their doorstep. "For some reason she could not immediately account for, the moment she got close enough to see the face, Sethe's bladder filled to capacity. . . . Not since she was a baby girl, being cared for by the eight-year-old girl who pointed out her mother to her, had she had an emergency that unmanageable. . . . Like flooding the boat when Denver was born . . . there was no stopping water breaking from a breaking womb and there was no stopping now" (63; compare 163, 249).[22]

Given the threatened descent into disremembering at the end of the novel, given Beloved's bodily presence as the consequence of an act of forgetting (when the baby ghost is banished from 124), and given the theft of so many individuals from their own history, we would think that such a revitalizing rememory as Beloved represents (which almost literally re-members the race) is necessary for the psychological and moral health of contemporary Americans and African Americans. This has been the thrust of several readings of the book.[23] And yet Beloved nearly kills the people who rememory her, and the family, which is struggling to construct or reconstruct itself at 124, is almost totally destroyed. The problem that Beloved poses to those at 124 is how the family, which has suffered so much loss and devastation, might remember the past without literally re-membering it, how, in other words, the family, under the pressure of loss, might secure both a present and a future without either forgetting or becoming possessed by what came before.

In response to the losses that Sethe has incurred, for her time has ceased to exist. By refusing to grant time its reality, Sethe is able to deny the absence of her loved ones, her many beloveds, including the child whom she has killed. But if those many beloveds whom the past has tried to take away from her continue to exist and if nothing ever dies, how does the past open up space for the present and future? "I'm not asking you to choose" between me and Denver, Paul D says to Sethe: "I thought—well, I thought you could—there was some space for me"; and he repeats, "Tell her it's not about choosing somebody over her—it's making space for somebody along with her" (56–57).

Nor is making space a problem only in relation to Paul D. For Sethe, if nothing ever dies, nothing ever grows older either. "A child is a child," Sethe explains to Paul D. "They get bigger, older, but grown? What's that supposed to mean? In my heart it don't mean a thing" (56). Given her particular experiences, Sethe has every reason in the world to want to "[beat] back the past" (90). Nonetheless, in "keeping her [daughter] from the past that was still waiting for her" (53), Sethe inevitably blocks Denver's access to the future. She denies her sexual and procreative maturity. When Denver finally does confront the future/past in the form of her resurrected sister, the past has already overwhelmed the present and is on the verge of possessing the future. The past-as-future threatens to de-create Denver herself. Beloved is not only Sethe's lost child recovered from the grave. She is also a potential substitute for the nearly grown Denver, whom she tries and to some degree succeeds in displacing from her mother's affections. For this reason, the scene of Beloved's birth, or, more accurately, rebirth, which is recalled several times in the text (pages 163 and 249, for example), explicitly recalls the scene of Denver's birth. It is as if Beloved's (re)birth displaces Denver's birth. (Morrison even tells us that Sethe believed Denver had died shortly before she is actually born—101–2; in reminding us that Sethe herself hasn't had an emergency that unmanageable since she herself was a baby, the scene recalls Sethe's birth). To add complexity to complexity, Beloved not only represents her mother's daughter(s) reborn, she is also her sister's daughter, Denver's child. Denver, we are told, is "expecting" her sister (51). In nursing Beloved, Denver plays the primary maternal role (67–69).

Were it not that what follows the (re)birth of Beloved (and Denver and Sethe) is not the story of a family restored to unity and integrity, nor the story of woman revitalized (the female restored to her procreative powers through the reexperiencing of her own birth), we might well be inclined to take this novel, as one critic has done, as about the recovery of lost mother-daughter bonds and therefore about the power of women to create history.[24] But Beloved is a "devil-child" (321). She would damn as easily as save. For this reason, Beloved's resurrection, even as it is the consequence of the family's getting on with the business of life, is simultaneously a revenge against the family for getting on. A spite ghost, Beloved would freeze history at the moment before her own cruel disappearance from it. Family, this book suggests, and therefore history as well, depends on making space. It depends on creating a future that, while not forgetting the past, does not reproduce it and that, remembering it, does not bodily re-member it.

The struggle of Sethe, Denver, and Paul D or of Sethe, Denver, Paul D, and Beloved to make themselves into a family (whether Beloved functions as an independent entity or as a duplication of Sethe or Denver or both of them) raises at least two questions: What constitutes family, and how does family recognize itself? How, in other words, does a family know itself to be a family, and how do family members recognize each other, as mother, father, daughter, and sister? One startling feature of the text is Paul D's sexual relationship with Beloved and her subsequent pregnancy by him. This relationship replicates Paul D's sexual relationship with Sethe, which in some sense produces the devil-child–succubus, Beloved. Insofar as Beloved is the child of Sethe and Paul D—either figuratively or through some new magical law of biology—the relationship between Paul D and Beloved (as Paul D's comments to her suggest— 143, 163) raises the same specter of incest that haunts other African American fictions. (At very least, Beloved is sleeping with her mother's lover; as Paul D himself realizes, Beloved is "young enough to be his daughter"—155). This may be related to the claim in the book that Halle's relationship to Sethe and Paul D's to her is more "brotherly" than sexual (9, 32).

What does it mean to recognize the members of one's family, and what are the consequences of a failure of recognition like the one that Paul D and Beloved experience? This question returns us to the question of what constitutes family, what creates it. Is what we seek in our relationships with our parents and our children a reflection of ourselves—as if our identities as individuals depended on our identification with other, recognizably like individuals, whom we biologically (re)produce or of whom we are genetic (re)productions? Or does family (and beyond it, community) provide the occasion for establishing relationships based on less physical or visual bonds?

What, in other words, is the force and function of family? Is it biological reproduction, which, recuperating the past, preserves it into the future, or something else, call it perhaps the desire for cohabitation or conversation or community? This question cannot be separated from the question of what draws men and women to each other in the first place. At one point in the novel, Paul D provides a rather curious definition of freedom: "Not to need permission for desire, well now, *that* was freedom" (199). This idea of needing permission for desire recalls an important aspect of the sexual abuse of African Americans under slavery.[25] We must nonetheless ask what it could mean to place—as in a hierarchy of values or human freedoms—the permission for desire over, say, possession of self. What would constitute permission? The word might here mean simply the permission to implement desire. But the text does not say so. Given the enormity of the issue of freedom, especially in relation to sexual abuse and thus in relation to the composition of family, how does Morrison permit herself to draw a distinction here between the freedom to desire and the freedom to reproduce?

By the time we meet Paul D he is a free man; he has won the ultimate freedom: not to need permission for desire. His relationship to Sethe seems to realize this freedom. And yet, from the moment of his arrival at 124 to the moment of his departure, Paul D is seeking permission for his desire. He is also resenting having to do so:

> Resigned to life without aunts, cousins, children. Even a woman, until Sethe.
>
> And then she moved him. Just when doubt, regret and every single unasked question was packed away, long after he believed he had willed himself into being, at the very time and place he wanted to take root— she moved him. From room to room. Like a rag doll. (272)

The "she" at the beginning of the second paragraph is ambiguous. The grammatical referent is Sethe, but because of the repetition of certain key phrases from earlier on and because we already know the story of Paul D's sexual relationship with Beloved, we recognize immediately that the word refers to Beloved. Paul D is thinking about "how he had come to be a rag doll—picked up and put back down anywhere any time by a girl young enough to be his daughter. Fucking her when he was convinced he didn't want to. . . . It was being moved, placed where she wanted him, and there was nothing he was able to do about it" (155). The "she" conflates Beloved and Sethe. It is as if Paul D's struggle is not against an inappropriate desire, such as the desire of a grown man for his lover's child or of a father for his own daughter, but against desire itself.

Like Denver and Sethe, Paul D experiences Beloved as a rememory. Most simply, Beloved is his rememory of the younger Sethe. Paul D has longed for Sethe ever since she first appeared at Sweet Home; he has been dreaming of her ever since (25–26). It is no surprise that the reality of her should disappoint him: "It was a good feeling—not wanting her. Twenty-five years and blip!" (30). But Paul D does want her. What he also wants is the intactness of his desire when he was twenty-five years younger, but this she cannot provide because it never existed. There is no such thing as the total possession and ownership of a desire unprohibited by constraints of any kind—de-prohibited from those constraints, wholly and exclusively within one's own power. There is no such thing as permission for desire. Insofar as desire (sexual desire especially) is always for or toward another person, neither is there legitimate desire that does not need to seek permission. Desire, in other words, cannot be subjected to simple rules and definitions. It cannot be rendered objective and concrete and thereby made knowable and controllable, as Paul D would wish.

In a perverse repetition of the terms of slavery, the paradox or dilemma of desire seems to Paul D to constitute a threat against his manhood. In Paul D's view, to be a man is to be in total control over oneself. To confess the unruliness of his desire to Sethe, he would, he believes, have to say to her nothing less than "I am not a man." But "he could not say to this woman who did not squint in the wind, 'I am not a man.'" (Could any man say this to any woman?) Instead he tells her: "'I want you pregnant, Sethe. Would you do that for me? . . . Think about it.' . . . And suddenly it was a solution: a way to hold on to her, document his manhood and break out of the girl's spell—all in one. . . . No motherless gal was going to break it up. No lazy, stray pup of a woman could turn him around, make him doubt himself, wonder, plead or confess" (158–59; the word *girl* here, though ostensibly referring to Beloved, contains the sense of Sethe as well, whom, throughout the novel, Paul D endearingly calls "Girl"; the text also stresses throughout the ways in which Sethe is also "motherless").

What would it mean for Paul D to stop doubting himself or to stop wondering, pleading, and confessing, especially in relation to something as intangible as desire? The question is not whether he needs to seek permission for desire but of whom he needs to seek it and what doubts he confesses in the seeking. In requesting Sethe to become pregnant Paul D would have her warrant his desire by allowing it to issue in an indisputable bond between them. By reproducing himself in the child, this bond would verify his manhood, which the intangibility and unruliness of his desire have thrown into question.

The question What is a man? in the specific, gender-linked form presented by Morrison's novel preoccupies African American writing, from slave narratives like *The Life and Times of Frederick Douglass* through twentieth-century fictions like Richard Wright's *Native Son* and Ralph Ellison's *Invisible Man*. Slavery, and later racism, threatened manhood by converting men into chattel and objects. *Beloved* makes explicit the sexual, progenerative significance of this aspect of enslavement. But it does more. It also demonstrates that the end of slavery and, should it come, the end of racism do not erase the question of manhood from among the issues that trouble but that can also—in a free society—enrich human existence. Paul D knows that manhood is nothing so simple as brute force: Southern men have declared their manhood from behind guns, and Paul D has pure contempt for this (199). But what manhood is, is another question, to which Paul D does not have an answer (see 271).

What does it mean for a human being, any human being, slave or free person, to be a man or a woman? What does it mean to come into possession of desire? Paul D's doubts about his manhood cause a recognizable response. He would have a child. This child would document his manhood. It would also bond the woman to him, not as his lover (making him subject to desires he cannot document or control) but as his wife (a relationship that certifies itself through a definition if not through an actual document). Sethe resists Paul D's desire to have a child. But she, too, knows "how good sex would be if that is what he wanted" (162). Sethe has also almost forgotten desire (25), but she links the rekindling of that desire with Paul D to the creation of family.

The relationship between Paul D and Sethe flies apart because neither of them is willing to recognize that desire and the bond it creates between men and women can never become subject to any external verification. Paul D would push aside doubt for the certainties that the conventionally constituted family might provide. To be a man, in other words, requires for Paul D that he be the head of a family uniquely, biologically, his own—hence the sliding between Sethe and Beloved, registered in the unreferenced "she." Paul D would subordinate desire, which he cannot know and cannot control, to a familial relationship that brings with it all kinds of certainties and assurances. In asking Sethe to become pregnant Paul D is only asking her to do what she has already done spiritually: bear him a child, Beloved. The problem, as I suggested, is that Paul D cannot recognize Beloved as his.

Beloved is no ordinary child. Her situation nonetheless evokes an aspect of the situation of all children in relation to their parents, especially after the children have grown and become sexually active men and women. How do parents account for the mystery of the birth connection? How do they recognize their children as separate and yet related human beings? The question mirrors the problem of desire in connection to the relationship between parents themselves: Who or what permits desire—children? the institution of marriage? oneself? some other?

Sethe's response to Paul D's desire that she bear him his child seems to understand Paul D in a way he does not understand himself. But Sethe's words mirror Paul D's. Sethe, too, would know her desire, and her pain, in ways to which human beings cannot really have access:

> What did he want her pregnant for? To hold on to her? have a sign that he passed this way? . . . He resented the children she had, that's what. Child, she corrected herself. Child plus Beloved whom she thought of as her own, and that is what he resented. . . . She had all the children she needed. If her boys came back one day, and Denver and Beloved stayed on—well, it would be the way it was supposed to be, no? Right after she saw the shadows holding hands at the side of the road hadn't the picture altered? And the minute she saw the dress and shoes sitting in the front yard, she broke water. Didn't even have to see the face burning in the sunlight. She had been dreaming it for years. (162–63)

Sethe cannot see that Paul D's desire for permanence and self-knowledge in the replication of self through children mirrors her own desire to confirm herself as mother and woman; Sethe would (re)construct, or rememory, herself through the (re)construction of her family. Both Sethe and Paul D want and try to achieve what both of them must forfeit in order to achieve the relationship that we call family: the physical confirmation of self (whether of manhood or of womanhood) that children can seem to provide. Sethe wants no more than the reconstitution of her original family: the two boys, Beloved, and Denver. This retrieval of the past, which would wholly exclude Paul D, is linked, through the concluding sentences of the paragraph, to the retrieval of another kind of knowledge that, were it to be acquired, would even more absolutely exclude Paul D (as it would any man) from the family. This is the woman's knowledge of her children's biological connection to her, to which the final sentences of the quotation allude.

The sentences from "Right after she saw the shadows" to "She had been dreaming it for years" are difficult to understand. On the one hand, they seem to follow through on the idea that she, Paul D, Denver, and Beloved already constitute a family. Implicitly, then, they acknowledge Paul D as Beloved's father and the father of this family, at least symbolically. His arrival is the event that caused the picture to change. On the other hand, the sentences also exclude Paul D from the family grouping: *she* had been dreaming this face for years; she alone creates it and knows it, and what she creates and knows is a child who is not actually Paul D's. The exclusion of Paul D from the family is reinforced later on when Sethe explains: "I would have known right away who you was . . . . I would have known at once when my water broke. The minute I saw you sitting on the stump, it broke. . . . I would have known who you were right away . . . I would have known right off, but Paul D distracted me. . . . I would have recognized you right off, except for Paul D" (249). The three hand-holding shadows, Sethe decides, "were not Paul D, Denver and herself, but 'us three.' . . . And since that was so—if her daughter could come back home from the timeless place—certainly her sons could, and would, come back from wherever they had gone to" (223).

The sense of these passages depends on the idea that women have uncontestable knowledge of their children's biological relationship to them. The idea is picked up in Baby Suggs's statement that "a mother would recognize [her children] anywhere" (171). From the beginning of the novel Sethe knows Beloved in this way. "Sethe loves you. Much as her own daughter. You know that," Paul D tells Beloved (143); the text independently confirms that Sethe "thought of" Beloved "as her own" (163). The maternal bond between Sethe and Beloved is strengthened through Denver, who mothers Beloved during the early stages of the story. Denver as mother reinforces our sense of Sethe's maternal function by reincarnating it in the daughter. It also extends Sethe's role from mother to grandmother. All of this reinforced maternal knowing points in a certain direction: that Sethe knows Beloved physically, biologically, through her body—hence the oft-repeated scene of Beloved's birth, which recalls Denver's birth. The sense of a special kind of knowing is enhanced by the conflation of Sethe and Denver: even if one part of Sethe does not immediately recognize Beloved as her daughter, another part of her does. Much of the action of the story involves Sethe's "unravel[ing] the proof for the conclusion she had already leapt to" (222).

Earlier I suggested that Beloved's birth is linked to Paul D's arrival at 124, specifically to his sexual relationship with Sethe. The text also holds out the possibility, however, that Beloved's birth is parthenogenic, proceeding solely through Sethe. This idea is reinforced in the name Beloved, which is another name for Christ. Christ also enters the world through a virgin birth. Like Beloved, he is subsequently resurrected. Morrison's text teases out of the Christian scriptures the suggestion that in achieving resurrection Christ further purifies himself of the taint of human birth: the resurrected Christ gives (re)birth to himself, without the benefit of any mother, even a virgin one. The fact that Beloved also represents Denver (as well as Denver's child) intensifies the idea of the solely matriarchal line, as does Beloved's pregnancy. In involving a spirit rather than a flesh-and-blood woman, the pregnancy might well be understood as self-generating.

Beloved, then, is the issue between Paul D and Sethe in more than one sense. She is their child. She is also "his shame" and "hers," "his cold-house secret" and "her too-thick love" (203). She is what each of them must accept about the other, the mystery of desire and love that can never be rendered visible and knowable, even through children. Like other African American writers—such as Gayl Jones (in *Corregidora*) or Gloria Naylor (in *Women of Brewster Place*, especially in the story "The Two")—Morrison moves beyond the reproductive imperatives of human sexuality to the desire that will never have issue in the form of concrete satisfactions or solutions and without which family becomes nothing more than the rememory of self. Given the circumstances of African American history, sexual reproduction as the sole or even primary motivation for family threatens to make family into a desperate and ultimately doomed effort to resurrect or at least compensate for or replace the irrevocably lost past.

Counting, Accounting, and the Commemoration of the Past

The home at 124 provides the riddle of what counts as family and of how one accounts for it. As the number itself suggests, something is missing at 124, some vital factor—of continuity or order, logic or history—without which a home cannot become a home. What does counting as family entail? What is the numerological system that will allow this family to count and be accounted for, both by itself and, as it turns out at the end of the novel, by the community and history? *Beloved* is veritably obsessed with counting, with taking account of, with counting for (see 6, 47, and 117, for example). From Morrison's dedication to "Sixty million and more" with which the text begins, to the introduction of that number into the text through the character "with a number for a name"—"Sixo" (Six-0), whose cry of freedom is "Seven-0! Seven-0!" (278;

ten more than 6–0, or ten million more)—this book pulls us toward the problematics of what and who count as family and as history, indeed, what counts as human (you have two feet, not four, Paul D tells Sethe).

How is it possible to measure time, for example (if, indeed, time exists)? How much time constitutes the natural cycle of fertility and reproduction is a puzzle: the "twenty-eight days of having women friends, a mother-in-law, and all her children" (212) that precede the death of Beloved or the eighteen years of haunting that follow those twenty-eight days, culminating in Beloved's rebirth (eighteen years conveniently brings Denver into her majority; it is also the doubling of the number nine, suggesting perhaps Beloved's double gestation). Counting correctly is important, the text seems to suggest, for on such mathematical accuracy depend the life and death of the community. Multiplying miscalculations put the family itself at risk: "From Denver's two thrilled eyes it grew to a feast for ninety people. . . . Baby Suggs' three (maybe four) pies grew to ten (maybe twelve). Sethe's two hens became five turkeys . . . two buckets of blackberries . . . ten, maybe twelve, pies," and so on. But "loaves and fishes were His powers" (168–69); and the family pays dearly for its failure to multiply correctly, that is, according to some modest system of human (ac)counting.

One straightforward explanation for the concern with numbers has to do with the way counting, like reading, represented for former slaves access to the sources of social and economic power in white America. "He could count on paper," Denver says of her father. "One of them with a number for a name said it would change his mind—make him forget things he shouldn't and memorize things he shouldn't and he didn't want his mind messed up. But my daddy said, If you can't count they can cheat you. If you can't read they can beat you" (256; Mrs. Garner invites the schoolteacher to Sweet Home because she needs someone who can take charge of the family's finances). The idea of counting draws out of the idea of reading a more specific sense of time and history as part of what constitutes full membership in the national community. It also suggests that at stake for African Americans if they do not break down the barriers between themselves and the majority culture is their reproduction into the future. If they are unable to count, Morrison suggests, black Americans might find themselves barred from the power of their own numbers, from the future generations who, counting, would have to be counted. (Consider that the word *cheat* in Halle's statement might carry with it sexual overtones.) Freed from slavery, the African American family must learn to count. It must learn to number itself among the nations.

But how to do this? The number and place at 124 signal many absences, not least of which is Beloved, the missing third child. To learn to count, the novel suggests, the family and, beyond it, the community, will have to accept (though emphatically not forget) the loss of its missing numbers. Recovering the missing third, which is to say reconstituting in the present what was lost in the past, will not, the book insists, restore order and logic to lives that have been interrupted by such loss. Neither will the reconstruction of the family around the magical number three, which is the minimum number for a biological family to create itself. As Morrison's *Bluest Eye* so powerfully suggests, this simple formula, mother, father, child, does not define a family. *Beloved* proposes several three-member families, none of them viable. Paul D would define the family as Sethe, Denver, and himself, or, barring that, he would have a child by Sethe and have the three of them constitute a new and separate family. Denver, Sethe, and Beloved would eliminate Paul D to become "us three," as Sethe calls them, the all-female family reminiscent of Sethe, Denver, and Baby Suggs (or, for that matter, of Pilate, Reba, and Hagar in *The Song of Solomon*). Whatever forces are at work to destroy the family at 124, it seems to work with "three—not two" (223, 298).

According to the logic of *Beloved,* the power of family resides in its ability to acknowledge a past and affirm a future without eliminating the gaps and absences and losses that define its essential structure. As a biological process, family necessarily reproduces elements of the past and present into the future. Individuals are therefore tempted to see family as a means of self-completion and self-extension. But if family reproduces only genetic features, it creates a future that is as barren as it is devoid of freedom. Like the rememory of Beloved, such a future would condemn family members to repeat past pain and suffering endlessly. The particular response that the novel calls upon Sethe to have, without which she cannot fully become mother or wife or whole person, is to recognize Beloved as her daughter and Paul D as her lover without being able to prove beyond the shadow of a doubt that Beloved is indeed her daughter or that Paul D is still a Sweet Home boy, whether he is called Halle or Paul D. To so recognize them, she must also be willing to accept the death of Beloved and the death of Halle, the permanent loss in the past of what was most beloved to her. Accepting loss means opening a space for others in the world. It means making a place in which we have room to become ourselves because we accept that that self is incomplete, in need of others similarly incomplete, who can help the self discover in family and in community such wholeness as exists. To go forth a woman in the world, Denver must "step off the edge of the world and die because if she didn't, they all would. . . . The job she started out with, protecting Beloved from Sethe, changed to protecting her mother from Beloved. Now it was obvious that her mother would die and leave them both. . . . Whatever was happening, it only worked with three—not two—and since neither Beloved nor Sethe seemed to care what the next day might bring . . . Denver knew it was on her. She would have to leave the yard; step off the edge of the world, leave the two behind and go ask somebody for help" (293–98).

The ultimate figure in *Beloved* for the deathliness of rememory is silence. With the departure of Paul D from 124, with Beloved's pregnancy substituting for Sethe's, the women at 124 embody an exclusively matriarchal line. They achieve a voiceless, transcendent unity of mother-daughter-sister. The consequence of the collapse of the women's identities into each other is not communion but possession. Reproduction creates nothing. It replicates the self as rememorying and disremembering collapse painfully into one another.

> Beloved, she my daughter. She mine. . . . I'll tend her as no mother ever tended a child, a daughter. Nobody will ever get my milk . . . . Nan had to nurse whitebabies and me too because Ma'am was in the rice. The little whitebabies got it first and I got what was left. Or none. There was no nursing milk to call my own. . . . And when I tell you you mine, I also mean I'm yours. . . . She come back to me, my daughter, and she is mine. (246–51)

> Beloved is my sister. I swallowed her blood right along with my mother's milk. . . . It's all on me. . . . It's all on me. . . . Maybe it's still in her the thing that makes it all right to kill her children. I have to tell her. I have to protect her. She cut my head off every night. . . . (252–58)

> I am beloved and she is mine. . . . I am not separate from her . . . Sethe's is the face that left me   Sethe sees me see her and I see the smile her smiling face is the place for me   it is the face I lost   she is my face smiling at me   doing it at last   a hot thing   now we can join   a hot thing . . . (259–63)

> Beloved
> You are my sister

You are my daughter
You are my face; you are me

. . .

You are mine
You are mine
You are mine (266)

The collapsing of individual identities corresponds to inarticulateness and incoherence, which ultimately dissolve into speechlessness: "I don't have to explain a thing," Sethe thinks to herself about Beloved. "She understands everything already" (246). Such mind reading is not communication. It is the silence of the tomb: "124 was quiet" (293).

The deathly silence of 124 eventually drives Denver into the world of other human beings and the conversation they create. What first takes Denver out of the yard are words that she tells herself, which she reconstructs from the remembered words of others, imaginary words, spoken to her by her grandmother: "You mean I never told you nothing about Carolina? About your daddy? You don't remember nothing about how come I walk the way I do and about your mother's feet . . . . I never told you all that? Is that why you can't walk down the steps?" (300). What enables her to continue on her journey and begin to make a life for herself in the outside world are the words spoken to her by others that also demand words of her own in return: "Nobody was going to help her unless she told it—told all of it" (311), Denver realizes. The response of Mrs. Jones is "the word 'baby,' said softly and with such kindness, that [it] inaugurated her life in the world as a woman" (304–5). "Take care of yourself, Denver," says another of the community's members, and "she heard it as though it were what language was made for" (310). By the time Paul D returns, Denver has opinions of her own, not to mention a young man at whom to direct her sexuality. Denver is no longer simply her mother's daughter (or her sister's sister), locked into a paralyzing and aphasic self-reflexivity. She is "her father's daughter after all" (309; "she looked more like Halle than ever"—326; compare 15). We might note here that Denver's name links her to Paul D as well. As her father's daughter, she recognizes her separateness from everyone, even or especially her mother, and therefore her need to establish relationships with other people.

The difference between "a little communication between . . . two worlds" and an "invasion" (315), in which one world (like one person) possesses the other, turns out to be the difference between speech and silence. Throughout the novel Morrison registers the importance of speaking and listening. According to Paul D, being "listened to" accounted for the Sweet Home boys' achievement of manhood despite slavery (154). Sethe herself recalls telling Mrs. Garner what the schoolteacher has done to her, because "somebody had to know it. Hear it" (248). Throughout most of the story Sethe and Paul D provide each other with a listening ear: "I never have talked about it," says Paul D, "not to a soul." Sethe responds, "Go ahead. I can hear it" (88). And hear she does, over and over again. In fact, the entire novel proceeds through the interlocking stories of Sethe, Paul D, and Denver, who collectively narrate the novel to each other, to Beloved, and to the reader. The reunion between Sethe and Paul D depends on their recovering this capacity for speaking and listening to each other. Speaking and listening is the opposite of the desire to merge with another human being or to confirm the self through its self-replication or self-reproduction. Instead, it involves putting one's story next to the story of someone else.

"She is a friend of my mind," Paul D recalls Sixo saying about the thirty-mile woman. "She gather me. . . . The pieces I am, she gather them and give them back to me in all the right order." Paul D remembers these words: "his hand limp between his knees." Sethe's confirmation of his "manhood," he realizes, has less to do with her ability to figure it forth bodily in the form of children than her willingness to address that desire, grant it, satisfy it. Similarly, Sethe's recovery depends equally on Paul D's ability to return Sethe to pure sexuality, pure desire, his ability thus to give Sethe back to herself. For this reason Paul D meets Sethe's claim that "the best thing she was, was her children" (308) with "You your best thing, Sethe. You are" (335).

At the end of the novel "his holding fingers are holding hers." The idea of holding on to and being held by—not intermingling or merging, as in sexual intercourse—corresponds to the idea of stories (and words) as not infiltrating each other but being next to and separate from yet intimate with each other. To love, to know, to remember—these are activities that depend on leaving open the spaces between people, even between lovers or between parents and children. "Sethe," Paul D says almost at the end of the novel, "me and you, we got more yesterday than anybody. We need some kind of tomorrow" (335). Men and women give each other tomorrow in this book, not through children, but by verifying each other's pain, each other's incompleteness. Children themselves may be important for the ways they remind parents that the future they create began with the recognition by each of them of their individual incompleteness and therefore of the need or desire for the other that preceded and perhaps prompted the sexual act.

The kind of remembering that *Beloved* performs is neither rememory nor disremembering but commemoration, as in "Dearly Beloved," we are gathered here today; it is to remember collectively, in words, the past, which we all accept as gone and buried (5). Like Hawthorne's final words in *The Scarlet Letter,* Morrison's in *Beloved* record a tombstone inscription: "Beloved." This inscription is also, again as in Hawthorne's novel, the title of the book.[26] Memory of the past must include an idea of loss: what the past has taken from us no present or future reality can restore. Such memory corresponds to an element in our everyday consciousness of ourselves as in some sense lost. The title of the novel and the final word, engraved on a tombstone, acknowledge in addition that our existence in this world is temporary and that we are preserved only by a communal will to remember us after we are gone. Beloved is beloved, not because of some supernatural will that she imposes, in the manner of one of Poe's Ligeia-like ladies, on the world. Rather, she is beloved because of the willingness of others that she be so. *Beloved* commemorates in words that, acknowledging absence and loss, enter into and help maintain the human conversation. This conversation is, for Morrison, the instrument of family and community. It binds past to present and individual to community in the recognition that what establishes human relatedness is nothing we can see or touch but only something we can feel and perhaps on occasion hear. Our participation in this world and ultimately our existence depend on our willingness to listen and to speak.

According to Morrison, there is no way to know, no way wholly to account for and take account of the world in which we exist. Our count will always be partial, deficient, inaccurate: 124. Insufficiency of the self and of the family motivates us, however, to step off the edge of our private world in quest of other people and the community and communication that they can provide. *Beloved* remembers. It does so not by telling a single story, whether Sethe's or Denver's or Paul D's, but by placing stories next to each other, insisting that each story register and respond to the other, hand holding hand. Morrison creates a story that is simultaneously the story of family, community, and history. The story remembers the past, not by re-membering it, but by gathering together its pieces, placing one next to the other, and letting these pieces freely generate a future that will remember them.

11

The Graceful Art of Conversation

Grace Paley

Most critics have hailed Grace Paley as the speaker of a unique, uniquely female voice. Her work has been understood as subverting the tradition of male discourse.[1] But Paley, I maintain, writes aversively, not subversively, in the special Cavellian, Emersonian mode that I have been considering a strategy of romance fiction generally. In other words, Paley, in my view, turns away from the society of white, male domination, not to overthrow that tradition but to return to it and to reaffirm and revise it from her own distinctive (female, Jewish) position. She writes into the male tradition, which she understands as already containing the terms of accommodation that she will attempt to isolate and develop. Like other authors in the romance tradition, Paley produces a skepticist text. She focuses the reader's attention not on what words mean (as if language were a symbolic code, which the reader could crack) but on *how* they mean, which is to say when and why they mean.

In Paley's stories of ordinary life, ordinary language plays a primary role. Such language is by no means beneath interpretation, as if Paley were the consummate realist, mimetically reproducing

the world through a nonfigural, nonsymbolic, perhaps even specifically feminine language. In fact, Paley's discourse seems to me anything but normative
human speech, although it catches the tone of daily conversation and forces us
to confront what we mean by conversation. Nor is her language the flourishing
of self-consciously self-reflexive rhetoric that characterizes postcontemporary
male writers (like John Barth and Thomas Pynchon). Rather, in the tradition of
Hawthorne, James, Faulkner, Ellison, and Morrison, Paley's language achieves
meaning because of the particular kind of place from which the author chooses
to speak her words. This is a place where linguistic self-consciousness joins a
fierce commitment to conversation and communication. A large theme
throughout Paley's stories is the failure of both women and men to make their
words mean in this way.

Fathers and Daughters, Mothers and Sons

In the dedication to her second collection of stories, *Enormous Changes at the
Last Minute,* Paley writes: "Everyone in this book is imagined into life except
the father. No matter what story he has to live in, he's my father, I. Goodside,
M.D., artist, and storyteller."[2] The dedication is almost as uninterpretable as
Paley's stories. It is also as precariously balanced between her twentieth-century feminist agenda and her more traditional community- and family-oriented
(even Jewish) concerns. Is Paley's work an attempt to imagine into life everyone
except the father—to write a text governed by any law but his? Many critics
have interpreted her work as subversive in just this way. Or is everyone in her
fiction imaginary except the father, who lives in every story, either as law or as
person or as both?

Paley's writings have been understood as writing in a feminist tongue wholly
discontinuous with and in defiance of the Law of the Father, which is to say the
tradition of symbolism and literary closure.[3] In "A Conversation with My
Father" Paley tackles head on what it might mean to write a wholly female discourse that succeeded in subverting language as we know it and in slipping
out of all connection both with the literary tradition and with the father himself. For Paley, as for Hawthorne, conversation has to do with acknowledgment. It involves speaking words to other people, assuming responsibility for
those words once spoken, and assuming the responsibility of listening. The
title of Paley's story conveys just this idea. Like Hawthorne announcing his personal commitment in "My Kinsman, Major Molineux," Paley in "A Conversa-

tion with My Father" recognizes the importance both of acknowledgment and communication.[4] Communication, this story insists, is conversation; and conversation is a form of acknowledgment. Conversation, acknowledgment, and communication, then, are what occur through Paley's story (primarily between Paley and her actual father or between the narrative voice and the father to whom the book is dedicated). They are not, however, what happen within the story itself.

In "A Conversation with My Father" the father voices stereotypical, limiting, and coercive male objections to feminist writing, such as Paley and the daughter-writer within the story write. The daughter-writer's response seems to represent a woman's attempt to claim her right to escape from the patriarchal tradition of literature. It appears to assert the legitimacy of her own feminist agenda, which is governed by other narrative and linguistic rules. In the daughter's view, female writing will take a course decidedly different from the course of male fiction. It will conform neither to the expectations of realism nor to the demands of closure. It will treat life irreverently and with no small amount of humor and optimism.[5] All of these claims and representations are fine as far as they go. Like any writer, the daughter insists on defining her own art; the text-within-a-text that the daughter writes constitutes an exemplum of female writing. (The father's allusion to "Faith in a Tree"—a story his daughter is supposed to have written—reinforces the exemplary status of the story-within-a-story as a feminist text.) But when the father objects to his daughter's response to his criticism that "that's not what I mean . . . . You misunderstood me on purpose" (EC, 162), he goes to the heart of the problem with his daughter's insistent feminism.

Stories, the father is saying, do not simply thematize subjects, which they then present in one kind of code or another. Rather, stories are acts of communication; they are parts of a conversation in which reader and writer traverse a certain distance between them to agree on a certain meaning and a certain relationship between storyteller and listener. The father's references to a male tradition of texts (EC, 162) may invoke the wrong tradition, from both the daughter-writer's and the real writer's—Paley's and the narrator's—points of view. But they do establish a connection between tradition and meaning. As Stanley Fish has insisted, a literary work does not exist except within an "interpretive community."[6] Therefore, for better or for worse, texts that completely evade interpretive community will remain largely uninterpretable, outside conversation and communication. Of course, new interpretive communities can constitute themselves and legitimize the appearance of new kinds of literary works. Murray Krieger has understood the history of criticism as an accommodation to new modes of literary expression that the scholarly community wishes to legitimize.[7] Paley herself contributes to this process in her stories with their self-conscious reflection on masculine versus feminine aesthetics. The daughter-writer's turn away from Chekov and Turgenev is a silencing rather than a retuning of tradition. The rejection is tantamount in this story to a rejection not simply of some theoretical masculinist tradition but of her own biological father.

The woman writer in Paley's story will not question whether her responsibility to her craft does not also include a responsibility to the audience into which she is born and which precedes the transformations that her texts will effect upon it. "I had promised the family," she explains, "to always let [her father] have the last word when arguing, but in this case I had a different responsibility. That woman [the woman in her story] lives across the street. She's my knowledge and my invention. I'm sorry for her. I'm not going to leave her there in that house crying" (EC, 167). Most readers would agree that letting the father have the last word is hardly the kind of advice the contemporary woman can accept. There is nonetheless a problem with the daughter's argument. The daughter-writer is unwilling to leave her character without consolation and hope, but she is all too willing to leave her listener, which is to say her father, in that condition.

The writer's argument that she is acting out of responsibility is problematic because the claims on her of a character whom she invents clash directly with more immediate human claims. The scene recalls the quarrel between Dr. Copeland and his daughter in The Heart Is a Lonely Hunter when the doctor proposes his theory of eugenics to his childless daughter. The writer-daughter will not attend to the emotionally fraught context in which her storytelling is proceeding. She is more than willing to interpret the scenes within her fiction. She is completely unwilling, however, to interpret the scene of her writing of the story, the scene, in other words, of the relationship between writer and reader, when writing enters into the process of communication. This is the larger scene created by Paley's story.

Immediately preceding the author's statement about her authorial versus her filial responsibility comes this passage:

"Jokes," he said. "As a writer that's your main trouble. You don't want to recognize it. Tragedy! Plain tragedy! Historical tragedy! No hope. The end."

"Oh, Pa," I said. "She could change."

"In your own life, too, you have to look it in the face." He took a couple of nitroglycerin. "Turn to five," he said, pointing to the dial on the oxygen tank. He inserted the tubes into his nostrils and breathed deep. He closed his eyes and said, "No." (*EC*, 166–67)

When the father points his daughter to tragedy, plain tragedy, he seems to her simply to be informing her (in the tradition of male realism that he has just cited) of some large cosmic truth, which he is obliging her to recognize. She therefore rejects his literary criticism. But the father, heavily dosed with nitroglycerin and hooked to an oxygen machine, is trying desperately to turn his daughter toward himself and his situation: "No hope. The end," he says about himself and his dying. "In your own life, too, you have to look it in the face."

The daughter understands the father's statement to be universal. Similarly, she takes the "you" and "your" as being exclusively personal and directly accusatory. To her, her father's statement is a large philosophical admonition with personal imperatives: *you* have to look tragedy in the face, her father seems to be saying to her, at all times and in all places. But the relation between the personal and the impersonal (or cosmic) may be just the reverse of what the daughter imagines. The father's "you" may be just as impersonal as personal; it may be directed as much to himself as to her; and the tragedy to which he refers may specifically refer to the termination of his existence, which he is now experiencing. We all have to look tragedy in the face, he is saying to himself, as well as to her, about his own tragic situation; and what *you*, my daughter, in particular have to look in the face right now is me and my tragedy. "When will you look it in the face?" he asks her a few moments later in the concluding line of the story (*EC*, 167).

This question turns us back to an earlier story in the volume, "Faith in the Afternoon." Here another daughter turns her face away from her father, unable to concede the terms of his tragedy or of her mother's. (The daughter in "Conversation" is the author of this story.) Like "A Conversation with My Father," "Faith in the Afternoon" would seem to be a story that in both form and content confirms a feminist as opposed to a masculinist or traditionalist aesthetic. It would seem, as the title implies, to be about the difference between faith or optimism, on the one hand, and pessimism and despair, on the other. This difference is one that "Conversation" also seems to be expressing. But like "Conversation," what the story thematizes and what it effects in the reader are two different things.

Throughout "Faith in the Afternoon," Faith's parents voice the same tragic pessimism as the father in "Conversation." Together the stories suggest what personal reality the writer of "Faith" is responding to in her story. Two elderly Jewish women—her mother, Mrs. Darwin, and Mrs. Darwin's friend, Mrs. Hegel-Shtein—bombard Faith with stories of human tragedy. These stories not only conform to the realism of the father in "Conversation" but provide both the themes and morals of conventional literature. All the stories, which range over such subjects as death, illness, abandonment, and despair, have in common a single message: that in youth (in the afternoon of being, as it were) a person cannot guess what tragedies lie in store (EC, 42–43). We know from the beginning of the story how deeply conscious of tragedy Faith really is. So deeply engrossed is she in the unfolding of her own tragedy with her husband that it comes as no surprise to us that after hearing all her mother's tales of woe "Faith bowed her head and wept" (EC, 44).

The effectiveness of her mother's stories in bringing Faith to tears puts into doubt Faith's (or the author's) real or apparent rejection of realistic narrative, perhaps even sentimental realism, as a potent storytelling form. The power of "Faith in the Afternoon" does not derive from its depiction of Faith's strength to resist the pull toward the tragic, whether the tragic is rendered realistically or surrealistically. Rather, the story painfully dramatizes the cost of insisting on happiness in the face of other people's tragedies ("I can't come until I'm a little happy," Faith tells her father at the end of the story—EC, 48). To refuse to hear other people's tragedies constitutes a new tragedy—the tragedy of denying relationships. Denial silences stories in their telling. It prevents conversations from coming into being. "To a Jew the word 'shut up' is a terrible expression, a dirty word, like a sin, because in the beginning, if I remember correctly, was the word" (EC, 41).

The storytelling that "Faith in the Afternoon" seems to criticize is almost prevented from coming into being by just such a command from Mrs. Darwin to Mrs. Hegel-Shtein to shut up: "Well, Ma," Faith asks, "what do you hear from the neighborhood?" clearly hoping to hear some cheery news. What follows is important for what the story dramatizes, which is not what a story means but what it means to tell a story.

"Ah, nothing much," Mrs. Darwin said.

"Nothing much?" asked Mrs. Hegel-Shtein. "I heard you correctly said nothing much. You got a letter today from Slovinsky family, your heart stuck in your teeth, Gittel, you want to hide this from little innocent Faith. Little baby Faithy. . . ."

"Celia, I must beg you . . . don't mix in. . . . Celia, I said shut up! . . . Shut up!" (EC, 39–40)

Mrs. Hegel-Shtein is hardly likable: Mr. Darwin describes her as an "insane, persecution, delusions-of-grandeur, paranoical" woman who "has a whole bag of spitballs for the world. And also a bitter crippled life" (EC, 47). Understandably he resents her intrusion into his life: "I don't have a soul to talk to. I'm used to your mother, only a funny thing happened to her, Faithy. . . . She likes to be with the women lately," especially Mrs. Hegel-Shtein (47). Nor is Mr. Darwin the only one who finds it hurtful that his wife should so enjoy the company of this bitter old lady. "It hurt [Faith's] most filial feelings that, in this acute society, Mrs. Hegel-Shtein should be sought after, admired, indulged." (EC, 39). What accounts for Mrs. Hegel-Shtein's popularity with the other women in the old-age home? Unlike the author of "Faith in the Afternoon" (the daughter in both "Conversation" and, by implication, this story too), Mrs. Hegel-Shtein is not a teller of stories. She is a listener to stories; that is, she facilitates the telling of stories by other people. She does this by discovering the connection between the storyteller's words (which almost arbitrarily describe one set of events or another) and the emotional realities that these events are meant to convey.

Mrs. Hegel-Shtein, in other words, represents the connection between writer and reader (speaker and listener) that the writer-daughter in "Conversation" is unwilling to acknowledge. "Your heart stuck in your teeth," she reminds Mrs. Darwin about the story she does not want to tell her daughter; "you want to hide *this* from little innocent Faith?" She understands that happiness maintained in withdrawal from knowledge can, like the indulgence in tragic consciousness, constitute an escape from human interaction. In the parent-child relationship, withdrawal may constitute a failure on the part of the parent to educate the child in the reality of the world, as well as a failure to allow the child into the private world of the parent's suffering and pain.

On the surface of it, "Faith in the Afternoon" is about the trivialization of storytelling, as Faith's mother and her elderly friend overwhelm Faith with one grotesque and exaggerated message of despair after another. The stories seem geared to produce the pat morals and cheap thrills that characterize one story-telling tradition, which Faith, not to mention Paley and the writer-daughter in "Conversation," seem to want to reject. And yet Paley's own story is no less tragic than the stories that she records. It just defines the tragedy differently. Take, for example, the storytelling event concerning the bad news that Mrs. Darwin has received and that she was actively keeping from her daughter.

> "Her husband, Arnold Lever, a very pleasant boy, got a cancer. They chopped off a finger. It got worse. They chopped off a hand. It didn't help. Faithy, that was the end of a lovely boy. That's the letter I got this morning just before you came."
>
> Mrs. Darwin stopped. Then she looked up at Mrs. Hegel-Shtein and Faith. "He was an only son," she said. Mrs. Hegel-Shtein gasped. "You said an only son!" On deep tracks, the tears rolled down her old cheeks. But she had smiled so peculiarly for seventy-seven years that they suddenly swerved wildly toward her ears and hung like glass from each lobe.
>
> Faith watched her cry and was indifferent. Then she thought a terrible thought. She thought that if Ricardo had lost a leg or so, that would cer-tainly have kept him home. This cheered her a little, but not for long.
>
> "Oh, Mama, Mama, Tessie never guessed what was going to happen to her . . . "
>
> "Who guesses?" screamed Mrs. Hegel-Shtein. "Archie is laying down this minute in Florida. Sun is shining on him. He's guessing? (EC, 41–42)

At first, Faith's indifference to Mrs. Hegel-Shtein's tears seems justified. She knows that Mrs. Hegel-Shtein hasn't the least concern for Arnold Lever and his family. Mrs. Hegel-Shtein is constantly melodramatic and insincere. She is a bully who thrives on the pain of others. But Mrs. Hegel-Shtein is not crying for Arnold Lever. She is crying for her own son, Archie, and for herself, for whom that son is as good as lost. Faith need not examine much more than her own response to her mother's story to understand that the stories we tell and the stories we hear are not about other people but about ourselves and about our relationships to each other, that through stories we communicate our own pain and warrant the pain of those whose stories we tell. Retelling our story to themselves, our listeners warrant our pain in turn.

Faith slaps a neat moral onto her mother's story: people never guess what is going to happen to them. But that is not the point of her mother's story, which simply expresses her pain, the pain of loss and dismemberment and encroaching death. Her story provides a vehicle by which she might communicate something to her daughter—something about herself, something about her fears for her daughter, something about her desires for her daughter. But her daughter will not listen. Faith responds to another of her mother's stories: "That's awful, Mama . . . The whole country's in a bad way." Like her indifference to Mrs. Hegel-Shtein's tears, this response is inadequate to the story being told, which is as much a story about Mrs. Darwin's sense of personal diminishment as about the Brauns of the story. "I'm sorry for the old people," her mother ends her narrative, pointing the story directly back to herself (42).

Faith's response to her father is likewise inadequate.

> "Listen, Faithl, I wrote a poem, I want you to hear. Listen. I wrote it in Yiddish, I'll translate it in my head:

Childhood passes
Youth passes
Also the prime of life passes.
Old age passes.
Why do you believe, my daughters,
That old age is different?

> "What do you say, Faithy? You know a whole bunch of artists and writers."
>
> "What do I say? Papa." She stopped stock-still. "You're marvelous. That's like a Japanese Psalm of David." (EC, 46)

Laudatory as Faith's literary criticism may be, it turns aside from hearing or listening to her father's lament. "Well, Pa, I guess I have to go now," she replies to his painful confession of loneliness and estrangement. "I loved talking to you" (EC, 47–48). When he asks her directly, "Can you come soon?" she says, "I can't come until I'm a little happy."

> "Happy!" He leaned over the rail and tried to hold her eyes. But that is hard to do, for eyes are born dodgers . . . .
>
> Mr. Darwin reached for her fingers through the rail. He held them tightly and touched them to her wet cheeks. Then he said, "Aaaah . . . ," an explosion of nausea, absolute digestive disgust. And before she could turn away from the old age of his insulted face and run home down the sub-

way stairs, he had dropped her sweating hand out of his own and turned away from her. (*EC,* 48–49)

Faith's flight from unhappiness, her unwillingness to confront tragedy, even the exaggerated, melodramatic tragedy of her mother's stories, is an affirmation of neither life nor faith; nor is it an expression of hope (to invoke the name of Faith's sister). Rather, her response slips away from responsibility and relationship. Faith will not face her father; she will not lend him her hand or accept a helping hand from him, even though his hand, holding hers, touches her own hand to her wet cheeks. The father feels his daughter's pain ("Oh . . . my darling girl," he gasps when he has inadvertently touched on a painful subject, "excuse me"); and he would put her in touch with her own pain as well as his. But Faith refuses the parental connection. Or, rather, she refuses to understand what her father is saying.

In "Conversation," the father, pressing for details about the daughter's story, asks whether the boy protagonist is (like so many of her other characters) "born out of wedlock?" The daughter responds: "Married or not, it's of small consequence." Her father answers: "It is of great consequence" (*EC,* 163). Peggy Kamuf says that reading a text like a woman is "reading it *as if* it had no [determined] father, *as if,* in other words, it were illegitimate, recognized by its mother who can only give it a borrowed name."[8] This idea applies to Paley's story and to her work in general. Like so much of Paley's fiction, the story-within-a-story in "Conversation" describes a mother and her deeply emotional relationship with her child. This relationship, which is unconditional and abiding and therefore beyond questioning, makes the question of the child's illegitimacy seem irrelevant. The father's insistence that it is of great consequence seems like one more imposition of male authority for the female text to resist. But is the father or even the wedlock through which he secures his relationship to his children of absolutely no consequence?

Many of Paley's stories dwell upon men's desertion of their wives and their children.[9] For fathers, it would seem, parenthood is a nonbinding, "occasional" obligation, as in "Enormous Changes at the Last Minute." (Another story is about "eleven unwed mothers on relief.")[10] There is no doubting Paley's accusation against men. They are often, in her fiction, selfish, unfeeling, heartless.[11] What disturb the easy accusations against men in these stories, however, are the depictions of fathers in other stories, such as "Conversation," "Faith in the Afternoon," "Enormous Changes," and "Dreamer in a Dead Language." Many of the same stories in which men come off so badly also contain accusations against women. In "A Woman, Young and Old," for example, the mother engages in a fierce sexual competition with her daughter, which is not unrelated to the desertion of the mother by the daughter's father.[12] Similarly in "Wants" the former wife is just as capable as her husband of trivializing both their relationship and the conversations in which they still engage: "Hello, my life," she says upon meeting him. "We had once been married for twenty-seven years, so I felt justified" (*EC,* 3). And in "The Story Hearer" the mother, not the father, deserts the children.[13] But it is the father-centered stories, I think, that most dramatically throw into relief what women will not grant men: that the terms of biology, which seem so to disadvantage women, making them (as in one of Paley's titles) "a subject of childhood" (*LDM*), disadvantage men as well. Men may not be able to know and experience their children in the same way. What, then, is the mother's obligation to the father of her children? the daughter's obligation to her own father? the responsibility of the woman writer to the male tradition?

In "Dreamer in a Dead Language," Paley picks up the story of Faith and her parents. Like so many of her stories, this one focuses on the painful complexity of communication between parents and children: Faith "was sorry so much would have to happen before the true and friendly visit." Again, "There was no way to talk" (*LSD,* 16, 22). But here Paley identifies an element in the problematics of parent-child communication that remains inchoate in her earlier stories: the daughter's unwillingness to discover her own words and thoughts in her father's discourse. "Oh Pa! Pa! . . . I can't stand your being here," she exclaims, bringing forward a major theme of "Faith in the Afternoon." This theme is Faith's disapproval of her parents' decision to entomb themselves in an old-age home. In the earlier story, "Faith in the Afternoon," their decision seems to highlight Faith's own faith in the afternoon of life as opposed to her parents' despair of the night. Here in "Dreamer," however, the relative positions of father and daughter drastically change. "Really?" the father responds. "Who says *I* can stand it?"

Then silence. . . .

Faith put her hand on her father's knee. Papa darling, she said.

Mr. Darwin felt the freedom of committed love. I have to tell the truth. . . . I have made a certain decision. Your mother isn't in agreement with me. The fact is, I don't want to be in this place anymore. . . . I have to go away. If I go away, I leave Mama. If I leave Mama, well, that's terrible. But, Faith, I can't live here any more. . . . You understand me, Faith?

Faith hoped he didn't really mean what she understood him to mean. (*LSD*, 27–29)

Faith does not want to understand her father. Furthermore, she does not want her own affirmations of life—expressed in her rejection of the old-age home—in any way compromised by his affirmation. When Faith's father then reveals that he and her mother were never really married, that they, like Faith, were "idealists" in their day, Faith enters fully into raw competition with her father: "Oh, *you* were idealists," she taunts him. "Then she sat down again and filled his innocent ear with the real and ordinary world. Well, Pa, you know I have three lovers right this minute" (*LSD*, 30–31).

Faith's desire not to have her father say to her exactly what she has been saying to him about the old-age home and then her desire to shock him—to outdo his idealism with her own—suggests the way the conversation between them, here and in "Faith in the Afternoon" and "Conversation," constitutes anything but an intimate exchange enabled by the freedom of committed love. When, at the end of the story, Faith's sons tell her that it is her "responsibility" to move her parents out of the old-age home and Faith asks her sons to bury her, albeit only in the sand, she plays out her own worst fears: that the parents' life forces can be preserved only at the expense of the child's, that their radicalism and idealism, like their very survival, diminish her own. The fact that Faith's father is a writer directs our attention to the way the father-daughter tension reflects as well a tension between women writers and the male literary tradition (it is revealed in *Later the Same Day* that Faith, too, writes poetry; and the father-daughter relationship in the Faith stories mirrors, as I have suggested, the analogous relationship in "Conversation" between the daughter-writer and her father). Anxiety of influence seems to take an especially nasty turn when it is cross-gendered.

The sequence of stories about Faith and her father, including the story about the fictionalized author of those stories ("Conversation"), also casts doubt on the ostensible meaning of the title story of Paley's second volume of stories, "Enormous Changes at the Last Minute." In this story Paley presents the female protagonist in the middle of a conflict between daughter and mother. Not only does the daughter double herself—appearing in some scenes with her father, in other scenes with Dennis, the father-to-be of her child—but the role of the father is doubled, too, in the father himself and in the lover, who is about to become a father. Alexandra's courage as a woman seems to consist in her ability to resist bowing either to her father's proprieties or to her lover's. Her father wants her to have a child only within the institution of marriage. Her lover is willing to expand the concept of marriage to include a "communal" marriage, but he, too, insists on the same kind of formalities and knowledge as Alexandra's father. However, Dennis's song with its pathetic lyrics, "Who is the father? I! I! I! I! I am the father," is more desperate than inane (EC, 135).

"Anyway," Alexandra asks him, "how do you know you're the father?" "Come on, he said, who else would be?" (EC, 134). Dennis may be arrogant, but Alexandra is cruel. And Dennis's voice carries more than a little moral weight when his final song, to his son, has the happy consequence of becoming "responsible for a statistical increase in visitors to old-age homes by the apprehensive middle-aged and the astonished young" (EC, 136). In "Enormous Changes" the male-authored work of art, which expresses archetypical male anxieties, effects enormous changes at the last minute—which is not a minute too soon. Nor is the apparently feminist solution that the story discovers for Alexandra's father anything less than horrifying. "Shortly before the baby's birth, he fell hard on the bathroom tiles, cracked his skull, dipped the wires of his brain into his heart's blood. Short circuit! He lost twenty, thirty years in a flood . . . but he was smart as ever, and able to begin again with fewer scruples to notice and appreciate" (EC, 134–35). Alexandra's assault against the male tradition (closely affiliated with that of the daughter-writer in "Conversation") infantilizes and annihilates it. The failure to find a language to share with the father seems to result either in the death of the parent or of the child, even if the death in the one case is simply a bad case of senility and in the other is only a temporary burial in the sand.

Paley's Writer-Response Criticism

Is there any way for men and women, parents and children (especially fathers and daughters), to speak to one another? Is there any way for a new generation, especially of women, to write into the tradition without compromising their own voices or destroying the tradition? Throughout her fiction Paley thematizes how and why and in what ways human conversations do not come into being. In the process she institutes the art of conversation that her characters fail to enjoy. She creates the relationships that they cannot establish.[14] Many critics have responded to the special quality of Paley's writing, which Ronald Schleifer has described as "storytelling as a form of listening." Schleifer quotes the following marvelous statement by Paley herself: "Before I wrote those stories, I was just stuck in my own voice. Until I was able to use other people's voices, that I'd been hearing all my life, you know, I was just talking me-me-me. While I was doing that, I couldn't write these stories. And when I was able to get into other voices consciously, or use what I was hearing, and become the story hearer—when I could do that I just suddenly wrote them."[15]

According to Schleifer and others, the problem with many of Paley's characters is that they "cannot listen and retell stories." But the critics get into trouble, I think, when they distinguish in Paley's fiction between characters and narrators. Paley's narrators, most of them speaking distinctly feminist voices, are themselves objects of her critique. "Mrs. Raferty has only her own voice, 'distanced' from others," write Schleifer, "while the narrator of 'A Conversation with My Father,' in *Enormous Changes at the Last Minute*, has learned the patience to wait and listen. 'Well,' she tells her father, 'you just have to let the story lie around till some agreement can be reached between you and the stubborn hero,' 'Aren't you talking silly, now?' her father answers."[16] The problem is that the father, to whom the writer-daughter makes this statement, *is* the stubborn hero of the same story in which the daughter-writer appears as character and narrator both. The narrator of the story does not display patience. She does not wait and listen. It is left to Paley herself to come to some agreement with this stubborn hero, and this she does.

Although the critical focus on Paley's feminist agenda is well placed, it has tended to occlude both the non-gender-specific concerns of her work and its antifeminist arguments. For Paley women must have their own voices. They must be listened to. They must also listen—to other women of other generations, like Mrs. Darwin and Mrs. Hegel-Shtein, who tell what seem to be patriarchal stories: realistic, tragic, and moral ("Don't laugh, you ignorant girl," Aunt Rose admonishes her niece in "Goodbye and Good Luck," *LDM*, 13)—and to men as well. When Schleifer prefers the daughter-writer's belief in hope and sympathy over her father's insistence on a linear meaning, he takes up residence within Paley's story on the daughter's side, on one side of a blocked conversation.[17] He does not take the side of Paley, the daughter, whose story is, indeed, a conversation with her father. "I had promised the family to always let him have the last word when arguing," the daughter-writer within the story tells us, only to immediately violate that promise out of devotion to her art.

Paley, however, does let the father have the last word. His is the last sentence spoken in the story. In a similar way, the father's words and actions are the final events recorded in "Faith in the Afternoon." In letting the father have the last word, Paley is not buckling under patriarchal pressure. She is recognizing in the father's question a question that she, too, is willing to ask herself.[18]

For Paley storytelling is not an amorphous, undifferentiated, democratic process in which everyone has a say and where truth consists in the multiplicity of voices, each going its own way. Paley is not as passive as her critics make her out to be; nor is she so completely tolerant of her characters and their foibles. Rather, like most writers Paley has a stake in what she writes. And that stake, for her, involves the dual responsibilities of the daughter-writer. Paley recovers, therefore, the power in the word, which tradition and convention have rendered impotent. Nicholas Humy makes the important point that the daughter-writer in "Conversation" "wants [her father] to see the process of storytelling anew, to see how, in the telling, the story becomes defamiliarized, becomes, not what it is about, but what it is." In this way, the daughter makes her father attend to the choices of which any story consists but which convention tends to naturalize.[19] What the father in turn would tell his daughter is that such choices involve decisions to accept or to reject responsibility for one's words—for the possible consequence of those words in the world. The world contains both the audience to which one writes and the literary tradition that comes prior to one's own writing. Paley's stories perform more than what Schleifer has called the "maieutic function of discourse, the role of the midwife in the dialectic of [in Paley's words] 'two events or two characters or two winds or two different weathers or two ideas or whatever bumping into each other' in stories."[20] Rather, Paley parents a tradition by acknowledging her own parents within that tradition, finding her own words in theirs, participating in the expression of their hopes and desires through her own.

Paley's is an Emersonian undertaking. She will discover the roots of words, the origins of things, not in themselves, but in language—hence the Whitmanesque quality of her consummately feminist story, "Faith in a Tree": "Just when I most needed important conversation, a sniff of the man-wide world, that is, at least one brainy companion who could translate my friendly language into his tongue of undying carnal love, I was forced to lounge in our neighborhood park, surrounded by children" (EC, 77). Other Whitmanesque allusions abound: "What a place in democratic time"—an allusion, I take it, to Democratic Vistas; "One God . . . who unravels the stars" and "Brooklyn . . .

Prospect Park"—77–78; not to mention the sailing imagery throughout the story, an imitation of "Crossing Brooklyn Ferry," which has affinities as well with Melville). "Faith in a Tree" does not simply discover the masculine world of epic adventure in the domestic reality of mother and children. It rediscovers America's own Emersonian, Whitmanesque relocation of the epic from the heroic to the ordinary, from the cosmic to the local. Paley may be a consummate woman writer, but she is also an active inheritor of an American tradition.[21] Like other twentieth-century female romancers, she recovers from the male tradition its latent content, which is its deep investment in telling the story of family and community and providing the possibility for the continued telling of that story.

Racism, Sexism, and Community

Later the Same Day, Paley's third volume of stories, has seemed to some critics the most radically feminist of her writings. I suggest that the book extends her earlier critique of feminism in the direction of reconciliation and conversation. In *Later the Same Day* the character who most grandly fulfills the requirements of responsibility is once again a father, indeed a grandfather. "Zagrowsky Tells" is not for Paley one more occasion to make the important point (articulated throughout Paley's work) that no single voice can suffice to tell a story. Nor is the story intended simply to suggest Faith's (and hence the author's) limitations as narrators or as narrative consciousnesses—although the suggestion is one important consequence of the story. Rather, "Zagrowsky Tells" draws an important line between moral statement and moral deed, between assuming responsibility for a theory of interpersonal relations and assuming responsibility for oneself and one's world. In Paley's view we must assume responsibility not only for our own words and stories but for other people's stories as well. To listen is not simply to hear but to respond; and to respond is to take an action in relation to another human being. It is also to be willing to discover oneself in another, to let one's words go and to be willing to find those words again where one least expects them in somebody else's entirely different discourse. To put it somewhat differently and to discover (perhaps) a development in Paley's three volumes, no matter how much we entertain the hopeful possibility of "enormous changes at the last minute" by which to soothe those "little disturbances of man," nonetheless we all must "later the same day" confront a reality that insists, without respite, on intruding itself, whatever our strategies for keeping it at bay.

Several of the stories in *Later the Same Day* explicitly call feminist ideologies into question. In "Friends," for example, Faith tries to convince her friends that her life, like theirs, has contained its unmitigated tragedies. "Well, some bad things have happened in my life," she says. "What?" her friend retorts. "You were born a woman? Is that it?" Faith continues, "She was, of course, mocking me this time, referring to an old discussion about feminism and Judaism. Actually, on the prism of isms, both of those do have to be looked at together once in a while" (*LSD*, 81). Ann's mocking of Faith picks up on an earlier story, "Lavinia: An Old Story," in which a mother laments her daughter's decision to go the way of motherhood. The mother makes the important and common feminist point that "what men got to do on earth don't take more time than sneezing. Now a woman walk away from a man, she just know she loaded down in her body nine months. She got that responsibility on her soul forever" (*LSD*, 63). But the mother's disappointment in her daughter ironizes this statement, for the mother can feel nothing for her happy and "busy" daughter (*LSD*, 68) but contempt and perhaps jealousy (in reminiscence of the mother in "A Woman, Young and Old"—*LDM*).

What it means to have responsibility on one's soul forever is more than Lavinia's mother with her casual and rather superficial feminist anger can understand. Nor does Faith herself grasp the depths of such responsibility when, in the butcher shop, she takes a cheap stab at correcting the butcher's male chauvinism, only to ignore his equally offensive anti-Semitism (*LSD*, 136–37). The story entitled "The Story Hearer," in which this incident occurs, is crucial to Paley's definition in *Later the Same Day* of what responsibility entails. Toward the end of the story, Faith tells Jack, "I want to have a baby," a desire Jack quickly and insensitively dismisses.

> Ha ha, he said. You can't. Too late. A couple of years too late, he said, and fell asleep. Then he spoke. Besides, suppose it worked; I mean, suppose a miracle. The kid might be very smart, get a scholarship to M.I.T. and get caught up in problem solving and godalmighty it could invent something worse than anything us old dodos ever imagined. Then he fell asleep and snored.
>
> I pulled the Old Testament out from under the bed where I keep most of my bedtime literature. I jammed an extra pillow under my neck and sat up almost straight in order to read the story of Abraham and Sarah with interlinear intelligence. There was a lot in what Jack said—he often

makes a sensible or thought-provoking remark. Because you know how that old story ends—well! With those three monotheistic horsemen of perpetual bossdom and war: Christianity, Judaism, and Islam.

Just the same, I said to softly snoring Jack, before all that popular badness wedged its way into the world, there *was first* the little baby Isaac. You know what I mean: looking at Sarah just like all our own old babies—remember the way they practiced their five little senses. Oh, Jack, that Isaac, Sarah's boy—before he was old enough to be taken out by his father to get his throat cut, he must have just lain around smiling and making up diphthongs and listening, and the women sang songs to him and wrapped him up in such pretty rugs. Right?

In his sleep, which is as contentious as his waking, Jack said yes—but he should not have been allowed to throw all that sand at his brother.

You're right, you're right. I'm with you there, I said. Now all you have to do is be with me. (*LSD*, 143–44)

There is no denying the feminist tilt of this scene: until he comes under his father's jurisdiction, Isaac is like any mother's son—a smiler, a listener, a maker of beautiful, poetic sounds. Faith's appeal to Jack to be with her on the side of her desire (we might say) is consummately affecting. If men had been with their wives, the statement implies, little male children would not have grown up to be the horsemen of perpetual bossdom and war.

But when Jack reminds Faith (or rather, Faith reminds herself—for Jack is by now asleep) that Isaac ought not to have been allowed to treat his brother the way he did, the core of the problem emerges. In the absence of male authority, women would have to draw up the moral rules, which might be every bit as stringent as male laws. By referring to the biblical desert as a sandbox and formulating Isaac's treatment of Ishmael as throwing sand in his brother's face, the story reminds us that mothers have always been in charge of policing their children; indeed, Old Testament authors portray women like Sarah and Rebecca as intimately concerned with their children's destinies. Sitting up straight in bed, understanding the Old Testament with interlinear intelligence, Faith is reading like a man; in articulating to herself Jack's probable comment to herself she is thinking like a man as well. Reading and thinking like a man might be the consequence of male domination. It may also represent the inevitable consequences of the assumption of authority. The question "Right?" is the exact question that women must ask themselves about their own assumptions about the feminine versus the masculine. Is it really true that there is smiling and singing and listening *without* entering into the brutal realities of violence and moral law? Is there, then, any way to rewrite the end of that old story of bossdom and war? Paley moves toward answers to these questions during the final sequence of stories in *Later the Same Day*.

In "Zagrowsky Tells" the female protagonist is made to switch positions with the male protagonist. As in "Dreamer in a Dead Language," in this story about a Jewish immigrant pharmacist and his African American grandson, Faith is the one who demands precision and moral meaning. It is Faith who has to understand how the story hangs together.

> She looks at me, this Faith. She can't say a word. She sits there. She opens her mouth almost. I know what she wants to know. How did Emanuel come into the story. When?
>
> Then she says to me exactly those words. Well, where does Emanuel fit in?
>
> He fits, he fits. Like a golden present from Nasser.
>
> Nasser?
>
> O.K., Egypt, not Nasser—he's from Isaac's other son, get it? A close relation. I was sitting one day thinking, Why? why? The answer: To remind us. That's the purpose of most things.
>
> It was Abraham, she interrupts me. He had two sons, Isaac and Ishmael. God promised him he would be the father of generations; he was. But you know, she says, he wasn't such a good father to those two little boys. Not so unusual, she had to add on.
>
> You see! That's what they make of the Bible, those women: because they got it in for men. Of *course* I meant Abraham. Abraham. Did I say Isaac? Once in a while I got to admit it, she says something true. You remember one son he sent out of the house altogether, the other he was ready to chop up if only he heard a noise in his head saying, Go! Chop! (*LSD*, 166–67)

For Zagrowsky, the purpose of Emanuel is the same as the purpose of the biblical text and "of most things." It is to remind us. Remind us, we ask, of what? The story refrains from saying. Faith's response to Zagrowsky, which is to remind him of something small and inconsequential—an error in his memory of biblical characters and events—is certainly not Paley's idea of a useful response.

Zagrowsky's slip reflects a pervasive aspect of the biblical text, especially in the stories of the patriarchs, of which these stories remind us. They tell us that biblical history (within the Old Testament and, we might add, in the relation between Old Testament and New) is the history of doublings and repetitions, which (depending on how they are viewed) either do or do not recognize the relatedness that binds siblings and cousins in the community of humankind. Zagrowsky's error, in other words, locates what Emanuel himself represents: the fact of human relatedness, of our joint origins in a single ancestry and a single story, a relatedness that has become painfully divisive and disjointed, one side of the family (male or female, black or white, Jewish, Christian, or Muslim) in opposition to and isolation from the other side. As Faith's comment in "The Story Hearer" reminds us, when she is contemplating bringing one more potential savior into the world, the "old story ends . . . with those three monotheistic horsemen of perpetual bossdom and war: Christianity, Judaism, and Islam," and there is little hope that her contribution to the family line will change things. Another story that calls into question the possibility that a new savior will bring the story to a new conclusion is "At That Time, or the History of a Joke" (*LSD*, 93–96). Here what is equally called into question is the idea that an all-female line will serve the purposes of redemption any better than the all-male line that Christianity seems to imagine. The final phrase of the story, about "a cheap but stunning garment for a wedding, birth, or funeral" (96), may constitute a direct invocation of Hawthorne's *Scarlet Letter*. Like Hawthorne investigating the Custom-House, Zagrowsky discovers in his grandson a reminder of something that was always there and that he has always known but that he—like so many of us—had painfully forgotten: the biblical story, however it ends, is a story of joint origins and interrelations and the painful problem of the displacements of cultures and peoples, one by the other.

"Zagrowsky Tells" exposes the racism of the Jewish Zagrowsky. Yet Faith and her friends, for all their civil rights activism, are not the heroes of the story. Like the feminism of the daughter-writer in "Conversation," their activism involves assuming one set of responsibilities at the expense of another set of equally valid obligations:

O.K.—you still listening? Let me ask you, if I did you so much good including I saved your baby's life, how come you did *that*? You know what I'm talking about. A perfectly nice day. I look out the window of the pharmacy and I see four customers, that I seen at least two in their bathrobes crying to me in the middle of the night, Help help! They're out there with signs. ZAGROWSKY IS A RACIST. YEARS AFTER ROSA PARKS, ZAGROWSKY REFUSES TO SERVE BLACKS. It's like an etching right *here*. I point out to her my heart. I know exactly where it is.

She's naturally very uncomfortable when I tell her. Listen, she says, we were right.

I grab on to Emanuel. You?

Yes, we wrote a letter first, did you answer it? . . . We said we would like to talk to you. We tested you. At least four times, you kept Mrs. Green and Josie . . . waiting a long time till everyone ahead of them was taken care of. Then you were very rude. . . . You remember?

No, I happen not to remember. There was plenty of yelling in the store. People *really* suffering. . . .

Then I thought, Why should I talk to this woman. . . . I tried to explain. Faith, Ruthy, Mrs. Kratt—a stranger comes into the store, naturally you have to serve the old customers first. Anyone would do the same. Also, they sent in black people, brown people, all colors, and to tell the truth I didn't like the idea my pharmacy should get the reputation of being a cut-rate place for them. They move into a neighborhood . . . I did what everyone did. Not to insult people too much, but to discourage them a little, they shouldn't feel so welcome. . . .

In the subway once [my wife] couldn't get off at the right stop. The door opens, she can't get up. . . . She says to a big guy with a notebook, a big colored fellow, Please help me get up. He says to her, You kept me down three hundred years, you can stay down another ten minutes. I asked her, Nettie, didn't you tell him we're raising a little boy brown like a coffee bean. But he's right, says Nettie, we done that. We kept them down.

We? We? My two sisters and my father were being fried up for Hitler's supper in 1944 and you say we? (*LSD*, 157–59).

I do not cite this passage in order to point out how classically it represents one aspect of racism—the excuses the racist brings to his defense, the way the victim becomes victimizer, and so on. Rather, I want to show how Paley's intention is to get behind people's words to the human realities that they reflect and to suggest why slogans and accusations (like Faith's and her friends' and like the hollow moralizing about China in "Somewhere Else") are in no way adequate to the challenge of community. Faith and her friends do owe Zagrowsky a debt that they cannot forget in paying off another debt. As Zagrowsky's comments to his wife remind us, the obligation of the Holocaust survivor to African Americans may be different from the obligations of other Americans.

To cite this obligation is not to say that the American Jew has no responsibility to the African American. It is, however, to insist that, just as Zagrowsky is going to have to get behind the words of the big colored fellow with the notebook (of grievances perhaps) to understand where his words are coming from, so the black man and Faith and her friends are going to have to get behind the reasons for Zagrowsky's behavior in the pharmacy to understand what motivates his words and responses. Faith and her friends, Mrs. Zagrowsky, and, in other stories, Faith's sons define morality abstractly, universally. Zagrowsky lives it immediately. There is a difference, he knows—linguistic as well as practical—between helping people up from their seats on the subway and keeping them down in history; and they require different kinds of responses. The immediate request of help can be responded to without forgetting larger injustices; larger injustices can be fought for without neglecting other, more immediate debts.

"Life is going on," says Mr. Zagrowsky; and "life don't have no opinion" (158). The wisdom of Paley's story, as of her work, is not that people do not have opinions, nor that they ought to refrain from expressing them. Nor is the point that one opinion cancels out another, so that if enough people have a chance to express an opinion, the world will right all inequalities. Paley suggests, rather, that opinions cannot substitute for commitments and affirmations. "My listener says to me, Right, Iz, you did the right thing. What else could you do? I feel like smacking her . . . who asked her?—Right, Iz." (*LSD,* 170). Faith's judgment that Iz is now doing the right thing for his grandson is no more valid than her verdict years earlier that he had done the wrong thing for his black customers. Faith cannot see that in both cases Zagrowsky is defining his allegiance, not abstractly, in terms of large issues of right and wrong, but practically, in terms of his responsibility to those whom he defines as family or community. And whereas his community did not include black people earlier, now it does: "In a few days, the rabbi came. He raised up his eyebrows a couple times. Then he did his job, which is to make the bris. In other words, a circumcision. This is done so that child will be a man in Israel. That's the expression they use. He isn't the first colored child. They tell me long ago we were mostly dark. Also, now I think of it, I wouldn't mind going over there to Israel. They say there are plenty black Jews. It's not unusual over there at all" (*LSD,* 171).[22]

Perhaps Zagrowsky had to know earlier what Faith and her picket signs could not or did not tell him: the fact of his relatedness to Mrs. Green and Josie, the fact that African Americans were not imported into his world as a judgment on him or as one more burden for the already overburdened Jew. They were, and always had been, a part of the very same neighborhood that he served. Perhaps Zagrowsky needed to confront the imperfection of our definitions of kinship and family. Community, for Paley, is an act of commitment, not an obligation of blood: "Gosh what a cute kid. Whose is he? . . . Really some cute kid," a passerby comments on Emanuel. "I just look in his face," Zagrowsky responds. "What does he want? I should tell him the story of my life? I don't need to tell. I already told and told. So I said very loud—no one else should bother me—how come it's your business, mister? Who do you think he is? By the way, whose kid you got on your back? It don't look like you" (*LSD,* 174). Human beings have to recognize that bloodlines, which are highly obscure and almost unreadable, do not count for everything. Who is to say that the Israelites were *not* black, that white culture and black did not originate in some joint culture to which they may still return. Emanuel reminds Zagrowsky of the uncertainty of origins; the circumcision of the black grandson recovers the kinship that was never lost, only forgotten.

By the end of the story Faith and her friends are "Laughing. Laughing." Zagrowsky continues: "So I say, What is going on, Emanuel, could you explain to me what just happened? Did you notice anywhere a joke? This is the first time he doesn't answer me. He's writing his name on the sidewalk. EMANUEL. Emanuel in big capital letters. And the women walk away from us. Talking. Talking" (*LSD,* 175). Zagrowsky repeats the father's objection in "Conversation": to you, he says to his daughter, everything is a joke. For Paley, life is not deadly serious; her stories are often riotously funny. But life is not a joke. Discovering one's responsibilities is a painful and serious process. In "Listening" Jack asks Faith, "Have you decided not to have a baby?" to which she responds "No, I've just decided to think about it, but I haven't given it up." Jack's response is important: "With the sweetness of old forgiving friendship, he took my hand. My dear, he said, perhaps you only wish that you were young again. So do I. At the store when young people come in waving youth's unfurled banner HOPE, meaning their pockets are full of someone's credit cards, I think: New toasters! Brand-new curtains! Soft convertibles! Danish glass! I hadn't thought of furniture from the discount store called Jack, Son of Jake as a song of beginnings. . . . Now listen to me, he said" (*LSD,* 203). In the end Faith will not have that baby. She will not begin again. Faith discovers that there is plenty of life, plenty to talk about, even "later the same day." The story proceeds as Faith listens to Jack, Jack listens to Faith's son, Richard, and so on. "I'm busy," Faith finally concludes about bringing more new life into the world. "I have an awful lot to do." In any event, "miracles don't happen, and if they do they're absolutely explainable" (*LSD*, 205). This conclusion is not gloomy. Nor is it, however, maintained in jest. Rather, it relocates the miracle from the realm of the divine, the inexplicable, or the nonbiological into the world of human busy-ness or business—the word recurs throughout Paley's fiction: Emanuel, Zagrowsky tells us, is his business, no one else's (*LSD*, 174).

Nor does the conclusion slip out from under responsibility. At the end of the book Jack approaches Faith with the sweetness of old forgiving friendship. Faith's friend, Cassie, however, in the concluding lines of the book, refuses to forgive Faith: "Forgive you? She laughed. But she reached across the clutch. With her hand she turned my face to her so my eyes would look into her eyes. You are my friend, I know that, Faith, but I promise you, I won't forgive you, she said. From now on, I'll watch you like a hawk. I do not forgive you" (*LSD*, 211). These lines turn us back to Zagrowsky and to the plot of bossdom and war that the white, male, Judeo-Christian tradition seems to tell. Forging friendships and assuming responsibility do not, for Paley, necessarily entail acts of forgiveness for past offenses. African Americans, Jews, and women (especially a lesbian woman like Cassie) have every right to retain their memories of injustice and suffering. But, like Denver in *Beloved*, they must at some moment enter the world and assume responsibility for it.

Carrying through on an idea that informs the whole of *Later the Same Day*, "Listening" explicitly rejects the idea of undoing the past—or of redoing it, an idea that solves the problem of feminist radicalism in "Enormous Changes" and that Faith herself fantasizes about in "The Story Hearer." As if remembering its own antecedent in the volume, which itself remembers the Old Testament text, the story reminds us that the human community does not lack stories. Instead it lacks hearers and listeners for those stories. Later the same day Paley opts to accept a world and a self no longer young, no longer capable of rebirthing reality.

Telling Stories, Saving Lives

In linking themselves to the Hawthorne tradition, twentieth-century women romancers discover hidden concerns in that tradition. The very act of engaging in conversation reveals conversation to be a central preoccupation of romance fiction writers from the nineteenth-century to the present day. What is conversation that it should seem so crucial to a literary tradition as to become one of its major subjects?

As I have argued in this chapter, conversation is not simply letting everybody have a say, although the idea of free and unhampered speaking is clearly important to Paley. Rather, the burden of conversation is placed by Paley, as by her predecessors in the tradition, on the art of listening, where listening (like speaking) is not neutral, either, but pointed toward and for someone or something else. Listening, for Paley, means responding. And responding means taking upon oneself a moral responsibility—not responsibility *for,* as if one were responsible for every grievance under the sun, but responsibility *to,* to a world that one did not make but into which one is born, to a language that is inadequate to most of our needs for articulation, to a tradition that seems poised to render us impotent to change anything.

Conversation, then, is also conversion, as Stanley Cavell stresses in relation to Thoreau. Conversion is religious, but not to a particular faith. "I am trying to curb my cultivated individualism," remarks Faith in "The Story Hearer" (*LSD,* 133), one of the most theological of Paley's stories. Conversion is a self-reliant turn away from what Cavell calls the attained self to the attainable self; it is an aversion of conformity, which yields and continues to yield consent.[23] It is a conversion, as in Emerson, Thoreau, and Hawthorne, away from faith in the old religious sense of the word and toward hope, which turns out to be toward grace as well. Grace Paley, naming her protagonist Faith and Faith's sister Hope, opens up a special way for the self to address the world: through a non-individualized identity that is always moving toward an attainable but never-to-be-attained self. Faith is always aspiring, through hope, to grace—and on through the chain of displacements, from grace through hope to faith restored.

Wolfgang Iser argues that fiction resides neither in the so-called quotidian world of the sociopolitical nor in the world of the imaginary and make-believe. It is, rather, the manifestation of what he calls play, a back-and-forth movement among the realms of the real, the fictive, and the imaginary. Nor are any of these realms static and existential. They are constructs that (in the fashion of fiction itself) manifest themselves in interactive transformations. Fiction, Iser concludes, is boundary crossing. It takes its vitality and its form from a movement that never ceases and that never leaves intact the elements that conspire in its construction.[24]

The path of resistance and affirmation that Iser charts can tell us much about the similar path traced in the romance tradition, both by its fiction writers (Hawthorne, Melville, James, Faulkner, Ellison, McCullers, O'Connor, Morrison, and Paley) and by its philosophers (Emerson, Thoreau, and Cavell). This path is not open-ended. Nor is it determined. It leads toward a freedom that is intellectual, psychological, and, finally, political. Play, I think, is the life force of the romance tradition.

Why do we create fiction? How might fiction serve the needs of human consciousness? Iser answers that fiction is the expression of the human. In the view of one group of writers, male and female, of many different ethnic and racial communities, romance fiction is one such expression of the human, especially self-conscious, self-reflexive, and poignant. It directly acknowledges that to be human is to imagine, and to imagine is to realize the possibility of crossing even the boundaries of self and, in so exceeding oneself, to realize with full vitality and force the potential of the human.

"Emanuel climbs up on my lap," Zagrowsky tells us. "He pats my face. Don't be sad, Grandpa, he says" (*LSD*, 165). Despite the apparent abundance of literary theories available today, there are perhaps only two schools of criticism: the party of hope and the party of despair. Faith's sister Hope is never given a voice in Paley's stories, yet almost all of Paley's fiction is infused with hope. Perhaps the nature of hope is that we cannot specify what it is, that it cannot speak to us directly. Hope cannot push tragedy aside, nor can it forgive us for our sins, nor can it assure us that the future will not repeat the past. On the contrary: hope is not likely to accomplish much more in this world than F/faith has done. But, Hope, as Faith's silent other, illuminates Paley's fiction. It resides next to faith, therefore making available to us the possibility of conversation as a constant two-way process of conversion and play—men with women, the young with the old, African Americans with Jews, Catholics with Protestants.

And just as hope resides next to faith and speaks through it, so, too, does G/grace, for which H/hope and F/faith speak. "I thought about our conversation," reports one of Paley's narrators. "Actually, I owed nothing to the lady who'd called. It was possible that I did owe something to my own family and the families of my friends. That is, to tell their stories as simply as possible, in order, you might say, to save a few lives" ("Debts," in *EC*, 10). But then the narrator goes on to tell the story of the lady to whom she owes nothing. Whoever saves a life, the Talmud says, saves the world. Grace Paley does not need to speak in her own individualized voice in order to achieve the moral impact of the personal. By encoding herself ostensibly as Faith and silently as Hope, Paley suggests that such grace as exists, exists in the transformative acts that her fiction produces. For Paley, as for the other romance writers in the Hawthorne tradition, there is no transcendental place for Faith, Hope, and Grace, no world of wholly autonomous, mutually independent capitalized selves. The real has no place separate from the place of the imaginary. There is only the self-reliant self next to itself, which can do no more than enter into a human conversation with other such selves, all of them consenting and affirming and acknowledging—across boundaries, which are constantly set into place and transcended—the human community in which they all reside.

Notes

Introduction

1   Other figures, in the male branch of the family, might include Washington Irving at the beginning of the tradition, Mark Twain later on, and in the twentieth-century such figures as F. Scott Fitzgerald, E. L. Doctorow, Ralph Ellison, and even postcontemporary writers like John Barth, Donald Barthelme, and Thomas Pynchon; female members of the tradition include Gloria Naylor, Gayl Jones, and many other African American women writers, as well as Maxine Hong Kingston and Cynthia Ozick.

2   An active component of the feminist debate has been whether or not men can be brought into the feminist circle as either critics or authors. For example, in a volume entitled *Men in Feminism*, ed. Alice Jardine and Paul Smith (New York: Methuen, 1987), a group of male and female critics raise serious objections to the participation of men in feminist criticism. This important issue raises as well the question Can a male author of fiction write about a woman or, for that matter, a woman writer about a man? can a female critic understand male writing, a male critic female writing? Elaine Showalter's distrust of male representations of the feminine, as in the movie *Tootsie* ("Critical Cross-Dressing: Male Feminist and the Woman of the Year," in ibid., 116–32), may be justified in terms of individual works of art (although I heartily disagree with her reading of the movie); but distrust cannot be allowed to permeate every reading of every text. More recently, feminist critics, gaining strength in the academy, have been more willing to yield some ground to the male critic. Showalter's subsequent collection of essays, *Speaking of Gender* (New York: Routledge, 1989), evidences this important shift.

3   Richard Chase, *The American Novel and Its Tradition* (New York: Doubleday, 1957), 12–13. Chase was building on the work of F. O. Matthiesson (*American Renaissance: Art and Expression in the Age of Emerson and Whitman* [London: Oxford University Press, 1941]); Charles Feidelson, Jr. (*Symbolism and American Literature* [Chicago: University of Chicago Press, 1953]); R. W. B. Lewis (*The American Adam: Innocence, Tragedy, and Tradition in the Nineteenth Century* [Chicago: University of Chicago Press, 1955]); and Lionel Trilling (*The Liberal Imagination: Essays on Literature and Society* [New York: Viking, 1950]); he was responding directly to F. R. Leavis's *Great Tradition* (New York: Anchor, 1954). However we choose to understand the reasons for Chase's description of American writing, the consequences for literary theory and history in the United States has been dramatic. A continuous stream of books published during the heyday of the New Criticism all accentuate the self-conscious self-reflexivity and language orientation of the tradition. See, e.g., Joel Porte, *The Romance in America: Studies in Cooper, Poe, Hawthorne, Melville, and James* (Middletown, Conn.: Weslyan University Press, 1969); Richard Poirier, *A World Elsewhere: The Place of Style in American Literature* (New York: Oxford University Press, 1966); Perry Miller, *The Raven and the Whale: The War of Words and Wits in the Era of Poe and Melville* (New York:

Harcourt, Brace, 1956); Harry Levin, *The Power of Blackness: Hawthorne, Poe, Melville* (London: Faber, 1958); and Maurice Bewley, *The Eccentric Design: Form in the Classic American Novel* (New York: Columbia University Press, 1963). These books were succeeded in the 1970s, 1980s, and 1990s by another series of like-minded works, especially Michael Davitt Bell, *The Development of American Romance: The Sacrifice of Relation* (Chicago: Chicago University Press, 1980); and Evan Carton, *The Rhetoric of American Romance: Dialectic and Identity in Emerson, Dickinson, Poe, and Hawthorne* (Baltimore, Md.: Johns Hopkins University Press, 1985). Also relevant here are Michael Davitt Bell, *Hawthorne and the Historical Romance of New England* (Princeton, N.J.: Princeton University Press, 1971); Richard Brodhead, *Hawthorne, Melville, and the Novel* (Chicago: University of Chicago Press, 1976); Emily Miller Budick, *Fiction and Historical Consciousness: The American Romance Tradition* (New Haven, Conn.: Yale University Press, 1989); Samuel Chase Coale, *In Hawthorne's Shadow: American Romance from Melville to Mailer* (Lexington: University of Kentucky Press, 1985); Edgar Dryden, *The Form of American Romance* (Baltimore, Md.: Johns Hopkins University Press, 1988); Edwin M. Eigner, *The Metaphysical Novel in England and America: Dickens, Bulwer, Melville, and Hawthorne* (Berkeley: University of California Press, 1978); Michael T. Gilmore, *The Middle Way: Puritanism and Ideology in American Romantic Fiction* (New Brunswick, N.J.: Rutgers University Press, 1977); Sam B. Girgus, *The Law of the Heart: Individualism and the Modern Self in American Literature* (Austin: University of Texas Press, 1979); Gordon Hutner, *Secrets and Sympathy: Forms of Disclosure in Hawthorne's Novels* (Athens: University of Georgia Press, 1988); John T. Irwin, *American Hieroglyphics: The Symbol of the Egyptian Hieroglyphics in the American Renaissance* (New Haven, Conn.: Yale University Press, 1980); Harold Peter Simonson, *Radical Discontinuities: American Romanticism and Christian Consciousness* (Rutherford, N.J.: Fairleigh Dickinson University Press, 1983); and, recently, Kenneth Dauber, *The Idea of Authorship in America: Democratic Poetics from Franklin to Melville* (Madison: University of Wisconsin Press, 1990); Michael P. Kramer, *Imagining Language in America: From the Revolution to the Civil War* (Princeton, N.J.: Princeton University Press, 1992); and Richard H. Millington, *Practicing Romance: Narrative Form and Cultural Engagement in Hawthorne's Fiction* (Princeton, N.J.: Princeton University Press, 1990). All of these studies differ in their individual arguments and readings. Indeed, they often define the tradition according to different member texts—Poe, for example, is variously in and out of the canon. Nonetheless, they—and other studies too numerous to list—share enough features to constitute a pattern in American literary criticism. For a recent overview, see George Dekker, "The Genealogy of American Romance," *ESQ: A Journal of the American Renaissance* 35 (1989): 69–83. I myself have discussed many of these issues in "Sacvan Bercovitch, Stanley Cavell, and the Romance Theory of American Fiction," *PMLA* 107 (1992): 78–91.

4   For critics who dispute the fiction-romance distinction, see, e.g., Nina Baym, "Concepts of Romance in Hawthorne's America," *Nineteenth-Century Fiction* 38 (1984): 426–43; and George Dekker, *The American Historical Romance* (Cambridge: Cambridge University Press, 1987).

5   Frederick Crews, "Whose American Renaissance?" *New York Review of Books* (Oct. 27, 1988): 68–81; Crews's review discusses seven recent works of New Americanist criticism: Sacvan

Bercovitch and Myra Jehlen, eds., *Ideology and Classic American Literature* (Cambridge: Cambridge University Press, 1986); Walter Benn Michaels and Donald E. Pease, eds., *The American Renaissance Reconsidered: Selected Papers from the English Institute, 1982–83* (Baltimore, Md.: Johns Hopkins University Press, 1985); Philip Fisher, *Hard Facts: Setting and Form in the American Novel* (New York: Oxford University Press, 1985); Donald E. Pease, *Visionary Compacts: American Renaissance Writings in Cultural Context* (Madison: University of Wisconsin Press, 1987); Jane Tompkins, *Sensational Designs: The Cultural Work of American Fiction, 1790–1860* (New York: Oxford University Press, 1985); David S. Reynolds, *Beneath the American Renaissance: The Subversive Imagination in the Age of Emerson and Melville* (New York: Knopf, 1988); Russell J. Reising, *The Unusable Past: Theory and the Study of American Literature* (New York: Methuen, 1986). One might well add to Crews's list several other forceful works of New Americanist revisionism: Sacvan Bercovitch, "Hawthorne's A-Morality of Compromise," *Representations* 24 (1988): 1–27; Bercovitch, "The A-Politics of Ambiguity in *The Scarlet Letter*," *New Literary History* 19 (1988): 629–54; Bercovitch, *The Office of the Scarlet Letter* (Baltimore: Johns Hopkins University Press, 1991); Bercovitch, "The Problem of Ideology in American Literary History," *Critical Inquiry* 12 (1986): 631–53; and Bercovitch, ed., *Reconstructing American Literary History* (Cambridge: Harvard University Press, 1986); Richard Brodhead, *The School of Hawthorne* (New York: Oxford University Press, 1986); Sharon Cameron, *The Corporeal Self: Allegories of the Body in Melville and Hawthorne* (Baltimore, Md.: Johns Hopkins University Press, 1981); Robert Clark, *History and Myth in American Fiction, 1823–52* (New York: St. Martin's Press, 1984); Dekker, *American Historical Romance*; Michael T. Gilmore, *American Romanticism and the Marketplace* (Chicago: Chicago University Press, 1985); Myra Jehlen, *American Incarnation: The Individual, the Nation, and the Continent* (Cambridge: Harvard University Press, 1986); Annette Kolodny, *The Lay of the Land: Metaphor as Experience in American Life and Letters* (Chapel Hill: University of North Carolina Press, 1975); Robert S. Levine, *Conspiracy and Romance: Studies in Brockden Brown, Cooper, Hawthorne, and Melville* (Cambridge: Cambridge University Press, 1989); John McWilliams, *Hawthorne, Melville, and the American Character: A Looking-Glass Business* (Cambridge: Cambridge University Press, 1984); Larry J. Reynolds, *European Revolutions and the American Literary Renaissance* (New Haven, Conn.: Yale University Press, 1988); Fred G. See, *Desire and the Sign: Nineteenth-Century American Fiction* (Baton Rouge: Louisiana State University Press, 1987); and Robert Weisbuch, *Atlantic Double-Cross: American Literature and British Influence in the Age of Emerson* (Chicago: Chicago University Press, 1986). Joining in the argument with romance theorists and including responses to Crews's essay is a recent volume of *Boundary 2*, 17 (1990), edited by Donald Pease, which contains two pertinent essays: Pease, "New Americanists: Revisionist Interventions into the Canon," 1–37; and John P. McWilliams, "The Rationale for 'The American Romance,'" 71–82. According to Pease, "The animus informing [Crews's review] can be reduced to a single complaint: the New Americanists have returned ideology to a field previously organized by an end to ideology consensus" (2).

6   For critics who tend toward implicating the text, see Jonathan Arac, "The Politics of *The Scarlet Letter*," and Myra Jehlen, "The Novel and the Middle Class in America," both in *Ideology and Classic American Literature*, ed. Bercovitch and Jehlen, 125–66.

7   Bercovitch, "Problem of Ideology," 635. Bercovitch's definition is shared by several New Americanists, including, for example, Donald Pease in *Visionary Compacts*.

8   Bercovitch, "A-Politics of Ambiguity," 629, 650. For like-minded readings, see Pease, *Visionary Compacts*, esp. 81–107; Larry J. Reynolds, *European Revolutions and the American Literary Renaissance* (New Haven, Conn.: Yale University Press, 1988); Leland S. Person, Jr., "Hester's Revenge: The Power of Silence in *The Scarlet Letter*," *Nineteenth-Century Literature* 43 (1989): 465–83.

9   Fish discusses this concept in *Is There a Text in This Class? The Authority of Interpretive Communities* (Cambridge: Harvard University Press, 1980).

10 Budick, *Fiction and Historical Consciousness*, ix–x, 79–84, 119–21.

11 Millicent Bell, "The Obliquity of Signs: *The Scarlet Letter*," in *Critical Essays on Hawthorne's The Scarlet Letter*, ed. David B. Kesterton (Boston: G. K. Hall, 1988), 157–69. See also Steven C. Scheer, *Pious Impostures and Unproven Words: The Romance of Deconstruction in Nineteenth-Century America* (Lanham, Md.: University Press of America, 1990).

12 I shall discuss the following of Stanley Cavell's works: *Conditions Handsome and Unhandsome: The Constitution of Emersonian Perfectionism* (Chicago: University of Chicago Press, 1990), esp. the opening essay, "Aversive Thinking," and the essay reprinted in the appendix, entitled "Hope Against Hope"—originally printed in the *American Poetry Review* (January–February 1986): 9–13; *In Quest of the Ordinary: Lines of Skepticism and Romanticism* (Chicago: University of Chicago Press, 1988), esp. the essay entitled "Being Odd, Getting Even (*Descartes, Emerson, Poe*)," 105–49, which originally appeared in *Reconstructing Individualism: Autonomy, Individuality, and the Self in Western Thought*, ed. T. C. Heller, M. Sosna, and D. E. Wellbery (Stanford, Calif.: Stanford University Press, 1986), 278–312; and *The Senses of Walden* (New York: Viking Press, 1972). Also relevant are *This New yet Unapproachable America: Lectures After Emerson After Wittgenstein* (Albuquerque, N.Mex.: Living Batch Press, 1989); and *The Claim of Reason: Wittgenstein, Skepticism, Morality and Tragedy* (Oxford: Claredon Press, 1979).

13 Cavell, *Senses of Walden*, 33–34, 64.

14 Cavell, "Being Odd, Getting Even," 135; Cavell, *Senses of Walden*, 33. I have discussed this issue to some extent in *Fiction and Historical Consciousness*, 119–21.

15 Cavell, "Hope Against Hope," 138.

16 Cavell, *Senses of Walden*, 62–63.

17 Nathaniel Hawthorne, *The Scarlet Letter*, in *The Centenary Edition of the Works of Nathaniel Hawthorne*, vol. 1, ed. William Charvat et al. (Columbus: Ohio State University Press, 1962), 263, 274; hereafter cited in the text.

18 See my "Sacvan Bercovitch, Stanley Cavell" for a fuller reading of *The Scarlet Letter* along these lines.

Chapter 1
The Romance of the Family: Hawthorne

1   Nathaniel Hawthorne, *The Scarlet Letter*, in *The Centenary Edition of the Works of Nathaniel Hawthorne*, vol. 1, ed. William Charvat et al. (Columbus: Ohio State University Press, 1962), 56; hereafter cited in the text. That Hester is referred to in the criticism by her first

name (Dimmesdale and Chillingworth by their patrinomials) is a holdover from sexist prac-
tices. Nonetheless, in a book also about tradition I have maintained the convention. By any
name, Hester is the power in this novel.

2   For feminist critiques of the novel see in particular Louise Desalvo, *Nathaniel Hawthorne*
(Brighton, Eng.: Harvester Press, 1987), 24–38, which summarizes the salient criticism for
and against the novel; and David Leverenz's two chapters on Hawthorne in his *Manhood and
the American Renaissance* (Ithaca, N.Y.: Cornell University Press, 1989), 227–78. The second
of these chapters, "Mrs. Hawthorne's Headache: Reading *The Scarlet Letter*," was originally
published in *The (M)other Tongue: Essays in Feminist Psychoanalytic Interpretation*, ed. Shirley
Nelson Garner, Claire Kahane, Madelon Springnether (Ithaca, N.Y.: Cornell University
Press, 1985), 194–216. Leverenz sees the novel as compromised feminism: it begins with a
strong feminist assertion, only to have that assertion defeated by the various male characters
and by Hawthorne himself ("A narrative that begins by challenging patriarchal punishment
ends by accepting punishment as a prelude to kindness"—270). Amy Shrager Lang comes
to similar conclusions in *Prophetic Woman: Anne Hutchinson and the Problem of Dissent in the
Literature of New England* (Berkeley: University of California Press, 1987), as does Jean Fagin
Yellin in *Women and Sisters: The Antislavery Feminists in American Culture* (New Haven,
Conn.: Yale University Press, 1990), 125–50. Other studies that take on the issue of the
novel's lack of feminism include Judith Fryer, *The Faces of Eve: Women in the Nineteenth-Cen-
tury American Novel* (New York: Oxford University Press, 1976); and Neal F. Doubleday,
"Hawthorne's Hester and Feminism," *PMLA* 54 (1939): 825–28. Nina Baym defends the
book on feminist grounds in several essays: "Thwarted Nature: Nathaniel Hawthorne as
Feminist," in *American Novelists Revisited: Essays in Feminist Criticism*, ed. Fritz Fleishmann
(Boston: G. K. Hall, 1982); "The Romantic *Malgré Lui*: Hawthorne in the Custom House,"
ESQ: A Journal of the American Renaissance 19 (1973): 14–25; and "Hawthorne's Women:
The Tyranny of Social Myths," *Centennial Review* 15 (1971): 250–71. Some of Baym's ideas
are also contained in her book-length study of Hawthorne, *The Shape of Hawthorne's Career*
(Ithaca, N.Y.: Cornell University Press, 1976). See also Leland S. Person, Jr., *Aesthetic
Headaches: Women and a Masculine Poetics in Poe, Melville, and Hawthorne* (Athens: University
of Georgia Press, 1988), 94–176; Cynthia S. Jordan, *Second Stories: The Politics of Language,
Form, and Gender in Early American Fictions* (Chapel Hill: University of North Carolina Press,
1989); and Joel Pfister, *The Production of Personal Life: Class, Gender, and the Psychological in
Hawthorne's Fiction* (Stanford, Calif.: Stanford University Press, 1991). David Stouck, "The
Surveyor of the Custom-House: A Narrator for *The Scarlet Letter*," *Centennial Review*" 15
(1971): 309–29, sees all the characters, including Hester, as aspects of the author's con-
sciousness, as does Charles Feidelson, Jr., in his *Symbolism and American Literature* (Chicago:
Chicago University Press, 1953), 10. Fruitful considerations of gender-construct and the
anxiety it engenders are T. Walter Herbert, "Nathaniel Hawthorne, Una Hawthorne, and *The
Scarlet Letter*: Interactive Selfhoods and the Cultural Construction of Gender," *PMLA* 103
(1988): 285–97; and Evan Carton, "'A Daughter of the Puritans' and Her Old Master:
Hawthorne, Una, and the Sexuality of Romance," in *Daughters and Fathers*, ed. Lynda E.
Boose and Betty S. Flowers (Baltimore, Md.: Johns Hopkins University Press, 1989),
208–32. On the strength and psychological astuteness of Hawthorne's depiction of the

mother-daughter relationship, see Lois A. Cuddy, "Mother-Daughter Identification in *The Scarlet Letter*," *Mosaic* 19 (1986): 101–15; and on the power of his portrait of the mother and woman, see Nina Baym, "Nathaniel Hawthorne and His Mother: A Biographical Speculation," *American Literature* 54 (1982): 1–27. In a recent essay that develops the quasi-feminist lines of the earlier "Footsteps of Ann Hutchinson: The Context of *The Scarlet Letter*," *ELH* 39 (1972): 459–94, Michael J. Colacurcio has demonstrated how the novel powerfully and explicitly responds to the hypocrisy of the Puritans' sexual views of women—"'The Woman's Own Choice': Sex, Metaphor, and the Puritan 'Sources' of *The Scarlet Letter*," in *New Essays on the Scarlet Letter*, ed. Colacurcio (Cambridge: Cambridge University Press, 1985), 101–35.

3   Mary O'Brien, *The Politics of Reproduction* (Boston: Routledge and Kegan Paul, 1983). See also Stanley Cavell, *Disowning Knowledge in Six Plays of Shakespeare* (Cambridge: Cambridge University Press, 1987), 15–19, 193–221; Mieke Bal, *Death and Dissymmetry: The Politics of Coherence in the Book of Judges* (Chicago: University of Chicago Press, 1988); and Lynda E. Boose, "The Father's House and the Daughter in It: The Structures of Western Culture's Daughter-Father Relationship," in *Daughters and Fathers*, ed. Boose and Flowers, 19–74.

4   Marianne Hirsch, *The Mother/Daughter Plot: Narrative, Psychoanalysis, Feminism* (Bloomington: Indiana University Press, 1989), 45. Hirsch is here quoting from Margaret Homans, *Bearing the Word: Language and Female Experience in Nineteenth-Century Women's Writing* (Chicago: University of Chicago Press, 1986). See also Christine van Boheemen, *The Novel as Family Romance: Language, Gender, and Authority from Fielding to Joyce* (Ithaca, N.Y.: Cornell University Press, 1987).

5   Three books that mount arguments concerning female otherness are Person, *Aesthetic Headaches*; Jordan, *Second Stories*; and Leverenz, *Manhood and the American Renaissance*. Leland Person, Jr., writes that the masculine poetics of Poe, Hawthorne, and Melville "reflect a tension between identification with women whose creative energy resists easy formalization and the containment of such women in artistic forms that subject creative energy to the artist's control—often to the detriment of the work as a whole." Person continues, contra Nina Baym, that "none of these three writers was very interested in examining the social and political status of women. Each writer was interested in gender and gender-related issues, but more from a psychological than from a social or political point of view" (2–5). Cynthia Jordan explores the concern in early American literature with "the patriarchal politics of language in America. . . . Franklin, Brackenridge, and Brown . . . believed with varying degrees of optimism that language could be used to maintain a patriarchal social order in the new nation. The narrative fictions they wrote to promote such a belief, however, are curiously doubled: their promotional surface narratives are constantly threatened by evidence of opposing views, and that evidence constitutes a rival second story which the authors try to suppress or defuse but which they find increasingly difficult to hold in check. In the romance period that followed, Cooper, Poe, Hawthorne, and Melville repeatedly criticized the patriarchal linguistic politics that tried to silence other views—'otherness' itself—in American culture, and their own experiments with narrative form reflect their attempts to unmask the fraud perpetrated by their cultural father: and to recover the long second story" (x).

David Leverenz's book differs from those of Person and Jordan in being more suspicious of the male writers. Concerned equally with the male and female constructs of gender in the nineteenth century (vis-à-vis each other) Leverenz suggests about the male-authored texts that the "American Renaissance writers did not liberate their voices from their class background and 'polite' English models until they began to struggle with, rather than dismiss, the middle-class ideology of manhood taking hold in American public life. They made a potentially hostile or indifferent audience, men preoccupied with competing for money and property, part of their rhetorical strategies" (15).

6   Leverenz, *Manhood and the American Renaissance*.

7   This is discussed in Desalvo, *Nathaniel Hawthorne*, 66; and Gloria C. Erlich, *Family Themes and Hawthorne's Fiction: The Tenacious Web* (New Brunswick, N.J.: Rutgers University Press, 1984), 26–27.

8   See Desalvo, *Nathaniel Hawthorne*, 58; and Erlich, *Family Themes and Hawthorne's Fiction*, 29. The most extensive treatment of the novel in relation to Hawthorne's mother is Baym's "Nathaniel Hawthorne and His Mother," in which Hawthorne's novel is read as a positive picture of the woman—which is how I read it, too.

9   Baym has discussed this sterility and its relation to the problem of authority and authorship in "Romantic *Malgré Lui*."

10   Cynthia Jordan develops the pun of the second story in *Second Stories*.

11   The root meaning of *purloin* is not "to steal" but "to put away" or "to render ineffectual."

12   On Poe's relation to the feminine in writing, see Person, *Aesthetic Headaches*, 19–47; and Jordan, *Second Stories*. For a lengthy debate over Poe's story and the philosophy of deconstruction, see John P. Muller and William J. Richardson, eds., *The Purloined Poe: Lacan, Derrida, and Psychoanalytic Reading*, (Baltimore, Md.: Johns Hopkins University Press, 1988); and Gregory S. Jay, *America the Scrivener: Deconstruction and the Subject of Literary History* (Ithaca, N.Y.: Cornell University Press, 1990), 170–204.

13   The critics who touch on this issue include T. Walter Herbert, in "Nathaniel Hawthorne, Una Hawthorne, and *The Scarlet Letter*"; Evan Carton, in "'Daughter of the Puritans'"; Nina Baym, in "Romantic *Malgré Lui*"; James D. Wallace, in "Hawthorne and the Scribbling Women Reconsidered," *American Literature* 62 (1990): 201–22; Leland S. Person, in *Aesthetic Headaches*, 94–145;, David Leverenz, in "Mrs. Hawthorne's Headache"; and Gloria Erlich, in *Family Themes and Hawthorne's Fiction*.

14   *The Standard Edition of the Complete Psychological Works of Sigmund Freud*, 24 vols., ed. James Strachey (London: Horgarth Press, 1953), 9:239.

15   Van Boheemen, *Novel as Family Romance*, 7, 33.

16   Hirsch, *Mother/Daughter Plot*, 56.

17   Ibid., 45. Hirsch also discusses Sandra M. Gilbert and Susan Gubar, *The Madwoman in the Attic: The Woman Writer and the Nineteenth-Century Literary Imagination* (New Haven, Conn.: Yale University Press, 1979).

18   Writes Mellard: "Pearl's development toward psychological maturity is . . . a paradigm case of the passage from infancy . . . through the steps of the mirror stage. She is at the *infans* stage when she is first seen, on the scaffold of the pillory with Hester at the novel's beginning; there, her response is directed totally by visual and auditory stimuli. Then she is

shown in the early chapters going through the first step of the mirror passage, where she finds images of identification and antagonism. Finally, in the last chapters, she is shown taking the climactic step of the mirror passage; this step takes her through recognition of the loss of the phallic symbol, through acceptance of symbolic castration, and at last through submission to the identity and authority of the father." "Pearl and Hester: A Lacanian Reading," in *Critical Essays on Hawthorne's* The Scarlet Letter, ed. David B. Kesteron (Boston: G. K. Hall, 1988), 197–98. This whole development proceeds under the sign of *A,* corresponding to Lacan's idea of psychic process as linguistically arranged. See also John T. Irwin, *American Hieroglyphics: The Symbol of the Egyptian Hieroglyphics in the American Renaissance* (New Haven, Conn.: Yale University Press, 1980), 239–59.

19   Beth Sharon Ash, "Frail Vessels and Vast Designs: A Psychoanalytic Portrait of Isabel Archer," in *New Essays on* The Portrait of a Lady, ed. Joel Porte (Cambridge: Cambridge University Press, 1990), 123–62. Hawthorne's *French Notebooks* contain a fascinating note that connects Una Hawthorne with James's Daisy Miller: "Una has taken what seems to be the Roman fever by sitting down to sketch in the Coliseum. It is not a severe attack, yet attended with fits of exceeding discomfort . . . . making the poor child talk in rhythmical measure, like a tragic heroine." *The French and Italian Notebooks,* in *The Centenary Edition of the Works of Nathaniel Hawthorne,* vol. 14, ed. Thomas Woodson (Columbus: Ohio State University Press, 1980), 495. Because Isabel is in many ways a version of Daisy, we might take this note as confirmation that there is a straight line connecting Hawthorne's protagonists and James's.

20   Alfred Habegger discusses the marriage of the woman to a father figure in relation to James's *Portrait* in *Henry James and the "Woman Business"* (Cambridge: Cambridge University Press, 1989), 150–81.

21   For a related reading of Hester's relationship to Pearl, see Michael Ragussis, "Family Discourse and Fiction in *The Scarlet Letter,*" *ELH* 49 (1982): 863–88.

22   Homans, *Bearing the Word,* 85.

23   Sandra M. Gilbert and Susan Gubar, *No Man's Land: The Place of the Woman Writer in the Twentieth Century,* vol. 1: *The War of the Words* (New Haven, Conn.: Yale University Press, 1988), 265–66. See Nancy Chodorow, *The Reproduction of Mothering: Psychoanalysis and the Sociology of Gender* (Berkeley: University of California Press, 1978), 92–129. According to Chodorow, in the case of both sons and daughters, "a mother is likely to experience a sense of oneness and continuity with her infant. However, this sense is stronger, and lasts longer, vis-à-vis daughters. Primary identification and symbiosis with daughters tend to be stronger and cathexis of daughters to be based on experiencing a daughter as an extension or double of a mother herself, with cathexis of the daughter as a sexual other usually remaining a weaker, less significant theme." "Because they are the same gender as their daughters and have been girls, mothers of daughters tend not to experience these infant daughters as separate from them in the same way as do mothers of infant sons" (109; see also 133). This bonding between mother and daughter, which makes separation so painful for both of them, is strengthened, according to Chodorow, by child-rearing habits that make the mother the primary caregiver—an idea poignantly developed in Hawthorne's novel.

24   In *The Reproduction of Mothering,* Chodorow alludes to female fantasies of parthenogenic

reproduction and discusses women's desires for maternity without marriage and sexuality (201–5). I will have more to say about this subject in my discussion of *The Portrait of a Lady*, in Chapter 2.

25   For a discussion of the possible, perhaps biologically determined asymmetry between male and female skepticism, having to do with their different relations to the question of parental knowledge, see Stanley Cavell, *Disowning Knowledge in Six Plays of Shakespeare* (Cambridge: Cambridge University Press, 1987), 15–19, 193–221; the "Recounting Gains" essay is reprinted as "Recounting Gains, Showing Losses (A Reading of *The Winter's Tale*)" in Cavell, *In Quest of the Ordinary: Lines of Skepticism and Romanticism* (Chicago: University of Chicago Press, 1988), 76–101. Cavell's ideas bear an interesting affinity to ideas expressed by Mieke Bal in her readings of biblical narratives in *Death and Dissymmetry* and to Lynda Boose's in "Father's House."

26   Some critics have even cast Hester's Pearl as Hawthorne's Una, intensifying our sense of Hawthorne's identification with his female hero, as if Hawthorne were struggling with the feminine-maternal-artistic within. See, again, Herbert's very fine "Nathaniel Hawthorne, Una Hawthorne, and *The Scarlet Letter*" and Carton's " 'Daughter of the Puritans.' "

27   This moment in the text may account for the image of the fierce female eagle, "a shield before her breast" (5), in "The Custom-House" sketch, which has yielded some feminist protest. Desalvo, *Nathaniel Hawthorne*, 59–60. The image of Hester's breastplate in the governor's breastplate does not, however, suggest that women are intrinsically demonic. It reflects, on the one hand, the way women are dominated by male images. On the other hand, it reveals how Hester has yielded herself to male domination.

28   "Rappaccini's Daughter" is another story about a female child who is created in the image of a single parent. In this case, the parent is male, as in the original biblical event. He is also a kind of god, although he embodies a principle of evil rather than good, and he outdoes the Christian God by at least seeming not to require the body of a woman, as if Beatrice were one more flower in his garden. By the end of the story, the male protagonist (Giovanni) has also been fashioned in the image of this father. In contradistinction to the original scriptural tale, however, this Adam takes his paternal nature through the woman. The male (as opposed to the female) yields to the Baglioni's (the serpent's) counsel and tempts the woman to partake of the forbidden drink (apple). The two of them thereby bring death into the Eden of this modern world, a death that is, however, unrelieved by any of the promises made to the first Adam and Eve in the first garden. Beatrice dies; and there is no saving union, which can bring history in the form of children into the world. In Milton's *Paradise Lost*, Eve suggests to Adam that they kill themselves in order to prevent the generations of misery that are destined to follow them. But Adam resists Eve's suggestion; having children, he insists, will eventually lead to redemption.

29   Cavell, "Being Odd, Getting Even," 129, 124.

30   Ibid., 129.

31   Leslie Feidler discusses the homosexual aspects of Dimmesdale and Chillingworth's relationship in *Love and Death in the American Novel* (New York: Dell, 1966), 227–28.

32   We might feel, especially in light of David Leverenz's sensitive discussion in "Mrs. Hawthorne's Headache," that Ernest Sandeen has overstated the case when he suggests that

Hawthorne's emotional response to reading the story to his wife reveals "the intimate rap-
port of the hour, the unspoken understanding between husband and wife that they were
sharing a love story offered as a tribute of praise and thanksgiving to their own love and to
their marriage." Nonetheless, for Hawthorne the relationship of husband and wife and the
procreative future that it ensures are crucial. See Sandeen, "*The Scarlet Letter* as a Love Story,"
PMLA 77 (1962): 425–35, quotation on 435. Sandeen continues: with Dimmesdale's kiss
"the illegitimate child has been made legitimate, an illicit passion has been converted into a
marriage . . . Pearl is brought into the human family by Arthur's act of public confession, so
Roger Chillingworth is morally excluded. . . . His last will and testament . . . suggests his
tacit admission that Dimmesdale in his last hour successfully usurped the role of father and
husband" (433). Only a year later, in *The House of the Seven Gables,* Hawthorne rewrites the
story of his Puritan ancestors with the appropriately happy ending. (He repeats this in the
conclusion to *The Marble Faun.*) The Custom-House of the Seven Gables has been redo-
mesticated, made a home, by female magic; see my discussion of this in *Fiction and Historical Consciousness: The American Romance Tradition* (New Haven, Conn.: Yale University Press,
1989), 119–42.

33   Peggy Kamuf, "Hawthorne's Genres: The Letter of the Law *Appliquée,*" in *After Strange Texts:
The Role of Theory in the Study of Literature,* ed. Gregory S. Jay and David L. Miller
(Tuscaloosa: University of Alabama Press, 1985), 83–84.

34   On Hawthorne's adding the *w* to his name, see Irwin, *American Hieroglyphics,* 276.

Chapter 2
A Portrait of Female Skepticism: James

1   On various connections between the conclusions to Hawthorne's and James's novels, see
Robert Weisbuch, *Atlantic Double-Cross: American Literature and British Influence in the Age of
Emerson* (Chicago: University of Chicago Press, 1986), 275–95; and Elissa Greenwald, *Realism and the Romance: Nathaniel Hawthorne, Henry James, and American Fiction* (Ann Arbor,
Mich.: UMI Research Publications, 1989), esp. 58–77. Both Weisbuch and Greenwald read
Isabel's return as signifying her affirmation of her identity (Weisbuch, 290), as "taking up
the burden of suffering, with which she can cross the doorway to experience" (Greenwald,
77). For a different reading, an argument that Isabel's return represents her capitulation to
her fears of freedom, power, and sexuality, see Carren Kaston, *Imagination and Desire in the
Novels of Henry James* (New Brunswick, N.J.: Rutgers University Press, 1984), 41–54. On
the connections between the *Letter* and the *Portrait,* see Weisbuch, *Atlantic Double-Cross;*
Greenwald, *Realism and Romance;* John Carlos Rowe, *The Theoretical Dimensions of Henry
James* (Madison: University of Wisconsin Press, 1984), esp. 29–57; and Laurence Holland,
The Expense of Vision (Princeton, N.J.: Princeton University Press, 1964), 20–27. Rowe summarizes previous discussions of the Hawthorne-James relationship on pp. 35–47. These are
only the most recent in a line of critics (including James himself) who have seen James in
the line of Hawthorne and Emerson. Richard Chase, for example, early on saw *The Portrait
of a Lady* as a "novel" in direct relation to the romance tradition from which it evolved:
"Part of James's great program for improving the novel consisted of the reconstitution, on

new grounds, of romance." Specifically, the *Portrait* is a "romance of the self." *The American Novel and Its Tradition* (Garden City, N.Y.: Doubleday, 1957), 117, 119, 131–32. Compare Rowe: "James . . . works to realize what is the undeniable goal of Hester's education and Hawthorne's romanticism: not just the secularization of Puritanism but also the historicization of idealism, which is an effective definition of James's realism. Pearl's ultimate voyage to Europe, and marriage into European aristocracy is Hawthorne's American telos: the discovery of a relation to the old world." *Theoretical Dimensions,* 34. Like several important literary critics from the 1950s on, Chase also reads James within a decidedly Emersonian context— the same context that is so richly developed by such eminent Americanists as Quentin Anderson in *The American Henry James* (New Brunswick, N.J.: Rutgers University Press, 1957) and that is verified and further enhanced by such non-Americanist perspectives as Dorothea Krook's, in *The Ordeal of Consciousness in Henry James* (Cambridge: Cambridge University Press, 1967). Among the other many distinguished studies of this kind are Leon Edel's biography of James, *Henry James,* 5 vols. (New York: Avon Books, 1972); Tony Tanner's "The Fearful Self," reprinted in *Henry James's* Washington Square *and* The Portrait of a Lady: *A Casebook,* ed. Alan Shelston (London: Macmillan, 1984), 162–79; Donald L. Mull's *Henry James's Sublime Economy: Money as Symbolic Center in the Fiction* (Middletown, Conn.: Wesleyan University Press, 1973). For a more recent Emersonian reading that takes account of gender issues, see Sharon Deykin Baris, "The Lady or the Scholar? 'Contending Lights' in James's Portrait of Isabel Archer," *HSLA* 18 (1990): 48–80; and Baris, "James's Pyrotechnic Display: The Book in Isabel's Portrait," *Henry James Review* 12 (1991): 146–53. Most recently, and utilizing more contemporary perspectives on literature, James's "ordeal of consciousness" has been taken up by Sharon Cameron in *Thinking in Henry James* (Chicago: University of Chicago Press, 1989)—her discussion of the *Portrait* is on pp. 53–63.

2 Henry James, *The Portrait of a Lady* (New York: Riverside, 1963), 206, 342; hereafter cited in the text.

3 See, e.g., Alfred Habegger, *Henry James and the "Woman Business"* (Cambridge: Cambridge University Press, 1989); Carolyn Porter, "Gender and Value in *The American,*" in *New Essays on* The American, ed. Martha Banta (New York: Cambridge University Press, 1987), 99–129; Beth Sharon Ash, "Frail Vessels and Vast Designs: A Psychoanalytic Portrait of Isabel Archer," in *New Essays on* The Portrait of a Lady, ed. Joel Porte (Cambridge: Cambridge University Press, 1990), 123–62; and Stephanie A. Smith, "The Delicate Organisms and Theoretic Tricks of Henry James," *American Literature* 62 (1990): 583–605.

4 Cameron, *Thinking in Henry James,* 56–59. In "Delicate Organisms," Stephanie A. Smith discusses the relationship between Isabel and Pansy on the one hand and between Isabel and Madame Merle on the other in terms of a motif of the mother-daughter relationship under the pressures placed on it by patriarchal culture. Although Smith's understanding of James's novel and her reasons for exploring the mother-daughter relationship are different from my own, some of her insights (especially into the way Isabel functions as Pansy's virgin mother) coincide with my own.

5 John Carlos Rowe attributes James's ability to represent women to his identification with their powerlessness. *Theoretical Dimensions of Henry James,* 91.

6   This portrait of Isabel as the Madonna has been extensively discussed in Baris, "Lady or the Scholar?" See also Baris, "Gender, Judgment, and Presumptuous Readers: The Role of Daniel in *The Portrait of a Lady,*" *Henry James Review* 12 (1991): 212–30.

7   Nancy Chodorow discusses female fantasies of asexual reproduction in *The Reproduction of Mothering: Psychoanalysis and the Sociology of Gender* (Berkeley: University of California Press, 1978), 201–5. I will discuss some related texts by women, such as Ellen Glasgow's *Barren Ground,* in Chapters 6 and 7. Writes Leon Edel: "Isabel and Osmond are, . . . for all their differences, two sides of the same coin, two studies in egotism—and a kind of egotism which belonged to their author." Again, "Isabel and Osmond had been attracted to one another because each saw in the other a mirror-image of self." "Two Studies in Egotism," in *Henry James,* ed. Shelston, 136. Similar ideas are developed in Tanner, "Fearful Self."

8   See, e.g., Habegger, *Henry James and the "Woman Question."* See also Nina Baym's carefully wrought exposition of James's revisions of the novel between 1881 and 1908, which moved the novel from a more to a less obvious connection with the women's tradition. Baym, "Revision and Thematic Change in *The Portrait of a Lady,*" in *Henry James,* ed. Shelston, 184–202. And see Habegger's own earlier study, *Gender, Fantasy and Realism in American Literature* (New York: Columbia University Press, 1982), 66–79. Another source, William Veeder's *Henry James — the Lessons of the Master: Popular Fiction and Personal Style in the Nineteenth Century* (Chicago: University of Chicago Press, 1975), has less to do with thematic than with stylistic continuities between James and nineteenth-century novels by women.

9   Following through on certain ideas first articulated in *Pursuits of Happiness: The Hollywood Comedy of Remarriage"* (Cambridge: Harvard University Press, 1981), Stanley Cavell has discussed the relationship between the parent and the daughter's desire in "Ugly Duckling, Funny Butterfly: Bette Davis and *Now, Voyager,*" *Critical Inquiry* 16 (1990): 213–47.

10   On the ways in which the novel deals with issues of sexuality, see Robert White, "Love, Marriage, and Divorce: The Matter of Sexuality in *The Portrait of a Lady,*" *Henry James Review* 7 (1986): 59–71. See also Annette Niemtzow, "Marriage and the New Woman in *The Portrait of a Lady,*" *American Literature* 47 (1975): 377–95.

11   Whether or not Isabel's psychological condition can be traced to the absent mother—I find Beth Sharon Ash's argument persuasive that it can—Isabel is, as Ash asserts, unable to warrant and therefore act on her own desire. She surrenders herself to Osmond, the idealized father-tyrant, not to the potential lover, Goodwood. See Ash, "Frail Vessels and Vast Designs."

12   Denis Donahue argues that the idea that "life is better, for in life there's love" gives the novel its "depth and reverberation": "Isabel's renunciation is her vision of responsibility, to herself and others." "Isabel's 'Yes' to Life," in *Henry James,* ed. Shelston, 182.

Chapter Three
Worlds Without Women: Melville and Poe

1   Henry James, *The Portrait of a Lady* (New York: Riverside, 1963), 458. See William Faulkner, *The Sound and the Fury,* ed. David Minter (New York: Norton, 1987), 91–95; Nathaniel

Hawthorne, *The Scarlet Letter*, in *The Centenary Edition of the Works of Nathaniel Hawthorne*, vol. 1, ed. William Charvat et al., (Columbus: Ohio State University Press, 1962), 166.

2   Judith Fetterley, *The Resisting Reader: A Feminist Approach to American Fiction* (Bloomington: Indiana University Press, 1978); and Mimi Reisel Gladstein, *The Indestructible Woman in Faulkner, Hemingway, and Steinbeck* (Ann Arbor, Mich.: UMI Research Press, 1986).

3   Elizabeth Ammons, "Cool Diana and the Blood-Red Muse: Edith Wharton on Innocence and Art," in *American Novelists Revisited: Essays in Feminist Criticism,* ed. Fritz Fleischman (Boston: G. K. Hall, 1982), 209–24. See also Diana Trilling, "*The House of Mirth* Revisited," in *Edith Wharton: A Collection of Critical Essays,* ed. Irving Howe (Englewood Cliffs, N.J.: Prentice-Hall, 1962), 103–18; and Judith Fetterley, "'The Temptation to Be a Beautiful Object': Double Standard and Double Bind in *The House of Mirth,*" in *Fiction by American Women: Recent Views,* ed. Winifred Farrant Bevilacqua (Port Washington, N.Y.: Associated Faculty Publications, 1983), 41–50. Fetterley focuses on Lily Bart's victimization in a society defined by patriarchal values that cause the woman to destroy herself: "The ultimate expression of the double standard as double bind lies in the fact that Lily can survive only at the cost of those qualities for which she is valued: or, to put the point in its legitimately tautological form, Lily can be what she is supposed to be only at the cost of being what she is supposed to be" (49).

4   Judi M. Roller, *The Politics of the Feminist Novel* (New York: Greenwood Press, 1986).

5   Alfred Habegger, *Henry James and the "Woman Business"* (Cambridge: Cambridge University Press, 1989). Also see Nina Baym, "Revision and Thematic Change in *The Portrait of a Lady,*" in *Henry James's* Washington Square *and* The Portrait of a Lady: *A Casebook,* ed. Alan Shelston (London: Macmillan, 1984), 184–201; and Habegger, *Gender, Fantasy and Realism in American Literature* (New York: Columbia University Press, 1982), 66–79. If Sandra M. Gilbert and Susan Gubar are correct in their analysis of Victorianism as a moment when gender conflict and redefinition were at some kind of peak, then it is difficult to imagine that an intellectually perceptive and responsive writer like James could have avoided the subject. Gilbert and Gubar, *No Man's Land: The Place of the Woman Writer in the Twentieth Century,* vol 1: *The War of the Words* and vol 2: *Sexchanges* (New Haven, Conn.: Yale University Press, 1988 and 1989). Mark Seltzer's *Henry James and the Art of Power* (Ithaca, N.Y.: Cornell University Press, 1984) provides powerful readings of several James novels in terms of how, in the guise of resisting political power, they reinscribe it through art.

6   Habegger, *Henry James and the "Woman Business,"* 4–8 (on "orphan-heroine"), 154–56 (on agonist premise), 230 (on female imagination). *Agonist* is Habegger's word for the female authors of the nineteenth century, who agonize over the woman's situation.

7   Carolyn Porter, for example, in an essay on *The American,* suggests that although in the *Portrait* James solves certain structural and conceptual problems presented by *The American*— such as the need for a feminized Newman or the bind created in the novel when Claire is placed outside the marketplace economy only to make her availability to Newman dependent on economic dynamics—"he frees [the woman] as subject from the commodity status she possesses as object only to become, in effect, *his* subject. His aim is to redeem value, the value conventionally inscribed in woman, from a world in which it has been threatened by commodification, but James's means of saving the value markedly resembles the behavior of

a patriarchal father who uses his authority both to protect and to control his daughter." Porter, "Gender and Value in *The American*," in *New Essays on* The American, ed. Martha Banta (New York: Cambridge University Press, 1987), 125–26. See also Martha Banta, *Imaging American Women: Idea and Ideals in Cultural History* (New York: Columbia University Press, 1987). Porter's argument has found further support recently in Stephanie Smith, "The Delicate Organisms and Theoretic Tricks of Henry James," *American Literature* 62 (1990): 583–605. In Smith's reading, the male author plays havoc with the range of his female characters, deepening the inscription of the woman into a male-ordered world. Related to both Porter's and Smith's readings is John Carlos Rowe's argument that "James's uncanny ability to represent the complex psychologies of women in the late nineteenth and early twentieth centuries is in part attributable to his identification with their marginal and powerless situations." But "James, the Master, uses feminism, uses the 'other sex' as part of his own literary power for the sake of engendering his own identity as Author." Rowe, *The Theoretical Dimensions of Henry James* (Madison: University of Wisconsin Press, 1984), 90–91. In the chapter entitled "Feminist Issues: Women, Power, and Rebellion" Rowe presents many interesting arguments concerning James's "feminism," especially on the anxiety of influence and its accompanying gender anxieties, which James experienced in relation to nineteenth-century women writers. Porter's, Smith's, and Rowe's readings enter into the conversation commonly associated in feminist criticism with such scholars as Mieke Bal (*Death and Dissymmetry: The Politics of Coherence in the Book of Judges* [Chicago: Chicago University Press, 1988] and *Murder and Difference: Gender, Genre, and Scholarship on Siser's Death* [Bloomington: Indiana University Press, 1987]) and Eve Kosofsky Sedgwick (*Between Men: English Literature and Male Homosocial Desire* [New York: Columbia University Press, 1985]). As Bal, following the lead of Barbara Johnson, has argued, "whoever became the object of writing, the textual thing to whom access to writing was denied, lost all power over her own life." *Death and Dissymmetry,* 244.

8   Hawthorne, *Scarlet Letter,* 30.

9   See David Leverenz, *Manhood and the American Renaissance* (Ithaca, N.Y.: Cornell University Press, 1989), 227–78; and Amy Shrager Lang, *Prophetic Woman: Anne Hutchinson and the Problem of Dissent in the Literature of New England* (Berkeley: University of California Press, 1987).

10   I again refer the reader to three works that I discussed in Chapter 1: Leverenz, *Manhood and the American Renaissance*; Cynthia S. Jordan, *Second Stories: The Politics of Language, Form, and Gender in Early American Fictions* (Chapel Hill: University of North Carolina Press, 1989); and Leland S. Person, Jr., *Aesthetic Headaches: Women and a Masculine Poetics in Poe, Melville, and Hawthorne* (Athens: University of Georgia Press, 1988).

11   Herman Melville, *Moby Dick or The Whale,* intro. Newton Arvin (New York: Holt, Rinehart, and Winston, 1961), 41; hereafter cited in the text.

12   Richard H. Brodhead, "Trying All Things: An Introduction to *Moby-Dick*," in *New Essays on Moby-Dick, or, The Whale,* ed. Brodhead (Cambridge: Cambridge University Press, 1986), 9–10. See also Sharon Cameron, *The Corporeal Self: Allegories of the Body in Melville and Hawthorne* (Baltimore, Md.: Johns Hopkins University Press, 1981), 42 ("Women are occasions for transferring sexuality to some other, person-transforming, person-eliding realm"

and hence are banished early from the book); and Joyce W. Warren, *The American Narcissus: Individualism and Women in Nineteenth-Century American Fiction* (New Brunswick, N.J.: Rutgers University Press, 1984). Michael Paul Rogin, in *Subversive Genealogy: The Politics and Art of Herman Melville* (New York: Knopf, 1983), presents a powerful New Historicist reading of Melville in terms of his engagement with issues of class, race, economy, and also gender. See also Leverenz's chapter on Melville in *Manhood and the American Renaissance,* 279–306.

13　He is, by Richard Chase's early account, neurotically self-dependent, characterized by "solipsism, hypnotic self-regard, imprisonment within the self." Chase, *The American Novel and Its Tradition* (New York: Doubleday, 1957), 105–7 On Ahab's selfishness compare Milton R. Stern, *The Fine Hammered Steel of Herman Melville* (Chicago: University of Chicago Press, 1968), 13. Thirty years of criticism have done little to change this portrait of Ahab. For more recent assessments of Ahab, see, e.g., Sharon Cameron, *Corporeal Self;* and David Simpson, *Fetishism and Imagination: Dickens, Melville, Conrad* (Baltimore, Md.: Johns Hopkins University Press, 1982). Simpson says: "Ahab's relation to the whale . . . is clearly . . . dependent upon substitution and reflection rather than upon achievement and conjunction" (80).

14　The homosexual nature of Queequeg and Ishmael's relationship, so richly developed in the early chapters of the book, has been understood as either revealing something about Melville's own sexual preferences or as reflecting a nineteenth-century cultural bias toward the essential maleness of human experience. The foundation for and still the most compelling reading of the novel along these lines is Leslie A. Fiedler's *Love and Death in the American Novel* (New York: Dell, 1960), 370–91.

15　On the novel as an expression of uncertainty, see, e.g., James Mcintosh, "The Mariner's Multiple Quest," in *New Essays on* Moby-Dick, ed. Brodhead, 23–52; and Richard H. Brodhead, *Hawthorne, Melville, and the Novel* (Chicago: University of Chicago Press, 1976), 134–62.

16　See Edwin Haviland Miller, "Infants, Boys, and Men and Ifs Eternally—*Moby Dick,"* in *Romanticism: Critical Essays in American Literature,* ed. James Burbour and Thomas Quirk (New York: Garland, 1986), 289–98, who notes that it is as if Ahab fathers Ishmael, who goes on to replace his father and tell his story, becoming a tyrant like Ahab.

17　Stanley Cavell, "Being Odd, Getting Even (*Descartes, Emerson, Poe*)," in Cavell, *In Quest of the Ordinary: Lines of Skepticism and Romanticism* (Chicago: University of Chicago Press, 1988), 105–49.

18　See esp. Person, *Aesthetic Headaches*; and Jordan, *Second Stories.*

19　Eve Kosofsky Sedgwick has dealt extensively with the use of women as brokers within the all-male economy in *Between Men*; Mieke Bal picks up elements of the argument in *Death and Dissymmetry.*

20　See, e.g., James D. Wallace, "Hawthorne and the Scribbling Women Reconsidered," *American Literature* 62 (1990): 201–22.

Chapter Four
The Material Reproduction of Culture: Faulkner

1　Other important writers are F. Scott Fitzgerald, Ralph Ellison, and E. L. Doctorow. I have discussed the relationship between Fitzgerald, Doctorow, and the romance tradition in *Fiction and Historical Consciousness: The American Romance Tradition* (New Haven, Conn.: Yale University Press, 1989).

2   Frederick L. Gwynn and Joseph L. Blotner, eds., *Faulkner in the University* (Charlottesville: University of Virginia Press, 1959), 71.

3   Ibid., 84.

4   William Faulkner, *The Sound and the Fury,* ed. David Minter (New York: Norton, 1987), 157; hereafter cited in the text.

5   Eric J. Sundquist, *Faulkner: The House Divided* (Baltimore, Md.: Johns Hopkins University Press, 1983).

6   See, e.g., Christine van Boheemen, *The Novel as Family Romance: Language, Gender, and Authority from Fielding to Joyce* (Ithaca, N.Y.: Cornell University Press, 1987).

7   John T. Matthews, *The Play of Faulkner's Language* (Ithaca, N.Y.: Cornell University Press, 1982); and Stephen M. Ross, *Fiction's Inexhaustible Voice: Speech and Writing in Faulkner* (Athens: University of Georgia Press, 1989).

See also other essays by Ross: "Shapes of Time and Consciousness in *As I Lay Dying,*" in *William Faulkner's* As I Lay Dying: *A Critical Casebook,* ed. Dianne L. Cox (New York: Garland, 1985), 33–48; "'Voice' in Narrative Texts: The Example of *As I Lay Dying,*" *PMLA* 94 (1979): 300–10; and "The 'Loud World' of Quentin Compson," in *William Faulkner's* The Sound and the Fury: *A Critical Casebook,* ed. André Bleikasten (New York: Garland, 1982), 101–14. And see Wesley Morris with Barbara Alverson Morris, *Reading Faulkner* (Madison: University of Wisconsin Press, 1989); Joseph Boone, "Creation by the Father's Fiat: Paternal Narrative, Sexual Anxiety, and the Deauthorizing Designs of *Absalom, Absalom!*" in *Refiguring the Father: New Feminist Readings of Patriarchy,* ed. Patricia Yaeger and Beth Kowalski-Wallace (Carbondale: Southern Illinois University Press, 1989), 209–37: "Sutpen used his children as a means of imposing his ego on the external world . . . effectually treat[ing] his family as a text . . . . What interests me is the fact that this family text, this paternal design, proves inherently self-subverting . . . . The story that Faulkner finally tells . . . ends up being less a demonstration of the ubiquity of the father than of the threats to paternal ubiquity that make the father's story an impossibility from its very inception" (211). Gail L. Mortimer, *Faulkner's Rhetoric of Loss: A Study in Perception and Meaning* (Austin: University of Texas Press, 1983), writes: "Absence enters the world, and our consciousness, at precisely the moment we become aware of the passage of time. It is . . . the occasion for our becoming symbolizing beings" (8). Compare the words of Juliet Mitchell: "Language speaks the loss which lay behind the first moment of symbolization." Quoted in Mimrose C. Gwin, *The Feminine and Faulkner: Reading (Beyond) Sexual Difference* (Knoxville: University of Tennessee Press, 1990), 17. See also Shlomith Rimmon-Kenan, "Under the Sign of Loss: A Reading of Faulkner's *The Sound and the Fury,*" in *Languages of the Unsayable: The Play of Negativity in Literature and Literary Theory,* ed. Sanford Budick and Wolfgang Iser (New York: Columbia University Press, 1989), 241–58.

For earlier interpretations of Faulkner that point the way toward some of these more deconstructionist readings, see André Bleikasten, *The Most Splendid Failure: Faulkner's* The Sound and the Fury (Bloomington: Indiana University Press, 1976), esp. 51–63; Arnold L. Weinstein, *Vision and Response in Modern Fiction* (Ithaca, N.Y.: Cornell University Press,

1974), esp. 91–92, 116, 126, 151; and Donald M. Kartiganer, *The Fragile Thread: The Meaning of Form in Faulkner's Novels* (Amherst: University of Massachusetts Press, 1979).

On the feminist implications of Faulkner's literary theoretic dimensions, see Gwin, *Feminine and Faulkner*, as well as Gwin, "(Re)reading Faulkner as Father and Daughter of His Own Text," in *Refiguring the Father*, ed. Yaeger and Kowalski-Wallace, 238–58; Karen Ramsay Johnson, "Gender, Sexuality, and the Artist in Faulkner's Novels," *American Literature* 61 (1989): 1–16; Deborah Clarke, "Gender, Race, and Language in *Light in August*," *American Literature* 61 (1989): 398–13; Gail L. Mortimer, "The Smooth, Suave Shape of Desire: Paradox in Faulknerian Imagery of Women," *Women's Studies* 13 (1986): 149–61; and Judith Bryant Wittenberg, "The Women in *Light in August*," in *New Essays on* Light in August, ed. Michael Millgate (New York: Cambridge University Press, 1987), 103–22. The feminist readings agree that Faulkner is not a feminist per se, registering (as in Wittenberg's and Mortimer's essays) Faulkner's ambivalence toward women, but they emphasize the ways in which his textual deconstructions represent the power of the woman to subvert male society and male discourse.

On the racial implications of Faulkner's style and content, see, in addition to Clarke, "Gender, Race, and Language," James A. Snead, "*Light in August* and the Rhetorics of Racial Division," in *Faulkner and Race: Faulkner and Yoknapatawpha, 1986,* ed. Doreen Fowler and Ann J. Abadie (Jackson: University Press of Mississippi, 1987), 156, 161; and Snead, *Figures of Division: William Faulkner's Major Novels* (New York: Methuen, 1986). Although Snead is primarily interested in the institution of racism, he relates the argument on division and signification to women as well: see, e.g., *Figures of Division*, 4–6, and, specifically on *As I Lay Dying*, 66–75. See also Sundquist, *Faulkner: The House Divided*; and Sundquist, "Faulkner, Race, and the Forms of American Fiction," in *Faulkner and Race*, ed. Fowler and Abadie, 1–34.

8   Gwin, *Feminine and Faulkner*, 25.
9   Snead, "*Light in August* and the Rhetorics of Racial Division"; and Snead, *Figures of Division*. Compare p. ix in the latter: "William Faulkner's major novels, written between 1929 and 1942, explored, earlier than most critics did, the systematic paradoxes within the fabric of literary discourse." And see Sundquist, *House Divided* and "Faulkner, Race, and Forms of American Fiction."
10 On Faulkner's indebtedness to Anderson, see his own essay "Sherwood Anderson: An Appreciation," in *The Achievement of Sherwood Anderson: Essays in Criticism,* ed. Ray Lewis White (Chapel Hill: North Carolina University Press, 1966), 194–201; also see William L. Phillips, "Sherwood Anderson's Two Prize Pupils," in ibid., 202–10; and Arthur F. Kinney, *Faulkner's Narrative Poetics: Style as Vision* (Amherst: University of Massachusetts Press, 1978), 39–40, in which the author specifically discusses Faulkner's adaption of the text that will concern me here, *Winesburg, Ohio*.
11 Noted in Gwynn and Blotner, eds., *Faulkner in the University*, 49–51. See also James B. Meriwether and Michael Millgate, eds., *Lion in the Garden: Interviews with William Faulkner, 1926–1962* (New York: Random House, 1968), 17, 21, 60.
12 Van Boheemen, *Novel as Family Romance*, 7–8; and Gwin, *Feminine and Faulkner*, 122–52. Van Boheemen is alluding here to the work of French feminist critics like Luce Irigaray and

Hélène Cixous who emphasize the indeterminacy and flow of female writing, which in the manner of lactating milk or menstrual blood creates motion and nonclosure. It is useful to read van Boheemen's discussion side by side with Edgar Dryden's interpretation of American romance fiction in *The Form of American Romance* (Baltimore, Md.: Johns Hopkins University Press, 1988), where the relation between romance fiction and the self-consciousness of its "textual productivity" is explored in detail. On Faulkner's affinities with Joyce, see Gwynn and Blotner, eds., *Faulkner in the University,* 57–60.

13   Gwin, *Feminine and Faulkner,* 27–28, 34–62; Sundquist, *Faulkner: House Divided;* Matthews, *Play of Faulkner's Language,* all discuss Caddy as the absent center of the novel. Writes Sundquist: The "'loss' of Caddy . . . represents the crucial generative event in the book—in fact the event that forecloses generation" (11); "the incestuous desire to father oneself or to be one's own family is here presented as correlative to, if not the cause of, the symbolic desire to absorb all creative energy into an invisible, ineffable presence. . . . Quentin's suicide, therefore, should not be interpreted as a reaction against his incestuous desires . . . [but] virtually *is* incest, the only act in which generation is thoroughly internalized (and prohibited) and the 'father,' as a consequence, killed": "In the final image of Benjy circling the Confederate statue we recognize that, although the plot has unfolded and advanced, its essence still lies in section one, to which we nervously return. The returning to stillness, as to death, is the book's primary movement, and the style of Benjy's section, stillness on the point of death, enacts in narrative the hard, bright flame of symbolic intensity that Quentin imagines incest to be, and Faulkner wanted his book to be, the burning out in passionate stillness of the power to generate a family, a life, a story" (17–18).

As John Matthews argues, in terms similar to those of van Boheemen (*Novel as Family Romance*): "The correspondence in Faulkner's fiction between verbal discourse and sexual intercourse is pronounced and explicit; it suggests that teller and listener, or writers and reader, surrender themselves to engagement, exposure, embrace, intimacy, and creation. . . . That individuals become themselves only in their words, that all representation is a kind of speaking and hearing and that language plays in its failure to present what it represents are all components of Faulkner's figure of marriage" (17). Sundquist's analysis locates the problem of the Compson men vis-à-vis their sister and therefore vis-à-vis the family itself, whereas Matthews notes an important feature of Faulkner's fiction in general. But *The Sound and the Fury,* I suggest, is not the fantasy of any one of its male protagonists. It manages to avoid what does overtake Faulkner later in his career: an unwillingness to grant the physical, material, maternal, specificity of women.

14   Faulkner refers to *The Sound and the Fury* as his "most splendid failure" in his introduction, where he also explains his preference for *The Sound and the Fury* over *As I Lay Dying,* which he devalues as a deliberate "tour-de-force." Faulkner, *Sound and the Fury,* ed. Minter, 218–19. All quotations from the two versions of the introduction (which are largely identical) will refer to this edition and are hereafter cited in the text.

15   William Faulkner, *Absalom, Absalom!* (New York: Random House, 1972), 9. Michael Millgate comments that "*The Sound and the Fury* is in part concerned with the elusiveness, the multivalence, of truth, or at least with man's persistent and perhaps necessary tendency to make of truth a personal thing: each man, apprehending some fragment of the truth, seizes upon

that fragment as though it were the whole truth and elaborates it into a total vision of the world, rigidly exclusive and hence utterly fallacious." *The Achievement of William Faulkner* (New York: Random House, 1966). Millgate specifically associates Faulkner's idea here with Anderson's *Winesburg* and the theory of the grotesque.

16 See, e.g., Olga W. Vickery's by now classic reading of the novel: *The Novels of William Faulkner: A Critical Interpretation* (Baton Rouge: Louisiana State University Press, 1959).

17 See, e.g., Sundquist, who suggests that "the timelessness of Dilsey's experience, the eschatological sublime of *Uncle Tom's Cabin,* validates the Christological structure of the plot only by declaring that, Negroes and idiots aside, it is of no real value whatsoever" (*Faulkner: A House Divided,* 13).

Chapter Five
Textual Indeterminacy: Faulkner and Anderson

1 For a feminist interpretation of Faulkner, which insists on the the feminine flooding and overflowing of Faulkner's text, see Mimrose C. Gwin, *The Feminine and Faulkner: Reading (Beyond) Sexual Difference* (Knoxville: University of Tennessee Press, 1990): she entitles a chapter "Flooding and the Feminine Text." A related reading is James Snead, "*Light in August* and the Rhetorics of Racial Division," in *Faulkner and Race: Faulkner and Yoknapatawpha, 1986,* ed. Doreen Fowler and Ann J. Abadie (Jackson: University Press of Mississippi, 1987). For a thoroughgoing analysis of Faulkner's language philosophy in the novel, see Carolyn Slaughter, "*As I Lay Dying:* Demise of Vision," *American Literature,* 61 (1989): 17–30.

2 William Faulkner, *As I Lay Dying* (New York: Random House, 1964), 165–66; hereafter cited in the text.

3 See, e.g., André Bleikasten, *Faulkner's* As I Lay Dying, trans. Roger Little (Bloomington: Indiana University Press, 1974), 18–20.

4 Compare Nathaniel Hawthorne, *The Scarlet Letter,* in *The Centenary Edition of the Works of Nathaniel Hawthorne,* vol. 1, ed. William Charvat et al. (Columbus: Ohio State University Press, 1962): "God gave me the child! . . . He gave her, in requital of all things else, which ye had taken from me. She is my happiness!—she is my torture, none the less. Pearl keeps me here in life! Pearl punishes me too! See ye not, she is the scarlet letter, only capable of being loved, and so endowed with a million-fold power of retribution for my sin?" (113).

5 For a discussion of a possible female language in another of Faulkner's novels, see Deborah Clarke, "Gender, Race, and Language in *Light in August,*" *American Literature,* 61 (1989): 398–13.

6 John Irwin, *Doubling and Incest / Repetition and Revenge: A Speculative Reading of Faulkner* (Baltimore: Johns Hopkins University Press, 1975), 113. See also André Bleikasten, "Fathers in Faulkner," in *The Fictional Father: Lacanian Readings of the Text,* ed. Robert Con Davis (Amherst: University of Massachusetts Press, 1981), 115–46.

7 Sherwood Anderson, *Winesburg, Ohio* (1919; reprint, New York: Viking, 1972), 32; hereafter cited in the text.

8 Again, although the terms of Eric J. Sundquist's discussion are somewhat different from my own, I find support for my reading in Sundquist's assertions that "pregnancy for Dewey Dell

and for Addie involves a confusion of identity that inverts the one expressed in the process of death, in which the impossibility of conceiving of the self as a singular identity is made paradoxically conspicuous in the sudden need to preserve those connections that define the self even as they pass away. Standing at the other end of death, as it were, the process of coming unalone [Dewey Dell's phrase for her impending motherhood] initiates in their most apparently physical form the connections without which one cannot fully imagine ever having been a lone, identical self existing apart from conscious and bodily ties to others. In extremity, the 'coming unalone,' the becoming more than one 'I,' leads to a threat of utter extinction through saturation." *Faulkner: The House Divided* (Baltimore, Md.: Johns Hopkins University Press, 1983), 37.

9   Androgynous images figure throughout *Winesburg*. For example, the first major representation of the artist-prophet, after the old man in the "Book of the Grotesque," is the latently homosexual Wing Biddlebaum, who is closely associated with the teacherly tradition of Plato and hence with the androgynous qualities of both art and teaching. Adolescent sexuality, as embodied by George and by Helen White, similarly represents an androgynous or at least premasculine or prefeminine sexuality. George's close relationship with Seth Richmond accentuates his not-yet-developed sexual identity early in the novel. In Faulkner images of bisexuality and androgyny abound, from his earliest novels, like *Mosquitoes,* right through the major fiction. On Faulkner's subversion of traditional gender categories, see Karen Ramsay Johnson, "Gender, Sexuality, and the Artist in Faulkner's Novels," *American Literature* 61 (1989): 1–15. Also see James A. Snead, *"Light in August* and the Rhetorics of Racial Division," in *Faulkner and Race: Faulkner and Yoknapatawpha, 1986),* ed. Doreen Fowler and Ann J. Abadie (Jackson: University Press of Mississippi, 1987), 156, 161; and Snead, *Figures of Division: William Faulkner's Major Novels* (New York: Methuen, 1986). One must also recall Carolyn G. Heilbrun's important study *Toward a Recognition of Androgyny* (New York: Knopf, 1973).

10   Marilyn Judith Atlas, in "Sherwood Anderson and the Women of Winesburg," suggests that the "nameless" woman in "Paper Pills" is "hardly more than a sacrifice." In *Critical Essays on Sherwood Anderson,* ed. David D. Anderson (Boston: G. K. Hall, 1981), 256.

11   The associations that I am drawing between the white dress and the white sheet of paper, the blood and the ink, and the doctor and the writer figure prominently in Michael Fried's readings of Thomas Eakins and Stephen Crane in *Realism, Writing, Disfiguration: On Thomas Eakins and Stephen Crane* (Chicago: University of Chicago Press, 1987), especially his discussions of an Eakins painting entitled *The Gross Clinic.* See also Susan Gubar's essay " 'The Blank Page' and the Issues of Female Creativity," in *The New Feminist Criticism: Essays on Women, Literature, and Theory,* ed. Elaine Showalter (New York: Pantheon, 1985), 292–313.

12   William Faulkner, *Absalom, Absalom!* (New York: Random House, 1972), 376, 378.

13   Sundquist, *Faulkner: The House Divided;* and Sundquist, "Faulkner, Race, and Forms of American Literature," in *Faulkner and Race: Faulkner and Yoknapatawpha, 1986,* ed. Doreen Fowler and Ann J. Abadie (Jackson: University Press of Mississippi, 1987), 1–34. A wealth of scholarly studies investigate Faulkner's relation to the issues of racism about which he writes. *Faulkner and Race* is a recent, excellent contribution to this area. Earlier studies include Charles H. Nilon, *Faulkner and the Negro,* University of Colorado Studies: Series in

Language and Literature 8 (Boulder: University of Colorado Press, 1962), the first book-length study; Lee Jenkin, *Faulkner and Black-White Relations: A Psychoanalytic Approach* (New York: Columbia University Press, 1981), in which much of the salient criticism is reviewed; Charles D. Peavy, *Go Slow Now: Faulkner and the Race Question* (Eugene: University of Oregon Press, 1971); and Myra Jehlen, *Class and Character in Faulkner's South* (Secaucus, N.J.: Citadel, 1978), esp. 75–96. Already in 1952, Irving Howe had faulted Faulkner for his lack of a politically useful position. *William Faulkner: A Critical Study* (New York, 1952), 134.

14   Sundquist, "Faulkner, Race," 7.

15   For a like-minded reading of miscegenation, see Marc Shell, "Those Extraordinary Twins," *Arizona Quarterly* 47 (1991): 29–76.

16   T. H. Adamowski, "Children of the Idea," *Mosaic* 10 (1976), 137.

17   Snead, "*Light in August* and the Rhetorics of Racial Division." This idea is picked up in Philip M. Weinstein's "Marginalia: Faulkner's Black Lives," also in *Faulkner and Race*, ed. Fowler and Abadie, 170–91. See also Craig Werner "Minstrel Nightmares: Black Dreams of Faulkner's Dreams of Blacks," in ibid., 35–57: in a novel like *Absalom*, he suggests, the characters can neither recognize likeness nor accept otherness.

18   Snead, "*Light in August* and the Rhetorics of Racial Division," 156. See also Judith Bryant Wittenberg's discussion entitled "The Women in *Light in August*," which discloses Faulkner's problem with women to be remarkably similar to his problem with African Americans: he desires to sympathize with them and thus to demarginalize them, but he cannot quite escape certain stereotypes and prejudices. In *New Essays on Light in August*, ed. Michael Millgate (Cambridge: Cambridge University Press, 1987), 103–22.

19   Matthews, *Play of Faulkner's Language*, 17, 121; see also 115–21. Here Matthews is in part following out the implications of Arnold L. Weinstein's assertion in *Visions and Responses in Modern Fiction* (Ithaca: Cornell University Press, 1974), 138, that meaning occurs in the "effort toward community" (quoted by Matthews on p. 120).

20   Stanley Cavell, *The Senses of Walden* (New York: Viking, 1972), esp. 61–65.

21   See Bleikasten, *Faulkner's As I Lay Dying*, 96–97, for a discussion of the fish image.

22   I have discussed this sentence at length in "Sacvan Bercovitch, Stanley Cavell, and the Romance Theory of American Fiction," *PMLA* 107 (1992): 199–211.

23   To bolster what might seem to be a fantastic claim about the scarlet letter, let me note that in *The Bell Jar*, Sylvia Plath inherits the *A* of Hawthorne's novel, associating it with red chalk, which is itself associated with menstrual bleeding. I have discussed this in "The Feminist Discourse of Sylvia Plath's *The Bell Jar*," *College English* 49 (1987): 872-85.

Chapter Six
Sentimentalism and Human Rights: Stowe and Melville

1   Nathaniel Hawthorne, *The House of Seven Gables*, in *The Centenary Edition of the Works of Nathaniel Hawthorne*, vol. 2, ed. William Charvat et al. (Columbus: Ohio University Press, 1965), 1.

2   Ibid.

3   Brook Thomas, *Cross-Examinations of Law and Literature: Cooper, Hawthorne, Stowe, and Melville* (Cambridge: Cambridge University Press, 1987).

4   Fred G. See, *Desire and the Sign: Nineteenth-Century American Fiction* (Baton Rouge: Louisiana State University Press, 1987). See's ideas are illuminated and verified by Winfried Fluck, who pushes back even further the scandalization of the sentimental. In an attempt to understand why *Uncle Tom's Cabin* continues to excite literary controversy despite its devaluation, Fluck has argued that the novel internalizes a struggle between a desire to represent, through language, an ineffable metaphysical order and an increasing awareness of the unrepresentability of such presence. That struggle, which generates a "permanent surplus of signification," finally makes the text accessible to a modern reader inimical to such ideas of representation. "The more the sentimental text becomes afraid of failing, the more it strains itself; the more it strains itself, however, the more it begins to undermine its own premise that an adequate representation of the moral order is still possible; and the more it undermines itself, the more it can be reappropriated by a postmodern sensibility." "The Power and Failure of Representation in Harriet Beecher Stowe's *Uncle Tom's Cabin*," *New Literary History* 23 (1992): 333–34.

5   Philip Fisher, *Hard Facts: Setting and Form in the American Novel* (New York: Oxford University Press, 1987). Fisher's thesis is that popular fiction does a certain kind of cultural work, which, when accomplished, makes the text obsolete—hence the disparity between the initial reception of a work like *Uncle Tom's Cabin* and its later rejection by the tradition. Essentially Fisher argues that a popular novel works to make room within the crowded realm of a culture's self-representations for a heretofore unrepresented part of the cultural picture, toward which the society is moving. Once the novel has done this work, thus forever changing that culture's picture of itself, the new self-representation is taken for granted as a hard fact of existence. The culture finds it trivial or excessive to indulge in representing what is obvious. Stowe's *Uncle Tom's Cabin,* in this reading, succeeds so well in transforming the public perception of blacks as to render its strenuous argumentation in this direction obsolete, self-annihilating. Nineteenth-century romance, I suggest, was aimed at exposing just this problem of cultural consensus, in which the work of popular fiction, according to Fisher's thesis, is involved. In other words, what Fisher sees as the positive energy of popular fiction to change society, the romance tradition sees as its troubling power to naturalize and conceal. The case is not only, as Fisher expresses it, that "high culture of the kind represented by Hawthorne, Melville, James, and Howells, remains unincorporated and therefore it remains as fresh and extraordinary as when it was written" (21). Rather, the American high culture of the nineteenth century—the romance tradition—made incorporation its subject.

6   Elizabeth Ammons, "Stowe's Dream of the Mother-Savior: *Uncle Tom's Cabin* and American Women Writers Before the 1920s," in *New Essays on* Uncle Tom's Cabin, ed. Eric. J. Sundquist (Cambridge: Cambridge University Press, 1986), 156–57. See Jane Tompkins, *Sensational Designs: The Cultural Work of American Fiction, 1790–1860* (New York: Oxford University Press, 1985); Fisher, *Hard Facts*; Ammons, "Heroines in *Uncle Tom's Cabin*" *American Literature*, 49 (1977): 161–79, and "Stowe's Dream of the Mother-Savior"; Gillian Brown, *Domestic Individualism: Imagining Self in Nineteenth-Century America* (Berkeley:

University of California Press, 1990); and Thomas P. Joswick, "'The Crown Without the Conflict': Religious Values and Moral Reasoning in *Uncle Tom's Cabin,*" *Nineteenth-Century Fiction* 39 (1984): 253–74. See also Leslie Fiedler, "The Many Mothers of *Uncle Tom's Cabin,*" in his *What Was Literature? Class, Culture and Mass Society* (New York: Simon and Schuster, 1982), 168–78; Joanne Dobson, "The Hidden Hand: Subversion of Cultural Ideology in Three Mid-Nineteenth-Century Women's Novels," *American Quarterly* 38, no. 1 (1986): 223–42; and Theodore R. Hovet, *The Master Narrative: Harriet Beecher Stowe's Subversive Story of Master and Slave in* Uncle Tom's Cabin *and Dred* (Lanham, Md.: University Press of America, 1989).

7   Harriet Beecher Stowe, *Uncle Tom's Cabin* (New York: Washington Square Press, 1971), 35; hereafter cited in the text.

8   These problems in the novel have not gone unnoticed by critics. Stowe scholarship, once so adamantly committed to defending the novel and recovering it from canonical oblivion, has already begun to constitute a critique of the novel's deficiencies. The intention here is not to banish Stowe's novel once again. Rather, what recent critics sympathetic to the novel have understood is what like-minded nineteenth-century romancers understood: the impossibility of guaranteeing human rights by propounding the cult of the sentimental. Writes Thomas Joswick, for example: "Once we have demonstrated the moral aims and aesthetic resourcefulness of *Uncle Tom's Cabin,* we may fairly assess the novel by pointing to conflicts and limitations that are created by the very forms of religious and moral values that sustain its coherence. The conflicts occur because the one form of social power sanctioned by the moral values in the novel severely limits the development of characters and the options for political action; moreover, the religious rhetoric that sustains the novel's aesthetic principles also encourages an aesthetic practice blind to its own implication in the moral evil it intends to expose and change. What follows, then, is that despite the novel's compelling and coherent claims for triumph, an internal dissonance makes its aesthetic, moral, and religious coherence inadequate to the professed aims to reform the world." "'The Crown Without the Conflict,'" 256. Specifically, in Joswick's reading, the book threatens to decrease the individual's sense of personal responsibility and even to persuade individuals that evil is a natural and therefore inescapable reality with which we must all learn to live (268ff). Going at the novel from a somewhat different perspective, Amy Schrager Lang locates the same political impasse to which Stowe's sentimentalism delivers her: "Stowe is unwilling finally to rely on the tearful prayers of women at home to end slavery, yet, having established tearful prayers as the limit of women's capability, she is unwilling to commit herself to an alternative form of moral action." Again: "Sentimentalism lends Stowe a framework which supports the idea that women and blacks are, by virtue of their circumstances if not innately, more Christian, more affectionate, more sympathetic, and more just than white men. But at the same time that sentimentalism proves that women have the emotional capacity to sympathize with the oppressed—the right feelings—it deprives them of the capacity to translate these into action." "Slavery and Sentimentalism: The Strange Career of Augustine St. Clare," *Women's Studies* 12 (1986): 34, 42. This conflict is central as well to Brook Thomas's reading in *Cross-Examinations.*

9   See Marc Shell's essay "Marranos (Pigs); or, From Coexistence to Toleration," *Critical Inquiry* 17 (1991): 306–35, where Shell questions whether the idea of universal brotherhood (asso-

ciated with Christianity) was less rather than more tolerant than the apparent separatism of Judaism and Islam.

10 Herman Melville, "Benito Cereno," in *Selected Tales and Poems*, ed. Richard Chase (New York: Holt, Rinehart, and Winston, 1950), 136.

11 James Kavanagh has suggested that "Benito Cereno" "can be read as a discourse about *discourse*, about how a mind *talks to itself*, giving itself the 'evidence' with which to 'perceive' and 'feel' its own ruthless brand of savagery as 'innocence' and 'moral simplicity.'" "'The Hive of Subtlety': Benito Cereno as Critique of Ideology," in *The Arts, Society, and Literature*, ed. Harry P. Garvin (Lewisburg, Pa.: Bucknell University Press, 1985), 131. See Brook Thomas's similarly ideological reading in "The Legal Fictions of Herman Melville and Lemuel Shaw," *Critical Inquiry*, 11 (1984): 24–51. The story, according to Kavanagh, effects "what Althusser calls an 'internal distantiation' of an ideology, displaying a dominant 'lived relation to the real' within itself as the lived experience of a fictional character (Delano) in a form that opens it to 'sight' and analysis" (132). See also Marianne Dekoven, "History as Suppressed Referent in Modernist Fiction," *ELH*, 51 (1984): 137–54.

12 Wolfgang Iser, *The Act of Reading: A Theory of Aesthetic Response* (Baltimore, Md.: Johns Hopkins University Press, 1978).

13 Fisher, *Hard Facts*, 87–127.

14 Stanley Cavell, *The Claim of Reason: Wittgenstein, Skepticism, Morality, and Tragedy* (Oxford: Oxford University Press, 1979), 376–77.

15 On this point see Jean Fagin Yellin, "Black Masks: Melville's 'Benito Cereno,'" *American Quarterly*, 22 (1970): 678–89.

16 Henry David Thoreau, *Walden; or, Life in the Woods*, intro. Norman Holmes Pearson (New York: Holt, Rinehart, and Winston, 1961), 4–5.

17 For a list of characteristics of sentimental fiction, see Fisher, *Hard Facts*, 99–101.

18 Joswick, "'The Crown Without the Conflict,'" 266.

19 Carol Bensick, "His Folly, Her Weakness: Demystified Adultery in *The Scarlet Letter*," in *New Essays on* The Scarlet Letter, ed. Michael J. Colacurcio (Cambridge: Cambridge University Press, 1985), 137–59.

20 Nathaniel Hawthorne, *The Scarlet Letter*, in *The Centenary Edition of the Works of Nathaniel Hawthorne*, vol. 1, ed. William Charvat et al. (Columbus: Ohio State University Press, 1962), 195.

21 See my *Fiction and Historical Consciousness: The American Romance Tradition* (New Haven, Conn.: Yale University Press, 1989), 58-62.

22 Herman Melville, *Billy Budd*, in *Selected Tales*, ed. Chase, 290.

23 "And good-bye to you . . . old *Rights of Man*," Billy exclaims when he is impressed into military service. Ibid., 296.

Chapter Seven
Literary Realism and a Woman's Strength: Wharton and Chopin

1 Edith Wharton, *The House of Mirth* (New York: Holt, Rinehart, and Winston, 1962), 376; hereafter cited in the text.

2   See Nina Baym, *Woman's Fiction: A Guide to Novels By and About Women in America, 1820–1870* (Ithaca, N.Y.: Cornell University Press, 1978), 11: "The many novels all tell . . . a single tale . . . the story of a young girl who is deprived of the supports she had rightly or wrongly depended on to sustain her throughout life and is faced with the necessity of winning her own way in the world." Faulkner's Caddy, whom (unlike Hester and Isabel) we meet as a child, reincarnates many of the qualities of the child-heroines of nineteenth-century fiction by women. She is independent, strong, and alive; and, because her mother is totally dysfunctional, she is something of an orphan, as are the somewhat older heroines of Hawthorne's and James's novels. Baym's book remains the definitive study of nineteenth-century women's fiction. See also her other study of women's fiction, *Novels, Readers and Reviewers: Responses to Fiction in Antebellum America* (Ithaca, N.Y.: Cornell University Press, 1984); and Ann R. Shapiro, *Unlikely Heroines: American Women Writers and the Woman Question* (New York: Greenwood, 1987). Susan Harris has significantly revised Baym's thesis, arguing that the nineteenth-century women's novels are far more subversive than Baym allows; see *Nineteenth-Century Women's Fiction: Interpretive Strategies* (Cambridge: Cambridge University Press, 1990). Another interesting qualification of Baym's thesis is in Hazel Carby's *Reconstructing Womanhood: The Emergence of the Afro-American Woman Novelist* (New York: Oxford University Press, 1987). Carby notes how women writers of nineteenth-century African American fiction are forced by the social condition of black people to revise the basic strategies of white fiction.

3   On the way the heroes of nineteenth-century women's fiction yield again to the dominant domestic ideology, see Alfred Habegger, *Henry James and the "Woman Business"* (Cambridge: Cambridge University Press: 1989). See also Joseph A. Boone, *Tradition Counter Tradition: Love and the Form of Fiction* (Chicago: University of Chicago Press, 1987). In *Nineteenth-Century Women's Fiction*, Susan Harris has argued that these texts do not retreat from the images of strength they present. On Chopin's relation to nineteenth-century women's writing, see Elaine Showalter, "Tradition and the Female Talent: *The Awakening* as a Solitary Book," in *New Essays on* The Awakening, ed. Wendy Martin (Cambridge: Cambridge University Press, 1988), 33–57.

4   Boone, *Tradition Counter Tradition*, 3, 4, 10. Boone identifies two major countertraditions of subversion. One, which works from within the genre, traces courtship into marriage and thus exposes the lack of harmony in which many marriages eventuate. Chopin's *Awakening*, according to Boone, is one such novel. The other countertradition subverts the norms of the genre by fantasizing a "society based on equality and brotherly [and sisterly] love rather than on sexual hierarchy" (247). Melville's *Moby Dick* and *Billy Budd*, Mark Twain's *Adventures of Huckleberry Finn*—three major American romances—and Sarah Orne Jewett's *Country of the Pointed Firs* are some of the novels that Boone discusses in this category.

5   Edith Wharton, *The Custom of the Country* (1913; reprint, New York: Scribner's, 1941), 206–7.

6   Judith Fetterley writes that "the objectification of her physical beauty" causes a "schism between . . . Lily's 'real self' and her cultural identity," increases her sense of powerlessness, and reveals her destiny to be that of "purchase." " 'The Temptation to Be a Beautiful Object': Double Standard and Double Bind in *The House of Mirth*," in *Fiction by American Women:*

Recent Views, ed. Winifred Farrant Bevilacqua (Port Washington, New York: Associated Faculty Press, 1983), 43. In connection with this discussion of *The House of Mirth* and the market economy, see Walter Benn Michaels, *The Gold Standard and the Logic of Naturalism: American Literature at the Turn of the Century* (Berkeley: University of California Press, 1987). Michaels emphasizes not so much Lily's objectification of herself as commodity as her fascination with the dynamics of speculation and risk taking.

7   Michaels, *Gold Standard,* 217–44.

8   Ibid., 87–112.

9   Michael T. Gilmore, "Revolt Against Nature: The Problematic Modernism of *The Awakening,*" in *New Essays on* The Awakening, ed. Martin , 60–61, 74.

10   Fetterley, " 'Temptation to Be a Beautiful Object,' " 50.

11   Showalter, "Tradition and the Female Talent," 33.

12   Kate Chopin, *The Awakening* (New York: Putnam, 1964), 190; hereafter cited in the text.

13   I am paraphrasing "Self-Reliance," in *The Selected Writings of Ralph Waldo Emerson,* intro. Brooks Atkinson (New York: Modern Library, 1950), 149.

14   See ibid., 148. See Gillian Brown's thesis on the ideology of individualism in nineteenth-century fiction by men and women alike. *Domestic Individualism: Imagining Self in Nineteenth-Century America* (Berkeley: University of California Press, 1990). Edna and Lily, we might say, abide by an idea of individualism that does not take into account the problematics of this term.

15   See Wendy Martin, "Introduction," in *New Essays on* The Awakening, ed. Martin, 7, where Martin reviews early reactions to the novel. She provides an excellent introduction to the novel.

16   See Cynthia Griffin Wolff, "Thanatos and Eros: Kate Chopin's *The Awakening,*" in *Fiction by American Women,* ed. Bevilacqua, 21–40.

17   C. L. Deyo, "The Newest Books," *St. Louis Post-Dispatch,* May 20, 1899, quoted in Kate Chopin, *The Awakening: An Authoritative Text, Context, and Criticism* (New York: Norton, 1974), 149. Many mothers, even feminist ones, might come to the reviewer's conclusion.

18   Sandra M. Gilbert and Susan Gubar, *No Man's Land: The Place of the Woman Writer in the Twentieth Century,* vol. 2: *Sexchanges* (New Haven, Conn.: Yale University Press, 1989), 109: "Because of the way it is presented, Edna's supposed suicide enacts not a refusal to accept the limitations of reality but a subversive questioning of the limitations of both reality and 'realism.' For, swimming away from the white beach of Grand Isle, from the empty summer colony and the oppressive imperatives of marriage and maternity, Edna swims, as the novel's last sentences tell us, not into death but back into her own life, back into the imaginative openness of her childhood." Gilbert's and Gubar's reading is consonant with the emphases of several critics, including Elaine Showalter in "Tradition and the Female Talent," 43; Cristina Giorcelli, "Edna's Wisdom: A Transitional and Numinous Merging" in *New Essays on* The Awakening, ed. Martin, 109–48; and Carole Stone, "The Female Artist in Kate Chopin's *The Awakening*: Birth and Creativity," in *The Female Imagination and the Modernist Aesthetic,* ed. Sandra M. Gilbert and Susan Gubar (New York: Gordon and Breach Science Publishers, 1986), 23–32. Stone writes: Edna's "regression" is in the "service of progression toward an artistic vocation" (24).

19 Gilbert and Gubar, *No Man's Land,* 142.

20 Giorcelli argues this in "Edna's Wisdom," 123. It is Joyce W. Warren's thesis that nineteenth-century male writers, because of their commitment to the values of individualism, tend narcissistically to exclude women from the arena of events. *The American Narcissus: Individualism and Women in Nineteenth-Century American Fiction* (New Brunswick, N.J.: Rutgers University Press, 1984). Edna Pontellier and Lily Bart, I suggest, are no less narcissistic in their individualism than most of the male protagonists with whom they might be compared.

21 Chopin's first description of the sea, early in the book, evokes Melville's in *Moby Dick.* She writes: "The voice of the sea is seductive; never ceasing, whispering, clamoring, murmuring, inviting the soul to wander for a spell in abysses of solitude; to lose itself in mazes of inward contemplation" (34). Compare Melville: "Let the most absent-minded of men be plunged in his deepest reveries—stand that man on his legs, set his feet a-going, and he will infallibly lead you to water . . . as every one knows, meditation and water are wedded for ever. . . . And still deeper the meaning of that story of Narcissus, who because he could not grasp the tormenting, mild image he saw in the foundation, plunged into it and was drowned. But that same image, we ourselves see in all rivers and oceans. It is the image of the ungraspable phantom of life; and this is the key to it all." *Moby Dick or The Whale* (New York: Holt, Rinehart and Winston, 1961), 2–3.

22 Gilbert and Gubar, *No Man's Land,* 109. Besides the discussion in Gilbert and Gubar, see Carole Stone's reading of Edna's regression to childhood in "Female Artist in Kate Chopin's *The Awakening.*"

23 See, e.g., Irving Howe, "The Achievement of Edith Wharton," in *Edith Wharton: A Collection of Critical Essays,* ed. Irving Howe (Englewood Cliffs, N.J.: Prentice-Hall, 1962), 1–18, plus three other essays in that collection: Edmund Wilson, "Justice to Edith Wharton," 19–31; Louis Auchincloss, "Edith Wharton and Her New Yorks," 32–42; and Q. D. Leavis, "Henry James's Heiress: The Importance of Edith Wharton," 73–88.

24 Most critics agree that what distinguishes Wharton as a novelist is her "rare and distinguished critical intelligence" and her ability to portray social manners. Percy Lubbock, "The Novels of Edith Wharton," in *Edith Wharton,* ed. Howe, 43. See also Q. D. Leavis, "Henry James's Heiress," in ibid., 73–88.

25 Nathaniel Hawthorne, *The House of Seven Gables,* in *The Centenary Edition of the Works of Nathaniel Hawthorne,* vol. 2, ed. William Charvat et al. (Columbus: Ohio State University Press, 1965), 307. I have discussed *The House of the Seven Gables* at length in my *Fiction and Historical Consciousness: The American Romance Tradition* (New Haven, Conn.: Yale University Press, 1989), 119–42.

26 Annette Kolodny, *The Lay of the Land: Metaphor as Experience in American Life and Letters* (Chapel Hill: University of North Carolina Press, 1975).

27 Ellen Glasgow, *Barren Ground* (New York: Harcourt, Brace, 1985), 526.

28 Michaels, *Gold Standard,* 27–28.

29 Ibid., 22–25.

Chapter Eight
The Mother Tongue: McCullers

1   Carson McCullers, *The Heart Is a Lonely Hunter* (1943; reprint, Middlesex, Eng.: Penguin, 1976), 312; hereafter cited in the text.

2   Carolyn G. Heilbrun, in *Toward a Recognition of Androgyny* (New York: Knopf, 1973), esp. 63–67, 95–97, traces the history of the motif of androgyny in British and American literature, including two of the texts that we have examined here: Hawthorne's *Scarlet Letter* and James's *Portrait of a Lady*. See also Mary Roberts, "Androgyny and Imperfect Love," *University of Hartford Studies in Literature*, 12 (1980): 73–98. McCullers's concern, writes Roberts, is the "incomplete androgyne" who, not whole in himself or herself, seeks completion in another (77–78).

3   Stanley Cavell, *The Senses of Walden* (New York: Viking Press, 1972), 62–63.

4   Henry David Thoreau, "On the Duty of Civil Disobedience," in *Walden; or Life in the Woods*, intro. Norman Holmes Pearson (New York: Holt, Rinehart and Winston, 1961), 291.

5   F. Scott Fitzgerald, *The Great Gatsby* (1925; reprint, New York: Scribner's, 1953), 99; hereafter cited in the text. I discuss this passage in somewhat different terms in *Fiction and Historical Consciousness: The American Romance Tradition* (New Haven, Conn.: Yale University Press, 1989), 143–63.

6   Marianne Hirsch, *The Mother/Daughter Plot: Narrative, Psychoanalysis, Feminism* (Bloomington: Indiana University Press, 1989).

Chapter Nine
Art and the Female Spirit: O'Connor

1   John Hawke, "Flannery O'Connor's Devil," *Sewanee Review* 70 (1962): 395. For such references see, e.g., Flannery O'Connor's essays "The Fiction Writer and His Country," "The Church and the Fiction Writers," and "The Catholic Novelist in the Protestant South." Quotations from O'Connor's essays and letters will be from O'Connor, *Collected Works*, ed. Sally Fitzgerald (New York: Library of America, 1988).

2   Richard Chase, *American Novel and Its Tradition* (New York: Doubleday,   1957). Arguments linking O'Connor to the romance tradition are so pervasive in the criticism as to defy citation. Major statements include Carol Shloss, *Flannery O'Connor's Dark Comedies: The Limits of Inference* (Baton Rouge: Louisiana State University Press, 1980), 12–13; Warren Coffey, Review of *Everything That Rises Must Converge*, reprinted in *Critical Essays on Flannery O'Connor*, ed. Melvin J. Friedman and Beverly Lyon Clark (Boston: G. K. Hall, 1985), 37–45; Louis D. Rubin, "Two Ladies of the South," in ibid., 25–28 (Coffey quotes Rubin [38], and Rubin also notes the link with McCullers, as does Alice Walker in "Beyond the Peacock: The Reconstruction of Flannery O'Connor," in ibid., 71); André Bleikasten, "The Heresy of Flannery O'Connor," in ibid., 138–58; Harold Bloom, Introduction to *Modern Critical Views: Flannery O'Connor*, ed. Bloom (New York: Chelsea House, 1986), 1–8, where Bloom focuses especially on O'Connor's relation to Faulkner's *As I Lay Dying*, a subject as well for Frederick Asals in *Flannery O'Connor: The Imagination of Extremity* (Athens: University of Georgia

Press, 1982), 18. Asals notes O'Connor's admiration for Richard Chase's *American Novel and Its Tradition* and her desire to write romance fiction (2) and traces the powerful affinities between O'Connor's *Wise Blood* and Poe's works (24–29) and between *The Violent Bear It Away* and *The Scarlet Letter* (163). This connection is also picked up by Leon V. Driskell and Joan T. Brittain in *The Eternal Crossroads: The Art of Flannery O'Connor* (Lexington: University of Kentucky Press, 1971), 14. On O'Connor's writing as "raising a structure of analogical meaning over the literal action of the stories, to construct natural tales that were sacred in implication," see Shloss, *Flannery O'Connor's Dark Comedies,* 11; see also also Richard Giannone, *Flannery O'Connor and the Mystery of Love* (Urbana: University of Illinois Press, 1989); and John F. Desmond, *Risen Sons: Flannery O'Connor's Vision of History* (Athens: University of Georgia Press, 1987), 117: "The metaphysical based upon an analogical view of reality is at the core of Flannery O'Connor's fictional vision and practice. . . . Her vision and practice are rooted specifically in the historical Christ event, the Incarnation and Resurrection of Jesus."

3   Shloss, *Flannery O'Connor's Dark Comedies,* 97. See also Desmond, *Risen Sons:* "What characterizes Tarwater's mind at the end is openness, possibility, and a sense of the mystery of being" (116).

4   See, e.g., Edward Kessler, *Flannery O'Connor and the Language of Apocalypse* (Princeton, N.J.: Princeton University Press, 1986); Bleikasten, who in the "Heresy of Flannery O'Connor," stresses the "irreducible ambiguity" of her work (147); and James Mellard, who, in "Flannery O'Connor's *Others:* Freud, Lacan, and the Unconscious," in *American Literature* 61 (1989): 625–43, argues that the stories dramatize psychological imbalance. Ben Satterfield argues vigorously that O'Connor's work has been overrated. "*Wise Blood,* Artistic Anemia, and the Hemorrhaging of O'Connor Criticism," *Studies in American Fiction* 17 (1989): 33–50.

5   O'Connor, "Fiction Writer and His Country," 805; and O'Connor, "Church and the Fiction Writer," 808. See also her "Catholic Novelist in the Protestant South."

6   O'Connor, "Fiction Writer and His Country," 805. For critics who interpret the violence recorded in O'Connor's stories and created by her language as essential to her enterprise, see Martha Stephens, *The Question of Flannery O'Connor* (Baton Rouge: Louisiana State University Press, 1973); Claire Kahane, "Flannery O'Connor's Rage of Vision," in *Critical Essays on Flannery O'Connor,* ed. Friedman and Clark, 119–30; Gilbert Muller, *Nightmares and Visions: Flannery O'Connor and the Catholic Grotesque* (Athens: University of Georgia Press, 1972); Giannone, *Flannery O'Connor and the Mystery of Love*; and Bleikasten, "Heresy of Flannery O'Connor." Bleikasten writes: "Instead of grace coming to complete and crown nature—as the mainstream Catholic tradition would have it—it breaks in on it . . . grace takes men by surprise. It . . . stabs them in the back . . . grace is not effusion but aggression" (152–53).

7   See especially Asals, *Flannery O'Connor,* 95–123. On the emphasis on fatalism in the stories, see Claire Kahane, "Flannery O'Connor's Rage of Vision," 126; and Bleikasten, "Heresy of Flannery O'Connor." Bleikasten writes: "The author plays God to her creatures, and foreshadowing becomes the fictional equivalent of predestination. . . . Not only does their rebellion fail, it also ends each time in unconditional surrender to the parental powers from which [the characters] had attempted to escape" (149).

8   Flannery O'Connor, *The Violent Bear It Away,* in *Three by Flannery O'Connor* (New York:

Signet, 1962), 337, 305; hereafter cited in the text. *The Violent Bear It Away* was originally published in 1955.

9 For example: "The face before [Rayber] was his own" (364) or "Rayber knew that the reason Bishop gave him pause was because the child reminded [Tarwater] of the old man" (371) or: "[Tarwater's] uncle's face was so familiar to him that he might have seen it every day of his life" (355). Compare Kahane, "Flannery O'Connor's Rage of Vision": "Searching for an identity in an isolating context, her characters bring to bear on that search all the psychological components of the desire to create oneself, of the impulse in the American character to become one's own parent, to break away from the limits of the past. . . . O'Connor's Christian theme provides [a] double solution: by submitting themselves to Christ, her characters acknowledge their powerlessness, yet share in the power of the parent-God" (129).

10 Leo Steinberg, *The Sexuality of Christ in Renaissance Art and in Modern Oblivion* (New York: Pantheon, 1984).

11 David Eggenschwiler, *The Christian Humanism of Flannery O'Connor* (Detroit, Mich.: Wayne State University Press, 1972), 30. Eggenschwiler identifies old Tarwater's problem as one of ego, although he brings to bear a sympathy for the man—which O'Connor herself seems to express—because old Tarwater is trying to cast out his evil nature.

12 Suzanne Morrow Paulson, in "Apocalypse of the Self, Resurrection of the Double: Flannery O'Connor's *The Violent Bear It Away*," *Literature and Psychology*, 30 (1980): 100–111, writes that to reject women is "to deny one's origin in the womb and to become the omphalos, which is to say, to be alive without knowledge of death" (102).

13 Emily Miller Budick, *Fiction and Historical Consciousness: The American Romance Tradition* (New Haven, Conn.: Yale University Press, 1989), 55–78.

14 See, e.g., John T. Irwin's *Doubling and Incest / Repetition and Revenge: A Speculative Reading of Faulkner* (Baltimore, Md.: Johns Hopkins University Press, 1975), esp. 125–35.

15 I have discussed these Hawthorne and Cooper scenes and their relation to each other in my *Fiction and Historical Consciousness*, 20–22, 36–58.

16 The feminist argument in the book would be much neater if Bishop's mother (who abandons him) weren't a worse parent even than his father. O'Connor's depiction of Bishop's mother, however, like some of Hawthorne's comments on Hester, suggests the way the desire for self-replication is not gender specific, even if its manifestations tend to differ in men and in women. Bishop's mother can discover neither in Bishop nor in young Tarwater any reflection of what she imagines herself to be, which is to say what she imagines to be natural and human. She deserts both of them, reneging on the responsibilities of motherhood.

17 O'Connor dismisses sentimentalism as an artistic strategy in "The Church and the Fiction Writer": "Sentimentality is an excess, a distortion of sentiment usually in the direction of an overemphasis on innocence and . . . innocence whenever it is overemphasized in the ordinary human condition, tends by some natural law to become its opposite. We lost our innocence in the Fall and our return to it is through the Redemption, which was brought about by Christ's death and by our slow participation in it. Sentimentality is a skipping of this process in its concrete reality and an early arrival at a mock state of innocence, which strongly suggests its opposite. Pornography, on the other hand, is essentially sentimental, for it leaves out the connection of sex with its hard purposes and so far disconnects it from its

meaning in life as to make it simply an experience for its own sake" (809). See also O'Connor, "Some Aspects of the Grotesque in Southern Fiction."

18 O'Connor, "Some Aspects of the Grotesque in Southern Fiction," 814–18.

19 O'Connor, "Catholic Novelist in the Protestant South," 854.

20 Wolfgant Iser, *The Implied Reader: Patterns of Communication in Prose Fiction from Bunyan to Beckett* (Baltimore, Md.: Johns Hopkins University Press, 1974), 1–29.

21 O'Connor, "The Fiction Writer and His Country," 804.

22 O'Connor, "The Regional Writer," 844; cf. O'Connor, "Catholic Novelist in the Protestant South," 856.

23 O'Connor, "Some Aspects of the Grotesque in Southern Fiction," 820.

24 Ibid., 816.

25 O'Connor comments about Hawthorne: "I cannot think of Mary Ann [a handicapped child who dies and to whose story O'Connor contributes an introduction] without thinking also of that fastidious skeptical New Englander who feared the ice in his blood. There is a direct line between the incidents in the Liverpool workhouse [when Hawthorne expresses this fear], the work of Hawthorne's daughter [the orphanage where Mary Ann lives is named for her], and Mary Ann. . . . [The work of the nuns] is the tree sprung from Hawthorne's small act of Christlikeness and Mary Ann is its flower. . . . Hawthorne gave what he did not have himself." "Introduction to 'A Memoir of Mary Ann,'" in *Mystery and Manners: Occasional Prose,* ed. Sally Fitzgerald and Robert Fitzgerald (New York: Farrar, Straus, and Giroux, 1969), 227.

26 Granville Hicks, "A Writer at Home with Her Heritage," *Saturday Review* 45 (May 12, 1962): 22, quoted in Eggenschwiler, *Christian Humanism of Flannery O'Connor,* 116.

Chapter Ten
Absence, Loss, and the Space of History: Morrison

1 Bernard W. Bell, *The Afro-American Novel and Its Tradition* (Amherst: University of Massachusetts Press, 1987), esp. xvi–xvii, 3–15. See also Jane Campbell, *Mythic Black Fiction: The Transformation of History* (Knoxville: University of Tennessee Press, 1986); and Molly Hite, "Romance, Marginality, Matrilineage: Alice Walker's *Color Purple* and Zora Neale Hurston's *Their Eyes Were Watching God,*" *Novel* 22 (1989): 257–73.

2 Zora Neale Hurston, "The Gilded Six-Bits," in *Spunk: The Selected Short Stories of Zora Neale Hurston* (1933; reprint, Berkeley: Turtle Island Foundation, 1985), 54; hereafter cited in the text.

3 For the classic formulation of the utilization of women within the economy of homosocial exchange, see Eve Kosofsky Sedgwick, *Between Men: English Literature and Male Homosocial Desire* (New York: Columbia University Press, 1985).

4 The first critic to couple these two stories is Werner Sollors, in "Modernization as Adultery: Richard Wright, Zora Neale Hurston, and American Culture of the 1930s and 1940s," *Hebrew University Studies in Literature and the Arts* 18 (1990): 109–55.

5 Ralph Waldo Ellison, *Invisible Man* (1947; reprint, New York: Random House, 1952), 12–14; hereafter cited in the text.

6   Michael Awkward, *Inspiriting Influences: Tradition, Revision, and Afro-American Women's Novels* (New York: Columbia University Press, 1989), 81–88; Houston A. Baker, Jr., *Blues, Ideology, and Afro-American Literature: A Vernacular Theory* (Chicago: University of Chicago Press, 1987), 172–99.

7   Stanley Cavell, "Being Odd, Getting Even (*Descartes, Emerson, Poe*)," in Cavell, *In Quest of the Ordinary: Lines of Skepticism and Romanticism* (Chicago: University of Chicago Press, 1988), 120–28. Among the many studies of the relationship between Emerson and Ellison, indeed, between Ellison and such other nineteenth-century writers as Hawthorne and Melville, see, e.g., Kimberly W. Benston, "I Yam What I Am: The Topos of Un(naming) in Afro-American Literature," in *Black Literature and Literary Theory,* ed. Henry Louis Gates, Jr. (New York: Methuen, 1984), 151–72; Alan Nadel, *Invisible Criticism: Ralph Ellison and the American Canon* (Iowa City: University of Iowa Press, 1988), which illuminates the many connections between Ellison and Melville, arguing that Ellison "was not trying to reject tradition but to return to it" (17), though by moving into terrain which the older writers resisted traversing; Robert G. O'Meally, *The Craft of Ralph Waldo Ellison* (Cambridge: Harvard University Press, 1980), which understands Ellison's major theme as the way consciousness creates freedom (O'Meally sees Ellison as responding to many traditions, including the symbolist tradition of Hawthorne and Melville but including as well the native folk tradition of African Americanism); Leonard Deutsch, "Ralph Waldo Ellison and Ralph Waldo Emerson: A Shared Moral Vision," *CLA Journal* 16 (1972): 159–78, which argues that Ellison was attracted by the visions of personal responsibility and democracy articulated by Emerson, Hawthorne, and Melville; Timothy Brennan, "Ellison and Ellison: The Solipsism of *Invisible Man,*" *CLA Journal* 25 (1981): 162–81, which stresses Ellison's participation in the multiethnicity of America; R. F. Dietze, "Crainway and Son: Ralph Ellison's *Invisible Man* as Seen Through the Perspective of Twain, Crane, and Hemingway," *Delta* 18 (1984): 25–46; Eleanor Lyons, "Ellison and the Twentieth-Century American Scholar," *Studies in American Fiction* 17 (1989): 93–106; and Bell, *Afro-American Novel,* 193–215. Bell writes: "*Invisible Man* traces a nameless black youth's journey from naive faith in the American Dream to an enlightened affirmation of self and society" (194). In "Indivisible Man," James Alan McPheron argues that all American culture reflects Afro-American culture. In *Speaking for You: The Vision of Ralph Ellison,* ed. Kimberly W. Benston (Washington D.C.: Howard University Press, 1987), 15–29. William W. Nichols, in contrast, argues that Ellison is satirizing Emerson. "Ralph Ellison's Black American Scholar," *Phylon* 31 (1970): 70–75. Benston has pointed out that "I yam what I am" formulates a central need in Ellison as in other African American writers to divest themselves of the arbitrary attributes by which white society has labeled and controlled them and to name themselves. The formulation "I yam what I am," echoing, as Benston notes, the Tetragrammaton, is replicated in many places in Ellison's text ("I'm your destiny, I made you"—500), as Ellison takes on what is another Emersonian imperative, to create his world by taking over the authority of naming it. See also Valerie Smith, "The Meaning of Narration in *Invisible Man,*" in *New Essays on Invisible Man,* ed. Robert O'Meally (Cambridge: Cambridge University Press, 1988), 23–53, in which the narrator is read as "assuming responsibility for naming himself by telling his own story" (27), thus placing the book in the tradition of slave narratives.

8   Stanley Cavell, *Conditions Handsome and Unhandsome* (Chicago: University of Chicago Press, 1990), 12.

9   Ibid., 138.

10 Toni Morrison, *Beloved* (New York: Signet, 1987), 198; hereafter cited in the text.

11 See Baker, *Blues, Ideology and Afro-American Literature.* On the relation between productivity and reproduction in the slave economy, see Anne E. Goldman, "'I Made the Ink': (Literary) Production and Reproduction in *Dessa Rose* and *Beloved,*" *Feminist Studies* 16 (1990): 313–30; and Mae G. Henderson, "Toni Morrison's *Beloved*: Re-Membering the Body as Historical Text," in *Comparative American Identities: Race, Sex, and Nationality in the Modern Text,* ed. Hortense J. Spillers (New York: Routledge, 1991), 62–86.

12 Most of the criticism on *Song of Solomon* has focused on the recovery of a black past that empowers contemporary African Americans to perpetuate their own cultural heritage. See Cynthia A. Davis, "Self, Society, and Myth in Toni Morrison's Fiction," *Contemporary Literature* 23 (1982): 323–42; Joseph T. Skerrett, Jr., "Recitation to the *Griot*: Storytelling and Learning in Toni Morrison's *Song of Solomon,*" in *Conjuring: Black Women, Fiction, and Literary Tradition,* ed. Marjorie Pryse and Hortense J. Spillers (Bloomington: Indiana University Press, 1985), 192–202; Dorothy H. Lee, "The Quest for Self: Triumph and Failure in the Works of Toni Morrison," in *Black Women Writers, 1950–80: A Critical Evaluation,* ed. Mari Evans (Garden City, N.Y.: Doubleday, Anchor 1984), 346–60; Genevieve Fabre, "Genealogical Archaeology, or the Quest for Legacy in Toni Morrison's *Song of Solomon,*" in *Critical Essays on Toni Morrison,*" ed. Nellie Y. McKay (Boston: G. K. Hall, 1988), 105–14; Susan Willis, *Specifying: Black Women Writing the American Experience* (London: Routledge, 1987); and Kimberly W. Benston, both "I Yam What I Am," 151–72, and "Re-Weaving the 'Ulysses Scene': Enchantment, Post-Oedipal Identity, and the Buried Text of Blackness in Toni Morrison's *Song of Solomon,*" in *Comparative American Identities,* ed. Spillers, 87–109. See also Valerie Smith, *Self-Discovery and Authority in Afro-American Narrative* (Cambridge: Harvard University Press, 1987); and Hazel Carby, *Reconstructing Womanhood: The Emergence of the Afro-American Woman Novelist* (New York: Oxford University Press, 1987).

13 Toni Morrison, *Song of Solomon* (New York: Signet, 1977), 126; hereafter cited in the text.

14 For a fascinating discussion of the "obliquity" of the father-daughter link in African American fiction, see Hortense J. Spillers, "'The Permanent Obliquity of an In(pha)llibly Straight': In the Time of the Daughters and the Fathers," in *Changing Our Own Words: Essays on Criticism, Theory, and Writing by Black Women,* ed. Cheryl A. Wall (New Brunswick, N.J.: Rutgers University Press, 1989), 127–49.

15 As Morrison herself comments, "Pilate is the ancestor . . . the apogee of all . . . of the best of that which is female and the best of that which is male, and that balance is disturbed if it is not nurtured, and if it not counted on and if it is not reproduced. That is the disability we must be on guard against for the future—the female who reproduces the female who reproduces the female." "Rootedness: The Ancestor as Foundation" in *Black Women Writers,* ed. Evans, 344.

16 On the idea of community in Morrison's work, see Kathleen O'Shaughnessy, "'Life Life Life Life': The Community as Chorus in *Song of Solomon,*" in *Critical Essays on Toni Morrison,* ed. McKay, 125–33, See also Dorothy H. Lee, "Quest for Self"; Cynthia Davis, "Self, Society, and

Myth"; and Barbara Christian, "Community and Nature: The Novels of Toni Morrison," *Journal of Ethnic Studies* 7 (1980): 65–78.

17 Considering how recently published *Beloved* is, it is remarkable how impressive a body of scholarship has been produced. Four essays in particular deal with the acts of historical recovery in the novel: Elizabeth B. House, "Toni Morrison's Ghost: The Beloved Who Is Not Beloved," *Studies in American Fiction,* 18 (1990): 17–26; Deborah Horvitz, "Nameless Ghosts: Possession and Dispossession in *Beloved,*" *Studies in American Fiction* 17 (1989): 157–68; Henderson, "Toni Morrison's *Beloved*"; and Goldman, "'I Made the Ink.'"

18 On rememory as female remembering, see, e.g., Henderson, "Re-Membering"; and Goldman, "'I Made the Ink.'"

19 House, "Toni Morrison's Ghost."

20 Baby Suggs is also re-remembered in Beloved, as is the baby Beloved, whom she ostensibly reincarnates. At a moment when Sethe feels ghost hands around her neck, Baby Suggs and Beloved are conflated into a single ghostly entity; Sethe also attributes to Baby Suggs a helping hand in pushing Beloved back to this side of death (246), while Baby Suggs's name also associates her with Beloved's identity as a baby. A reading of the novel that has taken into account some of its various patterns of repetition—which I am collecting under the idea of rememory—is Horvitz, "Nameless Ghosts."

21 On the ways in which the black family preserved the family during and after slavery, see Herbert G. Gutman, *The Black Family in Slavery and Freedom, 1750–1925* (New York: Pantheon, 1976).

22 Beloved's "birth" into the world as the child of Paul D and Sethe picks up on a curious fact about her burial: that her mother had sexual intercourse with the funeral director's son in order to pay for Beloved's stone, so that the rebirth of the daughter is almost the result of a painfully prolonged eighteen-year pregnancy. This idea is supported in the text by Beloved's spelling of out her name "slowly, as though the letters were being formed as she spoke them" (64). It is as if Beloved is the tombstone who is now coming to life, the letters being physically engraved on her.

23 See again Henderson, "Toni Morrison's *Beloved*"; and Goldman, "'I Made the Ink.'"

24 See Horvitz, "Nameless Ghosts."

25 For a recent, very fine discussion of this aspect of the novel, see Goldman, "'I Made the Ink.'"

26 The links between Morrison's *Beloved* and Hawthorne's *Scarlet Letter* are pervasive. Note, for example, Sethe's ostracism by the community, her going to jail with her baby, the representation of Beloved as a devil child, the concern with marks and marking expressed throughout *Beloved,* the emphasis on the mother-daughter relationship, especially the problem of mother-daughter separation, the idea of parthenogenic reproduction, and, finally and most significantly, the name Beloved, which, like Pearl, is a name for Christ.

Chapter Eleven
The Graceful Art of Conversation: Paley

1 A thoroughgoing and useful analysis of the way Paley's language dislodges the major assumptions of the dominant male discourse is Jacqueline Taylor, *Grace Paley: Illuminating*

the Dark Lives (Austin: University of Texas Press, 1990). A special 1982 issue of *Delta* (vol. 14) also contains some useful discussions of Paley's feminism and her linguistic style; see esp. Kathleen Hulley, "Grace Paley's Resistant Form," 3–18 (which reviews the essays in the journal); Nicholas Peter Humy, "A Different Responsibility: Form and Technique in G. Paley's 'A Conversation with My Father,'" 87–95; and Joyce Meier, "The Subversion of the Father in the Tales of Grace Paley," 115–27. Finally, see Ronald Schleifer, "Grace Paley: Chaste Compactness," in *Contemporary American Women Writers: Narrative Strategies,* ed. Catherine Rainwater and William J. Scheick (Lexington: University of Kentucky Press, 1985), 31–49.

2 Grace Paley, *Enormous Changes at the Last Minute* (1960; reprint, New York: Farrar, Straus, and Giroux, 1988), hereafter *EC.*

3 See especially Meier, "Subversion of the Father," which deals explicitly with the Lacanian elements of the story.

4 On Hawthorne see my *Fiction and Historical Consciousness: The American Romance Tradition* (New Haven, Conn.: Yale University Press, 1989), 113–18.

5 See again Taylor, *Grace Paley*; Schleifer, "Chaste Compactness," esp. 37; Humy, "Different Responsibility"; and Meier, "Subversion of the Father."

6 Stanley Fish, *Is There a Text in This Class? The Authority of Interpretive Communities* (Cambridge: Harvard University Press, 1980).

7 Murrary Krieger, *Arts on the Level: The Fall of the Elite Object* (Knoxville: University of Tennessee Press, 1981).

8 Peggy Kamuf, "Writing Like a Woman," in *Women and Language in Literature and Society,* ed. Sally McConnell-Ginet, Ruth Borker, and Melly Furman (New York: Praeger, 1980), 298.

9 See, e.g., Paley's stories "A Woman, Young and Old," "The Pale Pink Roast," "An Interest in Life," and "Two Short Sad Stories" in her *Little Disturbances of Man* (1956; reprint, New York: Viking Penguin, 1986), hereafter *LDM,* and "Wants," "Faith in the Afternoon," "Faith in a Tree," and "The Long-Distance Runner" in *EC.*

10 Paley, "Enormous Changes," in *EC,* 135; Paley, "Northeast Playground," in *EC,* 145. In "Two Short Sad Stories from a Long and Happy Life," Paley creates two fathers for Faith's children. Not only are the biological and legal fathers two different people—suggesting the difference between the paternal bond, which can be defined either by law or by genetics, and the maternal bond, which is exclusively biological—but for neither of these "used-boy raisers" are the boys an absolute or total responsibility. Livid (the biological father) can write to Pallid (the legal father): "I do think they're fine boys, you understand. I love them too, but Faith is their mother and now Faith is your wife. I'm so much away. If you want to think of them as yours, old man, go ahead." *LDM,* 127–28. "'Go say goodbye to your father,'" Faith whispers to her sons toward the end the first sad story. "'Which one?' they asked. 'The real father,' I said." *LDM,* 134. The story concludes with a series of goodbyes, most of them cold and formal, as the two fathers set off, leaving their sons and their wife. Their direction is the direction of most of the husbands and fathers in Paley's fiction: away from family. In contrast, in the second short tale in "Two Short Sad Stories" a third male companion also plays father to the two boys, only to leave, like the previous two fathers, in this case, bruised and battered after a bit of rough-and-tumble play gets out of hand. Indeed, in this story Faith,

too, has her hands full, for Tonto and Richard taunt each other and her. But if men travel outward, women move in the opposite direction. "'I love you, Mama,'" says Tonto. "'Love,' I said. 'Oh love, Anthony, I know.' I held him so and rocked him. I cradled him. I closed my eyes and leaned on his dark head. But the sun in its course emerged from among the water towers of downtown office buildings and suddenly shone white and bright on me. Then through the short fat fingers of my son, interred forever, like a black and white barred king in Alcatraz, my heart lit up in stripes" (*LDM,* 145).

11   The young female narrator in "A Woman, Young and Old" reports that her father "was a really stunning Latin. . . . They were deeply and irrevocably in love till Joanna and I revoked everything for them. . . . '. . . a wife,' he said, 'is a beloved mistress until the children come and then . . . '" (*LDM,* 26). Or, as the deserted wife in "An Interest in Life," reports, "My husband gave me a broom one Christmas. This wasn't right. No one can tell me it was meant kindly" (*LDM,* 81). Or take Faith's letter from Ricardo in "Faith in a Tree": "I am not well. I hope I never see another rain forest. I am sick. Are you working? Have you seen Ed Snead? He owes me $180. Don't badger him about it if he looks broke. Otherwise send me some to Guerra Verde c/o Dotty Wasserman. Am living her with her. . . . I *need* the money" (*EC,* 82).

12   "Mother doesn't want me to feel rejected, but she doesn't want to feel rejected herself, so she says *I* was too noisy and cried every single night. And then Joanna was the final blight and wanted titty all day *and* all night" (*LDM,* 26).

13   Paley, "The Story Hearer," in her *Later the Same Day* (Middlesex, Eng.: Viking Penguin, 1985), hereafter *LSD*.

14   In *Grace Paley,* Jacqueline Taylor usefully catalogues various strategies—such as "subjective narrative," "collective narration," and "collaborative narration"—whereby Paley achieves the open, conversational quality of her writing (108–29).

15   Schleifer, "Chaste Compactness," 34, 35. See also Taylor, *Grace Paley,* 106–29, where the same passage is quoted.

16   Schleifer, "Chaste Compactness," 35.

17   Ibid., 37.

18   In "Subversion of the Father," Joyce Meier suggests that "the fact that Paley's male characters can be open-hearted, and her women obsessed with power and control, indicates that her stories are not absolutely defined along sexual lines." Meier then interprets the pronoun-initial "I" in "I. Goodside, M.D." as incorporating the daughter within the father. And Meier concludes: "Since the Father is within Paley herself, her works do not really belittle men, but rather, the restrictions which the male naming and rhetoric involves" (125). I would say that Paley does not belittle male language at all, only the disuse into which it has fallen.

19   Humy, "Different Responsibility," 88–90.

20   Schleifer, "Chaste Compactness," 42. The brackets are Schleifer's.

21   Paley's writings seem to me strongly affiliated with Marilynne Robinson's *Housekeeping,* which also seems to design its feminist aesthetic on a male base. For a discussion of *Housekeeping* along these lines, see Martha Ravits, "Extending the American Range: Marilynne Robinson's *Housekeeping,*" *American Literature* 61 (1989): 644–66.

22   Zagrowsky's response here may create its own problems vis-à-vis African American culture,

for Zagrowsky does not so much recognize African Americans despite their differences from white Jews or Christians but discover their humanness in their similarity to himself.

23 Stanley Cavell, *Conditions Handsome and Unhandsome* (Chicago: University of Chicago Press, 1990), 12.

24 Wolfgang Iser, *The Fictive and the Imaginary: Charting Literary Anthropology* (Baltimore, Md.: Johns Hopkins University Press, 1993).

Index